Mobil

Travel Guide®

CANADA

ACKNOWLEDGEMENTS

We gratefully acknowledge the help of our representatives for their efficient and perceptive inspections of the lodging and dining establishments listed, the establishments' proprietors for their cooperation in showing their facilities and providing information about them, and the many users of previous editions who have taken the time to share their experiences. Mobil Travel Guide is also grateful to all the talented writers who contributed entries to this book.

CONTENTS

MAPS

CANADA

CELEBRATING 50 YEARS

Because time is precious and the travel industry is ever-changing, having accurate, reliable travel information at your has fingertips is essential. Mobil Travel Guide provided invaluable insight to travelers for 50 years, and we are committed to continuing this service into the future.

The Mobil Corporation (known as Exxon Mobil Corporation since a 1999 merger) began producing the Mobil Travel Guide books in 1958 following the introduction of the U.S.-interstate highway system in 1956. The first edition covered only five Southwestern states. Since then, our books have become the premier travel guides in North America, covering all 50 states and Canada.

Since its founding, Mobil Travel Guide has served as an advocate for travelers seeking knowledge about hotels, restaurants and places to visit. Based on an objective process, we make recommendations to our customers that we believe will enhance the quality and value of their travel experiences. Our trusted Mobil One- to Five-Star rating system is the oldest and most respected lodging and restaurant inspection and rating program in North America. Most hoteliers, restaurateurs and industry observers favorably regard the rigor of our inspection program and understand the prestige and benefits that come with receiving a Mobil Star rating.

The Mobil Travel Guide process of rating each establishment includes:
★ Unannouced facility inspections
★ Incognito service evaluations for
★ A review of unsolicited comments from the general public
★ Senior management oversight

For each property, more than 450 attributes, including cleanliness, physical facilities and employee attitude and courtesy, are measured and evaluated to produce a mathematically derived score, which is then blended with the other elements to form an overall score. These scores form the basis that we use to assign our Mobil One- to Five-Star ratings.

This process focuses on guest expectations, guest experience and consistency of service, not just physical facilities and amenities. It's fundamentally a rating system that rewards those properties that continually strive for and achieve excellence each year. The very best properties are consistently raising the bar for those that wish to compete with them.

Only facilities that meet Mobil Travel Guide's standards earn the privilege of being listed in the guide. Deteriorating, poorly managed establishments are deleted. A Mobil Travel Guide listing constitutes a positive quality recommendation. Every listing is an accolade, a recognition of achievement.

★★★★★The Mobil Five-Star Award indicates that a property is one of the very best in the country and consistently provides gracious and courteous service, superlative quality in its facility and a unique ambience. The lodgings and restaurants at the Mobil

Five-Star level consistently continues their commitment to excellence, doing so with grace and perseverance.

★★★★The Mobil Four-Star Award honors properties for outstanding achievement in overall facility and for providing very strong service levels in all areas. These award winners provide a distinctive experience for the ever-demanding and sophisticated consumer.

★★★The Mobil Three-Star Award recognizes an excellent property that provides full services and amenities. This category ranges from exceptional hotels with limited services to elegant restaurants with a less-formal atmosphere.

★★The Mobil Two-Star property is a clean and comfortable establishment that has expanded amenities or a distinctive environment. These properties are an excellent place to stay or dine.

★The Mobil One-Star property is limited in its amenities and services but provides a value experience while meeting travelers' expectations. Expect the properties to be clean, comfortable and convenient.

We do not charge establishments for inclusion in our guides. We have no relationship with any of the businesses and attractions we list and act only as a consumer advocate. We do the investigative legwork so that you won't have to.

Restaurants and hotels—particularly small chains and stand-alone establishments—change management or even go out of business with surprising quickness. Although we make every effort to update continuously information, we recommend that you call ahead to make sure the place you've selected is still open.

We hope that your travels are enjoyable and relaxing and that our books help you get the most out of every trip you take. If any aspect of your accommodation, dining, spa or sightseeing experience motivates you to comment, please contact us. Mobil Travel Guide, 200 W. Madison St., Suite 3950, Chicago, IL 60611, or send an e-mail to info@mobiltravelguide.com.

Happy travels.

HOW TO USE THIS BOOK

The Mobil Travel Guide Regional Travel Planners are designed for convenience. Each state has its own chapter, beginning with a general introduction that provides a geographical and historical orientation to the state and gives basic statewide tourist information. The remainder of each chapter is devoted to travel destinations within the state—mainly cities and towns, but also national parks and tourist areas—which, like the states, are arranged in alphabetical order.

THE STAR RATINGS
MOBIL RATED HOTELS

Travelers have different needs when it comes to accommodations. To help you pinpoint properties that meet your particular needs, Mobil Travel Guide classifies each lodging by type according to the following characteristics.

★★★★★The Mobil Five-Star hotel provides consistently superlative service in an exceptionally distinctive luxury environment, with expanded services. Attention to detail is evident throughout the hotel, resort or inn, from bed linens to staff uniforms.

★★★★The Mobil Four-Star hotel provides a luxury experience with expanded amenities in a distinctive environment. Services may include automatic turndown service, 24-hour room service and valet parking.

★★★The Mobil Three-Star hotel is well appointed, with a full-service restaurant and expanded amenities, such as a fitness center, golf course, tennis courts, 24-hour room service and optional turndown service.

★★The Mobil Two-Star hotel is considered a clean, comfortable and reliable establishment that has expanded amenities, such as a full-service restaurant on the premises.

★The Mobil One-Star lodging is a limited-service hotel, motel or inn that is considered a clean, comfortable and reliable establishment For every property, we also provide pricing information. The pricing categories break down as follows:

- ★   **$** = Up to $150
- ★   **$$** = $151-$250
- ★   **$$$** = $251-$350
- ★   **$$$$** = $351 and up

All prices quoted are accurate at the time of publication, however prices cannot be guaranteed. In some locations, special events, holidays or seasons can affect prices. Some resorts have complicated rate structures that vary with the time of year, so confirm rates when making your plans.

SPECIALITY LODGINGS

A Speciality Lodging is a unique inn, bed and breakfast or guest ranch with limited service, but appealing, attractive facilities that make the property worth a visit.

MOBIL RATED RESTAURANTS

All Mobil Star-rated dining establishments listed in this book have a full kitchen and most offer table service.

★★★★★The Mobil Five-Star restaurant offers one of few flawless dining experiences in the country. These establishments consistently provide exceptional food, service and décor.

★★★★The Mobil Four-Star restaurant provides professional service, distinctive presentations and wonderful food.

★★★The Mobil Three-Star restaurant has good food, warm and skillful service and enjoyable décor.

★★The Mobil Two-Star restaurant serves fresh food in a clean setting with efficient service. Value is considered in this category, as is family friendliness.

★The Mobil One-Star restaurant provides a distinctive experience through culinary specialty, local flair or individual atmosphere. The pricing categories are defined as follows, per diner, and assume that you order an appetizer or dessert, an entrée and one drink:

- ★ **$** = $15 and under
- ★ **$$** = $16-$35
- ★ **$$$** = $36-$85
- ★ **$$$$** = $86 and up

All prices quoted are accurate at the time of publication, but prices cannot be guaranteed.

MOBIL RATED SPAS

Mobil Travel Guide is pleased to announce its newest category, hotel and resort spas. Until now, these spas have not been formally rated or inspected by any organization. Every spa selected for inclusion in this book underwent a rigorous inspection process similar to the one Mobil Travel Guide has applied to lodgings and restaurants for five decades. After researching more than 300 spas and performing exhaustive incognito inspections of more than 200 properties, we narrowed our list to the best spas in the United States and Canada.

★★★★★The Mobil Five-Star spa provides consistently superlative service in an exceptionally distinctive luxury environment with extensive amenities. The staff at a Mobil Five-Star spa provides extraordinary service beyond the traditional spa experience, allowing guests to achieve the highest level of relaxation and pampering.

★★★★The Mobil Four-Star spa provides a luxurious experience with expanded amenities in an elegant and serene environment. Throughout the spa facility, guests experience personalized service. Amenities might include, but are not limited to, single-sex relaxation rooms where guests wait for their treatments, plunge pools and whirlpools in both men's and women's locker rooms, and an array of treatments, including at a minimum a selection of massages, body therapies, facials, and a variety of salon services.

★★★The Mobil Three-Star spa is physically well appointed and has a full complement of staff.

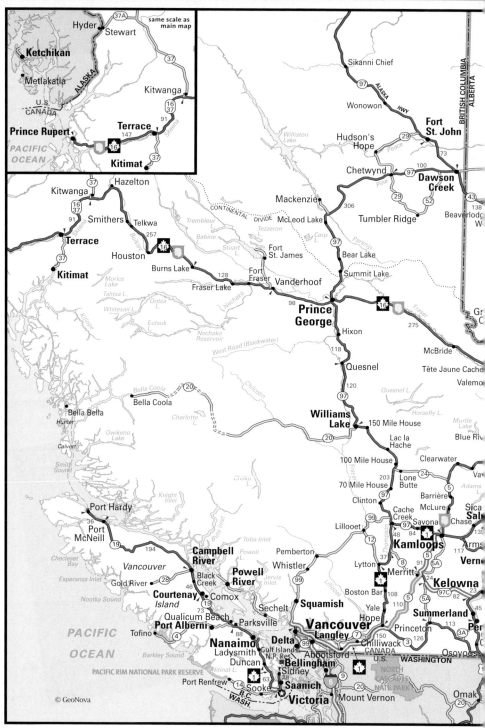

Inset map (top left):

same scale as main map

Hyder
Stewart
37A

Ketchikan
Metlakatla
37
ALASKA
U.S.
CANADA
Kitwanga
16
37
Prince Rupert
Terrace
147
91
Steena

PACIFIC
OCEAN
16
Kitimat
37

Main map:

Sikanni Chief

97
ALASKA HWY
Wonowon
Fort
St. John
BRITISH COLUMBIA
ALBERTA

Hudson's
Hope
29
Peace
73

Chetwynd
97
100
Dawson
Creek
43

Kitwanga
37
Hazelton
Mackenzie
Pine
29
52
138
Beaverlodge
W

16
37
91
Steena
Smithers
Telkwa
257
Bulkley
CONTINENTAL DIVIDE
Trembleur
McLeod Lake
306
Tumbler Ridge

Terrace
16
Babine
Carp
L.
Parsnip
Bear Lake
97

37
Houston
Stuart
L.
Fort
St. James
Summit Lake

Kitimat
Burns Lake
128
Fort
Fraser
Vanderhoof
Morice
Lake
Fraser Lake
Nechako
98
Prince
George
Fraser
16

Tahtsa L.
Ootsa
L.
Whitesail L.
Eutsuk
L.
Nechako
Reservoir
West Road (Blackwater)
Hixon
275

Gr
C

Bella Coola
Bella Bella
Chilcotin
20
Bella Coola
Charlotte
L.
118
Quesnel
McBride
Tête Jaune Cache
Valemo

Hunter
I.
120
97
Quesnel L.
Owikeno
Lake
Calvert I.
Williams
Lake
150 Mile House
Horsefly L.
Murtle L.
Blue Riv

Smith
Sound
20
Lac la
Hache
100 Mile House
Clearwater

Cinlau
203
Lone
Butte
24
Va

Knight
Inlet
70 Mile House
97
Barrière
5
Adams

Port Hardy
Clinton
McLure
Sica
Sal

36
Port
McNeill
Bute Inlet
Toba Inlet
Lillooet
99
Cache
Creek
Savona
97
Chase
135

Checleset
Bay
19
194
Campbell
River
Powell
L.
Pemberton
12
48
84
1
Kamloops
Arms

Vancouver
Whistler
37
8
91
5A
Vern
117

Esperanza Inlet
28
Black
Creek
Powell
River
Jervis
Inlet
Lytton
Merritt
Kelowna

Gold River
46
Comox
99
Boston Bar
108
5
5A
97C
5
45
Per

Nootka Sound
73
Courtenay
Island
19
Sechelt
Squamish
Yale
110
Summerland
113
3A

Qualicum Beach
Parksville
Hope
Princeton
126

PACIFIC
Port Alberni
4
88
Vancouver
Langley
7
150
Chilliwack
3
Osoyoos

Tofino
Nanaimo
99
Delta
CANADA
U.S.
WASHINGTON
Omak

OCEAN
Barkley Sound
Ladysmith
Duncan
Gulf Islands
N.P. Res.
Abbotsford
NORTH
CASCADES
20

PACIFIC RIM NATIONAL PARK RESERVE
Nitinat L.
Bellingham
Sidney
1
9
NAT'L PARK
20

© GeoNova
Port Renfrew
14
63
28
Sooke
Saanich
9
Mount Vernon

B.C.
WASH.
Victoria
20

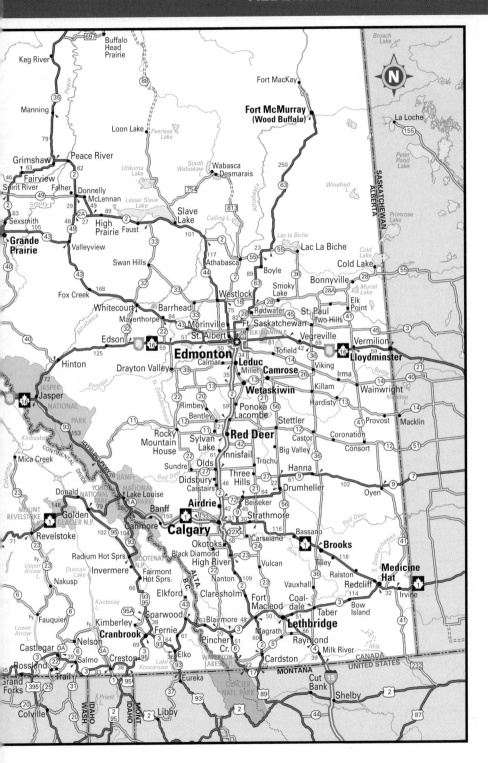

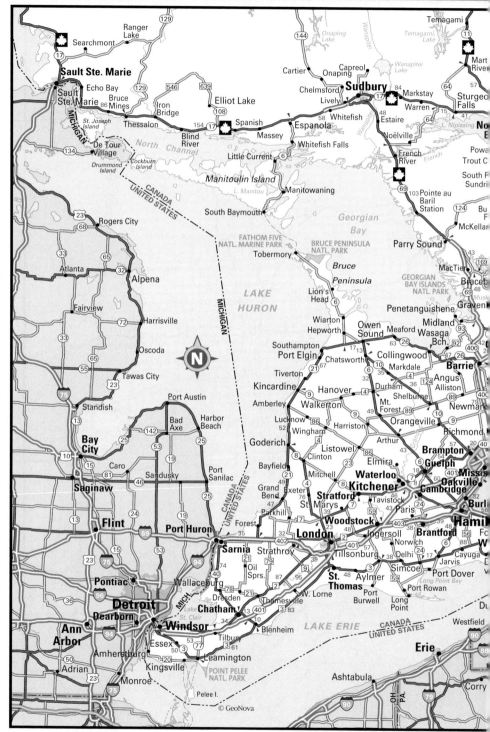

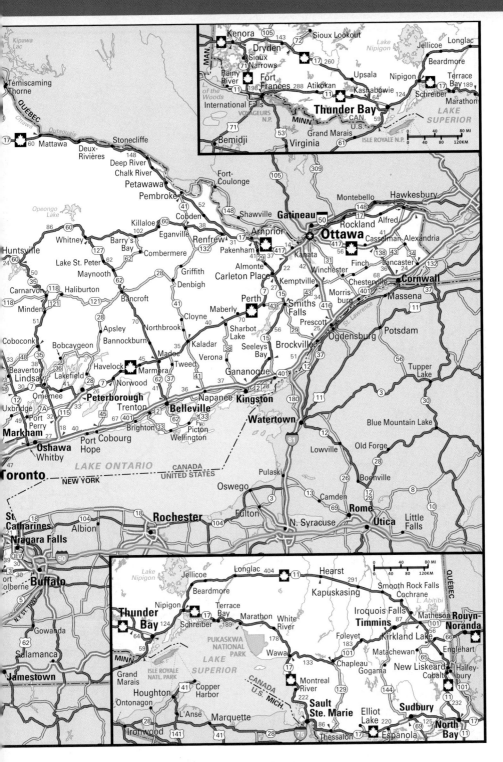

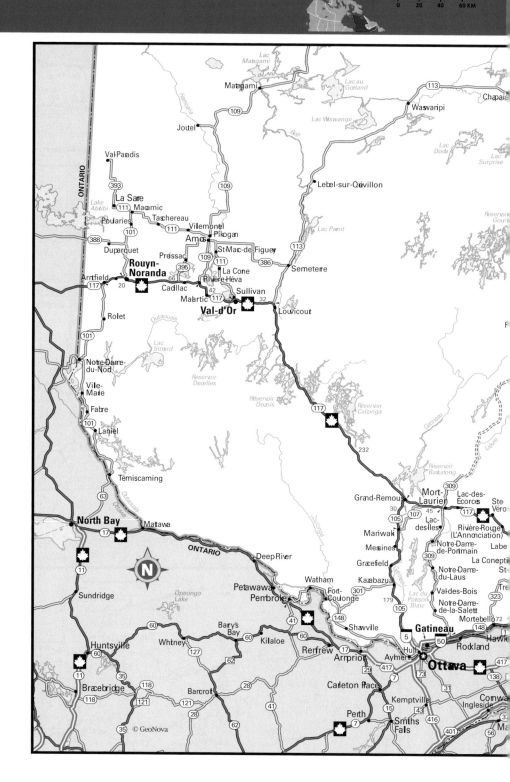

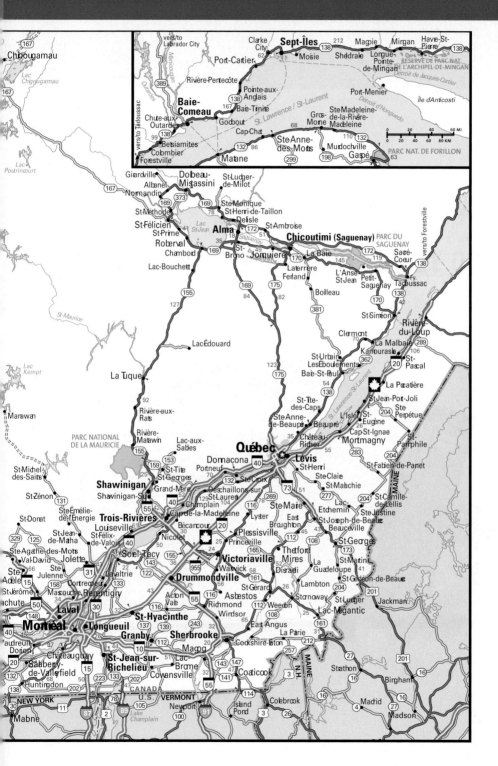

★CELEBRATING★
50 YEARS OF MOBIL TRAVEL GUIDE

1962 — **1964** — **1968** — **1971** →

← **1973** — **1976** — **1978** — **1979** →

1986 ——— **1988** ——— **1989** ——— **1992**

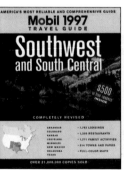

1994 ——— **1997** ——— **1998** ——— **2003**

ALBERTA

ALBERTA IS A RICH, RICH FRONTIER—CANADA'S ECONOMIC BOOMTOWN THANKS TO profitable oil sands—and home to some of the continent's most awe-inspiring scenery and outdoor adventure. Find sweeping plains, towering Rocky Mountains, sparkling emerald lakes, cowboys and cattle ranches, champagne powder snow, a colorful gold rush heritage and some of the most delectable steak in the world.

Alberta boasts the widest variety of geographical features of any province in Canada, including badlands rich in dinosaur fossils, rolling prairies and vast forests. All along its western border are the magnificent Canadian Rockies, which encompass six national and provincial parks, including the legendary Jasper and Banff.

Easily accessible from Montana, enter Alberta from Waterton Lakes National Park and drive north to Calgary, where you'll intersect with the Trans-Canada Highway and enjoy a variety of attractions. The view of the Rockies from the Calgary Tower and the excitement of the Calgary Stampede, a 10-day event held each July, are not to be missed. From Calgary, drive northwest to Banff, Lake Louise and Jasper National Park for some of the finest mountain scenery, outdoor activities and resorts and restaurants on the continent. Heading due north from Calgary, visit Red Deer, a town famous for agriculture, oil and its beautiful parkland setting. Farther north is the provincial capital, Edmonton. A multicultural city noted for its oil, Gold Rush past, parks, cultural celebrations, magnificent sports facilities and rodeos. Northwest of Edmonton, Alberta provides paved access to Mile 0 of the Alaska Highway at Dawson Creek, B.C. There is also paved access to the Northwest Territories—Canada's northern frontier land.

Drive southeast from Calgary and enter an entirely different scene: cowboy-and-Indian territory. Fort Macleod brings you back to the early pioneer days. Lethbridge is famous for its replica of the most notorious 19th-century whiskey fort, Fort Whoop-Up and the Nikka Yuko Japanese Gardens. Farther east, visit Medicine Hat, known for its parks, pottery and rodeos. Don't go to Alberta without plenty of space on your camera's memory stick.

Provincial Capital: Edmonton

Information: www.travelalberta.com

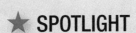

★ SPOTLIGHT

★ The world's largest herd of free-roaming bison is located in Wood Buffalo National Park.

1

ALBERTA

BANFF

As early as 1885, Albertans knew what treasure lay in their backyards. The Banff Hot Springs Reservation was incorporated to protect the steaming, healing grottos abundant to the area, and by 1887 that vision was expanded to become Rocky Mountains Park. Today the vast recreation area is known as Banff National Park—Canada's first national park, the second in North America and only the third in the world. A UNESCO World Heritage site, the park covers 2,564 square miles (6,641 square kilometers).

Banff comes alive each summer with its music and drama festival at Banff Centre. In winter, the Rockies provide some of the best skiing on the North American continent.

A fantastic blend of both culture and natural bounty, Banff offers exciting nightlife, sleigh rides, Western barbecues, gondola rides, boat and raft tours, concerts, art galleries, museums, hot springs, ice field tours, hiking and trail rides.

Snowy peaks tower over glassy alpine lakes. Massive canyons carved out of plain landscapes and more than 1,000 prehistoric glaciers await eco-warriors and everyday shutterbugs alike. Animals are so plentiful that traveling throughout the province (and camping and outdoor eating) requires special care. Watch for bighorn sheep, mountain goats, moose, elk, deer and grizzly and black bear.
Information: www.banfflakelouise.com

WHAT TO SEE AND DO

Banff Gondola
403-762-2523;
www.banffgondola.com
Travel up to 7,500 feet in elevation for spectacular vistas. Gift shop and restaurant at the top. Open year-round; hours vary by season

Banff National Park
403-762-1550;
www.pc.gc.ca/pn-np/ab/banff
Canada's first national park, Banff was initially famous for its hot springs, and visitors still flock here to check out the bubbling thermal waters at the Cave and Basin National Historic Site. The town is home to many of the park's resorts and lodges, perhaps the most notable being the opulent Fairmont Banff Springs, fashioned after a Scottish baronial castle. Upscale accommodations also can be found near the wondrous Lake Louise, its placid blue-green waters reflecting the sharply angled mountain peaks surrounding the shoreline. Budget-minded visitors to Banff National Park typically opt to sleep under the stars, with the park offering 2,468 campsites on a first-come, first-served basis.

Banff National Park stands tall among the spectacular peaks of the Canadian Rockies as one of the premier year-round vacation destinations in all of North America. Downhill skiers and snowboarders come from around the world to Banff's legendary slopes, with three major ski resorts serving the area. The summer months bring boot-clad hikers eager to take advantage of more than 1,000 miles (1,600 kilometers) of trails that cut across diverse but consistently striking terrain, winding through open meadows and dense forests, passing alongside ancient glaciers and glistening lakes. Other popular activities include mountaineering, fishing, canoeing/kayaking, golf, horseback riding and wildlife viewing.

Banff Park Museum
403-762-1558;
www.pc.gc.ca/lhn-nhs/ab/banff
One of the oldest museums in Canada. Displays animals, insects and other collections found in Banff National Park. Reading room, hands-on discovery room.

Banff Upper Hot Springs
403-762-1515, 800-767-1611;
www.hotsprings.ca
Originally built in 1932, the therapeutic waters of Canada's most revered hot spring average temperatures of 100 degrees, with an expansive outdoor pool and rich selection of spa indulgences.

Brewster Canada Motorcoach Tours
403-762-6767, 877-791-5500;
www.brewster.ca
Tours take passengers onto the Columbia Icefield for a glacier-bound SnoCoach tour.

Cave and Basin Centennial Centre
403-762-1557;
www.pc.gc.ca/lhn-nhs/ab/caveandbasin/index_E.asp
The birthplace of Canada's national park system and a national historic site. Hot springs, cave, exhibits, trails, theater.

Fairmont Banff Springs Golf Course
403-762-6801; www.fairmont.com

2

ALBERTA

This spectacular 27-hole golf course is situated along the Bow River and framed by the majestic peaks of the Canadian Rockies. Driving range, practice greens, pro shop. May-October.

Johnston Canyon
16 miles W. of Banff; www.banff.com/hiking/johnston_canyon.shtml
This self-guided, 3.5-mile (5.6 kilometer) walk through scenic canyon. View Ink Spots and six cool-water springs.

Natural History Museum
403-762-4652;
www.pc.gc.ca/lhn-nhs/ab/banff/natcul/index_e.asp
More than 60 displays; slide shows and films depict prehistoric life, precious stones, and trees and flowers, as well as the origins of the earth and the formation of mountains and caves.

Rocky Mountain Raft Tours
403-762-3632
Tranquil one- or two-hour float trips travel on the Bow River through Banff National Park.

Sunshine Village
403-762-6500, 877-542-2633;
www.skibanff.com
This legendary ski area offers 3,168 acres of terrain with an elevation of 8,954 feet (2,729 meters) and a vertical drop of 3,514 feet (1,071 meters). One high-speed six-passenger gondola, four high-speed detachable quads, one fixed quad, one triple chair, two double chairs, one T-bar, two magic carpets. Restaurants, lounges, ski and snowboard school, rental shop, day care, snowboard park and more.

SPECIAL EVENTS
Annual Banff/Lake Louise Winter Festival
403-762-8421; www.banfflakelouise.com
This two-week festival, including cultural events, winter athletic contests, a Town Party and bar socials has been a Banff tradition since 1916. Late January-early February.

Banff Summer Arts Festival
403-762-6301, 800-413-8368;
www.banffcentre.ca/bsaf
Mainstage productions and workshops in opera, ballet, music theater, drama, concerts, poetry reading and visual arts. May-September.

Banff Television Festival
403-678-9260; www.btvf.com
While this event is primarily for industry networkers, the public can view some of the best international television free of charge. June.

HOTELS
★Banff Ave. Inn
433 Banff Ave., Banff, 403-762-4499, 888-762-4499; www.banffavenueinn.com
18 rooms. Complimentary continental breakfast. $$

★★Banff Caribou Lodge
521 Banff Ave., Banff, 403-762-5887, 800-563-8764; www.banffcaribouproperties.com
195 rooms. Exercise Room. $$

★★Buffalo Mountain Lodge
700 Tunnel Mountain Rd., Banff, 403-762-2400, 800-661-1367; www.buffalomountainlodge.com
This mountain retreat lodge is perched above town on Tunnel Mountain (called "sleeping buffalo" by locals). Rooms have balconies or patios with fireplaces and private baths. The Buffalo Mountain Lodge Dining Room has been praised for its Victorian cooking and hearty meals prepared by Swiss and Austrian mountain guides.
108 rooms. Two restaurants, bar. Exercise. Busn. Center. $$

★★★Banff Park Lodge
222 Lynx St., Banff, 403-762-4433, 800-661-9266; www.banffparklodge.com
Stunning mountain views can be seen from any room of this full-service hotel located just two blocks from Banff's shopping district and near Bow River. Plenty of year-round activities to keep guests busy. After a long day at play,

enjoy a quiet dinner in the hotel's fine-dining restaurant, The Terrace. A casual dinner can be found at The Chinook where there are theme-night dinners such as "Seafood Italiano" and "Authentic Western Feasts."

211 rooms. Two restaurants, bar. Pool. Busn. Center. **$$**

★★Banff Ptarmigan Inn
337 Banff Ave., Banff, 403-762-2207, 800-661-8310; www.bestofbanff.com
134 rooms. Two restaurants, bar. Exercise. **$**

★★Brewster's Mountain Lodge
208 Caribou St., Banff, 403-762-2900, 888-762-2900; www.brewstermountainlodge.com
77 rooms. Restaurant, bar. Exercise room. Busn. Center. **$$**

★Douglas Fir Resort And Chalets
Tunnel Mt. Rd., Banff, 403-762-5591, 800-661-9267; www.douglasfir.com
133 rooms, all suites. Exercise room. Pool. Tennis. Busn. Center. **$**

★★★The Fairmont Banff Springs
405 Spray Ave., Banff, 403-762-2211, 800-441-1414; www.fairmont.com
A striking backdrop of snow-capped peaks and towering trees makes for a magical experience, with regal accommodations, luxurious amenities and plentiful activities— including world-class skiing and championship golf. The Willow Stream spa offers a well-rounded treatment menu to help guests further relax in this majestic setting.

770 rooms. Eight restaurants, two bars. Pet. Exercise. Swim. Golf. Tennis. Busn. Center. **$$$**

★★★Rimrock Resort Hotel
300 Mountain Ave., Banff, 403-762-3356, 888-746-7625; www.rimrockresort.com
Terraced into the side of a mountain in Banff National Park, this sophisticated hotel offers alpine vistas with world-class skiing only minutes away. A comprehensive health center and saltwater pools appeal to fitness-minded visitors, while the spa

indulges all. Three dining establishments echo the elegance of the hotel while catering to a variety of tastes.

349 rooms. Three restaurants, two bars. Exercise. Swim. Busn. Center. **$$$**

★★★Royal Canadian Lodge
459 Banff Ave., Banff, 403-762-3307, 800-661-1225; www.charltonresorts.com
In the serene setting of Banff, guest are charmed by this small, rustic hotel. The spacious guest rooms have high ceilings, Canadian maple furnishings, granite vanities and either gas fireplaces or views of the Alpine Garden. Evergreen, the restaurant, serves three meals daily and features Canadian cuisine, while the Grotto Spa includes a mineral pool and whirlpool and offers several types of treatments.

Restaurant, bar. Exercise. Swim. **$$**

RESTAURANTS

★★★★Banffshire Club
405 Spray Ave., Banff, 403-762-6860; www.fairmont.com
The jewel of the lavish Fairmont Banff Springs, the Banffshire Club prides itself on having one of the most extensive wine cellars in all of Canada. Warm up with one of many single malt scotches in view of Sulphur Mountain, and enjoy game dishes and a uniquely fresh, Alberta-inspired menu with hints of French cuisine. Reservations recommended. Contemporary North American cuisine. **$$$$**

★★Balkan
120 Banff Ave., Banff, 403-762-3454. Greek menu. **$$**

★★★Bow Valley Grill
405 Spray Ave., Banff, 403-762-6896; www.fairmont.com
Housed in the historic, castle-like Fairmont Banff Springs Hotel, this French restaurant was recently remodeled to restore its romantic brilliance. The formal, special-occasion space is the property's signature dining room and offers the excitement of tableside preparations and nightly dancing. **$$$**

ALBERTA

★★Buffalo Mountain Lodge Dining Room
Tunnel Mountain Rd., Banff,
403-762-2400, 800-661-1367;
www.crmr.com
Located in the Buffalo Mountain Lodge.
Canadian Rocky Mountain cuisine. **$$$**

★★Giorgio's Trattoria
219 Banff Ave., Banff, 403-762-5114;
www.giorgiosbanff.com
Italian cuisine. **$$**

★★★Le Beaujolais
212 Buffalo St., Banff,
403-762-2712;
www.lebeaujolaisbanff.com
A prestigious destination in a beautiful town, this restaurant is awash in fresh flowers, candlelight and mountain views. Comfortably formal service and occasional tableside preparations are a treat.
Classic French menu. Closed November-mid-December. **$$$**

★★★Seasons
1029 Banff Ave, Kananaskis Village,
403-591-7711;
www.rockymountainresort.com
This fireside café is housed at the Banff Rocky Mountain Resort and Conference Center in the heart of the Canadian Rockies. The atmosphere is casual, and the regionally influenced menu is broad. Views of the Rockies add drama to the experience. Canadian Cuisine. **$$**

★★★Ticino
415 Banff Ave., Banff,
403-762-3848;
www.ticinorestaurant.com
Named after the region in Switzerland that borders on Italy, this influence is reflected in Ticino's Swiss-Italian cuisine. The contemporary "Cucina Nostrana" emphasises hearty pasta meat and fish dishes with a variety local vegetables and herbs. The rustic, Italian alpine room has attracted diners for more than 30 years. **$$$**

★★★The Primrose
300 Mountain Ave., Banff,
403-762-1889, 800-661-1587;
www.rimrockresort.com
High on Sulphur Mountain, this restaurant is the more casual dining option at the Canadian Rockies Rimrock Resort Hotel. Enjoy great views and a straightforward American menu. **$$$**

SPAS

★★★★Willow Stream Spa
405 Spray Ave., Banff, 403-762-6860;
www.fairmont.com
Willow Stream Spa is a shining star in the world-class mountain paradise of Banff Springs. This top-rated facility has it all, along with an outdoor whirlpool, an indoor Hungarian mineral pool and three waterfall-style whirlpools. A diverse treatment menu is available, offering therapies customized for reawakening, balancing, rejuvenating, and revitalizing. Sport-specific treatments include massages designed for golfers and skiers, while those who want to enjoy their spa treatments a deux will enjoy massages and other therapies in the specially-designed couples suite. A full-service fitness center offers guided hikes and fitness consultations in addition to its two pools, cardiovascular equipment, and free weights. **$$$$**

5

ALBERTA

CALGARY

Calgary, the gateway to the Canadian Rockies, was founded in 1875 by the North West Mounted Police at the confluence of the Bow and Elbow rivers. Surrounding the city are fertile farmlands and to the west, the rolling foothills of the Rockies. A city couldn't be more ideally situated for both economic luster and gawk-value—lush ranchlands and profitable grain farming have made the city Canada's principle agribusiness center, while majestic peaks overlook the urban landscape to lure adventure-seekers.

Site of the 1988 Olympic Winter Games, Calgary offers endless pursuits for outdoor enthusiasts, with world-class golf, skiing, snowboarding, hiking, mountaineering and whitewater rafting in its foothills and alpine environs.

Powering Calgary's recent phenomenal growth is oil. Since 1914, the petroleum industry has centered its activities here. Today, more than 85 percent of Canada's oil and gas producers are headquartered in Calgary. Despite this influx of cash and ambition, Calgary retains a small town with a wild west atmosphere well demonstrated by the enthusiasm and pride that brims over during Stampede Week—arguably one of the most voracious parties in the entire country.

Information: www.tourismcalgary.com

WHAT TO SEE AND DO

Calgary Flames (NHL)
Pengrowth Saddledome, 14th Ave. and 5th St. S.E., Calgary, 403-777-4646; www.calgaryflames.com
Professional hockey team.

Calaway Park
Trans-Canada Hwy. 1 at Springbank Rd., Calgary. (6 miles/10 kilometers W. via Hwy. 1, Springbank exit), 403-240-3822; www.calawaypark.com
An amusement park with 30 rides, attractions, entertainment, games, shops and concessions. July-August: daily; late May-June and September-October: weekends.

Calgary Science Centre
701 11th St. S.W., Calgary, 403-268-8300; www.calgaryscience.ca
Discovery Dome, astronomy displays, exhibitions, observatory and self-guided tours; science and technology demonstrations.

Calgary Tower
101 9th Ave. S.W., Calgary, 403-266-7171; www.calgarytower.com
A 626-foot (191-meter) tower with a spectacular view of Calgary and the Rocky Mountains. Also a revolving restaurant, observation terrace, lounge and shopping.

The Calgary Zoo, Botanical Garden and Prehistoric Park
1300 Zoo Rd. N.E., Calgary, 403-232-9300; 800-588-9993; www.calgaryzoo.ab.ca
One of Canada's largest zoos, with more than 900 animals; botanical garden; Canadian

Wilds (25 acres) features Canadian eco-systems populated by their native species. Prehistoric Park.

Canada Olympic Park
88 Canada Olympic Rd. S.W., Calgary, 403-247-5452; www.coda.ab.ca
The premier site of the 1988 Olympic Winter Games. Olympic Hall of Fame and Museum, plus winter sports facilities with one double and two triple chairlifts, a t-bar, ski school and rentals. Summer facilities include mini-golf, beach volleyball, a summer bobsled ride, mountain biking and softball.

Devonian Gardens
7th Ave. and 2nd St. S.W., Calgary, 403-268-3830; www.calgary.ca/parks/devonian
A lush, welcoming oasis of green in the heart of the city with waterfalls, fountains and fish ponds as well as concerts, art displays, a playground and a reflecting pool. Below the gardens are stores and restaurants.

Eau Claire Festival Market
200 Barclay Parade S.W., Calgary, 403-264-6450; www.eauclairemarket.com
A two-story warehouse with boutique shops, specialty food stands, restaurants, bars and a five-screen cinema, including an IMAX theater.

EPCOR Centre for the Performing Arts
205 8th Ave. S.E., Calgary, 403-294-7455; www.epcorcentre.org
Four theaters noted for excellent acoustics house the Calgary Philharmonic, Orchestra Theatre Calgary and other performing arts.

Fort Calgary Historic Park
750 9th Ave. S.E., Calgary, 403-290-1875; www.fortcalgary.com
This vast riverside park is the site of the original North West Mounted Police (NWMP) fort at the meeting place of the Bow and Elbow rivers. Abandoned in 1914, the site of the fort is now being rebuilt. An interpretive center highlights NWMP and Calgary history. Adjacent is Deane House (1906), restored and open as a restaurant.

Glenbow Museum
130 9th Ave. S.E., Calgary, 403-268-4100; www.glenbow.org
Museum, art gallery, library and archives. Regional, national and international fine arts; displays of native cultures of North America and the development of the West; mineralogy, warriors, African and personal adornment. Museum shop.

Heritage Park Historical Village
1900 Heritage Dr. S.W., Calgary, 403-268-8500; www.heritagepark.ab.ca
Recreates life in western Canada before 1914. More than 150 exhibits; steam train, paddle wheeler, horse-drawn wagon and electric streetcars, wagon rides, antique midway.

Museum of the Regiments
4520 Crowchild Trail S.W., Calgary, 403-974-2850; www.themilitarymuseums.ca
One of North America's largest military museums, the Museum of the Regiments honors four Calgary regiments. Films, traveling art exhibits.

Royal Tyrrell Museum of Paleontology
Midland Provincial Park, 403-823-7707, 888-440-4240; www.tyrrellmuseum.com
The world's largest display of dinosaurs in a state-of-the-art museum setting. More than 35 complete dinosaur skeletons; Paleoconservatory with more than 100 species of tropical and subtropical plants that once thrived in this region; hands-on exhibits include interactive terminals and games throughout. Summer bus service from Calgary.

Spruce Meadows
18011 Spruce Meadows Way S.W., Calgary, 403-974-4200; www.sprucemeadows.com
Only internationally sanctioned outdoor horse jumping show held in North America; offers the world's richest show jumping purse. June-September.

7

ALBERTA

★
★
★
★
★

SPECIAL EVENTS

Calgary Stampede
Stampede Park, Olympic Way S.E. and
14th Ave., Calgary,
403-261-0101, 800-661-1260;
www.calgarystampede.com
Billed as "The World's Greatest Outdoor
Show," Stampede has been held every
year since 1912. Revelers gather with vivid
enthusiasm for parades, rodeos, chuck
wagon races, stage shows, exhibition,
square dances, marching bands and vaudeville shows. Ten days in early July.

Calgary Winter Festival
100-634 6th Ave. S.W., Calgary,
403-543-5480
Music, entertainment, sports competitions,
children's activities, carnival, dance. Eleven
days in mid-February.

HOTELS

★★**Blackfoot Inn**
5940 Blackfoot Trail S.E., Calgary,
403-252-2253, 800-661-1151;
www.blackfootinn.com
200 rooms, 7 story. Two restaurants, three
bars. Pet. Exercise. Swim. Busn. Center. **$**

★★★**Delta Bow Valley**
209 4th Ave. S.E., Calgary,
403-266-1980, 800-268-1133;
www.deltahotels.com
Guests have the choice of a room with a
city, mountain, or river view at this downtown full-service hotel which is located
east of the grand Canadian Rockies. Close
to local attractions give guests plenty to see
and do. The weekends feature the complimentary Children's Creative Centre. Elements Bistro emphasises regional cuisine
and Canadian wines are featured.
398 rooms, 21 story. Restaurant, bar, children's activity center. Pets accepted, fee.
Exercise room. Pool. Busn. Center. **$$**

★★★**Delta Lodge at Kananaskis**
1 Centennial Dr., Kananaskis,
403-591-7711; www.deltahotels.com
This resort is a paradise located amidst rug-
ged mountains. It is located close to Nakiska,

site of the 1988 Olympic Alpine events, so
guest can enjoy skiing or snowboarding. The
resort can also customize an activity package
for guests during their stay. Children have fun
at Kananaskis Kids Club. Have dinner at one
of the four restaurants, and enjoy a nightcap at
Bighorn Lounge.
321 rooms. Four restaurants, bar, children's
activity center. Pets accepted, fee. Exercise
room. Pool. Tennis. Busn. Center. **$$**

★★**Executive Resort at Kananaskis**
2 Terrace Dr., Kananaskis Village,
403-591-7500, 888-591-3932;
www.executivehotels.net
90 rooms. Exercise Room. **$$**

★★★**The Fairmont Palliser**
133 9th Ave. S.W., Calgary,
403-262-1234, 800-441-1414;
www.fairmont.com
This palace-style building is a city favor-
ite and its downtown location makes it a
convenient base for the business or leisure
traveler. This hotel is a masterpiece of tra-
ditional European styling. A skywalk con-
nects to the Telus Convention Centre, Cal-
gary Tower and Glenbow Museum. The
Oak Room and Rimrock restaurants feature
a variety of savory treats, while guests with
a sweet tooth look forward to the twice
weekly, all-chocolate buffets.
405 rooms. Restaurant, bar. Pets accepted,
fee. Exercise room. Pool. Busn. Center. **$$**

★★**Greenwood Inn Calgary**
3515 26th St. N.E., Calgary,
403-250-8855, 888-233-6730;
www.greenwoodinn.ca
210 rooms. Restaurant, bar. Airport. Pets
accepted, fee. Exercise room. Pool. **$**

★★★**Hyatt Regency Calgary**
700 Centre St. South, Calgary,
403-717-1234, 800-233-1234;
www.calgary.hyatt.com
This Hyatt's downtown location is ideal
for both leisure and business travelers.
Spacious rooms, vast amenities and 24-hour
room service as well as a fitness center and
indoor pool keep guests pampered. Relax-

ing dinners and small get-togethers can be had at Thomsons Restaurant and the Sandstone Lounge.
355 rooms. Restaurant, bar. Pets accepted, fee. Exercise room. Pool. Busn. Center. $$$

★★★International Hotel Suites Calgary
220 4th Ave. S.W., Calgary,
403-265-9600, 800-637-7200;
www.internationalhotel.ca
This high-rise hotel is conveniently located in the heart of the city center, within walking distance of area attractions. Although the hotel is known as "Calgary's Business Hotel," families and leisure travelers are warmly welcomed. A 4th Avenue Cafe, the hotel's on-site restaurant, features International cuisine and offers a children's menu. For lighter fare, head over to the 4th Avenue Lounge and order from the tapas menu.
248 rooms, all suites. Restaurant, bar. Exercise. Swim. $$

★★★Marriott Calgary
110 9th Ave. S.E., Calgary,
403-266-7331, 800-228-9290;
www.marriott.com
Situated in the heart of downtown Calgary, the Marriott is connected by skywalk to the Calgary Tower and Telus Convention Center and located near the Glenbow Museum and the Calgary Zoo. An array of amenities and services provides guests with the comforts of home
384 rooms. Restaurant, bar. Pet. Exercise. Swim. Busn. Center. $$

★★★Sheraton Cavalier Hotel
2620 32nd Ave. N.E., Calgary,
403-291-0107, 800-325-3535;
www.sheratoncalgary.ca
Many families choose the Sheraton Cavalier Hotel when staying in Calgary not only for its spacious guest rooms but for it indoor water park. But with a well-equipped business center and a cyber cafe on-site, the hotel attractions a number of business travelers as well. It is located only ten minutes from the airport and a complimentary shuttle is available to guests.

306 rooms. Restaurant, bar. Airport. Pets accepted, fee. Exercise room. Pool. Busn. Center. $$

★★★Sheraton Suites Calgary Eau Claire
255 Barclay Parade S.W., Calgary,
403-266-7200, 888-784-8370;
www.sheratonsuites.com
This downtown hotel facing Eau Claire Market is a great choice for both business and leisure travelers, and the indoor pool with waterslide is a hit with kids. Guest suites are spacious and dining options diverse, including the Irish pub Fionn McCool's and Barclay's, an upscale-casual restaurant.
323 rooms, all suites. Restaurant, bar. Pets accepted, fee. Exercise room. Pool. Busn. Center. $$$

SPECIALITY LODGING

Rafter Six Ranch Resort
Hwy. 1 and South Ranch Rd., Seebe,
403-673-3622, 888-267-2624;
www.raftersix.com
Wilderness camping facilities plus 30 rooms. Restaurant, bar. Swim. $$

RESTAURANTS

★★Atrium Steakhouse
2001 Airport Rd. N.E., Calgary,
403-250-6012, 800-268-1133;
www.deltahotels.com
Steak menu. Bar. $$$

★★★The Belvedere
107 8th Ave. S.W., Calgary, 403-265-9595;
Housed in the restored Union Bank building, this contemporary dining room has a plush, clubby feel. A seasonal, unhurried experience featuring globally inspired, creative cuisine.
French, seafood, steak, vegetarian. $$$

★★★Centini Restaurant and Lounge
160 8th Ave. S.E., Calgary,
403-269-1600; www.centini.com
Fresh, seasonal food is prepared and served with a passion at this Italian restaurant located in downtown Calgary's Telus Convention Center, near many businesses and

ALBERTA

shops. Housemade specialty pastas and an extensive wine list featuring 650 wines and 8,500 bottles.
Italian menu. Reservations recommended. **$$$**

★★Hy's Steak House
316 4th Ave. S.W., Calgary, 403-263-2222; www.hyssteakhoue.com
Legendary steak menu famed across Canada. **$$$**

★★★Panorama
101 9th Ave. S.W., Calgary, 403-508-5822; www.calgarytower.com
This revolving dining room has beautiful views of the city and surrounding mountains. An observation deck and souvenir store keeps tourists coming, but the locals still flock to this downtown perch for special-occasion dining.
American menu. **$$$**

★★Quincy's on Seventh
609 7th Ave. S.W., Calgary, 403-264-1000; www.quincysonseventh.com
Located in the city centre, a train runs directly outside, connecting to downtown points and farther destinations. Steak menu. Reservations recommended. **$$$**

★★★Rimrock Room
133 9th Ave. S.W., Calgary, 403-260-1219, 800-441-1414; www.fairmont.com
Located in the landmark Palliser Hotel, this regionally influenced restaurant has been serving guests for more than 80 years. The elegant dining room is a popular choice for special-occasion dinners and for seating during the lobby's Sunday buffet brunch. Canadian Regional menu. **$$$**

★★River Cafe
Prince's Island Park, Calgary, 403-261-7670; www.river-cafe.com
Canadian regional menu. Outdoor seating. **$$**

★Regency Palace
328 Centre St. S.E., Calgary, 403-777-2288.
Chinese menu. Reservations recommended on weekends. **$$**

★★The Keg Steakhouse and Bar
7104 MacLeod Trail S., Calgary, 403-253-2534; www.kegsteakhouse.com
Steak menu. Outdoor seating. **$$**

CANMORE

Canmore burst onto the tourist scene after hosting nordic events during the 1988 Calgary Winter Olympics. Today, it is an authentic Alpine village that's a destination for thrills and vistas alike, with a significant selection of exquisite galleries and unique gift shops. Most of Canmore can be traversed within an hour by foot; the town centre surrounds 8th Street, (or "Main Street," as it is known colloquially), originally a residential road boasting some of the oldest architecture in the town.

Much of the area to the northeast of Canmore is located in a critical wildlife corridor which hosts bears, cougars, wolves and elk as they move between habitats. A series of hiking and walking paths traverse this area, known as The Benchlands, and are watched over by various stakeholders (Bow Valley Mountain Bike Alliance, the B.V. Riding Association and local hiking groups) in order to protect wildlife and its habitat while providing high-quality recreational trails. Climbing is popular, with trad, sport and multi-pitch climbs throughout the Bow Valley, and the area is a world destination for ice climbing. Kayakers and canoeists can enjoy guided trips with one of the many local outfitters, or independently navigate the surrounding rivers and lakes. Caving enthusiasts will enjoy the extensive Rat's Nest Caves.
Information:www.tourismcanmore.com

SPECIAL EVENTS

The Canmore ArtsPeak Festival
Canmore, 403-996-0293;
www.artspeakcanmore.com
Celebrates Canmore's artistic spirit by featuring various artists, an art walk, a literary festival, film screenings and street performers. June.

Canmore Children's Festival
Canmore, 403-678-1878;
www.canmorechildrensfestival.com
A two-day event providing an array of children's entertainment, including acrobats, magicians, jugglers, music, theatre, storytelling, crafts, stilt-walking, dancing, face painting and clowns. Late May.

The Canmore Folk Music Festival
Canmore, 403-678-2524;
www.canmorefolkfestival.com
Held annually on the Heritage Day long weekend in August at Centennial Park on the Stan Rogers Stage. The festival is the longest running music festival in Alberta. Late August.

The Canmore Highland Games
Canmore, 403-678-9454;
www.canmorehighlandgames.ca
Presented annually by the Three Sisters Scottish Society on the September long weekend. The games host a heavy lifting competitions, piping, drumming and highland dance events. September.

The Canmore Ice Climbing Festival
Canmore, 403-678-4164;
www.canmoreiceclimbingfestival.com
An international event featuring an 18-meter (60-foot) manmade ice wall constructed on Canmore's downtown fringe from chicken wire, scaffolding and long hoses. Events include an exhibitor tent, climbing clinics and renowned guest speakers. December.

Festival of Eagles
Canmore; www.eaglewatch.ca
A celebration of the Golden Eagle autumn migration over Canmore and the Bow Valley. The weekend celebration includes guided hikes, bird walks, interpretive displays, theatrical performances and guest speakers. Spotting scopes are set up at Canmore Collegiat High School. Mid-October.

Mozart on the Mountain
Canmore, 403-571-0270;
www.cpo-live.com/main/
content.php?content_id=80
An outdoor concert presented annually by the Calgary Philharmonic Orchestra. Late August.

HOTELS

★★Chateau Canmore
1720 Bow Valley Trail, Canmore,
403-678-6699, 800-261-8551;
www.chateaucanmore.com
93 rooms, all suites. Restaurant, bar. Exercise room. Pool. Tennis. Busn. Center. $

★★Radisson Hotel And Conference Center Canmore
511 Bow Valley Trail, Canmore,
403-678-3625, 800-333-3333;
www.radisson.com
224 rooms. Restaurant, bar. Pets accpeted, fee. Exercise room. Pool. $

SPECIALITY LODGING

The Lady MacDonald Country Inn
1201 Bow Valley Trail, Canmore,
403-678-3665, 800-567-3919;
www.ladymacdonald.com
12 rooms. Complimentary full breakfast. $

RESTAURANTS

★★Chez Francois
1604 2nd Ave., Canmore,
403-678-6111.
French menu. Closed January 2-10. Outdoor seating. $$$

★★Sinclair's
637 Main St., Canmore,
403-678-5370.
American menu. Outdoor seating. $$$

ALBERTA

EDMONTON

As the capital of a province whose economic mainstays are petroleum and agriculture, Edmonton has all the brash confidence as a major supplier of one of the world's most sought-after resources. Yet at the heart this northern stalwart is rooted in a practical sensibility.

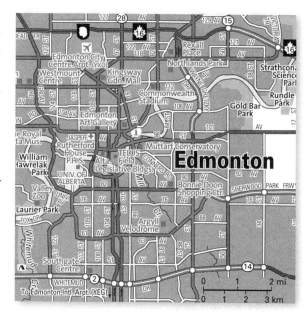

Established as a fort of operations during the fur trade era, Edmonton came into itself in the 1890s as a major supply depot for the Yukon gold rush—the highlight of the All-Canadian Route to the Klondike. Thousands of men stopped for days, weeks, or months before making the final 1,500-mile (2,400-kilometer) push for gold. Many decided to stay, transforming a quiet village into a prosperous city. Each July the city celebrates this era with Klondike Days.

Edmonton is a beautifully green city, with more park area per capita than any other city in Canada, primarily along the banks of the North Saskatchewan River. Visitors enjoy a perfectly Albertan blend of outdoor adventure, shopping, sports, arts, culture, dining, recreation and a wide variety of world-class attractions. "Canada's Festival City" also offers a calendar full of annual events and festivals celebrating jazz, folk, symphony, theatre, dance, visual arts, street performers, food and fun for every member of the family.

Information: www.tourism.ede.org

★ ## WHAT TO SEE AND DO

★ ### Canada's Aviation Hall of Fame
Wetaskiwin, Approximately 40 miles/64 kilometers S. of Edmonton via Hwy. 2A,
★ 403-361-1351;
www.cahf.ca

Features the inspiring stories and artifacts of more than 100 influential aviators. Vintage planes, free-standing exhibits and a large aviation library.

Capital City Recreation Park
95th St. and 97th Ave., Edmonton,
780-496-7275
Winding through the city's river valley, this is one of Canada's most extensive park systems. Bicycle, walking and cross-country ski trails link the major parks featuring barbecue and picnic facilities and food concessions.

Citadel Theatre
9828 101 A Ave., Edmonton,
780-425-1820
This five-theater complex located in downtown Edmonton is one of Canada's finest centers for the performing arts. Glass-enclosed atrium area; waterfall. Three theater series. September-May.

Commonwealth Stadium
11000 Stadium Rd., Edmonton,
780-944-7400
Built for the Eleventh Commonwealth Games, and now home of the Canadian Football League's Edmonton Eskimos. The

Stadium Recreation Centre houses a gym, weights and racquetball and squash courts.

Devonian Botanic Garden
Hwy. 60 and Garden Valley Rd., Devon, 6 miles/9.6 kilometers W. via Yellowhead Hwy. 16, then 9 miles/14 kilometers S. on Hwy. 60, 780-987-3054; www.discoveredmonton.com/devonian
An enormous, lush retreat including alpine and herb gardens, a peony collection and native plants, an extraordinary 5-acre (2-hectare) Japanese garden, nature trails, aspen and jack pine forests, a lilac garden, a butterfly pavilion and an orchid greenhouse. May-September, Daily.

Edmonton Art Gallery
2 Sir Winston Churchill Sq., Edmonton, 780-422-6223; www.edmontonartgallery.com
More than 5,000 works of contemporary and historical art from around the world live here, the largest art museum and longest-running cultural institution in Alberta.

Edmonton Oilers (NHL)
Rexall Place, 7424 118 Ave. N.W., Edmonton, 780-451-8000; www.edmontonoilers.com
Professional hockey team.

The Edmonton Queen Riverboat
9734 98th Ave., Edmonton, 780-424-2628; www.edmontonqueen.com
This riverboat runs along the North Saskatchewan River, which travels through many local parks. Packages include Sunday brunch, dinner, or cruise only.

Fort Edmonton Park
Whitemud Dr. and Fox Dr., Edmonton, 780-496-8787; www.gov.edmonton.ab.ca/fort
Canada's largest historical park encompasses Fort Edmonton (1846), the Hudson's Bay Company Trading Post that gave the city its name. Demonstrations, artifacts and costumed interpreters as well as steam trains and streetcar rides.

Francis Winspear Centre for Music
4 Sir Winston Churchill Sq., Edmonton, 780-428-1414, 800-563-5081; www.winspearcentre.com
Home of the Edmonton Symphony Orchestra.

John Janzen Nature Centre
Fox Dr. and Whitemud Dr., Edmonton, 780-496-2939
Natural history events and programs; hands-on exhibits; active beehive, gopher colony and nature trails; nature shop.

Kinsmen Sports Centre
9100 Walterdale Hill N.W., Edmonton, 780-496-7300
Swimming, diving; weight training, racquet sports.

Muttart Conservatory
9626 96A St., Edmonton, 780-496-8755; www.edmonton.ca/muttart
Glass pyramid house controlled growing environments: tropical, arid and temperate. A fourth pyramid is a floral showcase which is refreshed every few weeks.

Odyssium
11211 142nd St., Edmonton, Coronation Park, 780-452-9100; www.odyssium.com
An entertainment hub with a 275-seat IMAX theater, dome theater, Star Theater and six exhibit galleries featuring the latest discoveries in science, astronomy and space exploration. Artifacts (moon rock, telescopes) and space flight simulation.

Old Strathcona Farmers' Market
10310-83 Ave., Edmonton, 780-439-1844.
Shop for produce and local crafts at this indoor market. Saturday 8 a.m.-3 p.m.

13

ALBERTA

Reynolds-Alberta Museum

Wetaskiwin, Approximately 40 miles/64 kilometers S. of Edmonton via Hwy. 2A, 780-361-1351; www.machinemuseum.net

Interprets the mechanization of ground and air transportation, agriculture and selected industries in Alberta from the turn of the 20th century. More than 100 major artifacts in a vast museum building, hangars and grounds. Displays include vintage steam-powered farm equipment, automobiles and aircraft.

Royal Alberta Museum

12845 102nd Ave., Edmonton, 780-453-9100; www.royalalbertamuseum.ca

Excellent displays reflecting the many aspects of Alberta's heritage. Exhibits on natural and human history include information about aboriginal peoples, wildlife, geology, live insects, dinosaurs and Ice Age mammals.

Rutherford House

11153 Saskatchewan Dr., Edmonton, 780-427-3995; tprc.alberta.ca/museums/ historicsiteslisting/rutherfordhouse

This Jacobean Revival home was the residence of Alberta's first premier and has been restored and refurnished to reflect the lifestyle of the post-Edwardian era. Costumed interpreters reenact life in 1915 with activities such as woodstove baking, historical dramas, craft demonstrations and musical performances.

Valley Zoo

13315 Buena Vista Rd., Edmonton, 780-496-6911; www.gov.edmonton.ab.ca/valleyzoo

Features a wide variety of birds and mammals, fish and reptiles. Train, merry-go-round, pony and camel rides.

West Edmonton Mall

8882 170 St., Edmonton, 780-444-5308, 800-661-8890; www.westedmontonmall.com

Canada's largest shopping and entertainment complex features more than 800 stores and services, 110 eating establishments, 26 movie theaters, an aquarium, dolphin shows, a replica of a Spanish galleon, four submarines, a water park with wave pool and water slides, bungee-jumping, ice skating rink, casino, the Galaxyland amusement park with a 14-story looping rollercoaster, 18-hole miniature golf course and an IMAX Theatre.

SPECIAL EVENTS

Canadian Finals Rodeo

Rexall Place 7424 118th Ave. N.W. and 73rd St., Edmonton, 780-471-7210; www.canadianfinalsrodeo.ca

Professional indoor rodeo to decide the national championships. Mid-November.

Edmonton International Street Performers Festival

Sir Winston Churchill Sq., Edmonton, 780-425-5162; www.edmontonstreetfest.com

Performances by more than 60 international street acts at more than 1,000 free outdoor shows. July.

Edmonton's Klondike Days

Rexall Place 7424 118th Ave. N.W. and 73rd St., Edmonton, Northlands Park, 780-471-7210; www.northlands.com

Entertainment, exhibits, midway, parade; events include the Sourdough Raft Race, Sunday promenade, band extravaganza and chuckwagon races. Mid-late July.

Folk Music Festival

95th St. and 97th Ave., Edmonton, 780-429-1899; www.edmontonfolkfest.org

Three days of music at Alberta's largest outdoor music festival. Mid-August.

Fringe Theatre Festival

Old Strathcona district, 10330 84th Ave., Edmonton,

780-448-9000;
www.fringetheatreadventures.ca
Dance, music, plays, mime, mask, street entertainers. Over 1,200 performances of 140 productions on 30 stages, in the parks and on the streets. Mid-late August.

Heritage Festival
William Hawrelak Park, 9330 Goat Rd. N.W., Edmonton,
780-488-3378;
www.heritage-festival.com
More than 70 cultures show Alberta's multicultural heritage in pageantry of color and music. Music, dance, displays and demonstrations at 50 outdoor pavilions, plus arts and crafts and international cuisine. Early August.

Jazz City International Music Festival
780-432-7166;
www.allaboutjazz.com
Jazz concerts, workshops, outdoor events. Late June-early July.

HOTELS

★★★Delta Edmonton Centre Suite Hotel
10222 102nd St., Edmonton,
708-429-3900, 800-661-6655;
www.deltahotels.com
The location of this hotel is inside the Edmonton City Centre West shopping mall. It's also connected to City Hall and the Shaw Conference Centre. There's more to do in Edmonton than just hang out at the mall though as there's almost always a fantastic festival to check out. Cocoa's, the hotel's restaurant, features Continental cuisine with regional specialties and serves breakfast, lunch, dinner, Sunday brunch and late-night snacks. With its location overlooking the mall, Cocoa's Lounge is the perfect spot to relax and people-watch while enjoying a cocktail.
169 rooms. Restaurant, bar. Pets accepted. Exercise room. Busn. Center. $$

★★★The Fairmont Hotel Macdonald
10065 100th St., Edmonton,
780-424-5181, 800-441-1414;
www.fairmont.com

The Fairmont Hotel MacDonald reigns over Edmonton. This glorious château overlooks the scenic North Saskatchewan River Valley. From its formal high tea to its distinguished guest rooms and suites, this hotel recalls the grace and charm of the Victorian period. Its historic character is carefully preserved, yet this hotel also welcomes the modern day with complete fitness and business centers. Inventive nouveau cuisine is highlighted at Harvest Room, which also serves a Sunday brunch, and the Confederation Lounge is a nice spot for sipping a cocktail while soaking up the clubby atmosphere.
198 rooms. Restaurant, bar. Pets accepted, some restrictions; fee. Fitness room. Pools. Busn. Center. $$

★★Fantasyland Hotel
17700 87th Ave., Edmonton,
780-444-3000, 800-737-3783;
www.fantasylandhotel.com
355 rooms. Two restaurants, bar. Exercise room. Busn. Center. $$

★★Holiday Inn
4235 Gateway Blvd. N., Edmonton,
780-438-1222, 800-565-1222;
www.hipalace.com
136 rooms. Restaurant, bar. Pets accepted, fee. Exercise room. $$

★★★The Sutton Place Hotel
10235 101st St., Edmonton,
780-428-7111, 866-378-8866;
www.suttonplace.com
Connected by a walkway to Edmonton Centre, with over 400 stores, businesses and services, this hotel is also located near the Edmonton International Airport, the Space and Science Center, and many other area attractions. Within walking distance is the brand new Sir Winston Churchill Square as well as the Edmonton Art Gallery. Enjoy dinner at the Sutton Place's Capitals Restaurant with its a la carte menu or sip a drink or two at the open-air atrium of Central Park Lounge.

★
★
★
★
★

313 rooms. Restaurant, bar. Pets accepted, some restrictions; fee. Exercise room. Pool. Busn. Center. **$$**

★★★The Westin Edmonton
10135 100th St., Edmonton,
780-426-3636, 800-937-8461;
www.starwoodhotels.com
Conveniently located in downtown Edmonton, this hotel has a pedestrian walkway that connects to such area attractions as Edmonton Art Gallery, Shaw Conference Center and the Citadel Theater. Enjoy and unwind at the WestinWORKOUT® Powered gym or swim in the heated indoor pool. Pradera Café, the Westin's restaurant, focuses on regional and international cuisine.
416 rooms. One restaurants, bar, children's activity center. Pets accepted. Exercise room. Pool. Busn. Center. **$$**

★★Best Western Cedar Park Inn
5116 Gateway Blud.,
Edmonton,
780-434-7411, 800-780-7234;
www.bestwestern.com
190 rooms, 5 story. Restaurant, bar. Pet. Exercise. Swim. **$**

★Ramada
5359 Calgary Trail, Edmonton,
780-434-3431, 800-661-9030;
www.ramada.ca
127 rooms, 7 story. Complimentary full breakfast. Restaurant, bar. Exercise. Swim. **$**

RESTAURANTS
★★Cocoa's
10222 102nd St. N.W., Edmonton,
708-423-9650; www.deltahotels.com
French menu. **$$$**

★★La Boheme
6427 112th Ave., Edmonton,
780-474-5693;
www.laboheme.ca
French menu. Outdoor seating. **$$$**

★★★La Ronde
10111 Bellamy Hill, Edmonton,
780-428-6611;
www.chateaulacombe.com
This restaurant sits on the rooftop of the Crowne Plaza Hotel Chateau Lacombe. The revolving room has incredible views of the surrounding city.
Seafood, steak menu. **$$$**

★★La Spiga
10133 125th St., Edmonton,
780-482-3100.
Italian menu. Outdoor seating. Mansion built in 1915. **$$$**

★★★The Harvest Room
10065 100th St., Edmonton,
780-429-6424, 800-441-1414;
www.fairmont.com
Located in the historic, chateau-style Hotel MacDonald, this elegant dining room features contemporary Canadian cuisine using fresh, local ingredients such as Alberta beef and veal, farm-raised game and free-range poultry. The outdoor terrace overlooks the North Saskatchewan River Valley.
Seafood, steak menu. **$$$**

★Creperie
10220 103rd St., Edmonton,
780-420-6656;
www.thecreperie.com
French bistro menu. Reservations recommended. **$$**

★Fiore
8715 109th St., Edmonton,
780-439-8466.
Italian menu. Outdoor seating. **$$**

FORT MACLEOD
From a distance, Fort Macleod looks like any other town—but its rich history and national significance are apparent as soon as visitors wander through its streets. It is at a crossroads that once hosted Indian encampments, wagon trails and buffalo grazing grounds, in view of the

Porcupine Hills that front the Rocky Mountains. Known 150 years ago as Blackfoot Crossing, Fort Macleod became a North West Mounted Police barracks and trading post in 1874. From the fort spread the fame of the 'men in red' who stamped out the illegal whiskey trade and kept rowdy gold miners in check—and who eventually became known as the Canadian RCMP.

The town gradually took shape alongside the Oldman River, named for the grandfather of Blackfoot mythology and within easy view of the mountains. Fort Macleod draws you into a time when the North West Mounted Police, Blackfoot Indians and pioneer settlers were the only inhabitants. Main Street is dotted with gift shops, antique stores and restaurants that recapture this spirit.

Information: www.fortmacleod.com

WHAT TO SEE AND DO

Fort Museum
219 25th St., Fort Macleod,
403-553-4703;
www.nwmpmuseum.com
Experience the rich history of Fort Macleod, the first out-port in the Canadian west. Witness the history of the North West Mounted Police (the precursor to the national RCMP), plains tribes and pioneer life, and enjoy the spectacle of the Mounted Patrol Musical Ride. July-September: four times daily.

Head-Smashed-In Buffalo Jump Interpretive Centre
Hwys. 2 and 785, Fort Macleod,
403-553-2731;
www.head-smashed-in.com
This UNESCO World Heritage Site celebrates 6,000 year-old Native American hunting techniques as interpreted by members of Blackfoot Nation, built into the cliff where buffalo were herded to jump to their death.

Remington Carriage Museum
623 Main St., Cardston,
403-653-5139;
www.remingtoncarriagemuseum.com
Displays one of the largest collections of horse-drawn vehicles in North America, with over 200 carriages, wagons and sleighs. Gallery has interactive displays, multimedia productions and a carriage factory.

SPECIAL EVENTS

Powwow and Tipi Village
Head-Smashed-In Buffalo Jump, Hwys. 2 and 785, Fort Macleod,
403-553-2731
Celebration features open tepee village, traditional native dances, games, food. Third weekend in July.

Santa Claus Parade and Festival
3rd Ave. and 24th St., Fort Macleod,
403-553-2500
One of the oldest and largest Santa Claus parades west of Toronto. Last Saturday in November.

★
★
★
★
★
★

JASPER
Everywhere you turn in the resort town of Jasper, dramatic peaks crown the horizon. Established in 1907 in the heart of the Canadian Rockies, Jasper is one of Canada's largest and most scenic national parks—and unique in that the town of the same name is at its center, jointly governed by a municipal government and Parks Canada. In its more than 4,200 square miles (10,878 square kilometers) are waterfalls, lakes, canyons, glaciers and wilderness areas filled with varied forms of wildlife. The park has year-round interpretive programs, trips and campfire talks as well as guided wilderness trips, a sky tram, skating, skiing, ice climbing and rafting and cycling trips. While driving through Jasper, be prepared to be awestruck at every turn. Keep your camera poised—all the better if you've got a wide-angle lens for unmatched panoramas.

Information: jasper-alberta.com

WHAT TO SEE AND DO

The Icefields Parkway

www.pc.gc.ca/pn-np/ab/Jasper/visit/visit14_e.asp

One of the most famous mountain highways in the world, the Icefields Parkway travels between Lake Louise and Jasper along the crown of the Canadian Rockies. The scenery is phenomenal: soaring peaks still under the bite of glaciers, turquoise green lakes surrounded by deep forests, roaring waterfalls and at the very crest of the drive, the Columbia Icefield, the largest non-polar icecap in the world. Lakeside lodges offer canoe rentals, short horseback trail rides, whitewater rafting trips and trips onto the Columbia Icefield in specially designed snowcoaches. Just off the highway, by the Athabasca Glacier, the Columbia Icefield Centre provides information on the ice field and the glaciers (May-mid-October). Wildlife is also abundant: mountain goats, mountain sheep, elk, moose and bears are frequently sighted.

Maligne Tours

Hwy. 16 and Maligne Rd., Jasper, 780-852-3370; www.malignelake.com

Narrated boat cruise on Maligne Lake to world-famous Spirit Island (May-mid-October: daily). Fishing supplies and boat rentals. Whitewater raft trips.

Jasper Tramway

Hwy. 93 and Whistler Mountain Rd., 780-852-3093; www.jaspertraway.com

Two 30-passenger cars take 1 1/4-mile (2-kilometer) trip up Whistler's Mountain. Vast area of alpine tundra at summit; hiking trails, picnicking; restaurant, gift shop. April-mid-October: daily.

Marmot Basin

Hwy. 93 A and Marmot Basin Rd., Jasper, 780-852-3816; www.skimarmot.com

Quad, triple, three double chairlifts, two T-bars; patrol, school, rentals, repair shop; nursery, three cafeterias, bar. Vertical drop 3,000 feet (897 meters). Early December-late April.

Miette Hot Springs

Miette Rd. and Hwy. 16, Jasper, 780-866-3939, 800-767-1611; www.parkscanada.gc.ca/hotsprings

Pool uses natural hot mineral springs. Mid-May-early October.

Sightseeing tours

Jasper National Park, 607 Connaught Dr., Jasper, 780-762-6700

Various tours are offered by bus, raft, gondola and snowcoach to Lake Louise, Jasper, Calgary, Banff and the Athabasca Glacier.

HOTELS

★Alpine Village

Hwy. 93A N., Jasper, 780-852-3285; www.alpinevillagejasper.com

37 rooms. Closed mid-October-April. **$**

★★★Chateau Jasper

96 Geikie St., Jasper, 780-852-5644, 800-661-9323

This comfortable hotel is an ideal base for active travelers who enjoy skiing, snowboarding, snowshoeing and ice skating during the winter and hiking and guided nature tours during the summer. Spacious rooms feature lovely views, while the hotel's in-town location makes it perfect for dining and shopping.

119 rooms, 3 story. Restaurant, bar. Pool. **$$$**

★★★The Fairmont Jasper Park Lodge

Old Lodge Rd., Jasper, 780-852-3301; www.fairmont.com

The Fairmont Jasper Park Lodge is the sophisticated alternative in the Canadian Rocky Mountains. This rustic retreat consists of a series of cedar chalets and log cabins, with luxurious accommodations, fine dining and exceptional services.

390 rooms. Restaurant, bar, children's activity center. Pets accepted, some restrictions; fee. Exercise room. Pool. Golf. Tennis. **$$**

★★Lobstick Lodge

94 Geikie St., 780-852-4431, 888-852-7737;

www.mtn-park-lodges.com
139 rooms. Restaurant, bar. Pets accepted, fee. Pool. **$**

★★Marmot Lodge
86 Connaught Dr., Jasper,
780-852-4471, 888-852-7737;
www.mtn-park-lodges.com
10 rooms. Restaurant, bar. Pets accepted, fee. Pool. **$$**

★★Sawridge Inn & Conference Center
82 Connaught Dr., Jasper,
780-852-5111, 888-729-7343;
www.sawridgejasper.com
153 rooms. Restaurant, bar. Pool. **$$**

RESTAURANTS
★★★Edith Cavell Dining Room
Old Lodge Rd., Jasper,
708-852-6052, 800-441-1414;
www.fairmont.com

The gourmet fare, vintage wines and attentive service of Jasper Park Lodge's dining room are all eclipsed by breathtaking lake and mountain views.
French menu. Jacket required. **$$$**

★L & W
Hazel and Patricia St., Jasper,
780-852-4114.
American, Greek menu. Outdoor seating in a garden-like setting. **$$**

★Something Else
621 Patricia St., Jasper,
780-852-3850.
Italian, Greek menu. Outdoor seating. Homemade pizza. **$$**

★★Tonquin Prime Rib Village
100 Juniper, Box 1216, Jasper,
780-852-4966.
Steak menu. Outdoor seating. **$$$**

LAKE LOUISE

The blue-green glacial lake reflects a mirror image of the Victoria Glacier when the sun hits it at the right point and at the shore, nestled at the base of the mountain, sits the Chateau Lake Louise, one of the most elegant and classic hotel landmarks on the continent.

Lake Louise is the third in the must-visit trinity of Banff and Jasper. Its central Rocky Mountain location, longstanding history and lively resort atmosphere make it both an exciting and scenic destination. During the summer, the sightseeing gondola takes visitors high over the town to Mount Whitehorn, where a lodge serves as alpine home base for hiking, picnicking and exploration. Summer or winter, take in the fresh mountain air equipped with canoe, mountain bike, skis, snowboard, climbing rope or horse.
Information: www.banfflakelouise.com

★
★
★
★
★

WHAT TO SEE AND DO
Lake Louise Gondola
877-253-6888;
www.lakelouisegondola.com
Ascend to 6,810 feet (2,075 meters) in 14 minutes, to view Lake Louise Victoria Glacier and The Great Divide. Restaurant, cafeteria, deli bar; hiking trails, nature programs. Summer operation runs June 1-September 30.

Lake Louise Ski Area
403-522-3555, 800-258-7669;
www.skilouise.com

Canada's largest ski area with over 100 runs on four mountain faces across more than 4,200 acres (1,700 hectares) of skiing. Top elevation 8,650 feet (3,636 hectares); vertical drop 3,257 feet (993 meters). Four high-speed quads, one quad, one triple chair, two double chairs, one expert platter, one T-bar, one beginner rope tow, one magic carpet. Four restaurants, three cafeterias, three bars; rental shop, ski and snowboard school. Early November-mid-May.

Moraine Lake and Valley of the Ten Peaks

Lake Louise, 7.5 miles/12 kilometers E. of Lake Louise.

Towering mountain peaks frame the emerald green lake. Hiking trails, canoe rental.

HOTELS

★★Baker Creek Chalets

Hwy. 1A, Bow Valley Pkwy., Lake Louise, 403-522-3761;
www.bakercreek.com
35 rooms. Restaurant, bar. **$$**

★★Deer Lodge

109 Lake Louise Lodge, Lake Louise, 403-522-3991, 800-661-1595;
www.crmr.com
73 rooms. Restaurant, bar. Former trading camp (1921). Closed early October-early December. Busn. Center. **$$**

★★★Emerald Lake Lodge

1 Emerald Lake Rd., Field, 250-343-6321, 800-663-6336;
www.crmr.com
Located on 13 acres in Yoho National Park, the lodge has a formal dining room, reading and sitting rooms, conference facilities and a games room. The on-site restaurant, Mount Burgess Dining Room, serves rustic California cuisine with Native American influences and offers award-winning Canadian wines. There's plenty of activities from hiking and fishing in summer to skiing and ice fishing in winter.
25 cabin-style buildings, 85 rooms. Three restaurants, two bars. Exercise room. Busn. Center. **$$**

★★★The Fairmont Chateau Lake Louise

111 Lake Louise Dr., Lake Louise, 403-522-3511, 800-441-1414;
www.fairmont.com
This grand resort offers its guests a front-row seat to Banff National Park while overlooking the sparkling water of Lake Louise. Stunning panoramas are matched only by the sophistication and comfort offered inside, where European flair blends with Canadian hospitality.
550 rooms. Seven restaurants, three bars. Ski in/ski out. Pets accepted, fee. Exercise room. Pool. Skiing. Busn. Center. **$$$**

★★★Post Hotel

200 Pipestone Rd., Lake Louise, 403-522-3989, 800-661-1586;
www.posthotel.com
This historic alpine lodge shares the finer things with guests who savor gourmet European cooking, sip award-winning wines and sleep in total luxury. One of Canada's best ski areas is just a few minutes from the hotel.
96 rooms. Closed mid-October-mid-December. Two restaurants, two bars. Ski in/ski out. Pool. Skiing. Busn. Center. **$$$**

RESTAURANTS

★★★Fairview Dining Room

111 Lake Louise Dr., Lake Louise, 403-522-3511, 800-441-1414;
www.fairmont.com
This historic dining room, Chateau Lake Louise's original, is housed in a breathtaking Canadian Rockies location. One of several restaurants at the resort, the dining room serves classic continental cuisine during the summer months amidst original, 1913 grandeur. **$$$**

★★★★Post Hotel Dining Room

200 Pipestone Rd., Lake Louise, 403-522-3989, 800-661-1586;
www.posthotel.com
Tucked into the foothills of the Canadian Rockies is this gem of a dining experience. Set in one of Banff National Parks remaining historic log lodges, the Post Hotel Dining Room achieves an easy sense of old-fashioned charm with majestic mountain views and a blazing stone fireplace. The exceptional cuisine is matched by a highly acclaimed wine list with more than 28,500 bottles and more than 1,500 selections. Canadian menu. Closed late October-mid-December. Reservations recommended. **$$$$**

20

ALBERTA

★★Walliser Stube
111 Lake Louise Dr., Lake Louise,
403-522-3511, 800-441-1414;
www.fairmont.com
French menu. $$$

LETHBRIDGE

Lethbridge is one of the warmest and sunniest cities in Canada—and not just in terms of the weather. The community's pride for its recreation-driven lifestyle makes for a friendly, spirited and active community.

Originally known to the Blackfoot as Sik-okotoks or "place of black rocks," Lethbridge transformed from a coal-producing town to a lush parkland with gardens such as the Brewery Gardens at the western edge of town; Indian Battle Park, site of the last battle between Native American nations in North America (1870); and Henderson Lake Park. In 1869, traders from the United States came north and built so-called "whiskey forts" in and around the future city site, the most notorious of which was Fort Whoop-Up. The arrival of the North West Mounted Police in 1874 soon stamped out this illegal whiskey trade and brought order to this rambunctious corner of the west. The rebuilt fort now steeps visitors in this wily heritage, and the flag that signaled the arrival of the latest load of whiskey is now the city's official flag.
Information: www.lethbridgecvb.com

WHAT TO SEE AND DO
Alberta Birds of Prey Center
403-345-4262, 800-661-1222;
www.albertabirds.com
Living museum featuring hawks, owls, falcons and other birds of prey from Alberta and around the world. Interpretive center has educational displays, wildlife art. Daily flying demonstrations; picnicking. May-mid-October, daily, weather permitting.

Fort Whoop-Up
3rd Ave. S. and Scenic Dr.,
Lethbridge, Indian Battle Park,
403-329-0444;
www.fortwhoopup.com
Step into southern Alberta history at this replica of a booming, circa-1870s whiskey trading post. Interpretive gallery, theater, tours. Mid-May-September: daily; rest of year: Tuesday-Friday, Sunday afternoons.

Nikka Yuko Japanese Garden
Henderson Lake Park, Mayor Magrath Dr. and 9th S., Lethbridge,
403-328-3511;
www.nikkayuko.com
Built to commemorate Canada's centennial in 1967, the authentic garden is a symbol of Japanese-Canadian friendship. The garden is an art form of peace and tranquility. Mid-May 5-September 30: daily.

Sir Alexander Galt Museum
5th Ave. and Scenic Dr., Lethbridge,
403-320-3898;
www.galtmuseum.com
Displays relate to early development of area. Featured exhibits include indigenous culture, pioneer life, civic history, coal mining, farming history, irrigation, ethnic displays.

Waterton Lakes National Park
Hwys. 5 and 6, Waterton Park,
403-859-2224, 800-661-8888;
www.pc.gc.ca/edu/TRC/htm/
fwaterton_e.asp
Waterton is a rare gem tucked into the southwest corner of Alberta where the great Rocky Mountains rise suddenly out of the rolling prairies. Amid the peaks are the lakes of Waterton, carved out of the rock by ancient glaciers and forming a blend of unusual geology, mild climate, rare flowers and abundant wildlife.

In 1932 Waterton Lakes National Park was linked with neighboring Glacier

21

ALBERTA

★
★
★

National Park in Montana—the cross-border area is now known as Waterton-Glacier International Peace Park. This park contains 203 square miles (526 square kilometers) on the eastern slope of the Rocky Mountains, just north of the U.S.-Canadian border. Travelers from the United States can reach the park via the Chief Mountain Highway along the east edge of Glacier National Park (mid-May-mid-September). The trails are well-maintained and afford an introduction to much of the scenery that is inaccessible by car. The Red Rock Parkway goes from the town of Waterton Park to Red Rock Canyon after branching off Alberta Hwy. 5. A buffalo paddock is located on Hwy. 6, just inside the northeastern park boundary. Also from the town of Waterton Park, you can drive to Cameron Lake via the Akamina Parkway.

SPECIAL EVENTS

Ag Expo and the North American Seed Fair
Exhibition Park, 3401 Parkside Dr. S., Lethbridge,
403-328-4491;
www.exhibitionpark.ca
This annual event presents the latest in agricultural technology to the public and also includes a fashion show and Aggie Days for kids. Late February.

International Air Show
Hwy. 5 S. and McNally Rd., Lethbridge,
800-661-1222;
www.albertaairshow.com
The Canadian Forces Snowbirds are the highlight of this two-day airshow that includes several Canadian and international acts. August.

Whoop-Up Days
10th Ave. and 43rd St., Lethbridge,
403-328-4491;
www.exhibitionpark.ca/whoopup.htm
Fair, exhibitions, rodeo, grandstand show. Mid-August.

HOTELS

★★Best Western Heidelberg Inn
1303 Mayor Magrath Dr., Lethbridge,
403-329-0555, 800-791-8488;
www.bestwestern.com
65 rooms Restaurant, bar. Exercise room. Busn. Center. $

★★★The Kilmorey Lodge
117 Evergreen Ave., Waterton Lakes National Park,
403-859-2334, 888-859-8669;
www.kilmoreylodge.com
This historic lodge can be found on the lakeshore at Emerald Bay, tucked between mountain peaks in Waterton Lake. It offers uniquely decorated and well furnished rooms featuring fine antiques and other treasures from the past.
23 rooms. Two restaurants, bar. $

★★Lethbridge Lodge
320 Scenic Dr., Lethbridge,
403-328-1123, 800-661-1232;
www.lethbridgelodge.com
190 rooms. Two restaurants, two bars. Pets accepted, fee. Pool. Swim. $

★★Prince of Wales
117 Evergreen Ave.,
Waterton Lakes National Park,
403-859-2231;
www.princeofwaleswaterton.com
81 rooms. Closed mid-September-early June. Restaurant, bar. $$

RESTAURANTS

★★★Coco Pazzo
1264 3rd Ave. S., Lethbridge,
403-329-8979.
One of the trendiest spots in the area, this restaurant offers guests the best in Italian food in a casual, cafe atmosphere. With a variety of pasta dishes to suit every taste, fantastic red wine and a fun crowd, it is a delightful dining experience. Italian cuisine. Outdoor seating. $$$

★★★Sven Ericksen's
1715 Mayor Magrath Dr., Lethbridge,
403-328-7756.
Seafood, steak. $$

MEDICINE HAT

Despite its industrious roots, Medicine Hat is the ideal environ for natural bounty and beauty. Rich in clays and natural gas, the area was a natural site for brick, tile and petrochemical plants—but its hot summer temperatures make it ideal for beautiful market gardens and greenhouses.

The name Medicine Hat is a translation of the Blackfoot name Saamis, meaning "headdress of a medicine man," an item lost in the river by one such Cree during a fight with the Blackfoot. Natural gas was discovered here in 1883 and in 1909 the huge Bow Island gas field was founded, sending the town on a production frenzy that lasted for generations—the gas fields inspired the British poet Rudyard Kipling to refer to the settlement as "the town with all hell for a basement."
Information: www.city.medicine-hat.ab.ca

WHAT TO SEE AND DO

Cypress Hills Interprovincial Park
E. from Medicine Hat on Trans-Canada
Hwy. 1, then S. on Hwy. 41,
403-893-3777
An oasis of mixed deciduous and coniferous forests in the middle of a predominantly grassland region. At a maximum elevation of 4,810 feet (1,466 meters) above sea level, the hills are the highest point in Canada between the Rocky Mountains and Labrador. The area offers a swimming beach, boating, canoeing and fishing; camping (fee), golf course, hiking trails and nature interpretive programs.

Dinosaur Provincial Park
Approximately 25 miles/40 kilometers W. of Medicine Hat on Hwy. 1, then N. on Hwy. 884, W. on Hwy. 544,
403-378-4342;
www.gov.ab.ca/env/parks/prov_parks/dinosaur
Discoveries of extensive fossil concentrations in this area in the late 1800s led to the designation of this area as a provincial park and UNESCO World Heritage Site. More than 300 complete skeletons have been recovered and are now displayed in museums worldwide. The 22,000-acre (8,903 hectares) park consists mainly of badlands; large areas have restricted access and can be seen only on interpretive tours. Facilities include canoeing, fishing; interpretive trails, dinosaur displays (at the actual discovery site) along a public loop drive. Camping. Guided tours and hikes, amphitheater events and talks.

Medicine Hat Museum and Art Gallery
1302 Bomford Crescent S.W.,
Medicine Hat,
403-502-8580;
www.highway3.ca/attractions/mhartgallery.htm
Displays depict the history of the Canadian West, featuring pioneer items, local fossils, relics and Native artifacts. The archives contain a large collection of photographs and manuscripts.

SPECIAL EVENT

Exhibition and Stampede
Stampede Park, 2055 21st Ave. S.E.,
Medicine Hat,
403-527-1234;
www.mhstampede.com
Cattle and horse shows, professional rodeo, midway rides. Late July.

HOTELS

★Best Western Inn
722 Redcliff Dr., Medicine Hat,
403-527-3700, 888-527-6633;
www.bestwestern.com
122 rooms. Complimentary continental breakfast. Pets accepted, fee. Exercise room. Pool. $

★★Medicine Hat Lodge
1051 Ross Glen Dr. S.E.,
Medicine Hat,
403-529-2222, 800-661-8095;
www.medhatlodge.com
221 rooms. Restaurant, bar. Pets accepted, fee. Exercise room. Pool $

23

ALBERTA

RED DEER

Midway between Calgary and Edmonton is Red Deer, beautifully positioned from all possible perspectives in the lush, green parkland of central Alberta. A wealth of recreation and cultural programs keep visitors charmed, including famed dinner theatres by Central Alberta Theatre. Attend rodeos and authentic agricultural exhibitions alongside world-class sporting events such as the Sears Open Figure Skating Championship and the Scott Tournament of Hearts (curling).

In the early 1870s, the Calgary-Edmonton Trail crossed the river at Red Deer Crossing. With the coming of the railway, traffic increased and a trading post and stopping place were established. When the Northwest Rebellion broke out in 1885, a small regiment was stationed at Fort Normandeau, which still stands on the outskirts of the city. The river was originally called Was-ka-soo See-pi, the Cree word for elk, because of the abundance of these animals. Early Scottish fur traders thought the elk were related to the red deer of their native land, hence the present name for the river and city.
Information: www.city.red-deer.ab.ca

WHAT TO SEE AND DO

Canyon Ski Area
Ross St., Red Deer, 403-346-7003;
www.canyonski.net
Triple, double chairlifts, two T-bars, handle tow, nordic jump; patrol, school, rentals, snowmaking; day lodge, bar. Vertical drop 500 feet (164 meters). Cross-country skiing. November-March, daily.

Fort Normandeau
The C & E Trail and 32nd St., Red Deer, 403-346-2010;
www.waskasoopark.ca/ftnorm.htm
Rebuilt 1885 army fort and interpretive center with displays of cultural history. Slide program, living history interpreters. May-September: daily. Picnic area, canoe launch.

Red Deer and District Museum
4525 47 A Ave., Red Deer, 403-309-8405;
www.museum.red-deer.ab.ca
Displays cover prehistory and early settlement of Red Deer; changing exhibits. Also located here are Heritage Square and Red Deer and District Archives.

Waskasoo Park
49th St. and 48th Ave., Red Deer,
403-342-8159;
Large River Valley park extending throughout city. Includes 47 miles (75 kilometers) of bicycle and hiking trails, equestrian area, fishing, canoeing, water park, 18-hole golf course, camping. Natural and cultural history interpretive centers; other attractions located within park.

SPECIAL EVENTS

Fort Normandeau Days
Fort Normandeau, Range Rd. 280 and 32nd, Red Deer,
403-346-2010
Native American ceremonies and dances, parade, children's activities. Late May.

Highland Games
Westerner Exposition Park,
4847 19th St., Red Deer;
www.reddeerhighlandgames.ca
The annual Games began in 1947 and feature highland dancing, piping and drumming and shortbread baking competitions. Last Saturday in June.

Westerner Days
4847 A-19th St., Red Deer,
403-343-7800
Fair and exhibition, midway, livestock shows, chuckwagon races. Mid-July.

HOTELS

★★★Capri Conference Centre
3310 50th Ave., Red Deer,
403-346-2091, 800-662-7197;
www.capricentre.com
Although this Red Deer full-service hotel is primarily booked with convention travelers, families and leisure travelers are welcomed. Various types of rooms and suites are avail-

ble. Guests will find plenty of activities to keep their days busy. The hotel has a heated outdoor pool and deck, a whirlpool, a shopping concourse and the Capri Centre Spa & Health Club. Barbero's Restaurant is a great choice for a business lunch or quiet dinner and guests can kick up their heels at Billy Bob's Country Music Dance Hall or take a breather at Bellinis Lounge.

220 rooms. Two restaurants, three bars. Pets accepted, some restrictions; fee. Exercise room. Pool. **$**

★★**Holiday Inn**
6500 67th St., Red Deer,
403-342-6567, 888-465-4329;
www.ichotelsgroup.com
97 rooms. Complimentary continental breakfast. Restaurant, bar. Pets accepted, fee. Exercise room. Pool. Busn. Center. **$**

★**Holiday Inn Express**
2803 50th Ave., Red Deer,
403-343-2112, 800-465-4329;
www.ichotelsgroup.com
92 rooms. Complimentary continental breakfast. Pets accepted, fee. Exercise room. Pool. Busn. Center. **$**

25

ALBERTA

BRITISH

COLUMBIA

BRITISH COLUMBIANS LIVE IN A CORNER OF CANADA THAT SEES AN EXPLOSION OF DAFFODILS and cherry blossoms while the rest of the country is still shoveling snow. In this westernmost province, life is enormous—from thousand-year-old trees and everyday mountain vistas to towering city sunflowers and epic memories.

Five diverse regions make up the whole of the province, each pulling tourists a hundred different ways each day: Vancouver Island, Vancouver Coast & Mountains, Thompson Okanagan, the Kootenay Rockies, the Cariboo Chilcotin Coast and the vast Northern region.

Vancouver Island has one of the world's most diverse ecosystems: rainforests, marshes, meadows, beaches, mountains, oceans, rivers and lakes create habitats for multitudes of wildlife species. It all adds up to one of the world's premier locations for golf, whale watching, birding, and salmon and trout fishing. The island is blanketed in rare, old-growth rainforest and dramatic mountain ranges, picturesque cities and towns, and smaller island groups that invite ferry-bound adventures at an island pace.

Vancouver Coast and Mountains, slated to host the 2010 Olympic Games, is a phenomenal mountainous city—a mecca of peaks, ocean, lakes, rivers and beaches encircling a cosmopolitan gem that rivals the most spectacular cities in the world. Revel in the four-season resort town of Whistler, famed worldwide for skiing, great shopping and fine restaurants. Visitors and residents cycle, hike, camp, kayak, golf, ski and snowboard year-round—in fact, the mild climate is such that a "West Coast Special" is an everyday option: ski in the morning, then golf or sail in the afternoon.

The Thompson Okanagan region is as famous for its pastoral orchards and vineyards as it is for its wildly varied landscape—the highest mountain in the Canadian Rockies is here, as well as a waterfall twice the height of Niagara Falls and Canada's only true desert. The heart of BC's wine-growing region is located just a four-hour drive east of Vancouver, where more than 40 wineries are within a 150-mile (241-kilometer) range.

The Kootenays are a purer mountain play, a vast wilderness of rivers, lakes, waterfalls, beaches, mineral hot springs, alpine meadows and snow-capped mountains. Adventure connoisseurs tackle some of the world's most intense mountain biking, fishing, windsurfing, whitewater rafting and kayaking. Golfers come here for world-class courses with unbeatable scenery, and city slickers turn cowboy at dude and guest ranches that offer authentic cattle rides. Visit restored heritage towns, thriving arts communities and gold rush boomtowns, and in winter, take in the continent's finest powder skiing and snowboarding.

Thousands of lakes and rivers, plus a magnificent stretch of Pacific Ocean coastline, make the Cariboo Chilcotin Coast, which harkens back to the adrenaline-pumping gold rush era, an über-destination for fishing, boating, camping, swimming and kayaking. This is a region whose rich, fascinating history is perhaps only rivaled by its captivating present-day—complete with cowboys riding off into the sunset. Roam endless gentle trails or hike, ride and canter strenuous backcountry routes. Tramp through the volcanic mountains of Tweedsmuir Provincial Park, stand at the ancient hoodoos and shifting sand dune of Farwell Canyon and drive the original Cariboo Waggon Road on the historic Gold Rush Trail, taking in famed local rodeos and stampedes.

Northern BC's vast wilderness comprises more than half the province, a land of jagged mountain peaks, roaring rivers, serene lakes, green valleys, rugged coastlines and ancient island archipelagos. The region is known for its magnificent freshwater and saltwater fishing, canoeing, kayaking, whitewater rafting and in the winter, powder skiing. A wondrous system of national and provincial parks provides habitats and sanctuary for wildlife. The Queen Charlotte Islands are a living mystery within this region, an untamed, old-growth land rich in Haida culture and with distinct island flora and fauna that have evolved over thousands of years.

Provincial Capital: Victoria
Information: www.hellobc.com

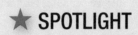

★ SPOTLIGHT

★ British Columbia is Canada's third-largest province after Quebec and Ontario. There are only 30 nations in the world and one US state (Alaska), larger in surface area than British Columbia.

DUNCAN

In addition to a thriving downtown with heritage buildings, shops and restaurants, Duncan, in the Cowichan region of Vancouver Island (just up from Victoria), is surrounded by vast tracts of unspoiled mountain, forest and coastal wilderness. Often referred to as the "City of Totems," Duncan has more than 40 examples of Aboriginal totem poles on display along its streets and walkways. The city is a good jumping-off point for touring valley wineries or recreational activities in nearby provincial parks.

Information: www.cowichan.bc.ca/visit/communities/duncan.htm

WHAT TO SEE AND DO

British Columbia Forest Discovery Centre
2892 Drinkwater Rd., Duncan,
250-715-1113;
www.bcforestmuseum.com
Logging and forest exhibits, equipment, train ride.

Pacific Northwest Raptor's
Bird of Prey Centre
1877 Herd Rd., Duncan,
250-746-0372;
www.pnwraptors.com
Learn about the aristocratic sport of falconry. Watch trained, free-flying birds of prey soar overhead. Hands-on courses,

demonstrations and activity days throughout the year.

Quw'utsun' Cultural & Conference Centre
200 Cowichan Way, Duncan,
250-746-8119, 877-746-8119;
www.quwutsun.ca
Learn about the First Nations heritage and the ancestral home of the Cowichan Tribes through interpretive tours, multimedia displays, hands-on carving experiences and locally made crafts at this tranquil setting along the river.

BRITISH COLUMBIA

KAMLOOPS

Thanks to more than 2,000 hours of annual sunshine, Kamloops trout are world famous, bountiful in over 200 lakes within an hour's drive of the city. Balmy summers encourage rapid plant and fish growth, making the area widely recognized as a freshwater fishing hotspot. In addition to hundreds of lakes, there are many areas of dry forest, hilly areas that are largely treeless (and well tracked-up by enthusiastic mountain bikers) and grasslands that support several endangered species.

Information: www.adventurekamloops.com

WHAT TO SEE AND DO

Kamloops Museum and Archives
207 Seymour St., Kamloops,
250-828-3576;
www.kamloops.ca/museum/index.shtml
Natural history; Shuswap culture; fur trade; Gold Rush eras.

Kamloops Wildlife Park
9077 E. Dallas Dr., Kamloops,
250-573-3242;
www.kamloopswildlife.org
More than 300 animals, both native and international. Nature trail, miniature railroad, park.

Secwepemc Native Heritage Park
355 Yellowhead Hwy., Kamloops,
N. across Yellowhead Bridge, then take the first right,
250-828-9801
Located on the Kamloops Reserve, this park interprets culture and heritage of the Secwepemc people. Includes archaeological site, full-scale winter village model, indoor museum exhibits and native arts and crafts.

SPECIAL EVENTS

International Air Show
Fulton Field, Kamloops,
250-554-0700
Concession, beer garden. Mid-July.

HOTELS

★★Accent Inn Kamloops
1325 Columbia St. W., Kamloops,
250-374-8877, 800-663-0298;
www.accentinns.com
83 rooms. Restaurant. Pets accepted, fee. Pool. $

★★★The Coast Canadian Inn
339 St. Paul St., Kamloops,
250-372-5201.
This hotel is located in downtown Kamloops, the center of the Thompson Valley recreation area. Perfect for the busines traveler with complimentary high speed Internet connection in each room. Enjoy a pint or two at Sgt. O'Flaherty's Pub or a light dinner at Pronto Grill.
98 rooms. Restaurant, bar. Pets accepted, fee. Exercise room. Pool. Busn. Center. $

★★Ramada Inn
555 W. Columbia St., Kamloops,
250-374-0358, 800-663-2832;
www.ramadainn.kamloops.com
90 rooms. Restaurant, bar. Pets accepted, fee. Pool. $

28

BRITISH COLUMBIA

KELOWNA

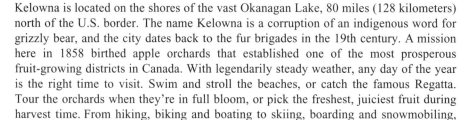

Kelowna is located on the shores of the vast Okanagan Lake, 80 miles (128 kilometers) north of the U.S. border. The name Kelowna is a corruption of an indigenous word for grizzly bear, and the city dates back to the fur brigades in the 19th century. A mission here in 1858 birthed apple orchards that established one of the most prosperous fruit-growing districts in Canada. With legendarily steady weather, any day of the year is the right time to visit. Swim and stroll the beaches, or catch the famous Regatta. Tour the orchards when they're in full bloom, or pick the freshest, juiciest fruit during harvest time. From hiking, biking and boating to skiing, boarding and snowmobiling,

every season holds promise. For golfers, Kelowna offers one of the longest and driest seasons in Canada.
Information: www.tourismkelowna.org

SPECIAL EVENTS

Black Mountain Rodeo Golf Tournament
Hwy. 33 and Brentwood, Kelowna,
250-763-7888,
Mid-May.

Kelowna Regatta
24-436 Bernard Ave., Kelowna,
250-860-0529, 877-973-4288;
www.kelownaregatta.com
Dating back to 1906, the Kelowna Regatta features many family-oriented land and water activities including a parade, rowing competitions, hydroplane races, water-skiing and an airshow. Mid-July.

Okanagan Wine Festivals
Kelowna, 250-861-6654; www.owfs.com
Dance, wine tasting at various locations around the Okanagan Valley. May and October.

HOTELS

★★Accent Inn Kelowna
1140 Harvey Ave., Kelowna,
250-862-8888, 800-663-0298;
www.accentinns.com
101 rooms. Restaurant. Pets accepted, fee. Exercise room. Pool. $

★★Best Western Inn-Kelowna
2402 Hwy. 97N., Kelowna,
250-860-1212, 888-860-1212;
www.bestwestern.com/ca/innkelowna
147 rooms. Restaurant, bar. Pool Tennis. $

★★★Coast Capri Hotel
1171 Harvey Ave.,
Kelowna,
250-860-6060, 800-663-1144;
www.coasthotels.com
Surrounded by mountains and orchards, this Kelowna landmark is located near golf courses, water sports and Lake Okanagan. Enjoy the year-round heated outdoor pool, hot tub and fitness center. End the evening with a visit to Bluelines Sport & Comedy Club for some fun.
85 rooms. Restaurant, bar. Pets accepted, fee. Pool Busn. Center. $

★★Sandman Hotel Kelowna
2130 Harvey Ave.,
Kelowna,
250-860-6409, 888-526-1988;
www.sandmanhotels.com
120 rooms. Restaurant, bar. Pets accepted, fee. Pool. $

NANAIMO

Nanaimo is located on Vancouver Island off across the strait of Georgia form Vancouver, a main entry port for ferries from Vancouver and Horseshoe Bay. Because of its location, it serves as a fine starting point to other attractions on the island, as well as being a vacation highlight in itself. A thriving arts, culture and sports scene kicks off your island adventure, a perfect mix of big city amenities with small town charm.
Information: www.tourismnanaimo.com

WHAT TO SEE AND DO

Bastion
Front and Bastion Sts., Nanaimo
Built in 1853 as a Hudson's Bay Company fort. Now restored as a museum; cannon firing ceremony (summer months at noon).

Bowen Park
500 Bowen Rd., Nanaimo, 250-756-5200;
www.nanaimoinformation.com/
bowen-park.php
Swimming pool; Tennis courts, fitness circuit, game fields, picnic shelters, recreation complex, lawn bowling; totem poles, rose

garden, rhododendron grove, petting farm, duck ponds, fish ladder.

BC Ferries
250-669-1211; www.bcferrries.com
Service between Nanaimo and Horseshoe Bay, north of Vancouver (1 1/2 hours); or Duke Point and Tsawassen, south of Vancouver, near U.S. border (2 hours).

Cyber City
1815 Bowen Rd., Nanaimo, 250-755-1828; www.cybercityadventures.com/home.html
Adventure park with laser tag, go-carts, paintball, miniature golf, virtual reality arcade, spaceball. Restaurant.

Nanaimo Art Gallery and Exhibition Centre
900 5th St., Nanaimo, Malaspina College campus, 250-755-8790
Gallery with changing exhibits of art, science and history.

Nanaimo District Museum
100 Cameron Rd., Nanaimo, 250-753-1821; www.nanaimomuseum.ca
Walk-in replica of a coal mine; turn-of-the-century shops, restored miner's cottage; dioramas; Chinatown display; changing exhibits.

Newcastle Island Provincial Marine Park
Nanaimo, 250-754-7893; www.newcastleisland.ca
Boat docking, camping, hiking and bicycle trails, picnicking; pavilion with historical displays, concession (May-September). Dance and barbecue events in summer. No land vehicle access. Access by foot/ passenger ferry from Maffeo Sutton Park (May-mid-October); by private boat the rest of the year.

Petroglyph Park
990 Island Hwy. S., Nanaimo, 250-391-2300; www.britishcolumbia.com/parks/?id=450
Ancient indigenous rock carvings.

Queen Elizabeth Promenade
Front and Bastion Sts., Nanaimo
Named to commemorate the vessel and landing of the first miner-colonists in the area (1854); boardwalk offers pleasant view of waterfront and tidal lagoon.

SPECIAL EVENTS
Boxing Day Polar Bear Swim
Departure Bay Rd., Nanaimo, 250-756-5200
Each Boxing Day, hardy souls take a dip in the frigid waters at Departure Bay Beach. All participants receive prizes as well as free ice cream, bananas and suntan lotion. December 26.

Nanaimo Marine Festival & International Bathtub Race
Front St. and Terminal Ave., Nanaimo, 250-753-7223; www.nanaimoinformation.com/nanaimo-marine-festival.php
A festival highlighted by a 34-mile bathtub race (third or fourth Sunday in July) across the Strait of Georgia to Vancouver. The festival begins one week prior to race day.

Vancouver Island Exhibition
Beban Park, Bowen and Northfield Rds., Nanaimo, 250-758-3247; www.viex.ca
For over 100 years this annual fair has attracted tens of thousands of visitors each year for beautiful artwork, baked goodies and prize-winning livestock. Early or mid-August.

HOTELS
★★★Coast Bastion Inn
11 Bastion St., Nanaimo, 250-753-6601; www.coasthotels.com
This downtown high-rise hotel offers breathtaking views of Nanaimo Harbour and nearby islands from every guest room. Its location is convenient to harbourfront shops, galleries, restaurants and the BC Ferry terminal. After a busy day, Minnoz Restaurant & Lounge is a great place for a delicious meal, the menu offers traditional

★
★
★
★

West Coast cuisine. The bar also offers a light tapas menu for lighter appetites.
179 rooms. Restaurant, bar. Pets accepted, fee. Exercise room. **$$**

★★★Crown Isle Resort
399 Clubhouse Dr., Courtenay,
250-703-5050; www.crownisle.com
The Crown Isle course meets the needs and playing levels of both novice and seasoned golfers. Accommodations include fairway rooms, one- and two-bedroom villas and loft villas. The resort is close to nearby Aquatics Centre and 5th Street shopping district as well as beaches and hiking.
56 rooms. Two restaurants, two bars. Exercise room. Golf. Airport transportation available. **$$**

★★Fairwinds Schooner Cove Resort & Marina
3521 Dolphin Dr., Nanoose Bay,
250-468-7691, 800-663-7060;
www.fairwinds.bc.ca
31 rooms. Restaurant. Pets accepted, fee. Pool. Tennis. Golf. **$$**

★★★Kingfisher Oceanside Resort And Spa
4330 S. Island Hwy., Courtenay,
250-338-1323, 800-663-7929;
www.kingfisherspa.com
Located on wooded grounds in Comox Valley, the Kingfisher has a heated outdoor pool, a sauna, canoe and kayak rentals and nearby golf. The spa offers many services. For a quiet dinner, guests can head to the resort's dining room, the Kingfisher Restaurant, West Coast cuisine, accented by views of Gartley Bay.
64 rooms. Restaurant, bar. Pets accepted, fee. Exercise room. Pool. Golf. Tennis. Busn. Center. **$**

RESTAURANT
★★The Mahle House Restaurant
2104 Hemer Rd., Nanaimo,
250-722-3621;
www.mahlehouse.ca
International menu. Reservations recommended. **$$$**

PENTICTON
Situated between the beautiful Okanagan and Skaha lakes on fertile orchard lands and rolling hills, this valley town is famous for summer heat, beaches, lakes, spectacular natural scenery, Canada's beast of legend Ogopogo and the Ironman Canada Triathlon.
Information: www.penticton.ca

WHAT TO SEE AND DO
Dominion Radio Astrophysical Observatory
717 White Lake Rd., Penticton,
250-493-2277
Guided tours (August). Visitor center (Daily).

Penticton Museum
785 Main St., Penticton,
250-490-2451.
Collection of Salish artifacts; taxidermy, ghost town and pioneer exhibits. Changing exhibits. At 1099 Lakeshore Dr. W are two historic 1914 steamships: SS Sicamous, a 200-foot (61-meter) sternwheeler and SS Naramata, a 90-foot (27-meter) steam tug. Monday-Saturday;.

Summerland Research Station Ornamental Gardens
Hwy. 97 and Johnson St., Penticton,
250-494-7711.
Beautiful display of ornamental gardens; canyon view; picnicking. Picnic grounds May-September: 8 a.m.-8 p.m. with shorter hours October-April; museum open daily 1-4 p.m.

Wonderful Water World
225 Yorkton Ave., Penticton,
250-493-8121
Water park with waterslides, miniature golf, slot car racing on 110-foot (33-meter) track. Concessions, picnic area. Campground on site. Late May-Labour Day.

SPECIAL EVENTS

Penticton Jamboree
Eckhardt Ave. and Hwy. 97, Penticton,
King's Park, 250-493-4055.
Dancing under the stars on what is perhaps North America's largest outdoor board floor. Early August.

Ironman Canada Championship Triathlon
Lake Shore Dr. and Main St., Penticton,
250-490-8787
Qualifier for Hawaiian Ironman. Late August.

Midwinter Breakout
Penticton, 250-493-4055
This winter festival celebrates the season with many events and activities, including ice carving and the Polar Bear Dip. Second and third week of February.

Okanagan Wine Festivals
1304 Ella St., Penticton, 250-861-6654;
www.owfs.com
Wine tasting, grape stomping, seminars and dinners. Various locations around the Okanagan Valley. Late April-early May; late September-mid-October.

Pacific Northwest Elvis Festival
Okanagan Lake Park, Penticton,
800-663-5052
Tribute shows, judged performances, impromptu entertainment, souvenir booths and more. Late June.

Peach Festival
Gyro Park, Main St. and Lake Shore Dr.,
Penticton, 800-663-5052;
www.peachfest.com
This five-day event celebrating the peach harvest has been taking place since 1947. Festivities include a parade, live entertainment, a fireworks display, and arts and crafts exhibits. Families especially love Kiddies Day, which features events and activities created especially with youngsters in mind. Mid-August.

HOTELS

★★Best Western Inn At Penticton
3180 Skaha Lake Rd., Penticton,
250-493-0311, 800-668-6746;
www.bestwestern.com
67 rooms. Restaurant. Pool. $

★★★Penticton Lakeside Resort and Conference Center
21 Lakeshore Dr. W., Penticton,
250-493-8221, 800-663-9400;
www.rpbhotels.com
This resort and conference center is located on the southern shore of Lake Okanagan. The hotel is close to local attractions and offers outdoor packages. Have some fun at the Barking Parrot, the waterfront bar and club.
204 rooms. Restaurant, bar. Pets accepted, fee. Exercise room. Pool. $$

REVELSTOKE

Located in the towering Monashee and Selkirk ranges of the Columbia Mountains between the scenic Rogers and Eagle passes, Revelstoke is the gateway to Mount Revelstoke National Park, with Glacier National Park just to the east. Visitors may enjoy many activities all year. Especially popular is the skiing. With an annual average of 40 feet (13 meters) of snow, Revelstoke offers multiple opportunities for downhill, cross-country, cat helicopter, ski touring adventures and snowmobiling. Tennis, fishing, hiking, golf, caving, mountaineering and swimming are also available throughout this exciting alpine city.
Information: www.revelstokecc.bc.ca

WHAT TO SEE AND DO

Beardale Castle Miniatureland
26 miles/42 kilometers W. of Revelstoke via Trans-Canada Hwy. 1 at Craigellachie,
250-836-2268;
www.3valley.com
Indoor attraction constructed in a European-style village setting. Handcrafted authentic miniature exhibits include prairie town, Swiss mountain village and medieval

German village, each with a model railway running through it. Also animated toyland exhibits. May-September: daily.

Three Valley Gap
12 miles/19 kilometers W. of Revelstoke on Trans Canada Hwy. 1,
250-837-2109;
www.bctravel.com/revelstoke/
heritageghosttown
Historic ghost town, lake, lodging, restaurant, cowboy show. Mid-April-mid-October: daily.

Revelstoke Winterlude
McKenzie and 1st, Revelstoke,
250-837-9351;
www.revelstokewinterlude.com
Outhouse races, parade, casino, dances, entertainment, cross-country skiing, downhill races, snow pitch, ice sculpture, snow Golf tournaments. January.

HOTELS

★★Best Western Wayside Inn
1901 La Forme Blvd., Revelstoke,
250-837-6161, 800-663-5307;
www.bestwestern.com
88 rooms. Restaurant, bar. Pool. $

★★Three Valley Lake Chateau
Trans-Canada Hwy. #1, Revelstoke,
250-837-2109, 888-667-2109;
www.3valley.com
200 rooms. Closed late October-early April. Restaurant. Pool. $

RESTAURANT

★Frontier
122 Hwy. 23 N., Revelstoke,
250-837-5119, 800-382-7763;
International menu. Outdoor seating. $$

VANCOUVER

Surrounded by the blue waters of the Strait of Georgia and backed by the mile-high peaks of the Coast Range, the most mundane of Vancouver moments elicits a gasp at the view—on public transit crossing one of many bridges or from the window of a hotel room, snow-capped peaks tower over the skyline with rainforest adventure and urban escape a short drive away. Aside from having a natural setting unsurpassed on this continent, Vancouver is one of Canada's largest cities—a major seaport, cultural center, tourist spot and gateway to Asia.

BRITISH COLUMBIA

★
★
★
★
★

Vancouver is on the Canadian mainland (not on Vancouver Island as some people think) but is so surrounded by waterfront that it certainly feels like it's on an island, or a series of them. The downtown area is a peninsula on a peninsula that juts out from the rest of the city into Burrard Inlet, making for plentiful urban beaches and marinas.
Information: www.tourismvancouver.com

WHAT TO SEE AND DO

Arts Club Theatre Company
1585 Johnston St., Vancouver,
604-687-5315;
www.artsclub.com
Having helped launch the careers of actors Michael J. Fox and Brent Carver, The Arts Club Theatre steals the Vancouver stage spotlight. In addition to its four annual mainstage productions at Stanley Theatre (Granville and 12th), the company mounts four productions at the Granville Island Stage.

Ballet British Columbia
677 Davie St., Vancouver,
604-732-5003;
www.balletbc.com
With a strong company of 14 dancers, this reigns as Vancouver's top dance troupe. Directed by John Alleyne, former dancer with the Stuttgart Ballet and the National Ballet of Canada, the company's repertoire includes dances by famed choreographers like William Forsythe and John Cranko, as well as commissioned works by Canadian talents. Ballet BC's home stage is the Queen Elizabeth Theatre (Hamilton at Dunsmuir). November-May.

BC Ferries
1112 Fort St., Victoria,
250-386-3432; www.bcferries.bc.ca
Trips to Nanaimo (2 hours) or to Swartz Bay near Victoria (1 1/2 hours); both destinations are on Vancouver Island. Terminals at Horseshoe Bay, north of Vancouver via Trans-Canada Hwy. 1 and Tsawwassen near U.S. border, south of Vancouver via Hwy. 99.

BC Lions (CFL)
777 Pacific Blvd., Vancouver,
604-589-7627; www.bclions.com
Professional football team.

Bites-on Salmon Charters
200-1128 Hornby St., Vancouver,
Granville Island, 604-688-2483;
www.bites-on.com
Coho, sockeye and chinook salmon school in the waters around Vancouver, which is convenient for urban-bound fishing fans. Granville Island-based Bites-On offers day trips of five or eight hours, during which you can sink a line into the Strait of Georgia on a yacht up to 40 feet (12 meters) long. The charters serve parties of one to 12 people. Peak fishing months are April-October, although charters operate year-round. Boat trips also allow fishermen to spot sea lion, porpoise and whale populations.

Burnaby Village Museum
6501 Deer Lake Ave., Vancouver,
604-293-6500;
www.burnabyvillagemuseum.ca
Living museum of the period before 1925 with costumed attendants; more than 30 full-scale buildings with displays and demonstrations. Closed January-April.

Capilano Suspension Bridge
3735 Capilano Rd., Vancouver,
604-985-7474;
www.capbridge.com
The 136 meters Capilano Suspension Bridge towers precariously 230 feet (70 meters) above the Capilano River gorge. Originally constructed in 1889 and rebuilt in 1956, the wooden bridge is engineered of wire rope cemented at either end. In addition to the bridge, the surrounding park provides walking trails, gardens, a totem pole collection and audiences with First Nations carvers at work. Arrive early in high season.

Chan Centre for the Performing Arts
University of British Columbia,
6265 Crescent Rd., Vancouver,
604-822-9197;
www.chancentre.com
In the University of British Columbia district, the Chan houses three venues for theater and music, all sharing the same light-flooded lobby. Built in 1997, the distinctive zinc-clad cylindrical building stands out amid the verdant campus. With superior acoustics, this is one of the best

BRITISH COLUMBIA

spots in town to hear concerts by touring soloists, UBC musicians and the Vancouver Symphony.

Chinatown

E. Pender and Gore Sts., Vancouver.

This downtown area is the nucleus of the third-largest Chinese community in North America (behind San Francisco and New York). At the heart lies the Chinese Market where 100-year-old duck eggs may be purchased; herbalists promise cures with roots and powdered bones. The Dr. Sun Yat-Sen Classical Chinese Garden provides a beautiful centerpiece. Chinese shops display a variety of items ranging from cricket cages to cloisonne vases. Offices of three Chinese newspapers and one of the world's narrowest buildings are located within the community's borders. Resplendent Asian atmosphere offers fine examples of Chinese architecture, restaurants and nightclubs.

CN IMAX Theatre

201-999 Canada Pl., Vancouver,
604-682-2384;
www.imax.com/vancouver

Under the white sails that distinguish waterfront Canada Place, CN IMAX screens wide-format documentary films on subjects ranging from space travel to wildlife conservation. Several shows are screened throughout the day, with a new film starting approximately every hour.

Cypress Mountain

Cypress Bowl and Hwy. 1, Vancouver,
604-419-7669;
www.cypressmountain.com

Covering two mountains with 34 runs and five lifts, Cypress Mountain claims the region's biggest vertical drop at 1,750 feet (533 meters). But the ski area's bigger claim to fame are its cross-country skiing facilities, which span 12 miles (19 kilometers) of groomed trails, nearly five of which are lit for night gliding. The region's most popular Nordic destination also offers private and group lessons as well as rental equipment. Snowshoers can tramp on designated trails solo or take a guided tour.

Dr. Sun-Yat-Sen Classical Chinese Garden

578 Carrall St., Vancouver,
604-662-3207

Unique to the Western Hemisphere, this garden was originally built in China circa 1492 and transplanted to Vancouver for Expo '86.

Ecomarine Ocean Kayak Centre

1668 Duranleau St., Vancouver,
Granville Island, 604-689-7575;
www.ecomarine.com

To get the full impact of Vancouver's magnificent setting on the coast, troll the waterways under paddle power with a kayak from Ecomarine. The outfitter rents both single and double kayaks at its Granville Island headquarters and at an outpost on Jericho Beach (Jericho Sailing Center, 1300 Discovery St.), where first-timers can take a three-hour lesson before getting started. Navigate from placid False Creek to more rugged inlets up the shore.

Fort Langley National Historic Site

23433 Mavis Ave., Fort Langley,
604-513-4777;
www.parkscan.harbour.com/fl

Originally one of a string of Hudson's Bay Company trading posts across Canada, Fort Langley in the Fraser Valley became the birthplace of modern-day British Columbia with the Crown Colony Proclamation, an act of protection by the British against an American gold rush influx, read there in 1858. In addition to preserving the restored buildings, Fort Langley is garrisoned by costumed re-enactors who demonstrate pioneer activities such as blacksmithing and open-fire cooking.

Gallery at Ceperley House

6344 Deer Lake Ave., Vancouver,
604-205-7332;
www.burnabyartgallery.ca

35

BRITISH COLUMBIA

Monthly exhibitions of local, national and international artists. Collection of contemporary Canadian works on paper. Housed in Ceperley Mansion, overlooking Deer Lake and the surrounding gardens.

Gastown
Columbia and Alexander Sts., Vancouver,
604-683-5650;
www.gastown.org
Vancouver's historic nucleus consists of a series of Victorian buildings rehabbed to shelter an array of shops, clubs and eateries. Among the highlights, the Gastown Steam Clock pipes up every 15 minutes and the Vancouver Police Centennial Museum covers the most notorious local crimes. To fully appreciate the neighborhood, show up for a free tour sponsored by the Gastown Business Improvement Society in Maple Tree Square (2 p.m. daily in summer).

Granville Island
A former industrial isle, Granville Island is an urban renewal case study, fashioning markets, shops, homes and entertainment out of decaying wharf warehouses beginning in the 1970s. Its hub is the Public Market, a prime picnic provisioner teeming with fishmongers, produce vendors, butchers, cheese shops, bakeries and chef demonstrations. A specialized Kids' Market and a free outdoor Water Park (May-September) appeal to children. The Maritime Market on the southwest shore serves as a dock for boat owners as well as those looking to hire a fishing charter, hop on a ferry, or rent a kayak. Three Granville Island museums showcase miniature trains, ship models and sport fishing. Dozens of bars and restaurants, many with views back across the water to the downtown skyline, drive the after-dark trade. An art school, artists' studios and several galleries lend bohemian flare to the Granville, abetted by several theaters and street musicians.
A 37-acre (15-hectare) area in the heart of the city, beneath the South end of the Granville Street Bridge, 604-666-5784; www.granvilleisland.bc.ca

Granville Island Kids' Market
1496 Cartwright St., Vancouver,
604-689-8447;
www.kidsmarket.ca
Vancouver's open food market turns its third floor into something kids can enjoy— beyond pastries on the market floor, that is. Twenty-five children's shops, including eight selling toys and another seven selling clothes, take aim at junior consumers, many of whom, of course, prefer Kids' Market's indoor play area. Strolling clowns and face-painters amplify the carnival-like setting.

Greater Vancouver Zoo
5048-264th St., Aldergrove,
604-856-6825;
www.greatervancouverzoo.com
Explore 120 acres housing more than 700 animals. Miniature train ride; bus tour of North American Wild exhibit.

Grouse Mountain
6400 Nancy Greene Way, North Vancouver,
604-984-0661;
www.grousemountain.com
For skiing in winter, hiking in summer and sightseeing year-round, Grouse Mountain draws legions of visitors to Vancouver's North Shore. The area's first ski mountain is still its most convenient, with ski and snowboard runs that overlook the metropolis, as well as a skating rink and sleigh rides available. Hikers have loads of trails to choose from, but the one to boast about is the Grouse Grind, a 1.8-mile (2.9 kilometers) hike straight up the 3,700-foot (1128 meter) peak. Look for mountain bike trails on the back side of the slopes. The Skyride gondola takes the easy route up in an eight-minute ride. At the top, all-season attractions include Theater in the Sky, a high-definition aerial film and several panoramic-view restaurants starring the Strait of Georgia and the twinkling lights of Vancouver.

Harbor Cruises Ltd.
1 North Foot Denman St., Vancouver,
departures from northern foot of Denman

★
★
★
★

St., 604-688-7246; www.boatcruises.com
Boat/train excursion (6 1/2 hours); also
sunset dinner cruises; harbor tours, private
charters. April-October.

Hastings Park
2901 E. Hastings St., Vancouver,
between Renfrew and Cassiar,
604-253-2311;
vancouver.ca/pnepark
Approximately 66-hectares (162 acres).
Concert, convention, entertainment facilities. Thoroughbred racing (late spring-early
fall) and Playland Amusement Park (April-
June: weekends; July-October: daily; also
evenings).

Hastings Park Racecourse
Renfrew and Dundas Sts., Vancouver,
800-677-7702;
www.hastingspark.com
Thoroughbreds run in Vancouver at Hastings Park on the city's east side. Although
the lengthy racing season runs late April-
November, most races are held on Saturday
and Sunday, with extra meets scheduled
for major holidays like Canada Day and
Labour Day. Two-dollar-bet minimums
encourage cheap dates, while self-service
betting terminals patiently acquaint you
with the track lingo.

HR MacMillan Space Centre
1100 Chestnut St., Vancouver,
604-738-7827;
www.hrmacmillanspacecentre.com
One of several museums in Vanier Park
tucked between Kitsilano Beach and
Granville Island, the MacMillan Space Centre appeals to would-be astronauts with a
space flight simulator, planetarium and interactive games. After hours, laser light shows
depart from the scientific, dramatizing music
by the likes of Pink Floyd and Led Zeppelin.

Inuit Gallery of Vancouver
206 Cambie St., Vancouver,
604-688-7323; www.inuit.com
Immerse yourself in the rich artistic
tradition of coastal natives with soapstone

sculptures, native prints, ceremonial masks
and bentwood boxes. One of Vancouver's
best sources for First Nations art, Inuit
represents tribes up and down the Pacific
Northwest. In the Gastown district, Inuit is
a short walk from the convention center and
cruise ship terminal.

Irving House Historic Centre
302 Royal Ave., Vancouver,
604-527-4640;
www.nwpr.bc.ca/parks%20web%20page/
irving%20hse.html
(1864) Fourteen rooms of period furniture
from 1864-1890. Adjacent is the New
Westminster Museum, on the back of
the property, which has displays on local
history, household goods and May Day
memorabilia.

The Lookout at Harbor Centre
555 W. Hastings St., Vancouver,
604-689-0421;
www.vancouverlookout.com
Glass elevators take you to a 360-degree
viewing deck 553 feet (167 meters) above
street level; multimedia presentation, historical displays, tour guides.

Old Hastings Mill
1575 Alma Rd., Vancouver, 604-734-1212;
www.findfamilyfun.com/hastingsmill.htm
One of the few buildings remaining after
the fire of 1886 now houses indigenous
artifacts and memorabilia of Vancouver's
first settlers.

Queen Elizabeth Park
Cambie St. and W. 33rd Ave., Vancouver,
604-257-8570;
www.city.vancouver.bc.ca/parks/parks/
queenelizabeth
Observation point affords a view of the
city, harbor and mountains; Bloedel
Conservatory has more than 100 free-flying
birds, plus tropical, desert and seasonal
displays.

Queen Elizabeth Theatre & Playhouse &
Orpheum Theatre
Vancouver, 604-665-3050;

37

BRITISH COLUMBIA

www.city.vancouver.bc.ca/theatres

A symphony orchestra, opera company and many theater groups present productions around town, especially at the Queen Elizabeth Theatre and Playhouse and Orpheum Theatre. Consult the local paper for details.

Robson Street

The epicenter of Vancouver's street chic, Robson makes a nice window-shopping stroll. A string of shops and sidewalk cafes runs several blocks in either direction from the intersection of Robson and Burrard streets. Retailers range from the posh Giorgio Armani and Salvatore Ferragamo to the playful Benetton on down to the divine ice cream at Cows. Jewelry stores, chocolatiers and craft galleries round out the offerings.

Royal City Star Riverboat Casino

788 Quayside Dr., New Westminster, 604-519-3660; www.royalcitystar.bc.ca

The late-model paddle wheeler "Queen of New Orleans," once stationed on the Mississippi, now calls the Fraser River its home port as the Royal City Star. Games of chance include pai gow poker, mini baccarat, blackjack, roulette and Caribbean stud poker. Several bars, a deli and a restaurant feed and water patrons. Between May and October, the boat schedules regular sailings.

Samson V Maritime Museum

New Westminster, moored on the Fraser River at the Westminster Quay Market 604-522-6891; www.nwpl.new-westminster.bc.ca/ nwheritage.org/heritagesite/orgs/samson/ index.htm

The last steam-powered paddle wheeler to operate on the Fraser River now functions as a floating museum. Displays focus on the various paddle wheelers and paddle wheeler captains that have worked the river and on river-related activities.

Science World British Columbia

1455 Quebec St., Vancouver,

604-443-7443; www.scienceworld.bc.ca

The massive, golf ball-shaped Science World attracts both architecture and museum fans. Modeled on the geodesic domes of F. Buckminster Fuller, the aluminum ball was erected for Expo '86 and now houses a science center devoted to interactive exhibits on nature, invention, ecology and optical illusions. A play space with a water table and giant building blocks engages the 3-to-6 set, while the dome-projection Omnimax theater entertains the whole brood.

Spokes Bicycle Rentals

1789 W. Georgia St., Vancouver, 604-688-5141; www.vancouverbikerental.com

Just across from the Stanley Park entrance on Georgia St., the cycle shop rents from a vast fleet that includes cruisers, tandems, mountain bikes and hybrid models. Spokes also offers bike tours of the Stanley Park perimeter (1 1/2 hours) and Granville Island (3 1/2 hours).

Stanley Park

2099 Beach Ave., Vancouver 604-257-8400; www.seestanleypark.com

One thousand acres of native British Columbia in the heart of the city, Stanley Park, the largest city park in Canada, is a green haven with few peers. Towering forests of cedar, hemlock and fir spill onto sand beaches, immersing visitors and residents alike in the wild just minutes from the civilized. Park-goers recreate along forest hiking trails, on three beaches and along the 5.5 mile (8.9 kilometer) 1920s vintage seawall, where in-line skaters, runners and cyclists admire skyline and ocean views. Man's hand distinguishes the park in gardens devoted to roses and rhododendrons and in a vivid stand of First Nations totem poles. Providing an appeal for every interest, Stanley Park also hosts the Vancouver Aquarium, Children's Farmyard, Miniature Railway, Theatre Under the Stars and several restaurants.

Vancouver Aquarium Marine Science Centre

845 Avison Way, Stanley Park, Vancouver, 604-659-3474.

With inviting, hands-on exhibits, Vancouver Aquarium in sylvan Stanley Park explores the undersea world from Amazon to Arctic, assembling 300 species of fish. For all its globetrotting interests, the aquarium is a top spot to study the local environment as well. In outdoor pools, graceful beluga whales, frisky sea lions and playful otters prove comfortable with the changeable Pacific Northwest climate (private encounters with the belugas and dolphins run $125 to $175 per parent/child pair). Progeny of salmon released by the aquarium in 1998 from a park river return each winter, roughly November to February, illustrating BC's rich salmon-spawning waterways. Behind-the-scenes tours with trainers (an extra $15 to $20) provide visitors a glimpse of the marine mammal rescue and rehab program for which the aquarium is lauded.

The Centre in Vancouver for Performing Arts

777 Homer St., Vancouver, 604-602-0616; www.centreinvancouver.com

Acclaimed Canadian architect Moshe Safdie designed the dramatic Centre in Vancouver with an arched glass facade and, punctuating the entry, a spiraling glass cone. The auditorium seats 1,800, accommodating major Broadway tours.

The Commodore Ballroom

868 Granville St., Vancouver, 604-739-4550; www.hob.com/venues/concerts/commodore

It's been swinging since the big band era, and the Commodore flaunts its age with brass chandeliers and polished wood stairs. A $3.5 million renovation in 1999 restored its elegance (and kept the spring-loaded dance floor) while modernizing its stage wizardry. U.S.-based House of Blues now programs the acts that come through the ballroom, ranging primarily from rock to blues with a smattering of world talent. HOB also operates a kitchen on site.

The Yale Hotel

1300 Granville St., Vancouver, 604-681-9253; www.theyale.ca

Built in 1889 as a hotel for rough-and-tumble miners, fishermen and loggers, The Yale, prizes its working-class roots and makes a fitting home for the city's best blues club. Past headliners include John Lee Hooker, Clarence "Gatemouth" Brown, Jeff Healey and Jim Byrnes.

Museum of Anthropology at the University of British Columbia

6393 N.W. Marine Dr., Vancouver, 604-822-3825; www.moa.ubc.ca

Built to reference a First Nations longhouse, the glass and concrete Museum of Anthropology makes a fitting shrine for the art and artifacts of West Coast natives. The Great Hall surrounds visitors in immense totem poles, canoes and feast dishes of the Nisgaa, Gitksan and Haida peoples, among others. An outdoor sculpture garden sets tribal houses and totem poles, many carved by the best known contemporary artists, against a backdrop of sea and mountain views. In its mission to explore all the cultures of the world, the Anthro also catalogs 600 ceramics works from 15th- to 19th-century Europe.

UBC Botanical Garden

6804 S.W. Marine Dr., Vancouver, 604-822-3928; www.ubcbotanicalgarden.org

Seven separate areas include Asian, Physick, Native, Alpine and Food gardens. Nitobe Garden, authentic Japanese tea garden located behind Asian Centre.

Vancouver Art Gallery

750 Hornby St., Vancouver, 604-662-4719; www.vanartgallery.bc.ca

Most visitors bound up to the Vancouver Art Gallery's fourth floor for a look at the largest collection of works by British

BRITISH COLUMBIA

Columbia's best known painter, Emily Carr. But the other galleries in western Canada's largest art museum, housed in an early 20th-century courthouse, are fantastic—subjects range from Group of Seven landscapes to photo conceptual art.

Vancouver Canadians
Nat Bailey Stadium in Queen Elizabeth Park, 4601 Ontario St., Vancouver,
604-872-5232;
www.canadiansbaseball.com
A-level Minor League Baseball in Northwest League. Mid-June-early September.

Vancouver Canucks (NHL)
800 Griffiths Way, Vancouver,
604-280-4100;
www.canucks.com
Professional hockey team.

Vancouver Maritime Museum
1905 Ogden Ave., Vancouver,
604-257-8300;
www.vancouvermaritimemuseum.com
Built around the St. Roch, the first ship to navigate Canada's Inside Passage from west to east, Vanier Park's Maritime Museum lets seafaring fans explore the 1928 supply ship from wheelhouse to captains quarters. In addition to the series of historic model ships housed inside the museum, several historic craft are tethered outside its waterfront Heritage Harbor, including two tugs, a rescue boat and the 1927 seiner once featured on Canada's $5 bill.

Vancouver Museum
1100 Chestnut St., Vancouver,
1 1/2 miles/2 1/2 kilometers S.W. via Burrard, Cypress Sts.,
604-736-4431;
www.vanmuseum.bc.ca
Keeper of city history and another Vanier Park attraction, Vancouver Museum takes a sweeping view of civilization, collecting everything from Egyptian mummies to local vintage swimming togs. In addition to the urban story, told in lifelike re-creations of an Edwardian parlor, ship's berth and trading post, the museum examines First Nations artifacts, the contributions of Asian Rim cultures and world history.

Vancouver Opera
835 Cambie St., Vancouver,
604-683-0222;
www.vancouveropera.ca
Vancouver Opera stages four productions annually. Established in 1958, the company has hosted a roster of greats, including guest singers Placido Domingo, Joan Sutherland and Marilyn Horne. Performances take place at the Queen Elizabeth Theatre.

Vancouver Police Centennial Museum
240 E. Cordova St., Vancouver,
604-665-3346;
www.city.vancouver.bc.ca/police/museum
For fans of the macabre, the Vancouver Police Centennial Museum in Gastown not only supplies the gruesome details of the city's most lurid crimes (such as bodies found in Stanley Park and the man who tried to murder his wife with arsenic-laced milkshakes) but also dramatizes them, crime-scene style. Run by the city's police department, the museum tells the history of local law-keeping and ushers visitors into an eerie mock-forensics lab in the former city morgue.

Vancouver Ravens
(National Lacrosse League)
800 Griffiths Way, Vancouver;
www.vancouverravens.com
Professional lacrosse team.

Vancouver Symphony Orchestra
601 Smithe St., Vancouver,
604-684-9100;
www.vancouversymphony.ca
Canada's third largest orchestra, the Vancouver Symphony presents more than 140 concerts annually, most of them at the ornate Orpheum Theatre. The symphony's featured programs broadly encompass classical, light classical, pops and children's works. Most concerts are on weekends with family-oriented matinees. September-June.

Vancouver Trolley Company Ltd
875 Terminal Ave., Vancouver,

604-801-5515; www.vancouvertrolley.com
Narrated trolley tours to top attractions and neighborhoods throughout the city. Get on and off at designated stops throughout the day.

VanDusen Botanical Garden
5251 Oak St., Vancouver,
604-878-9274;
www.vandusengarden.org
Approximately 55 acres (22 hectares) of flowers and exotic plants. Seasonal displays, mountain views, restaurant.

Whitecaps F.C.
Kingsway and Boundary Rd., Burnaby,
604-669-9283;
www.whitecapsfc.com
Professional soccer team in United Soccer League's 1st division. April-October.

Windsure Windsurfing School
1300 Discovery St.,
Vancouver,
604-224-0615;
www.windsure.com
Head to Jericho Beach to catch the offshore drafts in English Bay aboard a windsurfer. Windsure Windsurfing School, operating out of the Jericho Sailing Center, rents both boards and wetsuits, including rigs suitable for children. May-Labour Day, 9 a.m.-8 p.m.

Yaletown
From False Creek to Burrard Inlet on the N.W. and Georgia St. on the N.E.
A former rail yard, Yaletown once held the world record for the most bars per acre. With time and prosperity, the warehouse district is now one of Vancouver's hippest, drawing urban dwellers with an arty bent. The former loading docks along Hamilton and Mainland teem with cafes with umbrella-shaded tables onto concrete terraces. Tucked in between are a slew of shops, galleries and clothiers.

SPECIAL EVENTS
Alcan International Dragon Boat Festival
401-788 Beatty St., Festival Office,
Vancouver, 604-688-2382

Vancouver's considerable Asian community imports an eastern rite in dragon boat racing, the traditional Chinese rain ceremony that is equal parts pageant and competition. But don't tell that to the 100 or so crews that enter the False Creek event paddling boats with dragon figureheads representing the Asian water deity. Bring loads of film to the colorful event, which, in addition to racing, features a Taoist blessing of the fleet and on land, Asian entertainment, crafts and food. Mid-June.

Bard on the Beach Shakespeare Festival
Vanier Park, Whyte Ave., Vancouver,
604-739-0559;
www.bardonthebeach.org
The works of Shakespeare take the outdoor stage at Vanier Parks permanent seasonal theater, Bard on the Beach. Elizabethan-style tents cover the audience and actors, who play against an open backdrop of coastal landscape. The company mounts approximately three plays each summer, performed in repertory with several shows slated daily on two stages. June-September.

Caribbean Days Festival
Waterfront Park, North Vancouver,
take the Seabus from Canada Place to
Lonsdale Quay, 604-515-2400;
www.caribbeandaysfestival.com
The Trinidad and Tobago Cultural Society of BC throws the province's biggest island jump-up at this North Vancouver park. Its highlight parade kicks off Saturday morning with a slow, carnival-like promenade of bands and costumes, drawing crowds of pan-Caribbean expats. Head to the park festival grounds for calypso, steel drum, soca and reggae music, as well as island food and crafts. Late July.

HSBC Powersmart Celebration of Light
English Bay, Vancouver,
604-641-1193;
www.celebration-of-light.com
On four nights spread over two weeks, pyrotechnic fans gasp as the world's best fireworks designers compete for bragging rights in Vancouver's Celebration

★
★
★
★
★

of Light. Teams from China, Canada and Spain have competed on the basis of originality, rhythm, musical synchronization and color, leading up to the grand finale night on which all competitors restage their shows. For best viewing, park your beach towel along English Bay at Stanley or Vanier parks, Kitsilano or Jericho beaches. Come prepared for very large crowds, especially for the finale. Late July-early August.

Hyack Festival
1st and 3rd aves, New Westminster,
12 miles/19 kilometers S. of Vancouver
via Hwy. 1A,
604-522-6894;
www.hyack.bc.ca
Commemorates the birthday of Queen Victoria, held yearly since 1971; 21-gun salute; band concerts, parade, carnival, sports events. Ten days in mid-May.

Pacific National Exhibition Annual Fair
Exhibition Park, 2901 E. Hastings St.,
Vancouver, 604-253-2311;
www.pne.bc.ca
Second-largest fair in Canada. Hundreds of free exhibits, major theme event, concerts, thrill shows, world championship timber show; petting zoo, thoroughbred horse racing, commercial exhibits, roller coaster, agricultural shows, horse shows, livestock competitions, horticultural exhibits. Usually mid-August-early September.

Theatre Under the Stars
★ Stanley Park, Malkin Bowl,
2099 Beach Ave., Vancouver,
★ 604-687-0174; www.tuts.ca
Theatre Under the Stars puts the outdoors in outdoor theater. Towering forests of Douglas fir surround the 1,200-seat open-air Malkin Bowl theater in Stanley Park, binding art and nature in nightly performances. The short summer season generally presents two shows in every-other-night rotation, an annual repertory that hews to comedies and musicals. July-August.

Vancouver Fringe Festival
1402 Anderson St., Vancouver,
604-257-0350;
www.vancouverfringe.com
From comedies to musical acts to full-on drama, Vancouver Fringe trains the spotlight on fledgling theater troupes who come from around the globe to participate in the 11-day annual arts festival. Modeled on the oft-copied fringe festival in Edinburgh, Scotland, the Canadian organization mounts about 100 productions in a variety of venues including theaters, garages and even the Aquabus. Early-mid-September.

Vancouver International Children's Festival
Vanier Park, 1100 Chestnut St., Vancouver,
604-708-5655;
www.childrensfestival.ca
Though the 7-day slate of events programmed by the annual Children's Festival aims at school group audiences, its talent warrants broader attention. In a program ranging from music to theater, the performance lineup for young audiences might include Japanese dancers, Australia's teen troupe Flying Fruit Fly Circus, Aboriginal storytellers and clown companies. Aside from showtime, the festival engages kids with more than two dozen hands-on arts activities. Mid-May.

Vancouver International Jazz Festival
316 W. 6th Ave., Coastal Jazz and Blues
Society, Vancouver,
604-872-5200;
www.jazzvancouver.com
The Coastal Jazz and Blues Society runs this annual jazz festival over a 10-day span in several venues, climaxing in the headlining stage at the Orpheum Theatre. Past performers range from greats like Dizzy Gillespie to New Age interpreters like Pat Metheny to crooners such as Diana Krall. In addition to the main event, CJBS also sponsors 40 concerts between September and May each year (its 24-hour jazz hotline delivers a useful "what's-on-now" club report year-round). June.

BRITISH COLUMBIA

HOTELS

★★Best Western Downtown Vancouver
718 Drake St. at Granville,
Vancouver,
604-669-9888, 800-780-7234;
143 rooms. Restaurant, bar. Children's activity center. Pets accepted, fee. Exercise room. Busn. Center. **$$**

★★Best Western Sands
1755 Davie St., Vancouver,
604-682-1831, 800-663-9400;
www.bestwesternbc.com
121 rooms. Restaurant, bar, beach. Pets accepted, fee. Exercise room. **$$**

★★★Coast Plaza Suite Hotel
1763 Comox St., Vancouver,
604-688-7711, 806-716-6199;
www.coasthotels.com
This tower hotel is located just blocks from Stanley Park in Vancouver's West End, overlooking English Bay. Because of the range of amenities offered here, such as a fitness center, indoor pool, business center, Internet access, restaurants and a bar, this hotel is a nice choice for the business or leisure traveler. The hotel also offers many suites with kitchenettes and there is a mall on the lower floors of the building.
269 rooms. Two restaurants, bar. Pets accepted, fee. Exercise room. Pool. Busn. Center. **$$$**

★★Days Inn Vancouver Downtown
921 W. Pender St., Vancouver,
604-681-4335;
www.daysinnvancouver.com
85 rooms. Restaurant, Two bars. Busn. Center. **$$**

★★★Delta Vancouver Suites
550 W. Hastings St., Vancouver,
604-689-8188, 888-890-3222;
www.deltavancouversuites.ca
This high-rise, all-suite hotel is located in the middle of downtown Vancouver and just minutes from Gastown, Yaletown, Chinatown, Robson Square, Canada Place, Stanley Park and Kitsilano Beach.

225 rooms, all suites. Restaurant, bar. Pets accepted, fee. Exercise room. Pool. Busn. Center. **$$$**

★★★English Bay Inn
1968 Comox St., Vancouver,
604-683-8002, 866-683-8002;
www.englishbayinn.com
This relaxing, 20th-century Tudor-style escape is a short walk from the West End's Stanley Park and shops and restaurants on Denman Street. All guest rooms feature Ralph Lauren linens, featherbeds, antiques, reproductions, and some rooms have fireplaces. Take some time to lounge in the back garden.
6 rooms. Complimentary full breakfast. **$$**

★★★The Fairmont Hotel Vancouver
900 W. Georgia St., Vancouver,
604-684-3131, 800-441-1414;
www.fairmont.com/hotelvancouver
The Fairmont Hotel echoes the vibrancy of its home city. Grand and inviting, it has been a preeminent destination since 1939, when it opened to celebrate the royal visit of King George VI and Queen Elizabeth. The décor gives a nod to the past, but the dining and entertainment venues are cutting edge. Also home to world-renowned boutiques, including Louis Vuitton and St. John
556 rooms. Restaurant, bar. Pets accepted, fee. Exercise room. Pool. Busn. Center. **$$**

★★★The Fairmont Vancouver Airport
3111 Grant McConachie Way, Vancouver,
604-207-5200, 800-676-8922;
www.fairmont.com/vancouverairport
This stylish hotel is located inside the airport, accessed by the airport escalator The rooms and suites are the very definition of modern sophistication with elegant furnishings and thoughtful amenities. Airport dining is elevated to new levels at the Globe@ YVR, where diners marvel at the soaring jets while enjoying cosmopolitan cuisine.
392 rooms. Restaurant, bar. Airport Pets accepted, fee. Exercise room. Pool. Busn. Center. **$$**

BRITISH COLUMBIA

★★★The Fairmont Waterfront
900 Canada Way, Vancouver,
604-691-1991, 800-441-1414;
www.fairmont.com/Waterfront

With state-of-the-art conference facilities, a comprehensive health club and fine cuisine, this hotel is located beside an enclosed walkway to the Vancouver Convention and Exhibition Center, the Cruise Ship Terminal, and is within walking distance from Stanley Park and Gastown.

489 rooms. Restaurant, bar. Pets accepted, fee. Exercise room. Pool. Busn. Center. **$$$**

★★★★Four Seasons Hotel Vancouver
791 W Georgia St., Vancouver,
604-689-9333
www.fourseasons.com/vancouver

Located downtown in the commercial and cultural hub of the city, the Four Seasons Hotel Vancouver is a home-away-from-home for both business and leisure travelers. Families are welcome—children will love the indoor/outdoor pool and the in-room PlayStations. In addition to 24-hour room service, the hotel has three dining options: Chartwell restaurant, headed by executive chef Rafael Gonzalez, The Garden Terrace and the Terrace Bar. Chartwell. named after Chruchill's summer home, is famous for its exemplary service and West Coast cuisine.

376 rooms, Pets accepted, some restrictions. High-speed Internet access. Two restaurants, bar. Fitness room. Pools. Business center. **$$$**

★★Golden Tulip Georgian Court Hotel
773 Beatty St., Vancouver,
604-682-5555, 800-663-1155;
www.georgiancourt.com

180 rooms. Restaurant, bar. Pets accepted, fee. Exercise room. **$$**

★★Hampton Inn & Suites
111 Robson St., Vancouver,
604-602-1008, 877-602-1008;
www.hamptoninnvancouver.com

132 rooms. Restaurant, bar, children's activity center. Exercise room. **$$**

★★★Hilton Vancouver Metrotown
6083 McKay Ave., Burnaby,
604-438-1200, 800-445-8667;
www.hiltonvancouver.com

The Hilton Vancouver Metrotown is the perfect property for a business or leisure traveler. It's located in suburban Burnaby, a 20-minute drive from downtown and the airport, in the Metrotown Shopping Mall complex. A skytrain light rail station is across the street and offers high-speed travel to downtown. After a busy day, head to the hotel's small outdoor area with an outdoor lap pool, children's pool, whirlpool and sundeck for some relaxation.

283 rooms. Restaurant, bar. Pets accepted, fee. Exercise room. Swim. Busn. Center. **$$**

★★★Hyatt Regency Vancouver
655 Burrard St., Vancouver,
604-683-1234, 800-233-1234;
www.vancouver.hyatt.com

This hotel is located within the Royal Centre shopping complex, which also includes two levels of shops, restaurants and a Skytrain station. It is near many local attractions. After checking in, take a dip in the indoor pool or get a bite to eat in one of the three restaurants. Then later, relax in the guest rooms which all feature pillow-top mattresses and flat-screen televisions.

644 rooms. Three restaurants, two bars. Exercise room. Pool. Busn. Center. **$$**

★Hampton Inn Vancouver Airport
8811 Bridgeport Rd., Richmond,
604-232-5505, 800-426-7866;
www.hamptoninn-vancouver.com

111 rooms. Complimentary continental breakfast. Exercise room. Busn. Center. **$**

★★★Le Soleil Hotel & Suites
567 Hornby St., Vancouver,
604-632-3000, 877-632-3030;
www.lesoleilhotel.com

In the heart of the city's financial and business districts sits this charming boutique hotel. The stunning lobby boasts 30-foot gilded ceilings and a Louis XVI-style collection of imported Italian furniture. Complimentary bottled water and fruit

44

BRITISH COLUMBIA

★

★

★

★

★

upon arrival are welcome surprises, and the property's restaurant offers an eclectic Asian-Mediterranean cuisine.

119 rooms. Restaurant, bar. Pets accepted, fee. Busn. Center. **$$**

★★★Metropolitan Hotel

645 Howe Street, Vancouver,
604-687-1122;
http://metropolitan.com/vanc/

Located in the heart of Vancour's downtown, the hotel is convenient to all local sightseeing. The guest rooms are modern and spacious, with marble washrooms, down duvets and Frette linen and some have Juliet-balconies. Enjoy a dinner at the Diva at the Met, with its international/ Pacific Northwest influenced cuisine.

4 rooms. Complimentary full breakfast. Pets accepted, fee. **$**

★★★Opus Hotel

322 Davie St., Vancouver, 604-642-6787, 866-642-6787; www.opushotel.com

This hip, boutique hotel blends contemporary design with great service. Located in the Yaletown area, it close to all local attractions. The guest rooms have unique decor, ranging from modern and minimalist without ever losing warmth and comfort. Home to both home to the modern bistro, Elixir, and the hot spot, Opus Bar.

96 rooms. Restaurant, bar. Pets accepted, fee. Exercise room. Busn. Center. **$**

★★★Pacific Palisades Hotel

1277 Robson St., Vancouver,
604-688-0461, 800-663-1815;
www.pacificpalisadeshotel.com

This hotel underwent a total makeover in 2001 and now earns its reputation as one of the trendiest home bases on the legendary Robson Street. Fitness-minded guests enjoy complimentary yoga kits and a designated yoga channel, with personal trainers available for private yoga and Pilates sessions.

233 rooms. Restaurant, bar. Pets accepted. Exercise room. Pool. Busn. Center. **$$$**

★★★Pan Pacific Vancouver

300-999 Canada Place, Vancouver,
604-662-8111, 800-937-1515;
www.panpacific.com

Awe-inspiring waterfront views take center stage at Vancouver's Pan Pacific Hotel, only minutes from some of the best shopping in the city. Luxurious guest rooms look out over the unobstructed mountains and ocean and some rooms even feature private balconies. Four distinctive restaurants offer sushi, Italian and other international cuisine.

504 rooms. Three restaurants, bar. Pets accepted, fee. Exercise room. Pool. Busn. Center. **$$$**

★★Ramada Plaza Vancouver Airport Conference Resort

10251 St. Edwards Dr., Richmond,
604-207-9000, 800-272-6232;
www.ramada.com

438 rooms. Restaurant, bar. Children's activity center. Pets accepted, fee. Exercise room. Pool. Tennis. Busn. Center. **$$**

★★★Renaissance Vancouver Harborside Hotel

1133 W. Hastings, Vancouver,
604-689-9211, 800-905-8582;
www.renaissancevancouver.com

Located on the waterfront, and close to all local attractions, this is a great spot for both leisure and business travelers. Some room offer a balcony and all rooms have duvets and feather pillows along with Internet access. Enjoy a meal and the stunning views at Patina Restaurant or a light dinner and drink at the Coal Harbour Bar.

437 rooms. Two restaurants, bar, children's activity center. Pets accepted, fee. Exercise room. Pool. Busn. Center. **$$**

★★★River Run Cottages

4551 River Rd. W., Ladner,
604-946-7778; www.riverruncottages.com

Kayaking, canoeing, and rowboats are available for guests who want to watch eagles, seals, otters and beavers in their natural setting. Guests can pack a picnic and enjoy a romantic getaway on No Name Island.

4 rooms. Complimentary full breakfast. Pets accepted, fee. **$**

BRITISH COLUMBIA

★★Sheraton Guildford Hotel
15269 104th Ave., Surrey, 604-582-9288;
www.sheraton.com
278 rooms. Restaurant. Exercise room. Busn. Center. **$**

★★★★The Sutton Place Hotel - Vancouver
845 Burrard St, Vancouver, 604-682-5511;
www.vancouver.suttonplace.com
Located in the business and shopping core of downtown Vancouver, the hotel offers guest rooms that exude a European flavor, while the dining and lounge areas feature comforting old-world motifs. Business travlers are pampered with the business center that was renovated to provide state-of-the-art technology and efficiency. The hotel offers a serene spa, indoor swimming pool under a big sunroof, and a fitness center
397 rooms. Pets accepted, some restrictions; fee. High-speed Internet access. Two restaurants, bar. Fitness room, fitness classes available, spa. Indoor pool, whirlpool. Business center. **$$$**

★★★Wedgewood Hotel
845 Hornby St., Vancouver, 604-689-7777, 800-663-0666;
www.wedgewoodhotel.com
Tradition abounds at this independent boutique hotel. Bacchus, the on-site restaurant, offers a full menu plus sumptuous weekend brunch menus and traditional high tea served from 2-4 p.m. daily.
83 rooms. Restaurant, bar. Exercise room. Busn. Center. **$$$**

★★★The Westin Grand
433 Robson St., Vancouver, 604-602-1999, 888-680-9393;
www.westingrandvancouver.com
All of Vancouver is within reach of the Westin Grand. Sleek and stylish, this property introduces visitors to the hip side of this western Canadian city. Guests never leave behind the comforts of home here, where all rooms feature well-stocked kitchenettes. The hotel caters to the sophisticated, and many services are offered 24 hours daily.

Guests can dine on Pacific Rim dishes at the Aria Restaurant & Lounge.
207 rooms. Restaurant, bar. Pets accepted, fee. Exercise room. Pool. Busn. Center. **$$**

SPECIALITY LODGING
Barclay House in the West End
1351 Barclay St., Vancouver, 604-605-1351, 800-971-1351;
www.barclayhouse.com
6 rooms. Children over 12 only. Complimentary full breakfast. **$$**

O Canada House
1114 Barclay St., Vancouver, 604-688-0555, 877-688-1114;
www.ocanadahouse.com
7 rooms. Children over 11 only. Complimentary full breakfast. **$$**

West End Guest House
1362 Haro St., Vancouver, 604-681-2889, 888-546-3327;
www.westendguesthouse.com
8 rooms. Children over 11 years only. Complimentary full breakfast. **$$**

RESTAURANTS
★★Aqua Riva
200 Granville St., Vancouver, 604-683-5599;
www.aquariva.com
Pacific Northwest menu. Reservations recommended. **$$$**

★★★Beach House
150 25th St., West Vancouver, 604-922-1414;
www.atthebeachhouse.com
Originally built in 1912, this waterfront restaurant affords diners beautiful views of Burrard Inlet.
Seafood menu. Reservations recommended. Outdoor seating. **$$$**

★★★Bacchus
845 Hornby St., Vancouver, 604-608-5319, 800-663-0666;
www.wedgewoodhotel.com
This luxurious restaurant is adorned with richly upholstered furniture, décor from

Venice and of course, a large canvas depicting Bacchus, Greek god of wine and revelry.
French menu. Reservations recommended. $$$

★★★★Bishop's
2183 W. 4th Ave., Vancouver,
604-738-2025;
www.bishopsonline.com
Bishop's houses the most coveted tables in Vancouver. Intimate, modern and airy, this chic restaurant is known for West Coast continental menu that emphasizes seasonal, organic produce and British Columbia seafood. International menu. Reservations recommended. Outdoor seating. $$$

★★★C Restaurant
Z-1600 Howe St., Vancouver,
604-681-1164; www.crestaurant.com
Located along the boardwalk running under the Granville Building and overlooking the marina, this contemporary seafood house offers a raw bar, an enclosed patio area and more than 900 wines. Seafood menu. Reservations recommended. Outdoor seating. $$$

★★Cafe De Paris
761 Denman St., Vancouver,
604-687-1418
Cafe de Paris is the perfect choice for a wonderful gourmet meal in an authentic French bistro atmosphere. Located in the popular West End area of Vancouver, this charming restaurant offers three-course table d'hote meals.
French bistro. Reservations recommended. $$$

★★The Cannery
2205 Commissioner St., Vancouver,
604-254-9606, 877-254-9606;
www.canneryseafood.com
Although this award-winning seafood restaurant is isolated and somewhat difficult to find (it can be reached only through the Clark Drive and McGill Street gates on Port Vancouver), it is well worth the effort.

There is also a dock for diners who choose to travel by boat.
Seafood menu. Reservations recommended. $$$

★★★CinCin Ristorante
1154 Robson St., Vancouver,
604-688-7338; www.cincin.net
Located upstairs in a two-story building on trendy Robson Street, this Italian dining room has a mellow Tuscan atmosphere. A wood-fired brick oven emits a wonderful aroma throughout the restaurant and the extensive wine list offers the perfect complement to any meal.
Italian menu. Reservations recommended. Outdoor seating. $$$

★★Cloud 9
1400 Robson St., Vancouver,
604-687-0511, 800-830-6144;
www.cloud9restaurant.ca
Seafood, steak menu. Reservations recommended. $$$

★★Delilah's
1789 Comox St., Vancouver,
604-687-3424; www.delilahs.ca
Continental, tapas menu. Reservations recommended. $$$

★★Dockside Brewing Company
1253 Johnston St., Vancouver,
604-685-7070;
www.docksidebrewing.com
Seafood menu. Reservations recommended. Outdoor seating. $$$

★★★Fish House in Stanley Park
8901 Stanley Park Dr., Vancouver,
604-681-7275, 877-681-7275;
www.fishhousestanleypark.com
This Vancouver landmark seafood restaurant favored by both locals and tourists is located in Vancouver's West End at the south entrance to beautiful Stanley Park. Seafood menu. Reservations recommended. Outdoor seating. $$$

★★★Five Sails
300-999 Canada Pl., Vancouver,

BRITISH COLUMBIA

604-844-2855, 800-937-1515; www.dinepanpacific.com

Exceptional views of the harbor and neighboring mountains, a talented kitchen that produces creative Northwest/Asian fusion food and good service make this restaurant a favorite destination among locals.

International menu. Reservations recommended. **$$$$**

★★★Gotham Steakhouse and Cocktail Bar

615 Seymour St., Vancouver, 604-605-8282; www.gothamsteakhouse.com

It's worth the splurge for truly excellent steaks, smooth, friendly service and a sleek crowd at this downtown destination. The dining room, a converted bank, is modern and opulent with main floor and balcony dining.

Steak menu. Reservations recommended. Outdoor seating. **$$$**

★★★Hart House On Deer Lake

6664 Deer Lake Ave., Burnaby, 604-298-4278; www.harthouserestaurant.com

Known as having some of the best steaks in the Vancouver area, the Hart House Restaurant also offers one of the most charming dining atmospheres. The imaginative menu takes its inspiration from the flavors native to countries around the globe. In pleasant weather, the outdoor patio opens up to let diners enjoy the fresh air and views of Deer Lake.

International menu. Reservations recommended. Outdoor seating. **$$**

★★★Il Giardino di Umberto Ristorante

1382 Hornby St., Vancouver, 604-669-2422; www.umberto.com

This rustic room transports its young, established clientele to a Tuscan villa.

Italian menu. Reservations recommended. Outdoor seating. **$$$**

★★Imperial Chinese Seafood Restaurant

355 Burrard St., Vancouver, 604-688-8191;

www.imperialrest.com

At this contemporary Cantonese/Chinese restaurant, floor-to-ceiling windows and balcony seating offer breathtaking views of the bay and mountains.

Cantonese, Chinese menu. Reservations recommended. **$$$**

★★★★La Belle Auberge

4856 48th Ave., Ladner, 604-946-7717; www.labelleauberge.com

If you crave the glorious food of France's best kitchens, opt for a 30-minute drive from Vancouver to Ladner and enjoy dinner at La Belle Auberge. Set in a charming 1902 country inn, the restaurant is an intimate, five antique-filled salon-style dining rooms. The kitchen, led by chef/owner Bruno Marti, a masterful culinary technician, offers spectacular, authentic French cuisine.

French menu. Reservations recommended. Outdoor seating. **$$$**

★★★La Terrazza

1088 Cambie St., Vancouver, 604-899-4449; www.laterrazza.ca

This impressive restaurant feels like a classic villa with burnt-sienna walls, murals, massive windows and vaulted ceilings, as well as an impressive wine cellar.

Italian menu. Reservations recommended. Outdoor seating. **$$$**

★★Le Bistro Chez Michel

1373 2nd Floor, Marine Dr., Vancouver, 604-926-4913; www.chezmichelvancouver.com

French menu. Reservations recommended. **$$**

★★★Le Crocodile

909 Burrard St., Vancouver, 604-669-4298; www.lecrocodilerestaurant.com

A wonderful dress-up place, this downtown French bistro is worth a trip for the food alone—a great destination for a special occasion or romantic dinner.

French menu. Reservations recommended. Outdoor seating. **$$$**

BRITISH COLUMBIA

★★★Lumiere
2551 W. Broadway, Vancouver,
604-739-8185; www.lumiere.ca
Lumiere is a glossy, stunning and elegant restaurant that offers European-style dining of the most divine order. The inspired and innovative fare is French with Asian accents and a respect for regional ingredients. The global wine list is impressive and bartenders here recall a pre-Prohibition era where the craft of cocktail was taken as seriously as the mastery of the plate.
French menu. Reservations recommended. Outdoor seating. $$$$

★★Monk McQueens
601 Stamps Landing, Vancouver,
604-877-1351;
www.monkmcqueens.com
Seafood menu. Reservations recommended. Outdoor seating. $$$

★★Provence Mediterranean Grill
4473 W. 10th Ave., Vancouver,
604-222-1980;
www.provencevancouver.com
Casual Mediterranean bistro. Reservations recommended. Outdoor seating. $$

★★★Quattro on Fourth
2611 W. 4th, Vancouver,604-734-4444;
www.quattrorestaurants.com
This popular suburban Italian restaurant, located in the heart of Kitsilano near downtown, has an excellent selection of Italian entrees paired with fantastic wines.
Italian, Mediterranean menu. Reservations recommended. Outdoor seating. $$$

★★★Raincity Grill
1193 Denman St., Vancouver,
604-685-7337; www.raincitygrill.com
Located in Vancouver's West End, this eclectic, fine dining restaurant has views across a small park to English Bay. The delicious a la carte and chef's tasting menus draw almost exclusively on organic, regional sources. Don't miss brunch on Saturdays and Sundays.
International menu. Reservations recommended. Outdoor seating. $$$

★★★Saveur
850 Thurlow St., Vancouver,
604-688-1633;
www.saveurrestaurant.com
Located a block off Robson in downtown Vancouver, this warm and intimate French restaurant is the perfect spot for a special-occasion celebration. A French West Coast menu is served for lunch and dinner. Reservations recommended. $$$

★★★Seasons Hill Top Bistro
33rd and Cambie, Vancouver,
604-874-8008, 800-632-9422;
www.seasonshilltopbistro.com
This restaurant was the site of a Clinton-Yeltsin summit in 1993—come for the history and stay for the incredible International menu (and the view). Located on top of a hill in beautiful Queen Elizabeth Park in suburban Vancouver, there are magnificent views from the tiered dining room and attractive heated terrace.
International menu. Reservations recommended. Outdoor seating. $$$

★★Sequoia Grill
7501 Stanley Park Dr., Vancouver,
604-669-3281;
www.sequoiarestaurants.com
West Coast eclectic menu. Reservations recommended. Outdoor seating. $$$

★★Shijo Japanese Restaurant
1926 W. 4th Ave., Vancouver,
604-732-4676; www.shijo.ca
Japanese menu. Reservations recommended. $$$

★★Star Anise
1485 W. 12th Ave., Vancouver,
604-737-1485; www.staranise.ca
International menu. Reservations recommended. $$$

★★Sun Sui Wah Seafood Restaurant
3888 Main St., Vancouver,
604-872-8822, 866-872-8822;
www.sunsuiwah.com
Chinese menu. Reservations recommended. $$

★Tapastree
1829 Robson St., Vancouver,
604-606-4680; www.tapastree.ca
Spanish, tapas menu. Reservations recommended. Outdoor seating. $$

★★Tojo's
1133 W. Broadway, Vancouver,
604-872-8050; www.tojos.com
Japanese menu. Reservations recommended. Outdoor seating. $$

★True Confections
866 Denman St., Vancouver,
604-682-1292; www.trueconfections.ca
Desserts. Lunch, dinner, late night. $

★★Top of Vancouver
555 W. Hastings St., Vancouver,
604-669-2220; www.topofvancouver.com
International menu. Reservations recommended. $$$

★★★Villa Del Lupo
869 Hamilton St., Vancouver,
604-688-7436;
www.villadellupo.com
Tiny white lights and sparkling bay windows attract attention at this classic Italian restaurant housed in a charming, turn-of-the-century home. The menu highlights different regions of Italy using fresh, local ingredients in dishes such as osso bucco with risotto Milanese.
Italian menu. Reservations recommended. $$$

★★★★West
2881 Granville St., Vancouver, 604-738-8938; www.westrestaurant.com
West is one of those sleek, heavenly spots that makes sipping cocktails for hours on end an easy task. It is an ideal choice for gourmets in search of an inventive, eclectic meal, as well as those who crave local flavor and seasonal ingredients. Located in Vancouver's chic South Granville neighborhood, West offers diners the chance to sample the vibrant cuisine of the Pacific Northwest region. Stunning, locally sourced ingredients are on display here thanks to the masterful kitchen.
International menu. Reservations recommended. $$$

VANCOUVER ISLAND

The largest of the Canadian Pacific Coast Islands, Vancouver Island stretches almost 300 miles (480 kilometers) along the shores of western British Columbia. It is easily accessible by ferry from the city of Vancouver on the mainland as well as from other parts of the province and the state of Washington. With most of its population located in the larger cities on the eastern coast, much of the island remains a wilderness and is very popular with outdoor enthusiasts.

The Vancouver Island Mountain Range cuts down the middle of the island, providing spectacular snowcapped scenery, fjords and rocky coastal cliffs. The southern portion of the island contains more than half the island's total population and includes Victoria, British Columbia's capital. Here, countryside resembles rural Britain with its rolling farmland, rows of hedges and colorful flower gardens. Travelers go island-hopping among the Gulf Islands, located in the sheltered waters of the Strait of Georgia between the big island and the mainland. These beautiful, isolated islands are a mecca for artists, cottagers and tourists alike.

Nanaimo is the dominant town, an area known for excellent sandy beaches and beautiful parks. In the center of the island is the Alberni Valley, which includes several parks with excellent swimming and fishing and one of the tallest waterfall found in North America (Della Falls). From Port Alberni, the mountain highway winds its way to the peaceful fishing village of Tofino, the rugged northern boundary of the Long Beach section of the Pacific Rim National Park.

Information: www.seetheislands.com

WHAT TO SEE AND DO
Whale Watching

Vancouver Island is known as one of the best places to view migrating and resident whales. Whale-watching tours leave from Victoria and other large city centers on the island. View migrating gray whales during March and April, while Orca (killer) whales are best observed between May and October, with July and August as the key months for sightings. Three Orca pods totaling more than 80 whales make their home in the waters off of Victoria. North of Vancouver Island, a resident community of 217 whales patrol the Johnstone Strait in 16 pods. Other whales and marine mammals that can be seen off of Vancouver Island include humpback whales, Minke whales, otters, seals, sea lions and dolphins.

BC Forest Museum

40 miles/64 kilometers, N. of Victoria on Hwy. 1, near Duncan, 250-715-1113; www.bcforestmuseum.com

Logging museum; old logging machines and tools, hands-on exhibits, logging camp, 1 1/2 miles (2.4 kilometers) steam railway ride, sawmill, films, nature walk. May-September: daily.

HOTELS
★★★★The Aerie Resort

600 Ebedora Ln., Malahat, 250-743-7115, 800-518-1933; www.aerie.bc.ca

The Aerie Resort's hilltop perch looks out over Pacific fjords and snowcapped mountains. A multitude of activities, from biking and sailing to hiking and fishing, invite visitors to experience the natural splendors of this pristine island.

29 rooms. Complimentary full breakfast. Restaurant, bar. Pool. **$$$**

★★★Malahat Mountain Inn

265 Trans Canada Hwy., Malahat, 250-478-1979, 800-913-1944; www.malahatmountaininn.com

Just a short drive from Victoria brings guests to this inn's five ocean-view rooms and five ocean-view lofts. Take in dramatic views of the ocean and Saanich Inlet while dining on the outdoor patio.

10 rooms. Complimentary full breakfast. Restaurant, bar. **$$**

★★★★Wickaninnish Inn

500 Osprey Ln., Tofino, 250-725-3100, 800-333-4604; www.wickinn.com

Located on a rocky peninsula jutting out into the Pacific Ocean, this three-story cedar inn treats guests to a truly singular experience. In winter, 20-foot (6-meter) waves thrill storm chasers and surfers alike. Beachcombing on Chesterman Beach serves as therapy for some, while others head for the spa inspired by the nearby ancient rainforest.

75 rooms. Restaurant, bar, beach. Pets accepted, fee. Exercise room. Busn. Center. **$$$$**

SPECIALITY LODGINGS
Clayoquot Wilderness Resort & Spa

P.O. Box 130, Tofino, 250-726-8235, 888-333-5405; www.wildretreat.com

Tucked within the secluded inlets of Clayoquot Sound, this all-inclusive resort treats guests to luxurious accommodations amid snowcapped mountains, lush forests and pristine waters.

16 rooms. Restaurant, bar. Exercise room. Pool. Busn. Center. **$$$**

RESTAURANTS
★★★★Aerie Dining Room

600 Ebedora Ln., Malahat, 250-743-7115, 800-518-1933; www.aerie.bc.ca

Spectacular views of snowy mountaintops are among the many highlights of an evening at The Aerie Dining Room. The Aerie's kitchen is known for its use of superb local produce, sourcing its ingredients from a network of 60 small farms. The kitchen is loyal to classic French technique but brings plates to modern life with Pacific accents. The result is straightforward, yet innovative and sophisticated, fare. A lengthy wine list

51

BRITISH COLUMBIA

★
★
★
★
☆

features Vancouver's own, in addition to wines of the Pacific Coast.

French menu. Closed 10 days in January. Reservations recommended. Outdoor seating. **$$$**

★★★The Pointe Restaurant
Osprey Lane, Tofino,
250-725-3106, 800-333-4604;
www.wickinn.com

Perched above the crashing waves of Vancouver Island's west shore is the Pointe Restaurant at the Wickaninnish Inn. The cedar-beamed, circular dining room features a breathtaking 240-degree view of the Pacific Ocean. The adjoining On the Rocks Bar & Lounge is a perfect spot for a pre-or post-dinner cocktail, with a variety of wines by the glass and an extensive selection of single-malt scotches.

Reservations recommended. **$$$**

SPAS

★★★★Ancient Cedars Spa
500 Osprey Ln, Tofino,
250-725-3100

Resting on a rocky promontory jutting into the Pacific Ocean with an old-growth rainforest in the background, this is truly a one-of-a-kind hideaway. The interiors have been designed to bring the outdoors in, with slate tiles, dark colors and cedar decorating this serene space. This treatment menu focuses on relaxation and renewal. Thai, Lomi Lomi and hot stone massage are among the bodywork therapies available or the signature sacred sea treatment, which uses the renowned Bouvier Hydrotherapy tub. **$$**

VICTORIA

One of Canada's most temperate and eminently walkable cities, BC's capital has a distinctly British flavor, yet is a heartland of Pacific Northwest indigenous culture. This city of lush parks and gardens literally bursts with beauty in early spring, when even the five-globed Victorian lampposts are decorated with baskets of flowers. Take a horse-drawn carriage or double-decker bus tour through many historic and scenic landmarks, and wander through the bistros, boutiques and colorful alleys of a delightfully compact downtown and Chinatown district that sparkles with history.

Information: www.tourismvictoria.com

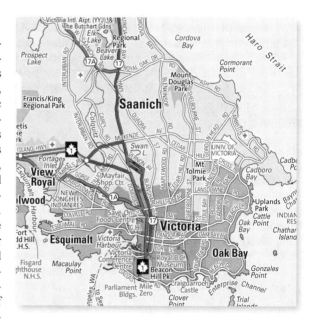

WHAT TO SEE AND DO

Art Gallery of Greater Victoria
1040 Moss St., Victoria,
250-384-4101; www.aggv.bc.ca

This gallery is said to have the finest collection of Japanese art in Canada; it includes major holdings of Asian ceramics and paintings. Also housed here are collections of Canadian and European art, with a focus on prints and drawings and decorative arts. The gallery is home to the only Shinto shrine outside of Japan and is the site of many lectures, film screenings and concerts.

Beacon Hill Park
Douglas St. and Dallas Rd., Victoria.,
From Douglas St. to Cook St. between
Superior St. and the Waterfront,
250-361-0370;
www.beaconhillpark.ca
Approximately 180 acres (75 hectares) with lakes, wildfowl sanctuary, children's petting farm, walks and floral gardens, cricket pitch; world's second-tallest totem pole; beautiful view of the sea.

Butchart Gardens
800 Benvenuto Ave., Victoria,
250-652-4422;
www.butchartgardens.com
Approximately 50 acres (20 hectares). The Sunken Garden was created in the early 1900s by the Butcharts on the site of their depleted limestone quarry with topsoil brought in by horse-drawn cart. Already a tourist attraction by the 1920s, the gardens now include the Rose, Japanese and Italian gardens; also Star Pond, Concert Lawn, Fireworks Basin, Ross Fountain and Show Greenhouse. The gardens are subtly illuminated at night (mid-June-mid-September) and on Saturday evenings in July and August, visitors enjoy fireworks displays.

Capital City Tally-Ho and Sightseeing Company
8615 Ebor Terrace, Victoria,
250-514-9257, 866-383-5067;
www.tallyhotours.com/contact.htm
English horse-drawn carriage sightseeing tour: of city highlights, departing from Inner Harbor beside Parliament Buildings, or past Victorian homes and through 200-acre (81-hectare) Beacon Hill Park and its extensive flower gardens (departs from Menzies and Belleville sts). Fully narrated. April-September: daily.

Carillon
Government and Belleville Sts., Victoria,
250-387-1616

Bells made in Holland; presented to the province by citizens of Dutch descent. Concerts.

Carr House
207 Government St., Victoria,
250-383-5843;
www.emilycarr.com
(1863) Italianate birthplace of famous Canadian painter/author Emily Carr. Ground floor restored to period. May-October: daily; rest of year: by appointment.

Chinatown
Chinese immigrants, used for railroad labor, established Canada's oldest Chinatown in 1858. Two key attractions are Fan Tan Alley, the narrowest street in North America and the Gate of Harmonious Interest, guarded by hand-carved stone lions from Suzhou, China. Visit shops with exotic merchandise and restaurants.

Craigdarroch Castle
1050 Joan Crescent, Victoria,
250-592-5323;
www.craigdarrochcastle.com
(1890) Historic house museum with beautifully crafted wood, stained glass; furnished with period furniture and artifacts.

Craigflower Farmhouse & Schoolhouse Historic Site
2709 Manor and Schoolhouse, Victoria,
250-383-4627;
www.conservancy.bc.ca/content.asp?
sectionack=craigflower
This farmhouse was built in 1856 in simple Georgian style. The adjoining 1854 schoolhouse is the oldest in western Canada. Some original furnishings.

Crystal Garden
713 Douglas St., Victoria,
250-953-8800;
www.crystalgarden.bcpcc.com
Glass building formerly housed the largest saltwater pool in the British Empire. Tropical gardens, waterfall, fountain, aviary, monkeys, free-flying butterflies, exotic fish pool; restaurant, shops.

BRITISH COLUMBIA

★
★
★
★
★

Dominion Astrophysical Observatory

5071 W. Saanich Rd., Victoria,
250-363-0001;
www.hia-iha.nrc-gc.ca

The observatory contains three telescopes, two of which are used for research by professional astronomers. The 72-inch Plaskett Telescope is used for public viewing on Saturday nights during "Star Parties" (April-October 31, 7-11 p.m.). Interactive exhibits, film presentations and other special programs are designed to entertain visitors while educating them about the universe.

Fort Rodd Hill and Fisgard Lighthouse National Historic Site

603 Fort Rodd Hill Rd., Victoria,
250-478-5849;
www.pc.gc.ca

A coastal artillery fort from 1895 to 1956; casemated barracks, gun and searchlight positions, loopholed walls. Historic lighthouse (1860) adjacent.

Hatley Castle

2005 Sooke Rd., Colwood,
250-391-2600;
www.hatleycastle.com

(Royal Roads University, 1908) Once the private estate of James Dunsmuir, former Lieutenant Governor of British Columbia. Buildings are noted for their beauty, as are the grounds, with their Japanese, Italian and rose gardens.

Helmcken House

10 Elliot Sq., Victoria,
250-356-7226

(1852) Second-oldest house in British Columbia; most furnishings are original. Extensive 19th-century medical collection.

Maritime Museum

28 Bastion Sq., Victoria,
250-385-4222;
www.mmbc.bc.ca

Depicts rich maritime heritage of the Pacific Northwest from early explorers through age of sail and steam; Canadian naval wartime history; large collection of models of ships used throughout the history of British Columbia. The Tilikum, a converted dugout that sailed from Victoria to England during the years 1901 to 1904, is here. Captain James Cook display.

National Geographic IMAX Theatre

675 Belleville St., Victoria,
250-480-4887

Pacific Undersea Gardens

490 Belleville St., Victoria,
250-382-5717;
www.pacificunderseagardens.com

Underwater windows for viewing of more than 5,000 marine specimens; scuba diver shows.

Point Ellice House Museum

2616 Pleasant St., Victoria,
250-380-6506;
www.victorialodging.com/pointellice/index.html

(1861) Original Victorian setting, furnishings. Afternoon tea served in restored garden.

Royal British Columbia Museum

675 Belleville St., Victoria,
250-356-7226, 888-447-7977;
www.royalbcmuseum.bc.ca

Three-dimensional exhibits include natural and human history, indigenous history and art; also a re-creation of a turn-of-the-century town. In the natural history gallery, the "Living Land-Living Sea" exhibit depicts the natural history of British Columbia from the Ice Age to the present.

Royal London Wax Museum

470 Belleville St., Victoria,
250-388-4461;
www.waxmuseum.bc.ca

More than 250 figures in theatrical settings.

Thunderbird Park

675 Belleville St., Victoria;
www.explorevancouverisland.com/Thunderbird_Park_Victoria_Vancouver_Island_BC.htm

Collection of authentic totem poles and indigenous carvings, representing the work of the main Pacific Coastal tribes. Indigenous carvers may be seen at work in the Carving Shed. May-September.

Whale-watching tours
950 Wharf St., Victoria

Whale-watching boats line both the Wharf St. waterfront and Inner Harbor. Half-day tours display marine life, including orcas, sea lions, seals and porpoises. Victoria Marine Adventures (250-995-2211) and Prince of Whales (250-383-4884) are two of the finer tour companies.

HOTELS

★★★Abigail's Hotel
906 McClure St., Victoria,
250-388-5363, 866-347-5054;
www.abigailshotel.com

This colorfully painted inn consists of an historic Tudor mansion and converted carriage house. The quiet setting belies the inn's location just three blocks from Victoria's Inner Harbor and main tourist attractions. A full gourmet breakfast is served overlooking the patio and English-style gardens.
23 rooms, 4 story. Children over 10 only. Complimentary full breakfast. Pet. **$$$**

★★★Beaconsfield Inn
998 Humboldt St., Victoria,
250-384-4044, 888-884-4044;
www.beaconsfieldinn.com

This three-story Edwardian mansion on Victoria's south side is a Registered Heritage Property. The gardens are kept in the English style, and high tea and sherry are served each afternoon. Each guest room boasts unique features such as canopied beds, beamed ceilings, stained-glass windows and wood-burning fireplaces.
9 rooms. Children over 11 only. Complimentary full breakfast. **$$$**

★★★Beacon Inn at Sidney
9724 Third St., Sidney,
250-655-3288, 877-420-5499;
www.beaconinns.com

Located in the center of BookTown, this elegant Edwardian-inspired property is the perfect romantic getaway. A complimentary gourmet breakfast in the breakfast room (or on the front patio) starts each day. Close to local attractions and Victoria is 20 minutes away. However, for guests who want pure relaxation, the Ocean Palm Spa is just a few minutes from the inn.
9 rooms. Complimentary full breakfast. **$$**

★★Bedford Regency Hotel
1140 Government St., Victoria,
250-384-6835, 800-665-6500;
www.bedfordregency.com
40 rooms. Restaurant, bar. **$$**

★★Best Western Carlton Plaza Hotel
642 Johnson St., Victoria,
250-388-5513, 800-663-7241;
www.bestwesterncarlton.com
103 rooms, 6 story. Restaurant. Pets accepted, fee. Exercise room. **$$**

★★★Coast Harborside Hotel & Marina
146 Kingston St., Victoria,
250-360-1211, 800-716-6199;
www.coasthotels.com

This location can't be beat. The hotel has an inner harbor location with a 42-slip private marina and close to Victoria International Airport. All rooms have balconies or terrace, some with marina side views, and complimentary high-speed Internet access. Guests can relax in one of the two pools or hot tub and enjoy a seafood dinner at the Blue Crab Bar & Grill.
132 rooms. Restaurant, bar. Pets accepted, fee. Exercise room. Pool. Busn. Center. **$$**

★★Chateau Victoria Hotel and Suites
740 Burdett Ave., Victoria,
250-382-4221, 800-663-5891;
www.chateauvictoria.com
177 rooms Restaurant, bar. Pets accepted, fee. Exercise room. Pool. **$$**

★★★Delta Victoria Ocean Pointe Resort and Spa
45 Songhees Rd., Victoria,
250-360-2999, 800-667-4677;
www.deltahotels.com

Located on a point between Victoria's Inner and Upper harbours, this elegant, modern hotel offers wonderful views of the water-

BRITISH COLUMBIA

front, Parliament Buildings and the Royal BC Museum. Take advantage of the full resort experience by participating in fitness classes, booking a tee time on a nearby golf course, and playing tennis on one of the hotel's two lighted courts.

239 rooms. Restaurant, bar. Pets accepted, fee. Exercise room. Pool. Tennis. Busn. Center. **$$**

★★★English Inn & Resort
429 Lampson St., Victoria,
250-388-4353, 866-388-4353;
www.englishinnresort.com

This unique resort was built to echo an English country village, and its buildings are set amidst 5 acres of beautifully landscaped English-style gardens.

30 rooms. Restaurant, bar. **$$$**

★★Executive House Hotel
777 Douglas St., Victoria,
250-388-5111, 800-663-7001;
www.executivehouse.com

181 rooms. Two restaurants, two bars. Pets accepted, fee. Exercise room. **$$**

★★★The Fairmont Empress
721 Government St., Victoria,
250-384-8111, 800-441-1414;
www.fairmont.com

The Fairmont Empress is one of Victoria's most cherished landmarks. Nearly a century old, this storybook castle resting on the banks of Victoria's Inner Harbor enjoys a legendary past, sparkling with royals, celebrities and a bygone era. Afternoon tea at The Fairmont Empress is a must for all visitors to Victoria.

477 rooms. Two restaurants, bar. Pets accepted, fee. Exercise room. Pool. Busn. Center. **$$$**

★★★★Hastings House
160 Upper Ganges Rd., Salt Spring Island,
250-537-2362, 800-661-9255;
www.hastingshouse.com

Snuggled on Salt Spring Island, the Tudor-style Hastings House captures the essence of the English countryside. Scattered throughout the lovely grounds, the rooms and suites

are housed within ivy-covered garden cottages and the timber-framed barn. High Tea and pre-dinner cocktails are served daily in the lounge. Hastings House boasts one of the most accomplished kitchens in British Colombia. Longtime Executive Chef Marcel Kauer and his brigade have the great fortune to draw on British Columbia's Pacific Northwest bounty. The wine list, although international in scope, features a slate of reds and white from B.C.'s Okanagan Valley.

18 rooms. Closed mid-November-mid-March. Restaurant. **$$$$**

★★Harbor Towers Hotel & Suites
345 Quebec St., Victoria,
250-385-2405, 800-663-5896;
www.harbourtowers.com

195 rooms Restaurant, bar, children's activity center. Pets accepted, fee. Exercise room. Pool. Busn. Center. **$$**

★★★Hotel Grand Pacific
463 Belleville St., Victoria,
250-386-0450, 800-663-7550;
www.hotelgrandpacific.com

Located at the southern tip of Vancouver Island, the hotel offers serene water views and easy access to historic Old Town and area businesses. The rooms and suites are light and airy. Fine dining is one of Victoria's hallmarks, and this hotel is no exception. The Pacific Northwest cuisine at The Pacific is a stand-out, while The Mark's regionally influenced dishes are equally delicious.

304 rooms. Three restaurants, bar, spa. Pets accepted, fee. Exercise room. Pool. Busn. Center. **$$**

★★★Laurel Point Inn
680 Montreal St., Victoria,
250-386-8721, 800-663-7667;
www.laurelpoint.com

Every room of this hotel has a balcony and a fabulous view of either the Inner or the Upper Harbor. The grounds include a Japanese-style garden and the Asian influence is felt in the decor. Relax in the cozy piano lounge, the fragrant garden or the outdoor patio.

★

★

★

★

★

200 rooms. Restaurant, bar. Pets accepted, fee. Pool. Busn. Center. **$$$**

★★★Magnolia Hotel and Spa
623 Courtney St., Victoria,
250-381-0999, 877-624-6654;
www.magnoliahotel.com
This luxury boutique hotel one block from the Inner Harbor provides comfort and pampering throughout. The spa offers a full range of beauty and relaxation regimens and prides itself on using natural products from renewable resources.
63 rooms. Complimentary continental breakfast. Two restaurants, two bars. Pets accepted. Exercise room. **$$$**

★★★Miraloma on the Cove
2306 Harbour Rd., Sidney,
250-656-6622, 877-956-6622;
www.miraloma.ca
This luxurious seaside property is located just 20 minutes from downtown Victoria and five minutes from ferries and the airport. Guests can choose from studios, one-bedroom suites, or two-bedroom suites. Each guest room also includes pillow-top mattresses, a balcony or patio, spa tubs and heated towel bars. Guests can enjoy a number of amenities such as hot chocolate, cookies, use of mountain bikes and a complimentary continental breakfast buffet.
22 rooms. Complimentary continental breakfast. Pets accepted, fee. Exercise room. **$$**

★★Oak Bay Beach and Marine Resort
1175 Beach Dr., Victoria,
250-598-4556, 800-668-7758;
www.oakbaybeachhotel.com
49 rooms. Complimentary continental breakfast. Restaurant, bar, beach. Pets accepted, fee. **$$**

★★Royal Scot Suite Hotel
425 Quebec St., Victoria,
250-388-5463, 800-663-7515;
www.royalscot.com
176 rooms. Restaurant, bar, children's activity center. Exercise room. Pool. **$**

★★★Sooke Harbor House
1528 Whiffen Spit Rd., Sooke,
250-642-3421, 800-889-9688;
www.sookeharbourhouse.com
Located on Vancouver Island by the sea, this bed-and-breakfast features beautifully designed guest rooms with fireplaces and spectacular ocean views. Guests can enjoy such area activities as hiking, whale-watching and cross-country skiing.
28 rooms Closed 3 weeks in January. Complimentary continental breakfast. Restaurant. Pets accepted, fee. **$$$**

★★★Swans Suite Hotel
506 Pandora Ave., Victoria,
250-361-3310, 800-668-7926;
www.swanshotel.com
Built in 1913, this hotel holds 30 one- and two-bedroom suites. Most of the guest rooms have a loft that contributes a spacious feeling, and some have skylights and private patios. All rooms boast full kitchens, duvets and original artwork. It's a lively place with its own brewery and two popular eating and drinking establishments.
30 rooms, all suites. Complimentary continental breakfast. Restaurant, bar. **$$**

★★Travelodge
229 Gorge Rd. E., Victoria,
250-388-6611, 800-565-3777;
www.travelodgevictoria.com
73 rooms. Restaurant, bar. Pets accepted, fee. Exercise room. Pool. Busn. Center. **$**

SPECIALITY LODGINGS
Andersen House
301 Kingston St., Victoria,
250-388-4565, 877-264-9988;
www.andersenhouse.com
4 rooms. Children over 11 years only. Complimentary full breakfast. **$$**

Gatsby Mansion B&B
309 Belleville St., Victoria,
250-388-9191, 800-563-9656;
www.gatsbymansion.com
20 rooms. Complimentary full breakfast. Restaurant. Spa. **$$**

57

BRITISH COLUMBIA

★
★
★
★
☆

Haterleigh Heritage Inn

243 Kingston St., Victoria,
250-384-9995, 866-234-2244;
www.haterleigh.com
This six-room inn, a heritage-designated property, was converted from a private residence built in 1901. The afternoon social hour provides an opportunity to mingle, browse the Internet, or relax on the covered veranda.
6 rooms, 2 story, all suites. Children over 9 only. Complimentary full breakfast. **$$$**

Prior House B&B Inn

620 St. Charles St., Victoria,
250-592-8847, 877-924-3300;
www.priorhouse.com
Set in a lovely residential area close to Craigdarroch Castle and within walking distance of many historic sites and shops, this Edwardian English manor-style home features ocean and mountain views. The property's beautifully manicured gardens are a wonderful place to relax after a formal three-course breakfast or afternoon sherry or tea.
6 rooms Complimentary full breakfast. **$$$**

Rosewood Victoria Inn

595 Michigan St., Victoria,
250-384-6644, 866-986-2222;
www.rosewoodvictoria.com
17 rooms, 3 story. Complimentary full breakfast. **$$**

RESTAURANTS

★★Blue Crab Bar and Grill

146 Kingston, Victoria,
250-480-1999;
www.bluecrab.ca
Seafood menu. Reservations recommended. **$$$**

★★Cedar Dining Room at Tigh-Na-Mara Resort

1155 Resort Dr., Parksville,
250-248-2333, 800-663-7373;
www.tigh-na-mara.com
International menu. Reservations recommended. **$$**

★★★Cafe Brio

944 Fort St., Victoria, 250-383-0009;
www.cafe-brio.com
This award-winning restaurant is located in downtown Victoria and offers West Coast/Continental cuisine featuring an abundance of fresh wild fish. The daily menu also offers local, seasonal, organic foods. For an exceptional value come for the early prix fixe menu.
International menu. Closed first two weeks in January. Reservations recommended. Outdoor seating. **$$$**

★★Camille's

45 Bastion Sq., Victoria,
250-381-3433;
www.camillesrestaurant.com
International menu. Closed Monday. Reservations recommended. **$$$**

★★★Deep Cove Chalet

11190 Chalet Rd., Sidney,
250-656-3541;
www.deepcovechalet.com
This charming and historic country inn has a great view overlooking the waters of the inside passage. Built in 1914, it was originally a teahouse for a railroad station.
French menu. Reservations recommended. Outdoor seating. **$$$**

★★★Empress Room

721 Government St., Victoria,
250-995-3615;
www.fairmont.com
Dine on classic cuisine in this richly appointed room of tapestries, intricately carved ceilings and live harp music. The 100-year-old hotel's waterfront location is full of European style, a great spot for a romantic meal.
International menu. Reservations recommended. **$$$$**

★★Gatsby Mansion

309 Belleville St., Victoria,
250-388-9191, 800-563-9656;
www.gatsbymansion.com
International menu. Reservations recommended. Outdoor seating. **$$$**

58

BRITISH COLUMBIA

★★★Herald Street Cafe
546 Herald St., Victoria,
250-381-1441.
International menu. Reservations recommended. Outdoor seating. **$$**

★★Hugo's
625 Courtney St., Victoria,
250-920-4846;
www.hugosbrewhouse.com
West Coast menu. Reservations recommended. Outdoor seating. **$$$**

★★Il Terrazzo
555 Johnson St., Victoria,
250-361-0028;
www.ilterrazzo.com
Italian menu. Reservations recommended. Outdoor seating. **$$$**

★★Japanese Village Steak and Seafood House
734 Broughton St., Victoria,
250-382-5165;
www.japanesevillage.bc.ca
Japanese menu with Teppan-grill cooking tables and a sushi bar. Reservations recommended. **$$**

★★Kingfisher Restaurant
4330 S. Island Hwy., Courtenay,
250-334-9600, 800-663-7929;
www.kingfisherspa.com
International menu. Reservations recommended. Outdoor seating. **$$**

★★★Lure
45 Songhees Rd., Victoria,
250-360-5873;
www.lureatoceanpointe.com
This contemporary, sophisticated seafood restaurant is located inside the Delta Ocean Pointe Resort and offers excellent water and downtown views.
Seafood menu. Reservations recommended. Outdoor seating. **$$$**

★★The Marina
1327 Beach Dr., Victoria,
250-598-8555;
www.marinarestaurant.com
International menu. Reservations recommended. **$$**

★★Old House Restaurant
1760 Riverside Ln., Courtenay,
250-338-5406;
www.theoldhouse.ca
International menu. Reservations recommended. Outdoor seating. **$$**

★★★★Restaurant Matisse
512 Yates St., Victoria,
250-480-0883;
www.restaurantmatisse.com
Restaurant Matisse is a gem of a dining room that has become a destination for simple, traditional French fare among Victoria's dining elite. While French wines dominate the list, a great selection of California bottles is also included.
French menu. Closed Monday-Tuesday and for two weeks in spring. Reservations recommended. **$$$**

★★Spinnaker's Brew Pub
308 Catherine St.,
Victoria,
250-386-2739, 877-838-2739;
www.spinnakers.com
Canada's oldest brewpub. Reservations recommended. Outdoor seating. **$$**

★★★Sooke Harbor House
1528 Whiffen Spit Rd., Sooke Harbor,
250-642-3421, 800-889-9688;
www.sookeharbourhouse.com
Considered one of the most unique restaurants in Canada, guests will enjoy fresh local organic seafood, meat and produce, with edible herbs and flowers from the garden.
International menu. Closed Monday-Wednesday from December to early February. Reservations recommended. Outdoor seating. **$$$**

★White Heather Tea Room
1885 Oak Bay Ave., Victoria,
250-595-8020.
Scottish menu, afternoon tea and delicious baked goods. Reservations recommended. **$**

BRITISH COLUMBIA

★
★
★
★
★

WHISTLER

The winning combination of Blackcomb and Whistler mountains makes this an internationally famous ski area—yet it's also packed full through the summer, as preppy golfers descend upon the village alongside mud-spattered, hardcore mountain bikers. Five lakes dot Whistler valley, offering ample opportunity to fish, swim, windsurf, canoe, kayak or sail. The alpine slopes for a time give way to extensive hiking and mountain biking trails, but even in summer there is skiing to be found—Whistler is where enthusiasts will find the only lift-serviced, summertime public glacier skiing in North America. Everything in Whistler is larger-than-life: the ideal getaway with opulent food and wine, an infectious party atmosphere and sumptuous accommodations, plus a staging ground for epics that is nothing short of extraordinary.
Information: www.mywhistler.com

WHAT TO SEE AND DO

Blackcomb Ski Area
4545 Blackcomb Way, Whistler,
604-687-1032, 866-218-9690;
www.whistlerblackcomb.com
Six high-speed quad chairlifts, three triple chairlifts, three handletows, two T-bars, platter lift, magic car lift. More than 100 runs; longest run 7 miles (11 kilometers), vertical drop 5,280 feet (1609 meters). Glacier skiing (mid-June-August, weather permitting). High-speed gondola.

Whistler Museum and Archives Society
4329 Main St., Whistler,
604-932-2019;
www.whistlermuseum.com
Discover the rich history of the thriving Whistler community through artifacts, photographs and stories from local community members.

Whistler Ski Area
4545 Blackcomb Way, Whistler,
604-687-1032, 866-218-9690;
www.whistlerblackcomb.com
Six high-speed quad, double, two triple chairlifts; two handletows, two T-bars, platter pull. More than 100 runs; longest run 7 miles (11 kilometers), vertical drop 5,020 feet (1530 meters). Two high-speed gondolas.

SPECIAL EVENTS

Cornucopia, Whistler's Food and Wine Celebration
www.whistlercornucopia.com

Enjoy wine from more than 70 wineries from the province, neighboring U.S. states and around the world. Food tastings, wine dinners and seminars. Early November.

TELUS World Ski & Snowboard Festival
www.whistlerblackcomb.com/todo/events/detail/twssf.htm
Ten-day festival features outdoor concert series, action-sports photography and film events, demonstration days and festive parties. Mid-April.

HOTELS

★★Best Western Listel Whistler Hotel
4121 Village Green, Whistler,
604-932-1133, 800-663-5472;
www.listelhotel.com
98 rooms. Restaurant, bar. Pets accepted, fee. Pool. $$

★★Crystal Lodge
4154 Village Green, Whistler,
604-932-2221, 800-667-3363;
www.crystal-lodge.com
137 rooms. Restaurant, bar. Pets accepted, fee. Exercise room. Pool. $

★★★★Four Seasons Resort Whistler
4591 Blackcomb Way, Whistler,
604-935-3400, 800-819-5053;
www.fourseasons.com
This resort is nestled in the foot of the Blackcomb and Whistler mountains offers a year-round getaway that features signature Four Seasons service and style. Located at the base of Blackcomb Mountain, so it a

mere five-minute walk to the ski lifts and a 10-minute stroll to the village center. The guest rooms are spacious, beautifully furnished and decorated. The dining room and lounge, Fifty Two 80, delight with flavorful food and an extensive wine list and specialty cocktails. After a day of activity, retreat to The Spa, where body wraps, hydro-therapy, facials and massages will help you unwind. 273 rooms. Restaurant, bar, children's activity center (winter only). Pets accepted, fee. Exercise room. Pool. Busn. Center. **$$$$**

★★★The Fairmont Chateau Whistler
4599 Chateau Blvd., Whistler,
604-938-8000, 800-606-8244;
www.fairmont.com
The Fairmont Chateau Whistler is a skier's nirvana. During summer, its golf course and David Leadbetter Golf Academy lend the same status for golfers. The Vida Wellness Spa soothes the tired muscles of active visitors. Taste buds are tantalized at the resort's three restaurants.
550 rooms. Two restaurants, bar. Ski in/ski out. Pets accepted, fee. Exercise room. Pool. Golf. Skiing Busn. Center. **$$$**

★★★Pan Pacific Whistler Mountainside
4320 Sundial Crescent, Whistler,
604-905-2999, 888-905-9995;
www.panpacific.com
Nestled at the foot of Whistler and Blackcomb mountains and facing Skier's Plaza, this all-suite boutique resort offers kitchens, fireplaces and balconies with beautiful views of the mountains of Whistler Village.
121 rooms, all suites. Two restaurants, bar. Exercise room. Pool. Busn. Center. **$$$**

★★Summit Lodge & Spa
4359 Main St., Whistler,
604-932-2778, 888-913-8811;
www.summitlodge.com
Located in the Whistler Marketplace development at the foot of the mountains, the Summit's lodge-like ambience features minimalist, Asian-inspired decor. The grounds feature a Japanese-themed spa, a

pool, underground parking and a shuttle bus to the slopes.
81 rooms. Restaurant, bar. Pets accepted, fee. Pool. **$$$**

★★★The Westin Resort and Spa
4090 Whistler Way, Whistler,
604-905-5000, 888-634-5577;
www.starwoodhotels.net
Dramatic views are enjoyed from the privacy of airy suites and guests retreat to the comfort of the FireRock Lounge apres-ski or the Aubergine Grille for fresh cuisine. The Avello Spa & Health Club entices visitors with more than 70 treatments and the latest fitness equipment.
419 rooms, all suites. Restaurant, bar. Children's activity center. Pets accepted, fee. Exercise. Pool. Busn. Center. **$$$**

RESTAURANTS
★★★Bearfoot Bistro
4121 Village Green, Whistler,
604-932-3433; www.bearfootbistro.com
Only a hard day of skiing can justify this four-hour, decadent feast for the senses. Each of eight courses is handcrafted from a huge range of rare, high-quality ingredients including caribou and pheasant. Add to this one of the most beautiful locations in North America and the result is a truly standout dining experience.
International menu. Reservations recommended. **$$$$**

★★La Rua
4557 Blackcomb way, 604-932-5011;
Seafood, steak menu. Closed six weeks in October-November. Reservations recommended. Outdoor seating. **$$$**

★★Rimrock Cafe
2117 Whistler Rd., Whistler, 604-932-5565;
www.rimrockwhistler.com
Seafood menu. Closed late October-mid-November. Reservations recommended. Outdoor seating. **$$$**

★★★Ristorante Araxi
4222 Village Sq., Whistler,
604-932-4540; www.araxi.com

★
★
★
★
★

Tables encircle a giant stone urn, the centerpiece of this warm and friendly dining room. A blend of French and Italian culinary styles and fine, regional ingredients have gained this resort-town restaurant continent-wide recognition.

International menu. Closed two weeks in early May, late October. Reservations recommended. Outdoor seating. **$$$**

★★Sushi Village
4272 Mountain Sq., Whistler,
604-932-3330;
www.sushivillage.com
Japanese menu. **$$**

★★Trattoria di Umberto
4417 Sundial Pl., Whistler, 604-932-5858;
www.umberto.com
Italian menu. Reservations recommended. Outdoor seating. **$$$**

★★★Val d'Isere
4314 Main St. #8, Whistler,
604-932-4666;
www.valdisere-restaurant.com
Impressive both for the food and the charming interior, this fine restaurant is located in the north village plaza.
French menu. Reservations recommended. Outdoor seating. **$$$**

★★★Wildflower Restaurant
4599 Chateau Blvd., Whistler,
604-938-2033, 800-606-8244;
www.fairmont.com
Tucked inside the Chateau Whistler, this restaurant features a local, organic-laden menu with weekly table d'hote signature dishes, an ever-popular coastal market buffet and a "Flavors of Asia" buffet on Friday and Saturday nights.
International menu. Reservations recommended. Outdoor seating. **$$$**

SPAS

★★★The Avello Spa
4090 Whistler Way, Whistler,
604-905-5000;

The Avello Spa takes a holistic approach in its well-being treatments. Massage accounts for most of the menu, with the signature massage treatments including the Avello hot rock massage, Thai and Chinese therapies. Asian approaches to balance include reiki, acupuncture, reflexology and shiatsu. A wide variety of hydrotherapy sessions are available, from herbal, milk, mustard, and mud to soaks using salts from the Dead Sea.

★★★★Spa at Four Seasons Whistler
4591 Blackcomb Way, Whistler,
604-935-3400;
www.fourseasons.com /whistler/spa
This contemporary spa located inside the Four Seasons Whistler offers a full-menu of massages and body treatments designed to sooth and restore sore muscles after a day on the slopes. Chilly feet are wrapped in warm towels while muscles are warmed with hot stones during the après-ski massage. The men's fitness facial restores wind- and sun-burned skin while the BC glacial clay wrap is a great way to warm up at the end of the day. Those who can't pry themselves from the comfort of their rooms can order up an in-room massage.

MANITOBA

MANITOBA IS LOCATED IN THE LONGITUDINAL CENTRE OF CANADA, THOUGH IT IS CONSIDERED part of Western Canada and is the easternmost of Canada's three prairie provinces. It is renowned for dramatic landscapes with golden fields, granite ridges and sparkling lakes, a lively cultural heritage of fur trade-era voyagers, accessible yet dramatic wildlife and warm, friendly people.

Sand dunes, ancient granite and amazing waterfalls are all woven through by extensive trail networks that attract hikers and bikers to broad valleys and lush Canadian Shield forests. More than 10,000 trophy-sized fish are pulled out of Manitoba's plentiful waters every year, with pristine fly-in as well as road-accessible lodges peppering the north. Arctic grayling, brook trout, lake trout, northern pike and walleye thrive here, and Winnipeg's Red River offers some of the best giant channel cat fishing in the world. Recognized as a birder's paradise, Manitoba attracts two-thirds of Canada's more than 500 species of birds. In spring, the birds fly north in amazing flocks in the hundreds of thousands over lakes, marshes and forests. North American birding hotspot, Oak Hammock Marsh Interpretive Centre, won the coveted 2002 British Airways Tourism for Tomorrow award for Best Environmental Experience.

In contrast to Manitoba's off-the-beaten-track experiences, Winnipeg is a multicultural city bursting with festivals, art, music and food. Restaurants serve everything from Ukrainian perogies to a fusion of regional and western cuisine.
Provincial Capital: Winnipeg
Information: www.travelmanitoba.com

★ SPOTLIGHT

★ Manitoba's lakes cover approximately 14.5% of its surface area, many with native-inspired names such as Lake Pekwachnamay-koskwaskwaypinwanik.

BRANDON

Brandon, Manitoba's second-largest city, has a rich agricultural heritage and reputation as a prosperous farming community, which it celebrates with the province's largest agricultural fair.
Information: www.tourism.brandon.com

WHAT TO SEE AND DO

Commonwealth Air Training Plan Museum
Hangar 1, McGill Field, Brandon, 204-727-2444;
www.airmuseum.ca
Display of WWII aircraft, vehicles; photos, uniforms, flags and other mementos of Air Force training conducted in Canada from 1940 to 1945 under the British Commonwealth Air Training Plan. Tours by appointment.

SPECIAL EVENTS

Manitoba Fall Fair
Keystone Centre, 18th St. and Richmond Ave., Brandon, 204-726-3590;

www.brandonfairs.com
Keystone Centre. Manitoba's largest live-stock show and sale; tractor pull, rodeo. November.

Manitoba Summer Fair
Keystone Centre,
18th St. and Richmond Ave., Brandon,
204-726-3590;
www.brandonfairs.com/
page.aspx?page_id=103&site_id=1
Competitions, children's entertainment, mid-way, dancing. June.

Royal Manitoba Winter Fair
Keystone Centre,
18th St. and Richmond Ave., Brandon,
204-726-3590;
www.brandonfairs.com
Manitoba's largest winter fair. Equestrian events, heavy horses, entertainment. Late March.

HOTELS
★Comfort Inn
925 Middleton Ave., Brandon,
204-727-6232;
www.choicehotels.ca
81 rooms. Pets accepted, fee. **$**

★★Royal Oak Inn & Suites
3130 Victoria Ave., Brandon,
204-728-5775, 800-852-2709;
www.royaloakinn.com
96 rooms. Restaurant, bar. Pets accepted, fee. Exercise room. Pool. **$**

★★Victoria Inn
3550 Victoria Ave., Brandon,
204-725-1532;
www.vicinn.ca
131 rooms. Restaurant, bar. Pets accepted, fee. Exercise room. Pool. **$**

CHURCHILL

Churchill is the only human settlement where visitors can come to see polar bears in the wild. Fast and dangerous at over 1,300 pounds (590 kilograms) and standing up to 10 feet (3 meters) tall, the bears are a marvel to behold when they frequent the area each fall. Wildlife admirers also come to this area of northern Manitoba to see some of the 250 species of birds that pass through, and in the summer to view beluga whales in the waters of the Churchill River.
Information: www.townofchurchill.ca

WHAT TO SEE AND DO
Eskimo Museum
242 Laverendrye Ave., Churchill,
204-675-2030;
www.museumsmanitoba.com/dir/
north/110.html
This museum contains an impressive collection of Inuit carvings and artifacts, considered some of the oldest and finest in the world. Artifacts date from 1700 B.C. to modern times.

Wapusk National Park of Canada
204-675-8863;
www.pc.gc.ca/pn-np/mb/wapusk/
index_E.asp
This park, southeast of Churchill, is home to one of the world's largest known polar bear denning sights. Wapusk, the Cree word for white bear, is dedicated to protecting the habitat for polar bears, as well as for the hundreds of thousands of birds that nest or migrate here each year. Unescorted visits to the park are not recommended. For the most current list of operators, contact the park office (888-773-8888; 204-675-8863).

WINNIPEG

Winnipeg, the provincial capital, is situated in the heart of the continent and combines the sophistication and friendliness of east and west. This formerly prairie-covered landscape was inhabited by Assiniboine, Cree and Ojibwa tribes over 6,000 years ago. These tribes met at the junction of the Assiniboine and Red rivers to trade. Today, Winnipeg, derived from the Cree word for "muddy waters," is home to Canada's largest city-dwelling aboriginal community. A historic gathering place, it is still a destination that foreigners and Canadians alike visit to enjoy a wide range of attrac-

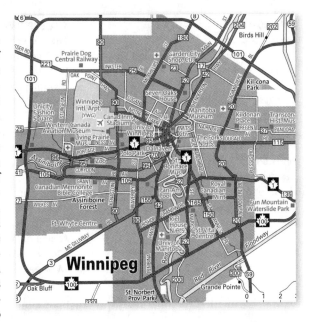

tions and cultural offerings. The city offers relaxing cruises on the Assiniboine and Red rivers, Rainbow Stage summer theater in Kildonan Park, the Manitoba Theatre Centre, the Winnipeg Symphony, the Manitoba Opera and the renowned Royal Winnipeg Ballet. Sports fans will enjoy the Blue Bombers football team and the Manitoba Moose hockey team.
Information: www.tourism.winnipeg.mb.ca

65

WHAT TO SEE AND DO

Assiniboine Forest Nature Park
2355 Corydon Ave., Winnipeg,
204-986-3989;
www.winnipeg.ca/publicworks/naturalist/
ns/AF/index.asp
This park features colorful English and formal gardens, the Leo Mol Sculpture Garden, a conservatory with floral displays, a duck pond, playgrounds, a cricket and field hockey area, a miniature train, bike paths and a fitness trail featuring more than 39 species of mammals and more than 80 species of birds. The Assiniboine Park Zoo has a collection of rare and endangered species, tropical mammals, birds and reptiles; the children's discovery area features a variety of young animals.

Assiniboine Park Conservatory
Assiniboine Park, Winnipeg,
204-986-5537;
www.winnipeg.ca/cms/ape/conservatory/
conservatory.stm
The longest established conservatory in western Canada gives visitors a chance to view tropical trees and plants, exotic flowers and foliage not indigenous to the country.

Birds Hill Provincial Park
8 miles/13 kilometers N. of Winnipeg
on Hwy. 59, Winnipeg,
204-222-9151;
www.gov.mb.ca/conservation/parks/
popular_parks/birds_hill/index.html
A 8,275-acre (3,350-hectare) park situated on a glacial formation called an esker. The park has a large population of white-tailed deer and many orchid species. Interpretive, hiking, bridle and bicycle trails; in-line skating path; snowshoe, snowmobile and cross-country skiing trails.

Centennial Centre
555 Main St., Winnipeg,

MANITOBA

204-956-1360;
www.mbccc.ca
Complex includes concert hall and Manitoba Theatre Centre Building.

Dalnavert Museum
61 Carlton St., Winnipeg,
204-943-2835;
www.mhs.mb.ca/info/museums/dalnavert/
index.shtml
Restored Victorian residence (1895) of Sir Hugh John Macdonald, premier of Manitoba, depicts the lifestyle and furnishings of the period.

Forks
Downtown Winnipeg, 204-943-7752;
www.theforks.com
Several key Winnipeg attractions are centered in the general location of what has been a gathering place for people for thousands of years. Come here to shop, dine, explore museums and historic sites, or simply stroll along the Riverwalk.

The Forks Market
Downtown Winnipeg, 204-942-6302;
www.theforks.com
Browse through more than 50 specialty shops for handicrafts, toys, gift items and more and dine on cuisine from around the world and on local specialties.

The Forks National Historic Site of Canada
401-25 Forks Market Rd., Winnipeg,
204-983-6757;
www.pc.gc.ca/lhn-nhs/mb/forks/
index_E.asp
Situated on 13.6 acres (5.5 hectares). Riverside promenade; walkways throughout. Historical exhibits, playground; evening performances. Special events. Adjacent area open in winter for skating, cross-country skiing.

Fort Whyte Centre for Family Adventure and Recreation
1961 McCreary Rd., Winnipeg,

204-989-8355; www.fortwhyte.org
Hike on self-guided trails through 400 acres (162 hectares) of marshes, lakes and forests that are home to 27 species of birds and mammals. Year-round fishing; canoe and boat rentals. Dine at Buffalo Stone Cafe and shop for souvenirs at The Nature Shop. A 10,000-square-foot (920-square-meter) interpretive center showcases a variety of exhibits. Don't miss the Bison Prairie, with the largest urban-based herd of Plains bison in the country, or the Prairie Dog Exhibit.

Leo Mol Sculpture Garden
Assiniboine Park, Winnipeg,
204-986-6531;
www.partnersinthepark.org/leomol.html
Garden and gallery to view the bronze sculptures and other artwork by this acclaimed local artist. An on-site studio allows visitors to see how bronze sculptures are created.

Lyric Theatre
Assiniboine Park, Winnipeg,
204-888-5466;
www.partnersinthepark.org/lyric.html
View performances by the Royal Winnipeg Ballet, the Winnipeg Symphony Orchestra and during assorted festivals.

The Manitoba Children's Museum
45 Forks Market Rd., Winnipeg,
204-924-4000;
www.childrensmuseum.com
Children explore and create in seven galleries, such as one that enables preschoolers to learn about the habitats of different animal species and to climb on a 17-foot (5.2-meter) oak tree, while older children can surf the Internet. Travel into the past on a 1952 diesel locomotive and passenger coach, or into a fairytale wonderland.

Manitoba Museum of Man and Nature
190 Rupert Ave., Winnipeg,
204-956-2830;
www.manitobamuseum.mb.ca
Galleries interpret Manitoba's human and natural history.

Manitoba Opera Association

Portage Place, 380 Graham Ave.,
Winnipeg, 204-942-7479;
www.manitobaopera.mb.ca

The strength of character of the Manitoba Opera comes from its ability to attract great international artists such as the Met's Leona Mitchell and La Scala's Eduard Tumagian, and to highlight local talent, such as Tracy Dahl and Phillip Ens. The Manitoba Opera Chorus is supported by Winnipeg Symphony Orchestra under the direction of internationally known conductors. Lavish sets and costumes bring the performances to life, while English subtitles, projected on an overhead screen, make foreign-language operas accessible and comprehensible to everyone.

Oak Hammock Marsh Wildlife Management Area

204-467-3300;
www.mb.ec.gc.ca/nature/whp/ramsar/
df02s09.en.html

More than 8,000 acres (3,238 hectares) of marshland and grassland wildlife habitat. Attracts up to 300,000 ducks and geese during spring (April-mid-May) and fall migration (September-October). Nature trails; picnic sites, marsh boardwalk, viewing mounds, drinking water. Conservation center with displays, interpretive programs.

Paddlewheel/River Rouge boat and bus tours

The Provencher Dock, Winnipeg,
204-944-8000;
www.paddlewheelcruises.com

Floating restaurant, moonlight dance and sightseeing cruises; also guided tours on double-decker buses. Bus/cruise combinations available.

Planetarium

190 Rupert Ave., Winnipeg,
204-943-3142;
www.manitobamuseum.ca/pl_info.html

Circular, multipurpose audiovisual theater. Wide variety of shows; subjects include cosmic catastrophes and the edge of the universe. Learn about science through hands-on exhibits.

Ross House

Joe Zuken Heritage Park,
204-943-3958;
www.mhs.mb.ca/info/museums/ross/
index.shtml

(1854) Oldest building in the original city of Winnipeg; first post office in western Canada. Displays and period-furnished rooms depict daily life in the Red River Settlement.

Royal Canadian Mint

520 Lagimodière Blvd., Winnipeg,
204-983-6429;
www.mint.ca/royalcanadianmintpublic

(1976) One of the world's most modern mints; striking glass tower, landscaped interior courtyard. Tour allows viewing of coining process; coin museum. May-August: Monday-Friday 9 a.m.-4 p.m.; September-April: Monday-Friday 10 a.m.-2 p.m. Tours by appointment only.

Royal Winnipeg Ballet

Centennial Concert Hall, 555 Main St.,
Winnipeg, 204-956-0183, 800-667-4792;
www.rwb.org

This nationally acclaimed company performs throughout the year in Winnipeg and also presents Ballet in the Park during the summer.

Seven Oaks House Museum

115 Rupertsland Blvd. E., Winnipeg,
West Kildonan, 204-339-7429.

Oldest house in Manitoba (1851). Log construction, original furnishings, housewares. Adjoining buildings include general store, post office.

The Splash Dash Water Bus

204-783-6633;
www.splashdash.ca

Explore the river on a half-hour boat tour, rent a canoe, or use the water taxi service to get to downtown locations. May-October.

St. Boniface Museum

494 Tache Ave., Winnipeg,
204-237-4500;

67

www.virtualmuseum.ca/Exhibitions/
Instruments/Anglais/msb_c_txt02_en.html
(1846) Located in the largest French-Canadian community west of Quebec, where Louis Riel, a founder of Manitoba, was born, this museum is housed in the oldest structure in the city, dating to the days of the Red River Colony; it's the largest oak-log construction in North America.

Winnipeg Art Gallery
300 Memorial Blvd., Winnipeg,
204-786-6641;
www.wag.mb.ca
Canada's first civic gallery (1912). Eight galleries present changing exhibitions of contemporary, historical and decorative art, plus world's largest public collection of Inuit Art. Free admission Wednesday evening and all day Saturday. Programming includes tours, lectures, films, concerts. Restaurant.

Winnipeg Symphony Orchestra
Centennial Concert Hall,
555 Main St., Winnipeg,
204-949-3950;
www.wso.mb.ca
Performances ranging from classical to pop to family-oriented music at Centennial Concert Hall. May-September.

SPECIAL EVENTS
Festival du Voyageur
Voyageur Park, St. Joseph and Messager Sts., Winnipeg,
204-237-7692;
www.festivalvoyageur.mb.ca
In St. Boniface, Winnipeg's French Quarter. Winter festival celebrating the French-Canadian voyageur and the fur trade era. Ten days in mid-February.

Folklorama
183 Kennedy St., Winnipeg,
204-982-6210, 800-665-0234;
www.folklorama.ca
Multicultural festival featuring more than 40 pavilions. Singing, dancing, food, cultural displays. August.

Red River Exhibition
3977 Portage Ave., Winnipeg,
204-888-6990;
www.redriverex.com
Large event encompassing grandstand shows, band competitions, displays, agricultural exhibits, parade, entertainment, midway, petting zoo, shows, food. Late June-early July.

Winnipeg Folk Festival
Birds Hill Provincial Park, 204-231-0096;
www.winnipegfolkfestival.ca
More than 60 regional, national and international artists perform; nine stages; children's village; evening concerts. Juried crafts exhibit and sale; international food village. Early July.

Winnipeg Fringe Theatre Festival
Old Market Square, 174 Market Ave.,
Winnipeg, 204-956-1340;
www.winnipegfringe.com
More than 100 theater companies perform during North Americas second-largest Fringe Festival. July.

HOTELS
★★Delta Winnipeg
350 St. Mary Ave., Winnipeg,
204-942-0051, 888-311-4990;
www.deltahotels.com
392 rooms. Restaurant. Exercise room. Pool. $$

★★★The Fairmont Winnipeg
2 Lombard Pl., Winnipeg,
204-957-1350, 800-257-7544;
www.fairmont.com
The Fairmont Winnipeg's stylish interiors and central location have earned it a loyal following among leisure and business travelers. The city's large historic district, cultural attractions, restaurants, shops, and businesses are all within walking distance from this hotel. The Velvet Glove restaurant is an ideal place for business meetings or private dinners with inspired Canadian cuisine and an exceptional wine list.
340 rooms. Restaurant. Exercise room. Busn. Center. $$

MANITOBA

★★Holiday Inn
2520 Portage Ave., Winnipeg,
204-885-4478, 800-465-4329;
www.holiday-inn.com/winnipeg-arpt
226 rooms, 15 story. Restaurant, bar, children's activity center. Exercise room. Pool. Busn. Center. **$$**

★★★Sheraton Winnipeg Hotel
161 Donald St., Winnipeg,
204-942-5300, 800-463-6400;
www.sheraton.com
This hotel is conveniently located three blocks from the convention center making it a star for business travelers. But all guests will enjoy the modern guest guest rooms with the Four Comfort Bed, complimentary Internet access and unwinding at Local Heroes Sports Bar.
271 rooms. Restaurant, bar. Pets accepted, fee. Pool. **$$**

★★Best Western Charter House Hotel
330 York Ave., Winnipeg,
204-942-0101, 800-782-0175.
90 rooms. Restaurant, bar. **$**

★Comfort Inn
1770 Sargent Ave., Winnipeg,
204-783-5627, 800-228-5150;
www.comfortinn.com
81 rooms. Pets accepted, fee. **$**

★★Radisson Hotel Downtown
288 Portage Ave., Winnipeg,
204-956-0410, 800-333-3333;
www.radisson.com
272 rooms. Restaurant, bar. Pets accepted, fee. Exercise room. Pool. Busn. Center. **$**

★★Victoria Inn Hotel Convention
1808 Wellington Ave., Winnipeg,
204-786-4801.
275 rooms. Restaurant, bar. Pets accepted, fee. Pool. **$**

RESTAURANTS

★★Amici
326 Broadway, Winnipeg,
204-943-4997;
www.amiciwpg.com
Italian menu. **$$$**

★★Hy's Steak Loft
216 Kennedy, Winnipeg,
204-942-1000;
www.hyssteakhouse.com
Steak menu. **$$$**

★★Ichiban Japanese Steakhouse and Sushi Bar
189 Carlton St., Winnipeg,
204-925-7400.
Teppanyaki/Japanese menu. **$$$**

69

MANITOBA

NEW BRUNSWICK

Triumph over tragedy personifies the great Acadian odyssey in New Brunswick—and through the Acadians' difficult historical journey, their "joie de vivre" (joy of life) has sustained them and the spirit of this province for 250 years. This indomitable spirit is celebrated in kitchen parties filled with fiddle music, traditional cuisine, lively dance and storytelling. While not a purely French population, New Brunswick's flavor is Acadian-inspired.

New Brunswick, the largest of Canada's three Maritime provinces, is bursting with the pride and colour of the Acadian French (Cajuns' northern cousins). New Brunswick's rich historic past is reflected in major restorations such as the Acadian Historical Village near Caraquet, Kings' Landing Historical Settlement near Fredericton and MacDonald Historic Farm near Miramichi. Despite the number of provinces with French-speaking locals, New Brunswick is Canada's only official bilingual province, with about 33 percent of the people speaking French.

There is much more to New Brunswick than history—the Bay of Fundy to the south (featuring some of the highest tides in the world and a great variety of whales), the Reversing Falls in Saint John, Magnetic Hill in Moncton, Hopewell Cape Rocks at Hopewell Cape, and always the sea. The four seasons of New Brunswick are some of the most vivid in the country. Summers are breezy and hot, with record-breaking tides and the warmest salt water north of Virginia, exposed ocean floors and vast expanses of sand dunes ripe for picnics and exploring. Fall brings brilliant colors and the bounty of the harvest amid some of the best whale-watching in the country. In winter, enjoy endless frozen ponds and lakes, alpine and cross-country skiing and the world's longest network of groomed snowmobile trails. Spring visitors feast on maple syrup and fiddleheads, and anglers are drawn to the world-famous Atlantic salmon river, Miramichi, for the opening of the fishing season.

Provincial Capital: Fredericton
Information: www.tourismnewbrunswick.ca

 SPOTLIGHT

★ The inventor of the ice cream cone was born in Sussex Corner, the dairy capital of Canada, midway along the Fundy Coastal Drive. Locals tell the story of baker Walter Donelly, who made a bad batch of dough. He was at a loss with what to do with his hard, crispy pastry. So he ran next door to the ice cream parlor... and the rest, as they say, is history.

★ The world's largest covered bridge was completed in Hartland in 1899. It is 1,282 feet (390 meters) long and spans the Saint John River.

EDMUNDSTON

Known as the Gateway of the Maritimes, Edmundston is in northwest New Brunswick, a few minutes from the province of Quebec, on the border of Maine and at the doorstep of Atlantic Canada. Acadian culture predominates in this cheerful and active town, with almost all of the population speaking French and English.
Information: www.ville.edmunston.nb.ca

WHAT TO SEE AND DO

Antique Auto Museum
35 Principale St., Edmundston,
506-735-2637.
Impressive display of vintage vehicles and mechanical marvels of the past 70 years Mid-June-Labour Day.

Edmundston Golf Club
570 Victoria St., Edmundston,
506-735-3086;
www.golfedmundston.nb.ca
This challenging 18-hole course within the city limits attracts golfers from a large area. May-September: daily

Grand Falls
40 miles (64 kilometers) S.E. of Edmundston,
506-475-7769;
www.grandfalls.com/english/fallsgorge.html
At 75 feet (23 meters) high, this is one of largest cataracts east of Niagara. Fascinating gorge and scenic lookouts along trail; museum. Stairs to bottom of gorge. Late May-October.

Les Jardins de la Republique Provincial Park
5 miles (8 kilometers) N. of Edmundston, via Trans-Canada Hwy. 2,
506-735-2525
(Gardens of the Republic) Park of 107 acres (43 hectares) overlooking the Madawaska River. Amphitheater, scene of music and film performances; 20-acre (8-hectare) botanical garden. Heated swimming pool, boat dock, launch; tennis, volleyball, softball, horseshoes, bicycling, playground.

Mont Farlagne
360 Mont Farlagne Rd., Saint-Jacques,
506-739-7669;

www.montfarlagne.com
Twenty trails open to downhill skiing and snowboarding, with five chair lifts, a snow park, restaurant and bar. December to March, weather permitting.

New Brunswick Botanical Garden
15 Principale St., Edmundston,
506-737-4444
Conceived and designed by a team from the prestigious Montreal Botanical Garden, the garden covers more than 17 acres (7 hectares). More than 30,000 annual flowers and 80,000 plants are on display. June-mid-October.

New Denmark Memorial Museum
6 Main New Denmark Rd., New Denmark,
45 miles/72 kilometers,
S.E. of Edmundston,
506-553-6724
Museum building is on the site of the original immigrant house built in 1872 to house settlers. Household articles, documents, machinery belonging to original settlers from Denmark. Mid-June-Labour Day: daily; rest of year: by appointment.

St. Basile Chapel Museum
321 Main St., St. Basile,
506-263-5971.
Parish church; replica of first chapel built in 1786. July-August: daily.

SPECIAL EVENTS

Festival aérien (radio-controlled planes and helicopters)
Edmundston Municipal Airport, Edmundston, at the Quebec/NB border on the #2 Hwy.
The aeromodeling club "Les ailes du Madawaska" have their annual Fun-Fly in August.

NEW BRUNSWICK

International Snowmobilers Festival
506-737-1866
Featuring snowmobile events on both sides of the International Border in Madawaska, Maine and Edmundston. Highlights include a two-day Lucky Run, Fun Night and many more events for Snowmobilers. Sledders from throughout the U.S. and Canada converge on the beautiful St. John Valley for three days of riding top rated trails. First week in February.

Jazz Festival
Canada Rd. and Rue St. Francois, Edmundston,
506-737-8188;
www.jazzbluesedmundston.com/index-english.php
Third weekend in June.

L'Acadie des Terres et Forêts en Fête
Republic Provincial Park, Saint-Jacques,
506-739-0919;
www.acadiedesterresetforets.com

The performance celebrates 400 years of Acadian history through song, dance and theater. The representations are held on a natural site (covered in the event of rain). Early July-mid-August.

La Foire Brayonne
215 Victoria St., Edmundston,
506-739-6608;
www.foirebrayonne.com
French heritage festival featuring concerts, crafts, cultural activities and sporting events. Late July-early August.

Marché Plein Air de Saint-Basile
Saint-Basile arena, Edmundston
The main street committee of Saint-Basile invites you to a weekend of animation for the whole family with more than 20 kiosks to visit, music and dancers. Mid-August.

NEW BRUNSWICK

★
★
★
★
★
★

FREDERICTON

In the 1950s, the patron of this city, the late Lord Beaverbrook, raised Fredericton from a quiet provincial capital to a major cultural center. Born in Ontario, this British newspaper baron maintained a strong loyalty to New Brunswick, the province of his youth. Wander the elm tree-lined streets through the Green, a lovely park along the St. John River, and admire examples of Beaverbrook's generosity that heighten the city's beauty. Nestled along the tree-shaded Green sits Christ Church Cathedral, an 1853 example of decorated Gothic architecture. And the art gallery that is Beaverbrook's namesake boasts a collection worthy of continent-wide pride.

Information: www.city.fredericton.nb.ca

WHAT TO SEE AND DO

Beaverbrook Art Gallery
703 Queen St., Fredericton,
506-458-8545;
www.beaverbrookartgallery.org
Collection includes 18th- to 20th-century British paintings, 18th- and early 19th-century English porcelain, historical and contemporary Canadian and New Brunswick paintings and Salvador Dalí Santiago el Grande; Hosmer-Pillow-Vaughan Collection of European fine and decorative arts from the 14th to 20th centuries.

Fredericton Golf and Curling Club
331 Golf Club Rd. off Woodstock Rd.,
506-458-0003;
www.fgcc.info/golf/index.asp
Eighteen holes.

Fredericton Playhouse
686 Queen St., Fredericton,
506-458-8345;
www.theplayhouse.nb.ca
Home of Theatre New Brunswick.

Historic Garrison District
Queen St., Fredericton,
between Regent and York Sts.,
506-460-2129, 888-888-4768;
www.tourismfredericton.ca/en/thingstodo/
HistoricGarrison.asp
In summer, daily outdoor theater and walking tours. Attractions include the New Brunswick School Days Museum, the York Sunbury Museum, the New Brunswick Sports Hall of Fame, the Guard House and the Casemate Artisans Shops.

Kings Landing Historical Settlement
20 Kings Landing Rd., Kings Landing,
23 miles/37 kilometers W. of Fredericton
on Trans-Canada Hwy. at exit 259,
506-363-4999;
www.kingslanding.nb.ca
Settlement of 70 buildings, costumed staff of 100; recalls Loyalist lifestyle of a century ago. Carpenter's shop, general store, school, church, blacksmith shop, working sawmill

and gristmill, inn; replica of a 19th-century wood river craft. All restoration and work is done with tools of the period. June-early October.

Mactaquac
1256 Rte. 105, Fredericton,
Mactaquac Provincial Park,
506-363-4926, 877-267-4653;
www.mactaquacgolf.com
Eighteen-hole championship course.

Mactaquac Fish Hatchery
114 Fish Hatchery Ln., French Village,
10 miles/16 kilometers W. of Fredericton
on Rte. 2/Trans-Canada Hwy.,
506-363-3021;
www.mar.dfo-mpo.gc.ca/science/
mactaquac
Sixty-seven rearing ponds with a potential annual production of 340,000 smolts (young salmon ready to migrate). Visitor center (mid-May-mid-October).

Mactaquac Generating Station
12 miles/19 kilometers W. of Fredericton
on Rte. 2/Trans-Canada Hwy. exit 274,
506-458-4448;
www.nbpower.com/en/commitment/
education/generating/hydro/mactaquac.
aspx
Hydroelectric dam has powerhouse with turbines and generators; fish collection facilities at foot of dam. Free guided tours. Mid-May-August: daily; rest of year: by appointment.

Mactaquac Provincial Park
1256 Rte. 105, Mactaquac, 15 miles/24
kilometers W. of Fredericton,
506-363-3011;
www.mactaquacgolf.com/thepark.html
Approximately 1,400 acres (567 hectares) of farmland and forest overlooking the head-pond of Mactaquac Dam. Boating (launch, marinas), swimming beaches, fishing; hiking, camping (hookups, dump station), golf, picnicking, playgrounds, restaurant, store, laundry. Also in the vicinity are a historic

NEW BRUNSWICK

village, a fish culture station and a generating plant.

Odell Park
End of Rookwood Ave., Fredericton,
506-458-8530;
www.tourismnewbrunswick.ca/en-CA/
Product/MunicipalPark.htm?pid=1498
Unique example of the primeval forest of New Brunswick; part of the original land grant. Approximately 400 acres (160 hectares) include lodge, picnicking, play area, walking paths through woods; deer and other animals; ski trails; arboretum with 1 3/4 mile (2.8 kilometers) trail.

Officers' Square
Queen and Carleton Sts., Fredericton,
506-460-2129
Park with Lord Beaverbrook statue; changing of the guard ceremonies (July-Labour Day); band concerts Tuesday and Thursday evenings (late June-August), theater in the park (July-August).

Old Officers' Quarters
Queen and Carleton Sts., Fredericton,
506-460-212.
Typical architecture of Royal Engineers in the Colonial period; stone arches, iron handrails and stone staircase. Older part (circa 1839-1840) near the river has thicker walls of solid masonry and hand-hewn timbers; later end (circa 1851) has thinner walls and sawn timbers.

York-Sunbury Historical Society Museum
571 Queen St., Fredericton,
506-455-6041
Permanent and changing exhibits of military and domestic area history; seasonal exhibitions of history, New Brunswick crafts and fine arts; mounted 42-pound (16-kilogram) Coleman frog.

Wilmot Park
51 Woodstock Rd., Fredericton.
Wading pool, lighted tennis, ball diamond, picnicking, playground, bowling green.

SPECIAL EVENTS
Atlantic Crew Classic Rowing Regatta
506-453-9428
The St. John River is the venue for this top-notch rowing regatta. Enjoy junior and senior rowing competitions, as well as a masters' competition and corporate challenge. Early July.

Canada Day Celebration
St. Anne Point Dr. and Regent St.,
Fredericton,
506-455-3866.
Last week in June-early July.

Fredericton Exhibition
359 Smythe St., Fredericton,
506-458-8819;
www.frex.ca
This 7 days exhibition showcases exhibits on agriculture, floriculture, horticulture and handicrafts; petting zoo, pony rides. First week in September.

Harvest Jazz and Blues Festival
King and Westmorland Sts., Fredericton,
506-454-2583, 888-622-5837;
www.harvestjazzandblues.com
Five days of performances from newer and more established local and international musicians. Mid-September.

New Brunswick Highland Games and Scottish Festival
Woodstock Rd., Fredericton (on the grounds of Old Government House),
506-452-9244, 888-368-4444;
www.highlandgames.ca
Immerse yourself in Scottish culture while listening to pipe bands, watching traditional dances, purchasing crafts and more. Last weekend in July.

New Brunswick Summer Chamber Music Festival
8 Bailey Dr., Fredericton,
506-453-4697;
extend.unb.ca/music/summerfestival.php.
Classical musicians celebrate chamber music at these outdoor concerts held throughout the downtown. Late August.

NEW BRUNSWICK

HOTEL

★★★Delta Fredericton Hotel
225 Woodstock Rd., Fredericton,
506-457-7000, 888-890-3222;
www.deltahotels.com
This brown stone hotel directly fronting the St. John River. The guest rooms are spacious, and the décor reflects a combination of styles. Half of the rooms overlook the river, and the other half overlooks a wooded area.
222 rooms. Restaurant, bar. Exercise room. Pool. $$

MONCTON

The Petitcodiac River and its branches twist and turn through this commercial and cultural center of the Atlantic provinces, becoming a mud flat clustered with sea gulls at the record-breaking low tides. Moncton is an excellent beginning for a tour to the northeast along the coast to beautiful Kouchibouguac National Park. Nearby, Shediac, "Lobster Capital of the World," boasts one of the finest beaches in Canada—Parlee Beach—with endless white sand dunes and the warmest ocean waters north of Virginia. Moncton, a bustling center with great shopping and plentiful amenities, hosts sailing regattas and hydroplane races, festivals, seafood and coastal relaxation.
Information: www.greater.moncton.nb.ca

WHAT TO SEE AND DO

Fundy National Park
P.O. Box 40, Alma, 506-887-6000;
www.canadianparks.com/brunswick/
fundynp/index.htm
On the coast between Saint John and Moncton sits an extraordinary parcel of land—80 square miles (207 square kilometers) of forested hills and valleys crisscrossed by miles of hiking trails. Cliffs front much of the rugged coastline, home of the highest tides in the world. To view this phenomenon, visit the beaches at Herring Cove, Point Wolfe and the picturesque town of Alma. Since the ocean water is cold enough for only the bravest of souls, swim in the heated saltwater pool or in one of the lakes; golf, tennis, lawn bowling, picnicking, camping (May-October) and cross-country skiing are also available. Ampitheater programs and guided beach walks (June-August).

Crystal Palace Amusement Park
499 Paul St., Dieppe,
506-859-4386, 877-856-4386;
www.crystalpalace.ca
Indoor and outdoor attractions including rides, miniature golf, science center, video games and go-karts.

Fort Beausejour National Historic Site
111 Fort Beauséjour Rd., Aulac,
approximately 37 miles/60 kilometers E. of Moncton on Hwy. 2, exit 550,
506-536-4399;
www.pc.gc.ca/lhn-nhs/nb/beausejour/
index_E.asp
Built by the French between 1751 and 1755 during their long struggle with England for possession of Acadia. Attacked in 1755, the fort was captured by the British under Colonel Monckton, who renamed it Fort Cumberland. Following its capture, the fort was strengthened and its defenses extended. During the American Revolution in 1776, it withstood an attack by revolutionaries under Jonathan Eddy. It was manned by a small garrison during the War of 1812. Three casements and a massive stone curtain wall have been restored; displays on history and culture of Isthmus of Chignecto; outdoor paintings showing garrison as it existed in 18th century. Panoramic view of site and surrounding salt marshes. (June-mid-October)

Magnetic Hill Zoo
175 Magic Mountain Rd., Moncton,
506-877-7718;

NEW BRUNSWICK

★
★
★
★
★
★

www.moncton.org/zoo
Wild animal park and petting zoo; many species represented, including wildfowl. May-October: daily.

Hopewell Rocks Provincial Park
Outside Moncton, across the Petitcodiac River, then 28 miles (45 kilometers) S.E. on Hwy. 114 to Rocks exit just S. of Hopewell Cape, 506-856-2940, 800-561-0123; www.thehopewellrocks.ca

Unique cliffs, caves and flowerpot-shaped pillars of conglomerate rock interspersed with shale and sandstone layers. The tourist information center has interpretive displays; tour guides are available. Visitors are advised to watch for caution signs, avoid loose cliff sections, stay off cliffs and return from the beach by the time posted at the stairs to avoid problems with rising tides. Picnicking, restaurant. May-October: daily.

Tidal Bore
King and Main Sts., Moncton, Main St. at Bore View Park, 506-853-3590; www.monctonkiosk.com/moncton-tour/Tidal-Bore.php

A small tidal wave running upstream to usher in the Bay of Fundy tides on the normally placid Petitcodiac River. The water level rises more than 25 feet in an hour. The bore arrives twice daily.

Parlee Beach Provincial Park
45 Parlee Beach Rd., in Shediac, Pointe-du-Chêne, 506-533-3363; www.tourismnewbrunswick.ca/en-CA/Product/ProvincialPark.htm?pid=2074

Parlee Beach boasts some of the warmest salt water north of Virginia, with vast sand dunes and clear swimming waters. Besides supervised swimming, enjoy volleyball, football and sand-sculpture competitions. On site are restaurants, a canteen, an amphitheater, showers, washrooms, a playground, picnic area and ample parking. Nearby you'll also find camping facilities, a marina, more restaurants, accommodations and cultural activities.

SPECIAL EVENTS
Shediac Lobster Festival
Shediac, 506-532-1122; www.shediaclobsterfestival.ca

Shediac, "Lobster Capital of the World," hosts five days of fantastic seafood and world-class entertainment. Started in 1949, the Shediac Lobster Festival draws visitors from all over the world to feast on succulent lobster and soak up Acadian and maritime culture. Ride the midway, join in the kids' parade and enjoy daily musical performances. Early July.

Atlantic Seafood Festival
506-855-8525; www.atlanticseafoodfestival.com

Enjoy all things seafood while listening to musicians from the Maritime provinces and observing the culinary skills of international celebrity chefs. Mid-August.

HOTELS
★★★Delta Beausejour
750 Main St., Moncton, 506-854-4344, 800-268-1133; www.deltahotels.com

This stylish urban hotel is located in the heart of downtown Moncton, overlooking the Petitcodiac River. The spacious guest rooms feature contemporary décor. Guests can take advantage of bicycle rentals and walking maps available through the hotel. 310 rooms. Three restaurants, bar. Pets accepted, fee. Exercise room. Pool. $$

SPECIALITY LODGING
Avalon Terrace
739 Frampton Ln., Moncton, 506-854-6494, 888-833-7177; www.avalonterrace.com

4 rooms, all suites. Complimentary full breakfast. $

NEW BRUNSWICK

SAINT JOHN

The largest and oldest city in the province, this deep-sea port was founded by the United Empire Loyalists after the American Revolution. Saint John is a vibrant arts and entertainment community with pristine parks, steep, history-lined streets, and quality dining, shopping and festivals. The highest tides in the world rise here, where the mighty Saint John River reverses its flow at the powerful Reversing Falls—a natural wonder to watch, but even more so to ride in a specially-designed jet boat. Day adventures from the city base include bird watching, whale watching, canoeing or kayaking the amazing Bay of Fundy ecosystem. Take a walking tour of the oldest incorporated city in Canada, and shop at the historic Old City Market.

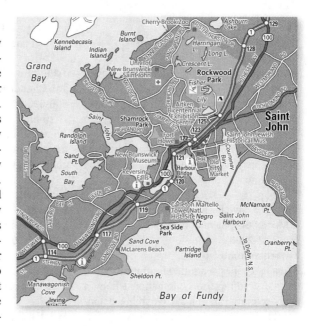

Information: www.tourismsaintjohn.com

WHAT TO SEE AND DO

Barbour's General Store
King and Water Sts., Saint John,
Market Slip area of downtown,
506-658-2855;
www.tourismsaintjohn.com

This restored general store reflects the period of 1840-1940; 2,000 artifacts and a wide selection of old-fashioned grocery items, china, yard goods, farm implements and cooking tools; re-created post office; barbershop with wicker barber's chair, collection of shaving mugs; pharmacy with approximately 300 samples of "cure-all or kill-alls," potbellied stove; staff outfitted in period costumes. Mid-June-mid-September: Daily.

Carlton Martello Tower National Historic Park
454 Whipple St., Saint John,
Hwy. 1, exit 107,
506-636-4011, 888-773-8888

These circular coastal forts were built for the War of 1812 and used in World War II as a fire command post for harbor defenses when a two-story superstructure was added. Restored 1840s powder magazine; barrack room (circa 1865). Panoramic view of the city, harbor and surrounding landscape. Guided tours of the tower (June-mid-October, daily).

Ferry Service to Digby, Nova Scotia
506-636-4048, 888-249-7245;
www.bayferries.com

Car and passenger ferry; 45 miles (72 kilometers). Reservations required.

Irving Nature Park
Sand Cove Rd. and Bleury St., Saint John,
506-653-7367;
www.ifdn.com/inp

Features winding coastal road and hiking trails. Harbor seals, porpoises and many species of migrating birds can be viewed offshore. Picnicking.

Loyalist House
120 Union St., Saint John,

★
★
★
★
★

506-652-3590;
www.saintjohn.nbcc.nb.ca/host/
loyalisthouse

Built by David Daniel Merritt, a United Empire Loyalist from New York. Six generations have lived in the house, a gracious Georgian mansion that remains much as it was when built with excellent craftsmanship in 1810-1817. July-August: daily; June and September: Monday-Friday; also by appointment.

New Brunswick Museum
1 Market Sq., Saint John,
506-643-2300;
www.nbm-mnb.ca

Canada's oldest continuous museum contains everything from international fine art and decorative art objects to exhibits detailing the human and natural history of New Brunswick. Exhibits include skeletons of a Right Whale, a mastodon and a geologic trail through time.

Old City Market
47 Charlotte St., Saint John,
506-658-2820;
www.tourismsaintjohn.com

This centralized market dating to 1876 sells fresh meats and vegetables as well as indigenous baskets and handicrafts.

Reversing Falls
Catherwood St., Saint John,
506-658-2937;
www.tourismsaintjohn.com/files/fuse.
cfm?section=10&screen=194

As the tides of the Bay of Fundy rise and fall, they cause the water of the St. John River to change the direction of its flow.

Rockwood Park
Off Mt. Pleasant Ave., Saint John,
506-658-2829;
www.new-brunswick.net/Saint_John/
rockwood/rockwood.html

Municipal park with 2,200 acres (890 hectares) of woodlands, lakes and recreational areas, including a golf course, aquatic driving range with floating golf balls collected by boat and campground.

Trinity Royal Heritage Preservation Area
115 Charlotte St., Saint John,
506-693-8558

A 20-block heritage area located in the city center; 19th-century residential and commercial architecture; handicrafts and specialty goods.

SPECIAL EVENTS
Festival by the Sea
Loyalist Plaza, 7 Market Sq., Saint John,
506-632-0086;
www.festivalbythesea.com

A 10-day performing arts festival featuring Canadian entertainers. Mid-August.

Loyalist Days' Heritage Celebration
109 Germain St., Saint John,
506-634-8123

Celebrates the arrival of the United Empire Loyalists in 1783 with a reenactment of the Loyalist landing; citizens in period costumes; parades, entertainment, sporting events. Five days in early July.

HOTELS
★★Delta Brunswick
39 King St., Saint John,
506-648-1981, 888-890-3222;
www.deltahotels.com

254 rooms Two restaurants, bar, children's activity center. Pets accepted, fee. Exercise room. Pool. $$

★★★Hilton Saint John
1 Market Sq., Saint John,
506-693-8484, 800-561-8282;
www.saint-john.hilton.com

Connected by an above ground, sheltered "pedway" to the Saint John Trade & Convention Center, Market Square shopping mall, New Brunswick Museum, and Canada Games Aquatic Centre, this hotel overlooking the Saint John Harbour and waterfront is centrally located. Guest rooms feature white duvet-covered beds, large-view windows, large work desks, and minibars.

197 rooms, Restaurant, bar. Exercise room. Pool. Busn. Center **$$**

ST. ANDREWS

Dramatic scenery frames this oceanside golf mecca, playground of the rich and famous through the years and long recognized as one of North America's premier destination towns. Much unchanged for over 100 years, St. Andrews is a town of character and charm, complemented by many historic sites, including the Algonquin Hotel, a War of 1812 Blockhouse, the Charlotte County Courthouse and an impressive collection of period homes. The old downtown commercial core is a shopper's paradise, especially renowned for handcrafts and woolen products. The Public Wharf at the center of town acts as the gateway to the abundant recreational water activities of Passamaquoddy Bay. The Fundy Isles dot the bay, the most famous of which is Campobello. Here, Franklin Delano Roosevelt spent his summers from 1905 to 1921 when he was stricken with infantile paralysis. Tours of Roosevelt's cottage in the International Park are available. Nearby, a ferry leaves for Grand Manan Island, a popular vacation destination with picturesque lighthouses and tiny fishing villages nestled in the barren seaside cliffs.
Information: www.townofstandrews.ca

WHAT TO SEE AND DO

Algonquin Golf Courses
464 Brandy Cove Rd., St. Andrews,
506-529-3062;
www.fairmontgolf.com/courses/index.
aspx?CourseID=105&I=0, 4, 13, 157, 158
Opened in 1894, this 18-hole championship course offers wooded glades and breathtaking shoreline views (fee). Executive 9-hole woodland course (fee). Late April-late October.

Blockhouse National Historic Site
Harriet St. and Joe's Point Rd.,
St. Andrews. Centennial Park,
506-529-4270;
www.pc.gc.ca/lhn-nhs/nb/standrews/
index_E.asp
Sole survivor of coastal defenses built during the War of 1812; restored in 1967. Mid-May-mid-October: daily.

Huntsman Marine Science Center Aquarium & Museum
1 Lower Campus, St. Andrews,
Brandy Cove Rd.,
506-529-1202;
www.huntsmanmarine.ca
Displays of coastal and marine environments with many fish and invertebrates found in waters of Passamaquoddy Region;

"Touch Tank" allows visitors to handle marine life found on local rocky beaches. Displays of live animals including local amphibians, reptiles and a family of harbor seals. Exhibits on local geology; seaweed collection. May-early October: daily.

Kingsbrae Garden
220 King St.,
St. Andrews,
506-529-3335, 866-566-8687;
www.kingsbraegarden.com
This garden contains 27 acres (11 hectares) of walking trails that pass more than 45,000 flowers, shrubs and other plants.

Ross Memorial Museum
188 Montague St.,
St. Andrews,
506-529-5124;
www.townsearch.com/rossmuseum
Private antique furniture and decorative art collection of the Rosses.

HOTELS

★★★★Kingsbrae Arms
219 King St., St. Andrews,
506-529-1897;
www.kingsbrae.com
This 1897 country house is intimate and elegant. It overlooks the breathtaking Pas-

79

NEW BRUNSWICK

samaquoddy Bay, a golf course, art galleries and the old town. Each suite has a gas fireplace, marble bathroom and a separate living room. Dining here is an event as the cuisine is based on the region's seasonal bounty. Dinner celebrates the seasonal delicacies and dishes are paired with selections from the award-winning cellar. There is no menu as everyone dines like they are a guest in someone's home.

14 rooms. Closed October-May. Complimentary full breakfast. Restaurant. Pet. Swim. Busn. Center. **$$$$**

★★★The Fairmont Algonquin
184 Adolphus St., St. Andrews,
506-529-8823, 800-441-1414;
www.fairmont.com
This seaside resort overlooks Passamaquoddy Bay, with an area of tidal changes that varies 28 feet between the high and low tides. Guest rooms are of period décor in the main historic building and a more contemporary style in the 1993 Prince of Wales wing. The fourth-floor rooms, originally the servants' quarters, offer the best views of the bay and surrounding countryside. Croquet, shuffleboard, and bocce ball are among the extensive activities offered.
234 rooms. Five restaurants, two bars, spa, beach. Exercise room. Pool. Golf. Tennis. **$$**

SPECIALITY LODGING
Pansy Patch
59 Carleton St., St. Andrews,
506-529-3834, 888-726-7972;
www.pansypatch.com
Built in 1911 and modeled after a French residence, this turreted cottage and its extensive gardens remain one of the most photographed homes in New Brunswick. The attached gallery showcases works of local artisans and rates for all rooms include afternoon tea.
9 rooms. Closed mid-October-April. Complimentary full breakfast. Restaurant. Exercise. Tennis. **$$$**

RESTAURANTS
★★The Library Lounge & Bistro
184 Adolphus St., St. Andrews by the Sea,
506-529-8823.
American menu. Reservations recommended. Outdoor seating. **$$**

★★Windsor House of St. Andrews
132 Water St., St. Andrews,
506-529-3330, 888-890-9463.
Seafood menu. Closed January-March. Reservations recommended. Outdoor seating. **$$**

★

★

★

★

★

NEWFOUNDLAND AND LABRADOR

NEWFOUNDLAND AND LABRADOR OFFER SO MANY ICONIC SOUNDS AND SCENES, IT'S ALMOST impossible to pick a representative few: thousand-year-old icebergs, multi-colored saltbox houses, fishing villages, fjords, lighthouses, whales, endless pubs and that Irish-origin lilt.

Wake up each day and walk outside, talk to the locals, tell them what mood you're in and see where it takes you. You might plan to tour the coastline by sea kayak one afternoon, but suddenly find yourself in a pub eating pan-fried cod and scrunchions. Or set out to tour a museum one morning and end up shopping along the oldest street in North America.

In Gros Morne National Park, exposed rock has been found that is 1.25 billion years old—as old as the planet itself. The mountains and fjords in this UNESCO World Heritage Site are 20 times older than the Rockies. Travel along some of the 10,500 miles (16,898 kilometers) of coastline to see 10,000-year-old icebergs drifting past, or humpback whales in their annual migration to the north. See the Northern Lights from Labrador more than 240 nights a year, where endless wilderness shelters wildlife such as moose, black bears and the largest caribou herd in the world.

Thirty-five million seabirds gather in this province every year. Human visitors hike, bike and kayak, fish for Atlantic salmon and brook trout, dogsled, snowmobile, ski, golf on more than 20 courses and visit archaeological and historic sites.

Provincial Capital: St. John's
Information: www.newfoundlandlabrador. com

 SPOTLIGHT

★ George Street, located in downtown St. John's, is closed to traffic twenty hours a day, and is widely understood to have the most pubs per square foot of any street in North America.

★ Newfoundland has its own time zone, which is half an hour later than Atlantic Time.

NEWFOUNDLAND AND LABRADOR

CORNER BROOK

Corner Brook is nestled among the folded and faulted Long Range Mountains, a continuation of the Appalachian Mountain belt. The landscape of the Corner Brook region is rugged and the scenery is spectacular. The surrounding coastline holds magnificent fjords, jagged headlands, thickly forested areas and many offshore islands. Wildlife, forest and water mingle with the city's borders on all sides and mountains fill the horizon in all directions.
Information: www.cornerbrook.com/tourism/tourmain.html

WHAT TO SEE AND DO
Marble Mountain
Rte. 1, Steady Brook,
709-637-7600, 888-462-7253;
www.skimarble.com
Some of the best skiing east of the Rockies, and certainly one of the top ski destinations of the Canadian east. 1,600-foot (488-meter) vertical drop. Downhill, cross-country and cat skiing. Lodging.

TNL (Theatre Newfoundland and Labrador)
709-639-7238;
www.theatrenewfoundland.com
Theatre Newfoundland and Labrador (TNL) is a not-for-profit organization dedicated to creating and producing professional theatre which reflects the lives and diversity of audiences on the province's west coast, extending to Labrador and across the island of Newfoundland. Through the Gros Morne Theatre Festival, youth theatre programming, main stage, courses in theater instruction, and touring productions to outport communities, TNL seeks to provide Newfoundlanders with thought-provoking and relevant entertainment, with an emphasis on regional and Canadian work.

SPECIAL EVENTS
Festival 500 Sharing the Voices
709-738-6013;
www.festival500.com
This international, biennial choral festival features choral groups from around the world and international guest performers. The festival occurs on several summer weekends in various places throughout the province. Mid-May-mid-July.

Corner Brook Winter Carnival
709-632-5343;
www.cornerbrookwintercarnival.ca
The Corner Brook Winter Carnival is an annual community festival dedicated to the celebration of winter, fostering of community spirit and pride. Enjoy an enlivening blend of sports, recreation, entertainment and culture within a 'snowfunland' theme. Mid-February.

GRAND FALLS-WINDSOR

With above average temperatures in the summer and beautiful, snow covered winters, this bustling town offers year-round vitality and entertainment. The Town's major event for the year is the Exploits Valley Salmon Festival, held each July and chosen as one the Top 100 Events by the American Bus Association.

WHAT TO SEE AND DO
Atlantic Salmon Interpretive Centre
On the banks of the Exploits River,
Grand Falls-Windsor,
709-489-7350;
www.asf.ca/interpretive.php
Located at Grand Falls Fishway. Exhibits on history, biology and habitat of the Atlantic Salmon. Underwater viewing windows and other live exhibits. Restaurant and gift shop.

Another Newfoundland Drama Company
Royal Canadian Legion (Branch 12),
Queen St., Grand Falls-Windsor,
1-877-822-7469; www.andco.nf.ca
This local theatre group entertains the town with their dinner theatre and lunch time show held at the Royal Canadian Legion.

NEWFOUNDLAND AND LABRADOR

Corduroy Brook Nature Trail

This nature trail offers serenity and an attractive setting suitable for all ages and abilities, and takes participants on a scenic journey along Corduroy Brook.

Exploits Valley Salmon Festival

Rte. 1, Grand Falls-Windsor,
709-489-0407;
www.salmonfestival.com

The annual Salmon Festival features an outdoor concert, stadium dances, a craft fair, salmon dinner and more. July.

ST. JOHN'S

For more than 500 years St. John's—the provincial capital and home of Canada's greatest number of per-capita pubs—has been visited by European explorers, adventurers, soldiers and pirates. First discovered in 1497 by John Cabot and later claimed as the first permanent settlement in North America for the British Empire by Sir Humphrey Gilbert, St. John's has a rich and colorful history. Cradled in a harbor carved from granite and surrounded by hills running down to the ocean, wander through quaint side streets of a thousand colors. This city is bursting with old world charm, unique architectural, historic and natural attractions and excellent facilities and services. And if that's not enough, a short drive brings visitors to spectacular coastlines, historic villages and a diverse selection of wildlife.

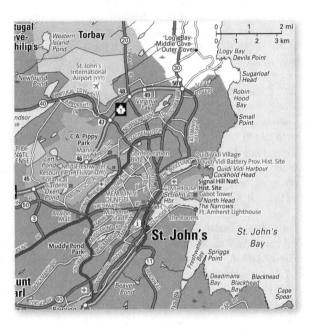

Information: www.stjohns.ca/visitors/index.jsp

WHAT TO SEE AND DO

Botanical Gardens

306 Mt. Scio Rd., St. John's,
709-737-8590;
www.mun.ca/botgarden

Memorial University's Botanical gardens cover 45 hectares of land close to the heart of St. John's. It is unusual in its dual purposes of botanical garden and natural reserve. The flower gardens include a rock garden, peat and woodland beds, cottage garden, perennial garden, rhododendrons and a display of Newfoundland heritage plants. Five nature trails meander through a 110-acre managed natural reserve.

Cape Spear National Historic Site

Rte. 11, Blackhead/Cape Spear,
709-772-5367;
www.pc.gc.ca/lhn-nhs/nl/spear/
index_e.asp

Just 11 kilometers from St. John's, Cape Spear National Historic Site is situated at the most eastern point in North America. Here, overlooking the North Atlantic, stands the oldest surviving lighthouse in Newfoundland, a World War II coastal defense battery and the place where the light of dawn is first seen in North America. Mid-May-mid-October.

83

NEWFOUNDLAND AND LABRADOR

The Fluvarium

Pippy Park, Nagle's Place (North Bank of Long Pond), St. John's,
709-754-3474;
www.fluvarium.ca

A unique facility on the shores of Long Pond in the heart of Pippy Park. A series of nine panoramic viewing windows gives visitors a chance to see the secret underwater life of a river. This is the only year-round public fluvarium in North America. Exhibits related to freshwater ecology. Guided tours year round.

Grand Concourse Walkways

709-737-1077;
www.grandconcourse.ca/noflash2004/
manual.htm

More than 74.5 miles (120 kilometers) of walkways connecting ponds, lakes and rivers in three municipalities make this one of the best walking networks in Canada.

Institute for Ocean Technology

Prince Philip Dr., St. John's,
709-772-4366;
iot-ito.nrc-cnrc.gc.ca

IOT is an innovative research facility for the ship technology and oil/gas industries. Learn how scale model ocean vessels are made and tested. See models of Hibernia and Terra Nova. View the ocean simulated indoors and the world's largest Ice Tank.

Johnson Geo Centre

175 Signal Hill Rd.,
709-737-7880, 866-868-7625;
www.geocentre.ca

The Johnson Geo Centre tells the story of "Our Earth and Our People" through the remarkable geology of Newfoundland and Labrador. The large, glass-encased entry is the only part of the building above ground. Most of the 33,600 square feet of floor space is underground.

Mile One Centre & St. John's Fog Devils

50 New Gower St.,
709-758-1111;
www.mileonecentre.com/main.asp

Mile One Centre is a first-class multi-purpose sports and entertainment facility located next to City Hall on New Gower Street in the heart of downtown St. John's. It is home to the Quebec Major Junior Hockey League (QMJHL), the St. John's Fog Devils and will host numerous entertainment events, including concerts by top artists from around the world, ice shows, family shows, conventions and local hockey events.

Newfoundland Science Centre

5 Beck's Cove, The Murray Premises,
709-754-0823;
www.nlsciencecentre.com

The Newfoundland Science Centre was created in 1993 to encourage interest and participation in science through informal education programs, interactive science displays and province-wide outreach programs. New exhibits arrive up to three times a year. The Centre also offers birthday parties, overnighters, science buskers, summer camps and more.

Ocean Science Centre of Memorial University

Marine Dr. (Rte. 30), Logy Bay,
709-737-3708;
www.mun.ca/osc/Home

The Ocean Sciences Centre is a cold ocean research facility operated in conjunction with Memorial University of Newfoundland. Located in Logy Bay, the Centre houses laboratories where research is conducted on the North Atlantic fishery, aquaculture, oceanography, ecology and physiology. Research is conducted on organisms ranging from bacteria to seals. In summer months, visitors experience an ocean life touch tank and Seal Facility.

The Rooms

9 Bonaventure Ave.,
St. John's (Fort Townsend),
709-757-8000;
www.therooms.ca

Visit the new home housing the combined collections of the Provincial Archives of Newfoundland and Labrador, the Provincial Museum of Newfoundland and Labra-

NEWFOUNDLAND AND LABRADOR

dor, and the Art Gallery of Newfoundland and Labrador. Sixteen galleries and exhibit halls, 180-seat multimedia theater and studio, restaurant, gift shop.

Signal Hill National Historic Site
Signal Hill Rd., St. John's,
709-772-5367;
www.pc.gc.ca/lhn-nhs/nl/signalhill
This site marks the spot where Marconi received the first transatlantic wireless signal in 1901. During the summer, watch cadets perform 19th-century British military drills.

St. John's Waterfront
Harbor Dr., St. John's
To get a real sense of St. John's, a walk along the waterfront is a must. The harbor, located in historic downtown, has provided shelter to explorers, merchants, soldiers, pirates and mariners of all kinds over the last 500 years. Historic buildings, coves, plaques and parks along the route help depict the history of St. John's.

NEWFOUNDLAND AND LABRADOR

NOVA SCOTIA

NATIONAL GEOGRAPHIC TRAVELER DESCRIBES NOVA SCOTIA AS A 'MUST SEE' DESTINATION, AND *Condé Nast Traveler* lauds Cape Breton as the world's most scenic island. All this is thanks to the surprising contradictions of this compact land: a slick and sophisticated urban scene populated with down-to-earth friendly folk; sumptuous accommodations with a rustic twist; and Zen-like oceanside relaxation alongside the kind of raucous parties and festivals epic to the most seasoned of sailors.

In Nova Scotia, a rich and diverse past is not just showcased at museums and heritage sites. It still lives and breathes in communities throughout the province—with ancient forts, cannons, saltbox houses and fishing villages standing unchanged. Cape Breton Island, in particular, offers a chance to truly explore this province's vivid Celtic culture and history. Here is where they say "Ciad mile failte," which means "a hundred thousand welcomes." Throughout each of Nova Scotia's scenic travelways, a cosmopolitan experience—from art galleries, live theatre, shopping, spas and major sports events—is presented against a setting of colorful history and rich tradition.

Historic waterfronts are home to great restaurants, live music and popular festivals that use the harbor as a backdrop, such as the International Buskers Festival, the Riverfront Music Jubilee and the Tall Ships Challenge. Spend the day shopping at a stylish boutique in Wolfville or Truro. Find the perfect souvenir to remember your trip with a stop at one of the many historic markets or quaint gift shops in the busy shopping districts in Yarmouth Sydney. or Spring Garden Road in Halifax, one of the country's oldest retail thoroughfares, is where you'll find the season's must-haves.

Visit the rugged Atlantic Coast and the rich Annapolis Valley which rolls down to the Bay of Fundy where the world's highest tides rise and fall. Follow the Northumberland Shore where you'll find the warmest waters north of Virginia and long, stretches of beach. Witness the Highlands of Cape Breton rising above the sea. And follow the south shore from Halifax, a chain of seaside villages peppered with hidden coves, beaches, antique stores, crafts and bistros, anchored by Lunenburg, home of the famed Bluenose schooner and UNESCO World Heritage Site. Two beautiful national parks (Kejimkujik National Park and National Historic Site of Canada and the Cape Breton Highlands National Park) and over a hundred provincial parks add to the bounty.

Provincial Capital: Halifax

Information: www.novascotia.com

 SPOTLIGHT

★ Marconi sent the first wireless (radio) message across the Atlantic Ocean, from Table Head, Cape Breton Island in 1902.

ANTIGONISH

This harbor town, the commercial and cultural home base for northeast Nova Scotia, was settled by Highland Scottish immigrants and American Revolutionary War soldiers and their families. As the Highland Heart of Nova Scotia, Antigonish is home to the oldest continuously run Highland Games in North America. Each year, the games bring together people from all over the world. Located just west of the Canso Causeway, the gateway to Cape Breton and its highlands, the town is surrounded by scenic rivers and hills.
Information: www.townofantigonish.ca/main.html

WHAT TO SEE AND DO

Sherbrooke Village
42 Main St., Antigonish, 40 miles/
64 kilometers S. via Hwy. 7, exit 32,
902-522-2400;
www.museum.gov.ns.ca/sv/index.php
Restored 1860s village reflects the area's former status as a prosperous river port. Historic buildings of that era are being restored and refurnished, including family homes, a general store, drugstore, courthouse, jail and post office; demonstrations of blacksmith forging, water-powered sawmill operation; horse-drawn wagon rides. Visitors can watch or try spinning, weaving and quilting. Restaurant. June-mid-October: daily.

St. Ninian's Cathedral
Antigonish,
902-863-2338;
www.antigonishdiocese.com/ninian1.htm
(1874) Built in Roman Basilica style of blue limestone and granite from local quarries. Interior decorated by Ozias LeDuc, Paris-trained Quebec artist. Gaelic words, Tigh Dhe (House of God), appear inside and out, representing the large Scottish population in the diocese who are served by the cathedral.

SPECIAL EVENT

Highland Games
Main St. and Columbus Field, Antigonish;
www.antigonishhighlandgames.com
This Scottish festival comprises the longest-running Highland Games in North America. Events include pipe band concerts, Highland dancing, traditional athletic events and a massed pipe band tattoo. Mid-July.

HOTEL

★★Best Western Claymore Inn
Church St., Antigonish,
902-863-1050; www.maritimeinns.com
75 rooms. Restaurant, bar. $

★★Maritime Inn
158 Main St., Antigonish,
902-863-4001, 877-768-3969;
www.maritimeinns.com
32 rooms. Restaurant, bar. Pets accepted, fee. $

RESTAURANT

★★Lobster Treat
241 Post Rd.,
Antigonish,
902-863-5465.
Seafood menu. Closed January-April. $$

NOVA SCOTIA

BADDECK

This tranquil, scenic village, situated midway between Canso Causeway and Sydney, is a good headquarters community for viewing the many sights on the Cabot Trail and around the Bras d'Or lakes. Fishing, hiking, swimming and picnicking are among favorite pastimes along the beautiful shoreline.
Information: www.baddeck.com

WHAT TO SEE AND DO

Alexander Graham Bell National Historic Park
559 Chebucto St., Baddeck,
902-295-2069;
capebretonisland.com/AGBell.html
Three exhibition halls dealing with Bell's numerous fields of experimentation. Includes displays on his work with the hearing impaired, telephones, medicine, marine engineering and aerodynamics.

Cape Breton's Celtic Music Interpretive Centre
Judique, 902-787-2708;
www.celticmusicsite.com
Learn about the heritage and tradition of local music through photos, vintage recordings, interviews with musicians, live performances and various exhibits. Guided tours. July-August, Monday-Friday; other times by appointment.

Cape Breton Centre for Craft & Design
322 Charlotte St., Sydney,
902-539-7491;
www.capebretoncraft.com/services/default.asp
Items of Scottish and Nova Scotian origins. Examples of handwoven blankets, ties, shopping bags, kilts, skirts.

Cape Breton Highlands National Park
16648 Cabot Trail, Cheticamp,
57 miles N. on Cabot Trail,
902-224-2306, 888-773-8888;
www.pc.gc.ca/pn-np/ns/cbreton/index_E.asp
The famous Cabot Trail, a modern 184-mile (294-kilometer) paved highway loop beginning at Baddeck, is among the most scenic drives in North America. It runs through this national park, offering visitors spectacular vistas, beaches and trails. The hiking trail system is large and diverse, providing access to the area's remote interior as well as allowing you to explore its rugged coastline. Beaches and campgrounds are plentiful and golf is also popular, with the Highlands Golf Links in Ingonish being one of the best 18-hole courses in Canada.

Fortress of Louisbourg National Historic Site
22 miles/35 kilometers S.
of Sydney via Hwy. 22;
www.fortress.uccb.ns.ca
This 11,860-acre (4,800-hectare) park includes the massive Fortress erected by the French between 1720 and 1745 to defend their possessions in the new world. It is the largest reconstructed 18th-century French fortified town in North America. Explore the governor's apartment, soldiers' barracks, the chapel, various guardhouses, the Dauphin Demi-Bastion, the King's storehouse, the engineer's house, the residence of the commissaire-ordonnateur, several private dwellings and storehouses and the royal bakery. Sample 18th-century food amongst costumed guides who interpret the town as it was in 1744. June-September, daily; May and October, limited tours.

Gaelic College
51779 Cabot Trail, St. Ann's,
13 miles/22 kilometers E. of Baddeck at exit 11 off Trans-Canada
Hwy. 105 in St. Ann's,
902-295-3411;
www.gaeliccollege.edu
The only institution of its kind in North America dedicated to preservation of Gaelic traditions; special summer and winter programs.

Glenora Distillery
Rte. 19, Glenville,
902-258-2662, 800-839-0491;
www.glenoradistillery.com
The only distillery in North America to produce single malt whisky. Museum, pub, restaurant, inn, gift shop. Distillery tours (May-October).

Great Hall of the Clans
51779 Cabot Trail, St. Ann's,
902-295-3411;
www.gaeliccollege.edu
Colorful historic display of Scot-origin clans, tartans and migrations. Genealogical and audiovisual section; life and times

of Highland pioneers, relics of Cape Breton giant Angus MacAskill.

HOTELS
★★★Keltic Lodge Resort and Spa
Middle Head Peninsula, Ingonish Beach,
902-285-2880, 800-565-0444;
www.signatureresorts.com
Perched high on a cliff overlooking the Atlantic Ocean, this resort provides a choice of accommodations in the main lodge, inn, or cottages. One of the top-rated golf courses in the world sits next door, and guests can also enjoy kayaking, hiking, whale-watching, beaches and complimentary bicycles. The Aveda concept spa is the perfect place to relax and rejuvenate. The views from this property are breathtaking, making this a special destination resort.
104 rooms, 3 story. Closed late October-mid-May. Two restaurants, bar, beach. Exercise room.Pool. $$$

★★Inverary Resort
Hwy. 205, Baddeck,
902-295-3500, 800-565-5660;
124 rooms. Restaurant, beach. Exercise room.Pool. Tennis. $$

★★★Auberge Gisele's Inn
387 Shore Rd., Baddeck,
902-295-2849, 800-304-0466;
www.giseles.com
Overlooking the Bras d'Or Lakes, the inn is close to the Bell Bay Golf Course, Highland Links and Usige Ban Falls Park. They offer bike rentals and picnic lunches as well sailing tours of the lake. Enjoy international cuisine at the award winning restaurant or a cocktail in the Lounge.
75 rooms. Closed mid-October-mid-May. Restaurant, bar. $

★★Silver Dart Lodge
Shore Rd., Baddeck,
902-295-2340, 888-662-7484;
www.silverdart.com
88 rooms. Closed mid-October-April. Restaurant, bar. Pool. Tennis. $

RESTAURANT
★★Grubstake
7499 Main St., Louisbourg,
902-733-2308
Steak menu. Closed October-mid-June. Early 1800s building. $$$

★
★
★
★
☆

DIGBY
Best known for its delicious scallops and harbor sights, this summer resort has many historic landmarks that date back to its founding in 1783 by Sir Robert Digby and 1,500 Loyalists from New England and New York. This Annapolis Basin town is the ideal headquarters for adventures down the Digby Neck peninsula, whose Bay of Fundy shores measure the highest tides in the world. Off Digby Neck are Long Island and Brier Island, reachable by ferry—both are popular sites for rock-hounding, whale-watching and bird-watching. Swim along sandy beaches and hike shoreline trails past dashing spray, lighthouses and wildflower-filled forests. A 35-mile (11-kilometer) drive to the northeast leads to Annapolis Royal and Port Royal, the first permanent European settlements in North America. Marking this is the restored fur trading fort, the Habitation of Port Royal, built by Samuel de Champlain. With high, imposing cliffs, gently rolling farmland and quiet woodland settings, this seacoast drive creates a study in contrasts.
Information: www.townofdigby.ns.ca

WHAT TO SEE AND DO
Fishermen's Wharf
Water St., Digby,
888-463-4429
View one of the largest scallop fleets in the world.

Fort Anne National Historic Site
St. George and Prince Albert Sts.,
902-532-2397;
www.pc.gc.ca/lhn-nhs/ns/fortanne/index_e.asp

Built between 1702 and 1708 in one of the central areas of conflict between the English and French for control of North America. Of the original site, only the 18th-century earthworks and a gunpowder magazine (1708) remain. Museum in restored officers' quarters. On the grounds is Canada's oldest English graveyard, dating from 1720.

Pines Golf Course
103 Shore Rd., Digby,
902-245-2511, 800-667-4637;
www.digbypines.ca
An 18-hole championship golf course on a provincially-owned and -operated resort.

Point Prim Lighthouse
Lighthouse and Bayview rds., Digby,
888-463-4429
Rocky promontory with a view of the Bay of Fundy.

Port Royal National Historic Site
53 Historic Ln., Annapolis Royal,
902-532-2898;
www.pc.gc.ca/lhn-nhs/ns/portroyal/index_e.asp
Reconstructed 17th-century fur trading post built by Sieur de Mons. Mid-May-mid-October: daily.

Trinity Church
109 Queen St., Digby,
902-245-6744;
www.unityserve.org/trinity
The only church in Canada built by shipwrights; the church cemetery is famous for inscriptions of pioneer settlers. Monday-Friday.

SPECIAL EVENT
Scallop Days
Water St., Digby,
902-245-4531;
www.digbyscallopdays.com
Scallop-shucking contests; grand parade, pet show, entertainment; sporting, fishing, water events. Second week in August.

HOTELS
★★Admiral Digby Inn
441 Shore Rd., Digby,
902-245-2531, 800-465-6262;
www.digbyns.com
46 rooms. Closed mid-October-mid-May. Complimentary continental breakfast. Restaurant, bar. Pets accepted, fee. Pool. $

★★Coastal Inn Kingfisher
111 Warwick Street, Digby, ,
902-245-4747
36 rooms. Restaurant. Business Center. $

★★★Digby Pines Golf Resort & Spa
103 Shore Rd., Digby,
902-245-2511, 800-667-4637;
www.signatureresorts.com
Built in 1929, the Digby Pines Golf Resort & Spa still holds true to its roots. With a magnificent setting on a terraced hillside, it overlooks the Annapolis Basin. The public rooms are large and gracious, with many of the original furnishings still in use in the "grande salon." Guest rooms reflect the period as well. The property is located approximately 1 mile from the Saint John's ferry terminal.
147 rooms. Closed mid-October-mid-May. Complimentary full breakfast. Four restaurants, two bars. Pool. Golf. Tennis. $$

RESTAURANT
★★Fundy Restaurant
34 Water St., Digby,
902-245-4950;
www.fundyrestaurant.com
Seafood menu. Outdoor seating. View of Annapolis basin. $$

90

NOVA SCOTIA

★
★
★
★
★

GRAND PRÉ

Grand-Pré is a heartland of Acadian culture in Canada—a rich tapestry of history in a pastoral setting of rolling hills, charming villages and vineyards. Founded by Acadian settlers who remained there until the expulsion that began in 1755 (immortalized by Henry Wadsworth Longfellow with his epic poem, "Evangeline"), the village of Grand Pré has provided a home for immigrant farmers and artisans for over 300 years. Today, the Grand-Pré National Historic Site commemorates the Acadian people. One of Nova Scotia's best known wineries, Domaine de Grand Pré, is an evocative culinary destination. Grand-Pré is also Canada's first designated Historic Rural District.
Information: www.valleyweb.com/grandpre

WHAT TO SEE AND DO

Acadian Memorial Church
1 Annapolis Valley RR, Grand Pré,
902-490-5946;
www.acadian-home.org/
grand-pre-church.html
Display commemorating Acadian settlement and expulsion. Old Acadian Forge; bust of Longfellow Evangeline statue; formal landscaped gardens with original French willows. Guides available.

Grand Pré National Historic Site
Grand Pré,
902-542-3631;
www.pc.gc.ca/lhn-nhs/ns/grandpre/index_
e.asp
Grand Pre commemorates the Acadian settlement from 1682 to 1755 and the Deportation of the Acadians, which began in 1755 and continued until 1762. Interpretive presentations and multimedia exhibits, Mid-May-mid-October. Grounds and gardens, all year.

HOTELS

★★Old Orchard Inn
Hwy. 101, exit 11, Wolfville,
902-542-5751, 800-561-8090;
www.oldorchardinn.com
105 rooms. Restaurant, bar, children's activity center. Pets accepted, fee. Pool. Tennis. $$

★★★Blomidon Inn
195 Main St., Wolfville,
902-542-2291, 800-565-2291;
www.blomidon.ns.ca
This inn, overlooking the Bay of Fundy, was built as a sea captain's mansion. With 4 acres (1.6 hectares) of Victorian gardens, it is a great place to relax.
28 rooms. Closed 10 days in December. Complimentary continental breakfast. Restaurant. Tennis. $$

★★★Tattingstone Inn
620 Main St., Wolfville,
902-542-7696, 800-565-7696;
www.tattingstone.ns.ca
This inn is located in the center of Wolfville. Victorian and Georgian period antiques fill the comfortable and inviting rooms. Meals incorporate the locally grown produce.
10 rooms. Complimentary full breakfast. Restaurant. Pool. Tennis. $

SPECIALITY LODGING

Victoria's Historic Inn
600 Main St., Wolfville,
902-542-5744, 800-556-5744;
www.victoriahistoricinn.com
15 rooms. Complimentary full breakfast. $

HALIFAX-DARTMOUTH

The capital of Nova Scotia, and the largest city in the Atlantic provinces offers a delightful combination of old and new. Founded in 1749 as England's stronghold in the North Atlantic, it is a bustling commercial, scientific and educational center. Centrally situated in the province, it is perfectly suited as the starting point for the Evangeline and Glooscap Trails, the Lighthouse Route and the Marine Drive with their scenic and historic sights. With the world's second-largest natural harbor and an array of histori-

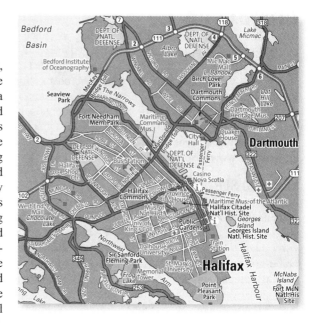

cal sites, fishing villages, beaches and pubs within its municipal borders, this city promises some of the most diverse explorations of any urban center in Canada.
Information: www.halifaxinfo.com

WHAT TO SEE AND DO

Art Gallery of Nova Scotia
1723 Hollis St., Halifax,
902-424-7542;
www.agns.gov.ns.ca
More than 2,000 works on permanent display, including folk art; changing exhibits.

Black Cultural Centre
1149 Main St., Dartmouth,
Rte. 7 at Cherrybrook Rd.,
902-434-6223, 800-465-0767;
www.bccns.com
History and culture of African Americans in Nova Scotia, which was the destination for many on the 'Underground Railroad' that led escaped slaves from American plantations—and not coincidentally, was also home to the first free black community in North America. Library, exhibit rooms, auditorium.

Chapel of Our Lady of Sorrows
Holly Cross Cemetery South and S.
Park Sts., Halifax;
www.mikecampbell.net/chapelofourlady.
htm

Built in one day by 2,000 men; altar carvings date from 1750.

Double Decker Bus Tours
Duke St. at Lower Water St., Halifax,
902-420-1155;
www.doubledeckertours.com
City tours on a double-decker, English-style bus. Tours last approximately 90 minutes and depart from multiple points. June-October: daily.

Halifax Citadel National Historic Park
5425 Sackville and Brunswick Sts., Halifax,
902-426-5080;
www.pc.gc.ca/voyage-travel/pv-vp/
itm2-/page3_e.asp
The most visited historic site in Canada. Star-shaped hilltop fort built 1828-1856. Excellent view of city and harbor. Audiovisual presentation "Tides of History" (50 minutes). Restored signal masts, library, barrack rooms, powder magazine, expense magazine, defense casement and garrison cell. Exhibits on communications, the four Citadels and engineering and construction.

Army Museum; orientation center. Coffee bar serving typical 19th-century soldiers' food; sales outlet; guided tours, military displays by uniformed students, bagpipe music, changing of the guard.

Harbour Hopper Tours

1751 Lower Water St., Halifax,
902-490-8687;
www.harbourhopper.com
Narrated tours in amphibious vehicles styled after World War II landing craft. May-late October: daily

Historic Properties (Privateers Wharf)

1869-1870 Upper Water St., Halifax,
902-422-3077;
www.historicproperties.ca/merch.htm
Variety of clothing, specialty shops, restaurants and pubs housed in several restored 18th-century buildings along the waterfront.

Maritime Museum of the Atlantic

1675 Lower Water St., Halifax,
902-424-7490;
www.museum.gov.ns.ca/mma
The museum contains 1,675 exhibits showcasing more than 24,000 artifacts that tell the nautical history of Nova Scotia, including **Titanic: The Unsinkable Ship.**

Murphy's on the Water

1751 Lower Water St., Halifax, Murphy's Pier next to Historic Properties,
902-420-1015;
www.murphysonthewater.com
Three harbor tour boats. Live narration and historical commentary; two-hour tour. May-mid-October: daily.

Neptune Theatre

1593 Argyle St., Halifax,
902-429-7070;
www.neptunetheatre.com
Home of the internationally recognized theater company; presents five main stage plays per season. Small, intimate theater with excellent acoustics. Reservations advised.

Nova Scotia Museum of Natural History

1747 Summer St., Halifax,
902-424-7353;
www.museum.gov.ns.ca/mnh
Permanent exhibits on man and his environment in Nova Scotia; changing exhibits.

Pier 21

1055 Marginal Rd., Halifax,
902-425-7770; www.pier21.ns.ca
Pier 21 is Canada's "Ellis Island." Between 1928 and 1971, more than 1 million immigrants and wartime evacuees took their first steps on Canadian soil here. Now a National Historic Site, the pier features traveling exhibits, live performances, the Wall of Ships, Immigrant Testimonial Stations and the Wall of Honor.

Point Pleasant Park

5718 Point Pleasant Dr., Halifax,
902-421-6519;
www.pointpleasantpark.ca
Perfect for scrambling and imaginary adventure, visit ruins of several historic forts in the heart of the city. Nature trail, monuments, public beach, picnic areas; cross-country skiing.

Prince of Wales Tower National Historic Park

S. Tower Rd., Point Pleasant Park,
Halifax, 902-426-5080;
www.pc.gc.ca/lhn-nhs/ns/prince/natcul/index_e.asp
Known locally as Martello Tower, this fort was built in the late 1790s to protect British batteries and is said to be first tower of its type in North America. Exhibits portray tower's history, architectural features and significance as a defensive structure. July-early September.

Province House

1726 Hollis St., Halifax,
902-424-4661; www.gov.ns.ca/legislature
Oldest provincial Parliament building in Canada; office of Premier; legislative library. Guided tours.

93

NOVA SCOTIA

★
★
★
★
☆

Public Archives of Nova Scotia
6016 University Ave., Halifax,
902-424-6060;
www.gov.ns.ca/nsarm
Provincial government records, private manuscripts, maps, photos, genealogies, film and sound archives; library.

Public Gardens
Spring Garden Rd. and South Park St., Halifax, 902-421-6550;
www.halifaxpublicgardens.ca
A 16 3/4-acre (7-hectare) formal Victorian garden begun by the Nova Scotia Horticultural Society in 1836, with trees, flower beds, fountains; bandstand; duck ponds; concession. The gardens were designated a National Historic Site in 1984. April-November.

Quaker Whaler's House
59 Ochterloney St., Dartmouth,
902-464-2253;
www.dartmouthheritagemuseum.ns.ca/quaker.html
Originally the home of William Ray, the house is considered one of the oldest domestic structures in the metro area. William Ray was a cooper (barrel maker) who came to Dartmouth as part of a community of Quakers who established a whale fishing industry of Dartmouth. Quaker House is restored and furnished to reflect its era of 1785. Guides provide tours. Herb garden backyard open to visitors. Pioneer Days Dress Up Trunk available to younger visitors July-August: daily.

Shearwater Aviation Museum
13 Bonaventure Ave., Dartmouth, Shearwater Airport,
902-460-1083;
www.shearwateraviationmuseum.ns.ca
Extensive collection of aircraft and exhibits on the history of Canadian Maritime Military Aviation. Art gallery; photo collection.

St. George's Round Church
2222 Brunswick St., Halifax,
902-423-1059;

www.roundchurch.ca
(1801) Anglican; Byzantine-style church built at the direction of Edward, Duke of Kent, father of Queen Victoria. Nearby is St. Patrick's Roman Catholic Church, a Victorian Gothic building still largely untouched by change. On Barrington Street is St. Paul's Church (1750), the first church in Halifax and oldest Protestant church in Canada. "Explosion window" on Argyle St. side; during a 1917 explosion that destroyed a large portion of the city, the third window of the upper gallery shattered, leaving the silhouette of a human head. Tours June-September: daily.

York Redoubt National Historic Site
Purcell's Cove Rd., Halifax,
6 miles/9.7 kilometers S.W. of Halifax,
902-426-5080;
www.pc.gc.ca/lhn-nhs/ns/york/index_e.asp
(1793) A 200-year-old fortification on a high bluff overlooking the harbor entrance. Features muzzle-loading guns, photo display, picnic facilities, information service. Grounds (daily). Mid-June-Labour Day: daily.

SPECIAL EVENTS
Atlantic Jazz Festival
Spring Garden Rd. and Queen, Halifax,
902-492-2225;
www.jazzeast.com
JazzEast's mandate runs from the promotion and presentation of soft-seat concerts and bar gigs to planning educational workshops (such as the renowned Creative Music Workshop). It features amateur musicians, established local artists and the local "jazz aristocracy," and also attracts world-famous performers from all over to a city which doesn't always find itself naturally on the maps of touring artists. July.

Dartmouth Natal Day
Lake Banook, Dartmouth,
902-490-6773; www.natalday.org
Parade, sports events, rowing and paddling regattas, entertainment, fireworks. First Monday in August.

Halifax Highland Games & Scottish Festival

Wanderer's Grounds base of Citadel Hill
Sackville St. and Bell Rd., Halifax,
902-469-2023;
www.halifaxhighlandgames.com

The Games are the centerpiece of five days celebrating Scottish culture, including competitions in piping, drumming, pipe bands and heavyweight events. Theme concessions, food vendors and beer tent with Celtic music on site. July.

International Buskerfest

Halifax, 902-429-3910; www.buskers.ca

Street performers from all over the world come to Halifax for this 10-day event along the waterfront, put on by the Atlantic Busker Festival Society. August.

Multicultural Festival

Alderney Landing, Alderney Dr. and
Ochterloney St., Dartmouth,
902-423-6534, 800-565-0000;
www.multifest.ca

The festival is an opportunity to celebrate Nova Scotia's diversity through performances, workshops, food vendors and visual displays. The three-day event takes place on the Dartmouth waterfront. Mid-June.

Nova Scotia International Air Show

Shearwater Airport Hines Rd. and
Pleasant St. (Hwy. 322), Shearwater,
902-465-2725;
www.nsairshow.ca

One of the premier air spectaculars in North America. September.

Nova Scotia International Tattoo

Halifax Metro Centre, 1800 Argyle St.,
Halifax, 902-451-1221;
www.nstattoo.ca

The world's largest indoor variety show, with more than 2,000 Canadian and international performers. The 10-day event features military bands, pipes and drums, choirs, gymnasts, dancers and military displays and competitions. Late June-early July.

HOTELS

★★★The Lord Nelson Hotel & Suites

1515 S. Park St., Halifax,
902-423-6331, 800-565-2020;
www.lordnelsonhotel.com

Conveniently located at the corner of Spring Garden Road and South Park Street in downtown Halifax, the Lord Nelson is across the street from the Halifax Public Gardens (Victorian-style), a block south of Citadel Hill and close to Dalhousie University.
260 rooms. Restaurant, bar. Pets accepted, fee. $$$

★★Blue Nose Inn & Suites

636 Bedford Highway, Halifax,
902.443.3171;
www.bluenoseinnandsuites.com/
51 rooms. Restaurant. $

★★Cambridge Suites Hotel

1583 Brunswick St., Halifax,
902-420-0555, 800-565-1263;
www.cambridgesuiteshotel.com
200 rooms, all suites. Complimentary continental breakfast. Restaurant, bar $$

★★★Delta Barrington

1875 Barrington St., Halifax,
902-429-7410, 888-890-3222;
www.deltahotels.com

Connected by the "Downtown Link"—an enclosed, above ground pedestrian walkway—to two shopping centers, this downtown hotel is also a block from the waterfront. Comfortable guest rooms feature Nova Scotia country pine furniture and pillow-top mattresses. An enclosed central courtyard provides a view of greenery to inner rooms and corridors.
200 rooms. Restaurant, bar. Pets accepted, fee. Exercise room.Pool. $$

★★★Delta Halifax

1990 Barrington St., Halifax,
902-425-6700, 888-890-3222;
www.deltahotels.com

Located in the heart of downtown, it is adjacent to the Scotia Square Shopping Centre and connected to the "pedway." The lobby

★
★
★
★
★

and ground floor public spaces reflect an elegance of days gone by. Guest rooms are comfortable and inviting with thoughtful amenities. Bathrooms provide a nice selection on Judith Jacobs items.
296 rooms. Restaurant, bar. Pets accepted, fee. Exercise room.Pool. Busn. Center. **$$**

★★★Halifax Marriott Harborfront
1919 Upper Water St., Halifax,
902-421-1700;
www.marriott.com
This hotel is the home of the only Halifax casino and is located right downtown. 352 rooms. Two restaurants, bar. Pets accepted, fee. Exercise room.Pool. Busn. Center. **$$**

★★Holiday Inn Select Halifax Centre
1980 Robie St., Halifax,
902-423-1161, 888-810-7288;
www.holiday-inn.com
232 rooms. Restaurant, bar. Pets accepted, fee. Pool. Busn. Center. **$$**

★★Holiday Inn Halifax-Harborview
101 Wyse Rd., Dartmouth,
902-463-1100, 888-434-0440;
www.holiday-inn.com/harbourviewns
196 rooms. Restaurant, bar. Pets accepted, fee. Pool. **$$**

★★Inn on the Lake
3009 Lake Thomas Dr., Waverley,
902-861-3480, 800-463-6465;
www.innonthelake.com
40 rooms. Restaurant, bar. Pool. Tennis. **$$**

★★★Oak Island Resort and Spa
51 Vaughan Rd., Western Shore,
902-627-2600, 800-565-5075;
www.oakislandinn.com
This oceanfront resort approximately one hour's drive from Halifax overlooks Mahone Bay and its many islands, including the famous Oak Island, rumored to be the hiding place of Captain Kidd's buried treasure.
120 rooms. Restaurant, bar. Pets accepted, fee. Pool. Tennis. Busn. Center. **$$**

★★Park Place Hotel & Conference Center Ramada Plaza
240 Brownlow Ave., Dartmouth,
902-468-8888, 800-561-3733;
www.ramadans.com
178 rooms, 5 story. Restaurant, bar. Pets accepted, fee. Pool. Busn. Center. **$$**

★★★Prince George Hotel
1725 Market St., Halifax,
902-425-6066, 800-565-1567;
www.princegeorgehotel.com
This downtown hotel is a favorite for business and leisure travelers alike. Guest rooms have mahogany furnishings and deftly accommodate the needs of business travelers. A covered walkway connects the hotel to the World Trade & Convention Centre, the Halifax Metro Centre, and the Halifax Casino.
203 rooms. Two restaurants, bar. Pets accepted, fee. Pool. Busn. Center. **$$**

★★★The Westin Nova Scotian
1181 Hollis St., Halifax,
902-421-1000, 888-679-3784;
www.westin.ns.ca
This historic brick hotel, originally built as a Canadian National Railway hotel, is located just above the Halifax Harbor Waterfront. A wide range of guest facilities are offered for both business and leisure travelers, including an Aveda concept spa, a lighted waterfront tennis court and conference and banquet facilities. The lobby is richly traditional in design and furnishings, and guest rooms are well stocked with amenities.
297 rooms. Restaurant, bar, children's activity center. Pool. Busn. Center. **$$**

★★★Citadel Halifax Hotel
1960 Brunswick St., Halifax,
902-422-1391, 800-565-7162;
www.citadelhalifax.com
Built in 1963, this comfortable property is nicely located for both business and leisure travelers. It is adjacent to the Citadel Hill National Historic Site and close to the World Trade and Convention Centre. This large, full-service urban hotel offers bud-

get-friendly rates and a good downtown location.

264 rooms. Restaurant, bar. Pets accepted, fee. Exercise room.Pool. Busn. Center. **$**

SPECIALITY LODGINGS

Dauphinee Inn
167 Shore Club Rd., Hubbards,
902-857-1790, 800-567-1790;
www.dauphineeinn.com
Approximately 40 minutes' drive from Halifax along the famed South Shore area. 6 rooms. Closed November-April. Complimentary continental breakfast. Restaurant. **$**

Waverley Inn
1266 Barrington St., Halifax,
902-423-9346, 800-565-9346;
www.waverleyinn.com
34 rooms, 3 story. Complimentary continental breakfast. Historic inn (1876); antiques. Near Halifax Harbor. **$**

RESTAURANTS
★Alfredo, Weinstein and Ho
1739 Grafton St., Halifax,
902-421-1977.
International menu. **$$**

★The Queen of Cups
44 Ochterloney Dr., Dartmouth,
902-463-1983;
www.queenofcups.ca
Light lunch/teahouse, reservations recommended, historic building, outdoor seating. **$$**

★★Rocco's
300 Prince Albert Rd., Dartmouth,
902-461-0211;
www.roccosrestaurant.ca
Italian menu. **$$**

★★★Salty's on the Waterfront
1869 Upper Water St., Halifax,
902-423-6818;www.saltys.ca
A blue-and-white-striped awning welcomes you to this casual seafood restaurant at the end of the Privateers, a 19th-century wharf, overlooking the Halifax Harbor in the Historic Properties area of downtown. American menu. Outdoor seating. **$$$**

★★Sou'Wester
178 Peggy's Cove Rd.,
Peggy's Cove,
902-823-2561;
www.peggys-cove.com
Seafood menu. On the oceanfront, approximately one hour drive from Halifax. **$$**

97

NOVA SCOTIA

TOWN OF LUNENBURG

Lunenburg, a UNESCO World Heritage Site founded in 1753 by German, Swiss and Montbeliardian Protestants under British patronage, is a mecca of architectural delights and rich marine history. Many of the homes and buildings date back to the mid-1700s, and are restored as such. Lunenburg is also the home of Canada's only tall ship, the Bluenose II, a replica of the legendary racing champion on the Canadian 10-cent piece. In 1992, the Government of Canada designated "Old Town" Lunenburg as a National Historic District. In 1995, the World Heritage Committee, under the auspices of UNESCO, recognized Lunenburg's cultural and natural heritage by adding it to their World Heritage List. Despite all this recognition, the town offers up a working, authentic heritage as opposed to a canned tourist experience—and some of the best fishcakes and sauerkraut in the country.
Information: www.town.lunenburg.ns.ca

WHAT TO SEE & DO

Bluenose II
Lunenburg waterfront,
800-565-0000;
www.bluenose2.ns.ca
Bluenose Preservation Trust. An exact replica of the famed racing schooner depicted on the Canadian dime; public cruises tour Nova Scotia's waters.

Fisheries Museum of the Atlantic
68 Bluenose Ave.,
Lunenburg (on the waterfront),
902-634-4794;
www.museum.gov.ns.ca/fma
Learn about offshore and inshore fisheries through exhibits, films and artifacts. Boat shop, model schooner. May-October: daily 9:30 a.m.-5:30 p.m.; off-season: Monday-Friday 8:30 a.m.-4:30 p.m.

SPECIALITY LODGINGS

1775 Solomon House B&B
69 Townsend St., Lunenburg,
902-634-3477;
www.bbcanada.com/5511.html
3 rooms. Inquire before bringing children. Full breakfast. $$

Boscawen Inn
150 Cumberland St., Lunenburg,
902-634-3325, 800-354-5009;
www.boscawen.ca
33 rooms. Full breakfast. $$

Kaulbach House
75 Pelham St., Lunenburg,
902-634-8818, 800-568-8818;
www.kaulbachhouse.com
3 rooms. Inquire before bringing children. Full breakfast. $$

Lunenburg Arms Hotel
94 Pelham St., Lunenburg,
902-640-4040, 800-679-4950;
www.lunenburgarms.com
26 rooms. Restaurant, bar. Spa. $$

RESTAURANTS

The Old Fish Factory
68 Bluenose Dr., Lunenburg,
902-634-3333, 800-533-9336;
www.oldfishfactory.com
Seafood. $$

The Grand Banker Seafood Bar & Grill
82 Montague St., Lunenburg,
902-634-3300;
www.grandbanker.com
Seafood. $$

Magnolia's Grill
128 Montague St., Lunenburg,
902-634-3287
Local favorite, home-style cuisine. Seafood. Closed through winter. $

The Knot Pub
4 Dufferin St., Lunenburg,
902-634-3334
Pub food in cosy atmosphere. Seafood. $

NOVA SCOTIA

TRURO

Truro, once known as the "Hub of Nova Scotia" for its location at the junction between the Canadian National Railway (running between Halifax and Montreal) and the Cape Breton and Central Nova Scotia Railway (running between Truro and Sydney), is one of those towns that's on the way to everywhere—or at least a stopping point from Halifax to everywhere. But Truro has a unique appeal of its own, with a charming heritage main street and a surprising number of attractions and dining establishments for a small town. When the town lost many trees after an outbreak of Dutch Elm Disease, folk here made a wonderfully imaginative effort and created unique wooden sculptures created from the stumps of lost trees throughout the downtown core.
Information: www.town.truro.ns.ca/main.htm

WHAT TO SEE AND DO

Acres of the Golden Pheasant
275 Greenfield, Truro,
902-893-2734
Contains over 50 species of birds, including pheasants, peacocks, parakeets, finches and doves.

Colchester Historical Society Museum
29 Young St., Truro,
902-895-6284;
www.genealogynet.com/colchester
Exhibits depict human and natural history of the county; changing exhibits. Archives, genealogy library.

Little White Schoolhouse Museum
On the campus of Nova Scotia Community College, 20 Arthur St., Truro,
902-895-5170;
www.lwsm.ednet.ns.ca
One-room schoolhouse built in 1871, furnished with desks, artifacts and textbooks from 1867-1952. June-August: daily; rest of year: by appointment.

Tidal Bore
Hwy. 102 and Tidal Bore Rd., Truro,
Viewing area on Tidal Bore Rd., just off Hwy. 102, exit 14,
902-426-5494
A wave of water rushes backward up the Salmon River before high tide. Bores range in height from a ripple to several feet. A timetable can be obtained from the Chamber of Commerce or by phoning "Dial-a-Tide."

Victoria Park
Brunswick St. and Park Rd., Truro,
902-893-6078;
www.town.truro.ns.ca
A 1,000-acre protected forest which contains hiking trails, an outdoor pool, a playground, tennis courts, picnic grounds and a baseball field, as well as Lepper Brook, which has two waterfalls that may be enjoyed from several walking trails.

SPECIAL EVENT

International Tulip Festival
577 Prince St., Truro,
902-895-9258;
www.nstulips.com
Over 250,000 tulips planted in flower gardens throughout the city. Picnics, art displays, entertainment. Late May.

HOTELS

★★Best Western Glengarry
150 Willow St., Truro,
902-893-4311, 800-567-4276;
www.bestwestern.com
90 rooms. Restaurant, bar. Pool. $

★Willow Bend Motel
277 Willow St., Truro,
902-895-5325, 800-594-5569;
www.willowbendmotel.com
27 rooms. Complimentary continental breakfast. Pool. $

NOVA SCOTIA

YARMOUTH

This historic seaport is the largest town southwest of Halifax and the gateway to Nova Scotia from New England. During the days of sail in the 1800s, this was one of the major shipbuilding and ship owning ports in the world. There is much evidence of this 'Golden Age of Sail' to be found in the architecture of many of its fine old homes as well as ship paintings and artifacts exhibited in museums. Travel north on the Evangeline Trail, which passes through French Acadian settlements, fishing centers and rich orchards and farmlands. South, follow the Lighthouse Route, which parallels the Atlantic coastline and passes near many picturesque lighthouses, beaches and fishing ports.
Information: www.aboutyarmouth.com

WHAT TO SEE AND DO

The CAT
58 Water St., Yarmouth
902-742-6800; www.catferry.com
Advance reservations required. Passenger and car ferry service to Bar Harbor, Maine. June-October.

Cape Forchu Lighthouse
Cape Forchu Island, 7 miles/11 kilometers S.W. of Yarmouth, linked by causeway to the mainland,
800-565-0000.
Entrance to Bay of Fundy and Yarmouth Harbor. Route travels along rocky coastline and through colorful fishing villages. County park, picnicking.

Firefighters' Museum of Nova Scotia
451 Main St., Yarmouth,
902-742-5525;
www.firefighters.museum.gov.ns.ca
Permanent display of history of firefighting service, including hand pumps, steamers and horse-drawn apparatus.

Yarmouth Arts Regional Centre
76 Parade St., Yarmouth,
902-742-8150; www.thyarc.ca
Center for visual and performing arts for southwestern Nova Scotia (356 seat capacity). Summer theater, drama, musical comedy, concerts, art shows, courses, workshops and seminars.

Yarmouth County Museum and Archives
22 Collins St., Yarmouth, 902-742-5539;
www.yarmouthcountymuseum.ednet.ns.ca

Displays detail the history of the county, with an emphasis on the Victorian period. Features marine exhibits, period rooms, blacksmith shop and a stagecoach. Of special interest is a runic stone found near Yarmouth Harbor in 1812, bearing a clear inscription alleged to be left by Leif Ericson on a voyage in 1007; Yarmouth Lighthouse lens.

SPECIAL EVENTS

Seafest
Waterfront Water and Lovitt Streets, Yarmouth, 902-742-7585;
www.playarmouthevents.com/html/seafest.html
Sporting events, entertainment, cultural productions, parade, Queen's Pageant. dory races, Fish feast. Mid-July.

Western Nova Scotia Exhibition
Western Nova Scotia Exhibition Grounds, Cottage Ln. and Forest St., Yarmouth, 902-742-8222.
Animal judging, equestrian events, agricultural displays, craft demonstrations and exhibits, midway and entertainment; Canada/U.S. ox hauls. Early August.

HOTELS

★Best Western Mermaid
545 Main Street, Yarmouth,
902-742-7821, 800-772-2774;
www.bwmermaid.com/
45 rooms, Restaurant, bar. Pool. $

★★Rodd Colony Harbor Inn
6 Forest St., Yarmouth,
902-742-9194, 800-565-7633;
www.rodd-hotels.ca

NOVA SCOTIA

65 rooms, Restaurant, bar. Pets accepted, fee. **$**

★★★Rodd Grand Yarmouth
417 Main St., Yarmouth,
902-742-2446, 800-565-7633;
www.rodd-hotels.ca
This hotel is located in the downtown core of Yarmouth. Many of the guest rooms have full views of the waterfront.
138 rooms. Restaurant, bar. Pet Pool. Busn. Center. **$**

★★★The Manor Inn
417 Main St., Route 1, Hebron,
902-742-2487, 800-626-6746;
www.manorinn.com
This resort on the shores of Doctors Lake was once the summer cottage of Commodore H. H. Raymond, an American shipping magnate. Now a country inn with an extensive rooster of activities, including fishing, bicycle rentals and boating. The guest rooms in the main house are Victorian in style and the adjacent two-story "coach house" offers several rooms.
53 rooms. Closed mid-October-late May. Complimentary continental breakfast. Restaurant, bar. Pool. Tennis. **$**

RESTAURANTS

★★Austrian Inn
Hwy. 1, Yarmouth,
902-742-6202.
German menu. Closed mid-December-March. **$$**

★★Lotus Garden
67 Starrs Rd., Yarmouth,
902-742-1688;
www.lotusgarden.ca
Chinese menu. Lunch, dinner, Sunday brunch. Bar. Children's menu.**$$**

★Prince Arthur Steak and Seafood House
73 Starrs Rd., Yarmouth,
902) 742-1129
Seafood, steak menu. Lunch, dinner, Sunday brunch. Bar. Children's menu. **$$**

101

NOVA SCOTIA

★
★
★
★
★

ONTARIO

WHILE THE REST OF CANADA LOVES TO TEASE TORONTO FOR ITS BIG-CITY GRAVITY, THIS HUB and its surrounding province justifies its ego. A colorful and endless mishmash of wilderness adventure, diverse cultures, urbane cosmopolitanism, and rustic rural scenery, the province of Ontario has it all.

The vast province of Ontario can be divided into north and south—the far northern wilderness dominated by lakes, forests and logging camps, and the southern agricultural, industrial and commercial hive inhabited by 90 percent of the population.

Toronto, the provincial capital and Ottawa, the nation's capital, offer tourists a wide spectrum of vibrant and world-class theater, restaurants, galleries, museums and recreational facilities. The Stratford Festival in Stratford, the Shaw Festival in Niagara-on-the-Lake and Upper Canada Village in Morrisburg are not to be missed, and the same goes for the spectacular Niagara Falls. Ontario's many recreational areas, such as Algonquin and Quetico provincial parks and St. Lawrence Islands National Park, offer a bounty of camping, hiking and all varieties of outdoor adventure. To the north lie Sudbury and Sault Ste. Marie; to the northwest, Thunder Bay, Fort Frances and Kenora, with canoeing, fishing and hunting. Perhaps more appealing than any one attraction is the vast, unspoiled nature of the province itself. More than 400,000 lakes and magnificent forests form a huge vacationland just a few miles from the U.S. border stretching all the way to Hudson Bay.

Provincial Capital: Toronto
www.ontariotravel.net

> ## ★ SPOTLIGHT
>
> ★ Currently, Niagara Falls wears its way back approximately one foot a year.
>
> ★ Yonge Street is the world's longest road, stretching 1,178 miles (1,896 kilometers) from the shores of Lake Ontario in Toronto to Rainy River on the border of Manitoba.

ONTARIO

BRANTFORD

Brantford offers world-class gardens, museums and cultural attractions, scenic trails and paddling—all one hour's drive from Toronto. Home to the Alexander Graham Bell Homestead National Historic Site, it was here that the great inventor conceived his idea for the telephone. Brantford is also the hometown of hockey legend Wayne Gretzky—and for the ultimate dose of Canada's national sport and spirit, view memorabilia from the career of The Great One alongside other local sports legends at the Gretzky Sports Hall of Recognition.

Information: www.visitbrantford.ca

WHAT TO SEE AND DO

Big Creek Boat Farm
14321 Hwy. 54 W., Caledonia,
Hwy. 54, 4 miles/6.4 kilometers
W. of Caledonia,
905-765-4107
Dinner cruises on the Grand River. Mid-May-September; reservations required.

Brant County Museum
57 Charlotte St., Brantford,
519-752-2483;
www.brantmuseum.ca
Collection of Native American artifacts, life histories of Captain Joseph Brant and Pauline Johnson. Also displays of pioneer life in Brant County, including Brant Square and Brant Corners, where former businesses are depicted.

Glenhyrst Art Gallery of Brant
20 Ava Rd., Brantford,
519-756-5932;
www.glenhyrst.ca
Gallery with changing exhibits of paintings, sculpture, photography and crafts surrounded by 16-acre 7-hectare. estate overlooking the Grand River. Beautiful grounds and nature trail.

Her Majesty's Royal Chapel of the Mohawks
190 Mohawk St., Brantford,
519-756-0240;
www.mohawkchapel.ca
1785. The first Protestant church in Ontario, the Mohawk Chapel is the only Royal Native Chapel in the world belonging to Six Nations people. May-June: Wednesday-Sunday afternoons; July-Labour Day: daily; early September-mid-October: Saturday and Sunday afternoons.

Myrtleville House Museum
34 Myrtleville Dr., Brantford,
519-752-3216;
www.myrtleville.ca
(1837) This Georgian house is one of the oldest in Brant County; original furniture of the Good family, who lived here for more than 150 years. On 5 1/2 acres 2 hectares. of parkland. Picnicking. Mid-April-mid-September.

Sanderson Centre for the Performing Arts
88 Dalhousie St., Brantford,
519-758-8090, 800-265-0710;
www.sandersoncentre.on.ca
This 1919 vaudeville house has been restored and transformed to a theater featuring music, dance and dramatic performances.

Woodland Cultural Centre
184 Mohawk St., Brantford,
519-756-8767;
www.woodland-centre.on.ca
Preserves and promotes the culture and heritage of the First Nations of eastern woodland area. Education, research and museum programs; art shows, festivals.

SPECIAL EVENTS

International Villages Festival
320 N. Park, Unit 2, Brantford,
519-756-8767;
www.brantfordvillages.ca
Ethnic villages celebrate with ethnic folk dancing, pageantry and food. Early July.

Riverfest
Lions Park Arena, 12 Edge St., Brantford,
519-751-9900
Three-day festival celebrates the Grand River. Entertainment, fireworks, crafts. Children's activities. Last weekend in May.

"Six Nations Fall Fair & Powwow"
Ohsweken Fairgrounds, Fourth Line and Chiesswood, Brantford,
519-445-0783
Native dances, authentic craft and art exhibits. Weekend after Labour Day.

Six Nations Native Pageant
Seneca Rd. and Sour Springs Rd.,
Brantford, 519-445-4528;
www.sixnationspageant.com
Forest Theatre at Six Nations reserve. Six Nations people reenact their history and

104

ONTARIO

culture in natural forest amphitheater. First three weekends in August.

HOTELS

★★Best Western Brant Park Inn And Conference Centre

19 Holiday Dr., Brantford,
519-753-8561, 877-341-1234;
www.bestwestern.com
158 rooms. Restaurant, bar. Children's activity center. Pool. **$**

★★★Holiday Inn Brantford

664 Colborne St. E., Brantford,
519-758-9999, 800-465-4329;
www.holiday-inn.com/brantfordon
98 rooms. Restaurant, bar. Pool. **$**

RESTAURANT

★★★Olde School Restaurant

Hwy. 2W. and Powerline Rd. W., Brantford,
519-753-3131, 888-448-3131;
www.theoldeschoolrestaurant.ca
This steak and seafood restaurant, located in a relatively rural area, is housed in a 1850s schoolhouse with a bell tower and beautifully landscaped grounds. Before or after dinner, stop by the piano lounge offered six nights a week..
Steak, seafood, European menu. **$$$**

BROCKVILLE

Brockville, one of the oldest and most beautiful communities in Ontario, is the eastern gateway to the 1000 Islands and features Victorian homes and a historic downtown. The streetscape, floral displays and local hospitality make shopping a delight. Specialty stores showcase unique works from artists, artisans, and clock-makers. One-of-a-kind gifts can be found at the many wonderful boutiques. Once you've stocked up in the town center, retreat to the nearby 1000 Islands, summer home for many of North America's elite since the 1800s, for hidden coves, granite cliffs and scenic sunrises.
Information: www.brockvilletourism.com

105

ONTARIO

WHAT TO SEE AND DO

Brockville Museum

5 Henry St.,
Brockville,
613-342-4397;
www.brockvillemuseum.com
Devoted to history surrounding the city. Exhibits, workshops, afternoon teas.

Thousand Island Cruises

30 Blockhouse Island Pkwy.,
Brockville, 14 miles/23 kilometers W. of Brockville via Hwy. 401 to 1000 Islands Pkwy,
613-549-5544, 800-848-0011;
www.1000islandscruises.on.ca
Aboard the General Brock. Shallow-draft boat makes trips one hour. through the heart of the region, including Millionaires' Row and many smaller channels inaccessible to larger boats. May-late October: daily.

SPECIAL EVENTS

Poker Run

Water and Kate Streets, Gananoque,
613-382-8413;
www.1000islandsinfo.com/pokerrun/index.htm
A Poker Run is not a race but a game of chance and a assembly of some of the hottest, fastest and exotic boats in North America. Mid-August.

Riverfest

Water St. and Market St. W., Brockville,
Waterfront,
613-345-0660;
www.brockvilleriverfest.ca
Over the past 25 years, Riverfest has grown to become one of the longest and most successful family-oriented festivals in Eastern Ontario. Having hosted some of the biggest names in entertainment for the young and young at heart. Mid-June-early July.

★
★
★
✩
✩

HOTELS

★Best Western White House Inn
1843 Hwy. 2 E., Brockville,
613-345-1622;
www.bestwestern.com
56 rooms. Complimentary continental breakfast. Restaurant. Pets accepted, fee. Pool. **$**

★★Days Inn
160 Stewart Blvd.,
Brockville,
613-342-6613, 800-325-2525;
www.daysinn.com
56 rooms. Restaurant, bar. Pool. **$**

★★Quality Inn
100 Stewart Blvd., Brockville,
613-345-1400;
www.qualityinn.com
72 rooms. Restaurant, bar. Children's activity center. Pool. Tennis. **$**

COLLINGWOOD

Collingwood, on the southern shore of Georgian Bay, is at the foot of Ontario's highest ski hill, Blue Mountain. As the heart of one of Ontario's most attractive year-round recreation destinations, Collingwood offers an array of outdoor pursuits, as well as outstanding events and festivals, some of Ontario's best-known trail systems and the province's longest beach.
Information: www.collingwood.ca/visiting_tourism.cfm

WHAT TO SEE AND DO

Blue Mountain
Jozo Weider, Blvd.,
Take Hwy. 400 N. to Barrie, exit 98,
Bayfield St., Follow signs to Hwy. 26 W,
in Craigleith, turn left onto Blue Mountain
Rd./County Rd. 19,
705-445-0231, 877-445-0231;
www.bluemountain.ca
Ontario's largest mountain resort offers a plethora of activities. In winter, skiers and snowboarders hit Blue Mountain's 34 runs of varying difficulty, while those who long for warmer days turn to the indoor tennis courts. When the world turns green again, visitors can swim, sail, mountain bike, or just bask at the beach. The resort also has an 18-hole golf course that doubles as an Audubon sanctuary.

Tube Town at Blue Mountain
18 Jozo Weider Blvd.,
705-445-0231, 877-445-0231;
www.bluemountain.ca
Tube Town, on the south side of the mountain, is a section that's specifically groomed to take the tumult of inner tubes. Guests are towed up the mountain via a ground lift and then set free to swoosh down one of four runs with banked turns and slippery chutes.

Scenic Caves Eco Adventure
Collingwood,
705-446-0256;
www.sceniccaves.com
Scenic caves, zip cable gliding, suspension bridge, cross-country skiing. Activities during summer and winter.

CORNWALL

Cornwall is a thriving community buzzing with community theaters, art galleries and concert halls on the banks of the St. Lawrence River. Many museums and historical sites celebrate this center of what was once called "Upper Canada," and outdoorsy types enjoy nature parks, golf courses and sailing from one of many marinas, while fairs and festivals pepper each season with sparkling fun.
Information: www.visit.cornwall.on.ca

WHAT TO SEE AND DO

Inverarden Regency Cottage Museum
3332 Montreal Rd., Cornwall,
613-938-9585;
www.museumsontario.com/museums/
onlineguide/details.aspx?ContactID=995
1816. Retirement home of fur trader John McDonald of Garth. Collection of Canadian and English Georgian furniture; houses local picture archives. Tea room. April-mid-November: daily; rest of year: by appointment.

United Counties Museum
731 Second St. W.,
Cornwall,
613-932-2381
Old stone house has displays showing early life of the United Empire Loyalists. April-late November: daily.

Upper Canada Village
13740 County Road 2,
Morrisburg, 25 miles/40 kilometers
W. of Cornwall on Hwy. 2 in Morrisburg,
613-543-4328, 800-437-2233;
www.uppercanadavillage.com/home.htm
Escape to the sights and sounds of an 1860s village. Over 40 heritage buildings include mills, trades shops, farms, churches, homes, factories and even a one-room schoolhouse. Enjoy horse-drawn wagon and boat rides, shopping and food.

SPECIAL EVENTS

Cornwall Lift-Off
Lamoureaux Park, Cornwall,
613-938-4748;
www.lift-off.ca
Annual hot air balloon festival on the site of Canadian National Hot Air Balloon Championships in 1996 and 1997. Extensive balloon roster plus a mainstage with live music. Mid-July.

Raisin River Canoe Races
Hwy. 138 and County Rd. 18,
Cornwall,
613-938-3611
On Raisin River. Mid-April.

Williamstown Fair
Hwys. 17 and 19, Williamstown,
613-347-2841;
williamstownfair.com
Canada's oldest annual fair, with talent contests, livestock and agricultural events, arts, crafts, baking and more. Mid-August.

Worldfest/Festimonde
Cornwall Civic Complex,
100 Water St. E., Cornwall,
613-938-9400;
www.realontario.ca/listings/listing.
asp?id=10478
International folk festival; ethnic music, dancing, displays, costumes. Six days in early July.

HOTEL

★★Best Western Parkway Inn & Conference Centre
1515 Vincent Massey Dr., 2nd St. E.,
Cornwall,
613-932-0451, 800-932-0451;
www.bestwestern.com
91 rooms. Restaurant, bar. Pets accepted, fee. Pool. $

ONTARIO

FORT FRANCES

Fort Frances, the largest town in the Rainy River District and one of Canada's major tourist entry points, is a prosperous, full-service town across the international bridge from its sister city, International Falls, Minn. Sailors enjoy a variety of lake conditions while families picnic, sun, swim, fish and boat at one of many secluded beaches. A new waterfront development, including the Sorting Gap Marina, provides an excellent place to dock and then tour the many historical attractions and sites of the town. During winter months, join the locals to snowmobile through bush trails and over lakes, fish through the ice, curl, cross-country ski and play broomball and hockey.

Information: www.fortfranceschamber.com

WHAT TO SEE AND DO

Fort Frances Museum
259 Scott St., Fort Frances,
807-274-7891;
www.museum.fort-frances.com
This small museum has changing displays dealing with the indigenous era, the fur trade and later settlement.

Noden Causeway
Fort Frances, E. on Hwy. 11.
Excellent island views may be seen from this network of bridges.

Pither's Point Park
Rainy Lake, Fort Frances,
807-274-5087.
This beautiful park has a reconstructed fort, logging tugboat and a lookout tower with a pioneer logging museum at its base. Tower, fort and boat mid-June-Labour Day: daily.. Campground with swimming beach, fishing, boating; playground, fitness trail, cafe. Late June-Labour Day.

SPECIAL EVENTS

Culturama Festival
720 Gillon St., Fort Frances,
807-274-5773
Early May.

Fun in the Sun Festival
Lake Rd. and Idylwild Dr., Fort Frances,
807-274-5773
Late June.

HOTEL

★★La Place Rendez-vous
1201 Idylwild Dr., Fort Frances,
807-274-9811, 800-274-9811;
www.rendezvoushotel.com
54 rooms. Restaurant, bar. $

RESTAURANT

★★La Place Rendez-vous
1201 Idylwild Dr., Fort Frances,
807-274-9811;
www.rendezvoushotel.com
Outdoor seating. $$

GANANOQUE

Nestled in the heart of the 1000 Islands, Gananoque is homebase for endless boating, sailing, canoeing, kayaking, jet skiing, scuba diving, water taxis and charters. St. Lawrence Islands National Park, made up of nearly two-dozen beautiful islands, features nature trails, parks, beaches and island camping. Visitors can enjoy unique exhibits at the Historic 1000 Islands Village, a heritage centre located on the waterfront. The Thousand Islands Playhouse is one of the region's most acclaimed professional theatres, featuring stage productions from May until October.

Information: www.1000islandsgananoque.com

WHAT TO SEE AND DO

1000 Islands Camping Resort
1000 Islands Pkwy., Gananoque,
613-659-3058;
www.1000islandsinfo.com/camping.htm
Campground area with pool; tent and trailer sites, playground, nature trails, miniature golf.

1000 Islands Skydeck
123 Lake Aldwell Rd., Lansdowne,
613-659-2335;
www.1000islandsskydeck.com
The 400-foot 146-meter. tower offers views of the 1000 Islands and the St. Lawrence River. Visitors ride an elevator that takes 40 seconds to reach the first of three observation decks. Mid-April-late October, daily 8:30 a.m.-dusk.

Gananoque Boat Line
Water St., Gananoque, 613-382-2144;
www.ganboatline.com
Three-hour tours through the 1000 Islands with a stop at Boldt Castle. Mid-May-mid-October; one-hour trips. July-August.

Gananoque Historical Museum
10 King St. E., Gananoque,
613-382-4024
Former Victoria Hotel 1863.; parlor, dining room, bedroom, kitchen furnished in Victorian style. Military and indigenous artifacts; china, glass, 19th- and 20th-century costumes. June-October: daily.

Giant Waterslide
1000 Islands Pkwy., Gananoque,
613-659-3058.
A 175-feet 53-meter. water slide. Mid-June-Labour Day: daily.

St. Lawrence Islands National Park
14 miles/30 kilometers E. of Gananoque,
613-923-5261, 800-839-8221;
www.pc.gc.ca/pn-np/on/lawren/index_E.asp
Established in 1904, this park lies on a 50-mile 80-kilometer. stretch of the St. Lawrence River between Kingston and Brockville. It consists of 21 island areas and a mainland headquarters at Mallorytown Landing. The park offers boat launching facilities, beaches, natural and historic interpretive programs, island camping, picnicking, hiking and boating. A visitor reception center and the remains of an 1817 British gunboat are at Mallorytown Landing mid-May-mid-October, daily; rest of year, by appointment.. The islands can be accessed by water taxi or by rental boats at

numerous marinas along both the Canadian and American sides.

HOTELS
★★★Gananoque Inn
550 Stone St. S., Gananoque,
613-382-2165, 800-465-3101;
www.gananoqueinn.com
This historic inn is located on the banks of the St. Lawrence River in the heart of the Thousand Islands.
50 rooms. Restaurant, bar. $

★★★Trinity House
90 Stone St. S., Gananoque,
613-382-8383; www.trinityinn.com
In the heart of the famous Thousand Islands, this fully restored 1859 home has antiques mixed together with modern amenities. Guests can wander through Victorian perennial gardens with herbs and flowers used by the chef in preparing meals.
8 rooms. Complimentary continental breakfast. Restaurant, bar. $

★★Quality Inn
650 King St. E., Gananoque,
613-382-1453, 800-228-5151;
www.qualityinn.com
34 rooms. Restaurant. Pool. $

★★Ramada Provincial Inn
846 King St. E. Hwy. 2., Gananoque,
613-382-2038, 800-272-6232;
www.ramadaprovincialinn.ca
78 rooms. Closed November-February. Restaurant, bar. Pool. Tennis. $

RESTAURANT
★★Golden Apple
45 King St. W., Gananoque,
613-382-3300;
www.gananoque.com/goldenapple
Seafood menu. Closed January-March. Outdoor seating. Converted 1830 mansion; antiques. $$$

ONTARIO

HAMILTON

Hamilton, linked to Toronto by the majestic Skyway Bridge, is a vibrant community with excellent dining, galleries and shopping. Emerging artists make their home downtown, a bustling engine of creative energy with a thriving gallery scene. Browse for antiques and collectibles, or wander through cobbled streets for a club scene that swings till the wee hours. The waterfront is a mecca for hikers, boarders and water sports enthusiasts, while buyers flock to the cornucopia of ethnic food stores and shops on Ottawa Street. Circling the cosmopolitan pleasures of the city are the splendor of the Royal

Botanical Gardens, the famous Bruce Trail and an abundance of conservation areas, water parks and walking paths.

Information: www.hamiltonundiscovered.com

WHAT TO SEE AND DO

African Lion Safari
1386 Cooper Rd., Flamborough,
W. on Hwy. 8 between Hamilton and
Cambridge, on Safari Rd.,
519-623-2620, 800-461-9453;
www.lionsafari.com
Drive-through wildlife park; exotic animal and bird shows, demonstrations. Admission includes large game reserves, African Queen boat, shows, scenic railway; play areas.

Art Gallery of Hamilton
123 King St. W., Hamilton,
905-527-6610;
www.artgalleryofhamilton.on.ca
Collection of more than 8,000 sculptures and photographs covering several centuries by American, Canadian, British and European artists. Impressive building; many international, national and regional exhibitions.

Battlefield House and Monument
77 King St., Stoney Creek,
QEW exit at Centennial Pkwy.,
905-662-8458;
www.battlefieldhouse.ca/monument.asp
Devoted to the Battle of Stoney Creek, this 1795 settler's home and monument honors one of the most significant encounters of the War of 1812. Some rooms furnished as a farm home of the 1830s. Guides in period costumes.

Ben Veldhuis Limited
154 King St. E., Hamilton,
905-628-6307
More than two acres one hectare. of greenhouses; thousands of varieties of cacti, succulents, St. Paulias and hibiscus; flowering tropical plants. Hibisci bloom all year.

Canadian Football Hall of Fame and Museum
58 Jackson St. W., Hamilton,
905-528-7566;
www.footballhof.com
Sports museum and national shrine tracing 120 years of history of Canadian football.

Children's Museum
1072 Main St. E., Hamilton,
905-546-4848;
www.myhamilton.ca
Participatory learning center where children ages two to 13 can expand sensory awareness of the world. Hands-on exhibits.

Dundurn Castle
610 York Blvd., Hamilton,
905-546-2872;
www.hamilton.ca
Home of Sir Allan Napier MacNab, Prime Minister of the United Provinces of Canada 1854-1856.. The 35-room mansion is restored to its former splendor. Exhibits, programs, special events featured all year.

Flamboro Downs
967 Hwy. 5, Flamborough,
905-627-3561;
www.flamborodowns.com
Harness racing all year.. Grandstand seats 3,000; restaurants, lounges. Confederation Cup race for top three-year-old pacers in North America held here August..

Hamilton Place
10 MacNab St. S., Hamilton,
905-546-3100;
www.hecfi.on.ca
Live theater and concerts featuring international artists in a spectacular cultural center. All year.

Hamilton's Farmers' Market
55 York Blvd., Hamilton,
905-546-2096;
www.hamilton.ca
Fresh produce, flowers, meat, poultry, fish, cheese and baked goods are brought from all over the Niagara garden belt. Tuesday, Thursday-Saturday.

Hamilton Military Museum
Dundurn Park, 610 York Blvd., Hamilton,
905-546-4974
Displays Canadian uniforms, equipment and weapons circa 1800.

McMaster Museum of Art
Alvin A. Lee Bldg., McMaster University,
1280 Main St. W., Hamilton,
905-525-9140;
www.mcmaster.ca/museum
On McMaster University campus 27,328 students.. Houses the university's collection of 6,000 works of art, changing public programs and the Herman H. Levy Collection of Impressionist and Post-Impressionist paintings.

Museum of Steam and Technology
900 Woodward Ave., Hamilton,
905-546-4797;
www.hamilton.ca
An 1859 pumping station contains unique examples of 19th-century steam technology; gallery features permanent and temporary exhibits on modern technology; also special events.

Ontario Workers Art & Heritage Centre
51 Stuart St., Hamilton,
905-522-3003;
www.wahc-museum.ca
Canada's only museum dedicated to preserving the legacy of labor and working people. Includes public resource center, cafe, reading room and gift shop. Closed Sunday & Monday.

Royal Botanical Gardens
680 Plains Rd. W., Hamilton,
at Hwys. 2, 6 and 403.,
905-527-1158;
www.rbg.ca
Colorful gardens, natural areas and a wildlife sanctuary. Rock Garden with seasonal displays; Laking Garden herbaceous perennials.; Arboretum world-famous lilacs in late May.; Rose Garden; Teaching Garden; woodland, scented and medicinal gardens. At Cootes Paradise Sanctuary trails wind around more than 1,200 acres 486 hectares. of water, marsh and wooded ravines.

Whitehern Historic House & Garden
41 Jackson St. W., Hamilton,
905-546-2018;
www.hamilton.ca

★
★
★
★
★

Former home of the McQuesten family; 19th-century Georgian mansion furnished with original family possessions. Landscaped gardens.

SPECIAL EVENTS

Around the Bay Road Race
905-624-0046
Canada's oldest footrace 1894.. Late March.

FestItalia
1 Summers Ln., Hamilton,
905-546-5300
Opera, concerts, bicycle race, fashion shows, ethnic foods. Mid-September.

Festival of Friends
Main St. and Gage Ave., Hamilton,
905-525-6644;
www.creativearts.on.ca
Musicians, artists, craftsmen, puppets, dance, mime and theater. Second weekend in August.

Hamilton International Air Show
Hamilton Civic Airport, 9300 Airport Rd.,
Hamilton, 905-528-4425
Large international air show. Mid-June.

Hamilton Mum Show
Main St. and Gage Ave., Hamilton,
905-546-2424
Gage Park, in greenhouses. More than 6,000 blooms. First two weeks in 2nd 2 weeks in October.

★
★
★

★

★

HOTELS

★★Admiral Inn
149 Dundurn St. N., Hamilton,
905-529-2311, 866-236-4662;
www.admiralinn.com
60 rooms. Restaurant. Pets accepted, fee. $

★★★Sheraton Hamilton Hotel
116 King St. W., Hamilton,
905-529-5515, 888-627-8161;
www.sheraton.com
Located in downtown Hamilton, this contemporary hotel has direct access to a shopping mall, the Convention Centre and Hamilton Place Concert Hall. Business travelers will appreciate the fitness room, business center and the high-speed and wireless Internet access.
301 rooms, 18 story. Restaurant, bar. Pets accepted, fee. Pool. Busn. Center. $$

RESTAURANTS

★★★Ancaster Old Mill Inn
548 Old Dundas Rd., Ancaster,
905-648-1827;
www.ancasteroldmill.com
Originally this building was a gristmill, built in 1792. Tour available.
American menu. Outdoor seating. $$$

★★Shakespeare's Dining Lounge
181 Main St. E., Hamilton,
905-528-0689; www.shakespeare.ca
Seafood, steak. Reservations recommended. $$$

KENORA

An attractive and prosperous town, Kenora is also a popular resort center and gateway to both Lake of the Woods to the south and a great wilderness to the north. Fishing, hunting, boating, sailing and excellent resort accommodations may be found here, along with 14,500 islands and 65,000 miles (104,600 kilometers) of shoreline on the lake. Winter offers up ice fishing, snowmobiling, downhill and cross-country skiing, curling and hockey, while summer sees a plethora of festivals along the downtown harbor front.
Information: www.lakeofthewoods.com

WHAT TO SEE AND DO

Lake Navigation, Ltd. Cruises
Harbor front Wharf, Kenora,
807-468-9124.

The MS Kenora makes three 18-mile 29-kilometer. cruises through the many islands and channels of Lake of the Woods. Included is Devil's Gap, with its "spirit rock" painting. Lunch, mid-afternoon and dinner cruises. Restaurant, bar. Mid-May-early October: daily.

Lake of the Woods Museum
300 Main St., S., Kenora,
807-467-2105;
www.lakeofthewoodsmuseum.ca
Houses more than 15,000 articles reflecting local, native and pioneer history.

Rushing River Provincial Park
Kenora, 12 miles/20 kilometers E. on Hwy., 17 and 4 miles/6 kilometers S. on Hwy. 71, 807-468-2501.
Approximately 400 acres 160 hectares.. Beautiful natural setting with a long and photogenic cascade. Swimming, fishing, boating; nature and cross-country skiing trails, picnicking, playground, camping, museum.

SPECIAL EVENTS
ESCAPE Exciting, Scenic, Canadian/American Powerboat Excursion.
Golf Course Rd. and Miikenna Way, Kenora,
807-467-4650.
Lake of the Woods. Four-day event for powerboats to explore the many channels, islands and historic features of the lake.

Canadian and U.S. participants meet in the vicinity of Flag Island, Minn. Early July.

Kenora Agricultural Fair
Kenora Recreation Centre Complex, 1st Ave. S. and 2nd Ave. S., Kenora, 807-467-4650;
www.kbfishing.com
Three days of competitions and cultural exhibitions include a midway show. Mid-August.

Kenora International Bass Fishing Tournament
Bernier Dr. and Lakeview Dr., Kenora, 807-467-4650;
www.kbfishing.com
Three-day competition. Early August.

HOTELS
★★Best Western Lakeside Inn
470 1st Ave. S., Kenora,
807-468-5521, 800-465-1120;
www.bestwestern.com
94 rooms, 11 story. Restaurant, bar. Pool. $

★Comfort Inn
1230 Hwy. 17E., Kenora,
807-468-8845;
www.comfortinn.com
77 rooms. Pets accepted, fee. $

KINGSTON
Nestled where the Rideau Canal and the St. Lawrence River meet Lake Ontario, Kingston is a freshwater sailor's dream, a city that exquisitely blends history and modern sophistication. Stroll through the bustling downtown and its boutiques and bistros, through its meandering waterfront with heritage-filled neighborhoods and breath-taking parklands.
Information: www.kingstoncanada.com

WHAT TO SEE AND DO
Agnes Etherington Art Centre
University Ave. and Queen's Crescent, Kingston, 613-545-2190
Changing exhibitions of contemporary and historical art.

Canadian Empress
253 Ontario St., Kingston,
departs from the front of City Hall,
613-549-8091, 800-267-7868.

This replica of a traditional steamship cruises the St. Lawrence and Ottawa rivers on six different routes; trips span four or five nights, some reaching Montréal and Québec City. Mid-May-November. Ages 12 and up.

Bellevue House National Historic Site
35 Centre St., Kingston,
613-545-8666.

Italianate villa 1840. was home of Sir John A. Macdonald, the first prime minister of Canada. Restored and furnished with period pieces. Multimedia display and video presentation at the visitor center.

Confederation Tour Trolley
209 Ontario St., Kingston. Leaves from Confederation Park,
613-548-4453
50-minute, 10-mile (16-kilometer) narrated tour of Kingston. Victoria Day-Labour Day, daily on the hour; charters available.

Correctional Service of Canada Museum
555 King St. W., Kingston,
613-530-3122;
www.csc-scc.gc.ca/text/organi/org
05-3_e.shtml
The museum displays a variety of artifacts and documents related to the early history of Canadian penitentiaries. It includes displays of contraband weapons and escape devices.

Fort Frederick & College Museum
Kingston. Martello Tower,
613-541-6000
Exhibits depict the history of the college and the earlier Royal Dockyard circa 1789-1853.; Douglas Collection of small arms and weapons that once belonged to General Porfirio Diaz, president of Mexico from 1886-1912. Late June-Labour Day: daily.

Fort Henry
1 Fort Henry Dr., Kingston, E. at the junction of Hwys. 2 and 15,
613-542-7388, 800-437-2233;
www.forthenry.com
One of Ontario's most spectacular historic sites, the present fortification was built in the 1830s and restored during the 1930s. Guided tour; 19th-century British infantry and artillery drills; military pageantry; exhibits of military arms, uniforms, equipment; garrison life activities. Mid-May-early October: daily 10 a.m.-5 p.m.

Grand Theatre
218 Princess St., Kingston,
613-530-2050

Century-old, renovated theater. Live theater, dance, symphonic and children's performances by professional companies and local groups; summer theater.

Geology Museum
Union St., Kingston. Miller Hall,
613-545-6767
Collection of minerals from around the world.

International Ice Hockey Federation Museum
445 Alfred St., Kingston,
613-544-2355;
www.ihhof.com
Displays trace history of hockey from its beginning in Kingston in 1885 to the present.

Island Queen
6 Princess St., Kingston,
departs from Kingston Harbor, downtown,
613-549-5544
Showboat of the 1,000 Islands. Offers three-hour river cruises through the Islands. May-October: daily.

MacLachlan Woodworking Museum
2993 Hwy. 2 E., Kingston,
613-542-0543
circa 1850. "Wood in the service of humanity" is the theme of the museum; highlights the life of the pioneer farmer in both the field and kitchen, as well as workshops of a cooper, blacksmith, cabinetmaker.

Marine Museum of the Great Lakes at Kingston
55 Ontario St., Kingston,
613-542-2261;
www.marmuseum.ca
Ships have been built in Kingston since 1678. This museum explores the tales, adventures and enterprise of Inland Seas history. Ship building gallery, 1889 engine room, with dry dock engines and pumps; artifacts; changing exhibits. Library and archives. The Museum Ship Alexander Henry, a 3,000-ton icebreaker,

★
★
★
★
★

is open for tours and bed-and-breakfast accommodations.

Murney Tower Museum
King and Barrie Sts., Kingston, 613-544-9925.
(1846) Martello tower is now a museum with exhibits of the area's military and social history.

Pump House Steam Museum
23 Ontario St., Kingston, 613-542-2261.
Displays on steam technology, model trains, small engines. June-September: daily 10 a.m.-4 p.m.

SPECIAL EVENTS
It's a Grand Summer
Grand Theatre, 218 Princess St., Kingston, 613-530-2050
Late June-Labour Day.

Pittsburgh Sheepdog Trials
Grass Creek Park, 2993 Hwy. 2 E., Kingston, 888-855-4555
Includes sheep-shearing demonstrations and a variety of related activities. Early August.

HOTELS
★★Best Western Fireside Inn
1217 Princess St., Kingston, 613-549-2211; www.bestwestern.com
77 rooms. Restaurant, bar. Pool. $

★First Canada Inn
1 First Canada Ct., Kingston, 613-541-1111.
74 rooms. Complimentary continental breakfast. Pets accepted, fee. $

★★Howard Johnson
237 Ontario St., Kingston, 613-549-6300, 888-825-4656; www.hojo.com
94 rooms, 6 story. Restaurant. Pets accepted, fee. Pool. $

★Knights Inn
2327 Princess St. Hwy. 2. and Sybenham Rd., Kingston, 613-531-8929, 800-843-5644; www.knightsinn.com
32 rooms. Pets accepted, fee. Pool. $

★★★Isaiah Tubbs Resort & Conference Centre
RR 1, W. Lake Rd., Picton, 613-393-2090; www.isaiahtubbs.com
This resort is located on the shores of West Lake and is open year-round. Adjacent to Sandbanks Provincial Park
60 rooms. Restaurant, bar. Children's activity center. Pool. Tennis. $$

★★★Merrill
343 Main St. E., Picton, 613-476-7451; www.merrillinn.com
This Victorian house was built in 1878 for Edwards Merrill, one of Canada's top barristers. Guest rooms are all decorated with period antiques.
14 rooms. Complimentary continental breakfast. Restaurant. $$

★Seven Oakes
2331 Princess St. Hwy. 2., Kingston, 613-546-3655.
40 rooms. Pets accepted, fee. Pool. Tennis. $

★★Travelodge
2360 Princess St., Kingston, 613-546-4233; www.travelodge.com
69 rooms. Restaurant, bar. Pool. $

SPECIALITY LODGING
Green Acres Inn
2480 Princess St. Hwy. 2., Kingston, 613-546-1796, 800-267-7889; www.greenacresinn.com
31 rooms. Complimentary continental breakfast. Pool. $

Hochelaga Inn
24 S. Sydenham St., Kingston, 613-549-5534; www.hochelaga.com
23 rooms. Complimentary continental breakfast. $

115

ONTARIO

★
★
★
★
☆

Rosemount Inn
46 Sydenham St. S., Kingston,
613-531-8844, 888-871-8844;
www.rosemountinn.com
10 rooms. Closed mid-December-early January. Children over 13 years only. Complimentary full breakfast. **$**

RESTAURANT
★★**Aunt Lucy's**
1399 Princess St. Hwy. 2., Kingston,
613-542-2729
Seafood, steak menu. **$$**

KITCHENER-WATERLOO
The twin cities of Kitchener-Waterloo were settled in the early 1800s by Mennonites, Amish and Germans whose cultural heritage is still widely celebrated. Not far to the north in Elmira is the heart of Ontario's Pennsylvania German country, with a Maple Sugar Festival and tours of Mennonite country. A vigorous spirit of youth and industry pervades both cities, which sparkle with a dynamic nightlife, fabulous restaurants, world-class cultural facilities, over 200 kilometers of community trails and lovely golf courses.
Information: www.kwtourism.ca

WHAT TO SEE AND DO
Bingeman Park
1380 Victoria St. N., Kitchener,
519-744-1555
Recreation center on banks of Grand River; swimming pool, wave pool., water sliding, bumper boats; go-cart track, arcade, roller skating, miniature golf, golf driving range, batting cages, cross-country skiing; picnicking, restaurant; playground, camping.

Doon Heritage Crossroads
Hwy. 401 exit 275, Homer Watson Blvd., Kitchener, 519-748-1914.
Re-creation of early 20th-century village circa 1915. includes museum, grocery store, post office/tailor shop, blacksmith, church, two farms and several houses. May-late December.

Farmers' Market
Frekerick and Duke Sts., Kitchener, Market Sq., downtown, 519-741-2287
More than 100 vendors sell fresh produce, meat, cheese and handicrafts. Mennonite specialties featured. All year: Saturday; mid-May-mid-October, also Wednesday..

Glockenspiel
King and Benton Sts., Hamilton

Canada's first glockenspiel tells the fairy tale of Snow White. Twenty-three bells form the carillon. Performance lasts 15 minutes. Four times daily.

Joseph Schneider Haus
466 Queen St. S., Kitchener-Waterloo, 519-742-7752
Pennsylvania German Mennonite house 1820., one of area's oldest homesteads, restored and furnished; living museum with costumed interpreters; daily demonstrations. Adjacent Heritage Galleries, includes Germanic folk art; exhibits change every three months. Victoria Day-Labour Day: daily; rest of year: Tuesday-Sunday.

Kitchener-Waterloo Art Gallery
101 Queen St. N., Kitchener-Waterloo, 519-579-5860; www.kwag.on.ca
Six exhibition areas cover all aspects of the visual arts. Gift shop. Tuesday-Sundy.

Laurel Creek Conservation Area
N.W. corner of Waterloo, bounded by Westmount Rd., Conservation Dr. and Beaver Creek Rd., 519-884-6620
Approximately 750 acres 305 hectares. of multipurpose area. Dam, swimming beach, boating no motors.; hiking, sports fields, camping fee., picnicking, reforested areas, bird-watching. May-mid-October.

★
★
★
☆
☆

Museum & Archive of Games
B.C. Matthews Hall, 200 University Ave.,
W., Waterloo, 519-888-4567;
www.gamesmuseum.uwaterloo.ca
On the University of Waterloo campus. Collection includes more than 3,500 games. Many hands-on exhibits drawn from collection range from Inuit bone games to computer games. Exhibits change every four months. Archive contains documents pertaining to games and game-playing.

Pioneer Memorial Tower
Pioneer Tower Rd. and Lookout Ln.,
Kitchener-Waterloo, 519-571-5684
Tribute to industrious spirit of pioneers who first settled Waterloo County. Cemetery on grounds includes the graves of several original founders. Excellent view of Grand River. May-October.

Waterloo Park
Albert St. N. and Young St., Waterloo,
519-747-8733
Log schoolhouse built in 1820 is surrounded by picnic area and lake; playground. Small zoo and band concerts in summer. Sunday..

Waterloo-St. Jacobs Railway
10 Father David Bauer Dr., Kitchener-
Waterloo, 519-746-1950.
Streamliner tourist train rolls into the heart of Mennonite farm country. Stops allow exploration of the quaint village of St. Jacobs and the St. Jacobs Farmers Market. Ninety minutes, round-trip. May-October: daily; November-April: weekends.

Woodside National Historic Site
528 Wellington St. N., Kitchener,
519-742-5273.
Boyhood home of William Lyon Mackenzie King, Canada's tenth prime minister. 1890s Victorian restoration. Interpretive center has theater and display on King's early life and career. Picnicking. May-December.

SPECIAL EVENTS
Ale Trail
Guelph Visitor and Convention Services,
55 Wyndham St. N., Guelph,
800-334-4519
Showcases region's brewing industry and allows visitors to experience the craft of brewing at six different area breweries. Mid-June.

Kitchener-Waterloo Multicultural Festival
Victoria Park, Park St. and David St.,
Kitchener-Waterloo,
519-745-2531
Late June.

Sounds of Summer Music Festival
Waterloo Park, Waterloo
Three days in mid-June.

Waterloo Busker Carnival
King and William Sts., Kitchener-Waterloo,
519-747-8769.
International showcase of street performers. Late August.

Waterloo County Quilt Festival
519-699-5628, 800-265-6959
Quilt exhibits, displays, workshops and demonstrations. Nine days in mid-May.

Wellesley Apple Butter & Cheese Festival
519-656-2222
Pancake breakfast, farmers market, free tours of farms, cider mill; horseshoe tournament, quilt auction, smorgasbord dinner, model boat regatta, antique cars and tractors. Last Saturday in September.

HOTELS
★Best Western Cambridge Hotel
730 Hespeler Rd., Cambridge,
519-623-4600;
www.bestwestern.com
106 rooms, 7 story. Complimentary continental breakfast. Pool. $

★★Elora Mill
77 Mill St. W., Elora,
519-846-9118, 866-713-5672;

117

ONTARIO

★
★
★
★
★
★

www.eloramill.com

32 rooms. Complimentary continental breakfast. Restaurant, bar. **$$**

★★Holiday Inn
30 Fairway Rd. S., Kitchener,
519-893-1211;
www.holiday-inn.com/kitcheneron
182 rooms, 6 story. Restaurant, bar. Pets accepted, fee. Pool. **$**

★★★Langdon Hall Country House Hotel & Spa
1 Langdon Dr., Cambridge,
519-740-2100, 800-268-1898;
www.langdonhall.ca
This antebellum-style inn has been restored and decorated with period furniture. It is located a few miles from downtown Cambridge in the heart of the Mennonite countryside on beautiful grounds. Toronto and the Shakespearean Festival are an easy drive. If you don't feel like leaving the property, there's always something to do on the grounds: walking, hiking, biking trails, skiing, croquet, bastennis and nearby golf.
53 rooms, 3 story. Restaurant, bar. Pet. Exercise. Swim. Tennis. **$$$**

★★Walper Terrace Hotel
1 King St. W., Kitchener,
519-745-4321, 800-265-8749;
www.walper.com
79 rooms. Complimentary continental breakfast. Restaurant, bar. **$**

★★★Waterloo Inn
475 King St. N., Waterloo,
519-884-0220, 800-361-4708;
www.waterlooinn.com
This hotel is close to the famous St. Jacob's Farmers Market, the Elora Gorge, and the Stratford festival.
155 rooms. Restaurant, bar. Pets accepted, fee. Exercise. Pool. **$**

RESTAURANTS

★★★Charcoal Steak House
2980 King St. E., Kitchener,
519-893-6570;
www.charcoalsteakhouse.ca
Consistently delicious steaks and a relaxing, serene atmosphere have made the Charcoal Steak House a Kitchener favorite for more than 50 years. The menu, which highlights Canadian AAA steaks and fresh seafood, offers choices for all. A number of cocktails choices are offered in addition to an award-winning wine list.
Steak menu. **$$$**

★★Benjamin's
1430 King N., St. Jacobs,
519-664-3731;
www.stjacobs.com/benjamins
Contemporary menu. **$$$**

★★Waterlot
17 Huron St., New Hamburg,
519-662-2020;
www.waterlot.com/spevents.html
This gourmet bed-and-breakfast, located close to the Stratford Festival, is in a Victorian house built in 1845. French menu. **$$$**

118

ONTARIO

LONDON

London is a busy, modern city with charming small-town atmosphere. Located on the Thames River, its street names echo "the other" London, as does the contrast of Victorian architecture and contemporary skyscrapers.

Near to the downtown core are historic sites, theatres, provincial parks and some of the best freshwater beaches in the world. Every summer evening, the lights dim and the curtain rises on stages throughout the area for the famous Stratford Festival, London's entertainment flagship.

Information: www.londontourism.ca

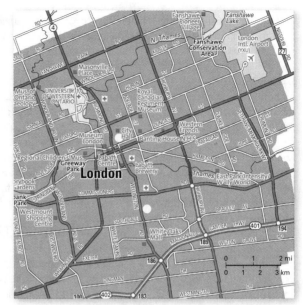

WHAT TO SEE AND DO

Double-decker bus tours
300 Dufferin Ave.,
London,
519-661-5000, 800-265-2602.
Two-hour guided tour aboard authentic double-decker English bus with stops at Storybook Gardens in Springbank Park and Regional Art Museum. Departs City Hall Wellington St. and Dufferin Ave. July-Labour Day: daily. Reservations suggested.

Eldon House
481 Ridout St. N., London,
519-661-5169
1834. Oldest house in town; occupied by same family until donated to the city. Furnished much as it was in the 19th century with many antiques from abroad. Spacious grounds, lawns, brick paths, gardens, conservatory-greenhouse.

Fanshawe Pioneer Village
2609 Fanshawe Park Rd. E., London,
N.E. edge of town, E. end of Fanshawe
Park Rd.,
519-457-1296;
www.fanshawepioneervillage.ca

Living history museum of 24 buildings moved to this site to display artifacts and re-create the life of a typical 19th-century crossroads community in southwestern Ontario. Log cabin, barns and stable; blacksmith, weaver, harness, gun, woodworking and barber shops; general store, church, fire hall, school and sawmill; costumed interpreters. Also at Fanshawe Conservation Area is Ontario's largest flood control structure; swimming, sailing, fishing walleye.; camping, various sports activities and nature trails.

Grand Theatre
471 Richmond St.,
London,
519-672-8800, 800-265-1593;
www.grandtheatre.com
Contemporary facade houses 1901 theater, built by Colonel Whitney of Detroit and Ambrose Small of Toronto. Restored interior, proscenium arch, murals and cast plasterwork. Professional stock theater. October-May.

Guy Lombardo Music Centre
205 Wonderland Rd. S.,
London,
519-473-9003

ONTARIO

Institution housing artifacts belonging to London-born musician. Exhibits on other big-band era greats.

Indian Village
Ongoing excavation and reconstruction of authentic 500-year-old Neutral village located on original site.

London Museum of Archaeology
1600 Attawandaron Rd., London,
519-473-1360
Traces prehistory of southwestern Ontario; more than 40,000 artifacts show how indigenous people lived thousands of years before Columbus was born; archaeological and ethnographic exhibits from southwestern Ontario. Gallery, theater and native gift shop. May-September: daily.

London Regional Art and Historical Museums
421 Ridout St. N., London,
519-672-4580
Changing exhibits on art, history and culture of the London area; regional, national and international art.

London Regional Children's Museum
21 Wharncliffe Rd. S., London,
519-434-5726
Hands-on galleries allow children to explore, touch and discover. Artifacts to touch, costumes to put on and crafts to make; also special events.

Royal Canadian Regiment Museum
650 Elizabeth St., London, Wolseley Hall, Canadian Forces Base,
519-660-5102.
Displays include artifacts, battle scenes from 1883-present, weapons and uniforms. Tuesday-Sunday; closed holidays.

Ska Nah Doht Indian Village
London, 20 miles/32 kilometers W. via Hwy. 2 in the Longwoods Road Conservation Area,
519-264-2420
Re-created Iroquoian village depicting native culture in southwest Ontario 800-

1,000 years ago. Guided tours, slide shows, displays; nature trails, picnicking, group camping.

Storybook Gardens
1958 Storybook Ln., London,
Springbank Park, Thames River Valley,
519-661-5770;
www.storybook.london.ca
Family-oriented theme park, children's playworld and zoo, 8 acres 3 hectares. within London's largest park of 281 acres/114 hectares. Early May-mid-October: daily.

SPECIAL EVENTS

Dragon Boat Race Festival
Fanshawe Conservation area. Clark and Huron Sts., London, 519-872-6961.
Mid-August.

Home County Folk Festival
Victoria Park. Charles and Water Sts., London, 519-432-4310.
Three-day outdoor music fest. Mid-July.

London Fringe Theatre Festival
476 Richmond St., London,
519-433-3332; www.londonfringe.ca
Citywide theatrical event. Mid-August.

Panorama Ethnic Festival
Open house of ethnic clubs; music, dance, food, crafts. Three days in late September.

Sunfest
Victoria Park, Charles and Water Sts., London, 519-663-9170, 800-265-2502.
Features 25 music and dance ensembles from around the world, plus 70 food and craft vendors. Early July.

Western Fair
Western Fairgrounds. 900 King St., London, 519-438-7203.
Entertainment and educational extravaganza; horse shows, musicians, exhibits, livestock shows. Ten days in early September.

HOTELS

★★Delta London Armories Hotel
325 Dundas St., London,

ONTARIO

519-679-6111, 800-668-9999;
www.deltahotels.com
245 rooms, 20 story. Restaurant, bar. Children's activity center. Pets accepted, fee. Pool. Busn. Center. **$**

★**Ramada Inn**
817 Exeter Rd., London,
519-681-4900, 800-303-3733;
www.ramadainnlondon.com
124 rooms. Restaurant, bar. Pool. **$**

★★★**Hilton London Ontario**
300 King St., London,
519-439-1661; www.hiltonlondon.com
An attached heated walkway makes access to the convention center easy from this hotel.
322 rooms, 22 story. Restaurants, bar. Exercise. Pool. **$$**

RESTAURANTS
★**Fellini Koolini's**
155 Albert St., London,
519-642-2300.
Italian menu. Outdoor seating. **$$**

★**Marienbad**
122 Carling St., London,
519-679-9940.
American menu. Outdoor seating. **$$**

★★**Marla Jane's**
460 King St. E., London,
519-858-8669.
Cajun/creole menu. Reservations recommended. Outdoor seating. **$$$**

★★**Michael's on the Thames**
1 York St., London,
519-672-0111;
www.michaelsonthethames.com
French and Italian menu. Reservations recommended. **$$$**

MORRISBURG

Morrisburg is nestled in the township of South Dundas, just west of Cornwall and within an hour's drive of Ottawa. It is near the site of Upper Canada Village, a living museum which depicts 19th century life in Upper Canada. It also hosts Upper Canada Playhouse, a repertory theatre housed in an old toothbrush factory. The town was partially flooded by the creation of the St. Lawrence Seaway in 1958. Unlike the region's Lost Villages, however, the parts of the town to be flooded were simply moved to higher ground in the same townsite, and the former Highway 2 was shifted onto the former Canadian National Railway's right of way.
Information: www.southdundaschamber.com

ONTARIO

WHAT TO SEE AND DO
Crysler Farm Battlefield Park
Morrisburg, 7 miles/11 kilometers E. on Hwy. 2.
Scene of a decisive battle of the War of 1812, where 800 British and Canadians defeated 4,000 American troops. Also here are Crysler Park Marina, Upper Canada Golf Course, Crysler Beach fee., Battle of Crysler's Farm Visitor Centre and Memorial Mound, Pioneer Memorial, Loyalist Memorial, Air Strip and Queen Elizabeth Gardens. Varying fees.

Upper Canada Village
613-543-3704
Authentic re-creation of rural 1860s riverfront village. Demonstrations by staff in period costumes. Historic buildings include an operating woolen mill, sawmill and gristmill; Willard's Hotel; blacksmith's, tinsmith's, dressmaker's, shoemaker's and cabinetmaker's shops; tavern, churches, school, bakery, working farms, canal. May be seen on foot, by carryall, or bateau.

Prehistoric World
5 miles/7 kilometers E. via Hwy. 401, on Upper Canada Rd., exit 758,

613-543-2503;
www.c360.ca/mornsburg/pw
Life-size reproductions of prehistoric animals along a 3/4-mile (1-kilometer). nature trail. More than 40 exhibits com-pleted, including Brontosaurus and Tyrannosaurus Rex; others in various stages of construction. Late May-Labour Day.

NIAGARA FALLS

To more than 12 million annual visitors, Niagara is magic—either for the spectacle of Niagara Falls, or for the bounty of ripening grapes and the taste of heavenly fresh fruit. In particular, the Canadian side of Niagara Falls offers viewpoints different from, and in many ways superior to, those on the American side. With over 40 world-class golf courses, over 70 award winning wineries and over 200 kilometres of spectacular cycling and hiking trails, the greater Niagara region offers more than one of the world's most incredible views.
Information: www.tourismniagara.com

WHAT TO SEE AND DO

Canada One Factory Outlets
7500 Lundy's Ln., Niagara Falls,
905-356-8989;
www.canadaoneoutlets.com
This outlet sells many nationally recognized brands of merchandise. Stores here include The Body Shop, Club Monaco, Guess, Tommy Hilfiger and Reebok.

Greenhouse
7145 Niagara Pkwy., Niagara Falls,
905-354-1721
Tropical and native plants; animated fountain, garden shop.

Great Gorge Adventure
4330 River Rd., Niagara Falls,
905-356-2241
Niagara River at its narrowest point. Elevator and 240-foot 73-meter. tunnel takes visitors to the boardwalk at edge of whirlpool rapids. April-October: daily.

Guinness World of Records Museum
4943 Clifton Hill, Niagara Falls,
905-356-2299
Based on the popular book of records; hundreds of original exhibits, artifacts; laser video galleries; re-creations of many of the world's greatest accomplishments. Daily.

IMAX Theatre Niagara Falls
6170 Fallsview Blvd., Niagara Falls,
905-358-3611; www.imaxniagara.com
Six-story-high movie screen shows Niagara: Miracles, Myths and Magic, a film highlighting the Falls. Daredevil Adventure has displays, exhibits and some of the actual barrels used to traverse the Falls.

Journey Behind the Falls
6650 Niagara Pkwy., Niagara Falls,
1 mile/1.6 kilometers S. of Rainbow Bridge on Niagara Pkwy. in Queen Victoria Park,
905-354-1551
Elevator descends to a point about 25 feet 8 meters. above the river, offering an excellent view of the Falls from below and behind; waterproof garments are supplied.

Louis Tussaud's Waxworks
4915 Clifton Hill, Niagara Falls,
905-356-2238
Life-size, historically-costumed wax figures of the past and present; Chamber of Horrors.

Lundy's Lane Historical Museum
5810 Ferry St., Niagara Falls,
905-358-5082;
www.lundyslanemuseum.com
1874. On the site of the Battle of Lundy's Lane 1814.. Interprets the early settlement and tourism of Niagara Falls; 1812 war militaria; Victorian parlor, early kitchen, toys, dolls, photographs; galleries and exhibits.

Maid of the Mist
Niagara Falls, 905-358-0311;
www.maidofthemist.com

122

ONTARIO

Maid of the Mist leaves from the foot of Clifton Hill on the Niagara River Pkwy. near Rainbow Bridge.

Marineland
7657 Portage Rd., Niagara Falls,
905-356-8250;
www.marinelandcanada.com
Performing killer whales, dolphins and sea lions; wildlife displays with deer, bears, buffalo and elk; thrill rides, including one of the world's largest steel roller coasters; restaurants, picnic areas.

Minolta Tower Centre
6732 Oakes Dr., Niagara Falls,
905-356-1501; www.niagaratower.com
This awesome 325-foot 99.06-meter. tower offers a magnificent 360-degree view of the Falls and surrounding areas. Eight levels at top; specially designed glass for ideal photography; Minolta exhibit floor; Waltzing Waters water and light spectacle; gift shops; incline railway to Falls; Top of the Rainbow dining rooms overlooking Falls reservations suggested..

Niagara Falls Aviary
5651 River Rd., Niagara Falls,
866-994-0090;
www.niagarafallsaviary.com
Wander through this 15,000-square-foot 1,394-square-meter. conservatory amidst lush foliage. The environment simulates a tropical rainforest in which free-flying birds soar overhead. Guided and self-guided tours; cafe, restaurant.

Niagara Falls Museum
5651 River Rd., Niagara Falls,
416-596-1396
One of North America's oldest museums, founded in 1827. Twenty-six galleries of rare, worldwide artifacts, including Niagara's Original Daredevil Hall of Fame; Egyptian mummy collection; dinosaur exhibit.

Niagara Parks Botanical Gardens
2565 Niagara Pkwy., Niagara Falls,
905-356-8554, 877-642-7275;
www.niagaraparks.com
Nearly 100 acres 40 hectares. of horticultural exhibits. Nature shop.

Niagara Parks Butterfly Conservatory
2565 Niagara Pkwy., Niagara Falls,
905-358-0025, 877-642-7275
Approximately 2,000 butterflies make their home in this 11,000-square-foot 1,022-square-meter., climate-controlled conservatory filled with exotic greenery and flowing water. Nearly 50 species of butterflies can be viewed from a 600-foot 180-meter. network of walking paths. Outdoor butterfly garden. Gift shop.

Niagara Spanish Aero Car
Niagara Falls. 3 1/2 miles/5 kilometers N. on Niagara Pkwy.,
905-354-5711
The 1,800-foot 549-meter. cables support a car that crosses the whirlpool and rapids of the Niagara River. Five-minute trip each way. Mid-April-mid-October: daily.

Old Fort Erie
350 Lake Shore Rd., Fort Erie,
905-871-0540
Site of some of the fiercest fighting of the War of 1812; restored to the period. Guided tours of the Glengarry Light Infantry by interpreters dressed in uniform. May-November, daily 10 a.m.-6 p.m..

Skylon Tower
5200 Robinson St., Niagara Falls,
905-356-2651, 866-434-4202;
www.skylon.com
Stands 775 feet 236 meters. above the base of the Falls. Three-level dome contains an indoor/outdoor observation deck and revolving and stationary dining rooms served by three external, glass-enclosed Yellow Bug elevators. Specialty shops at base of tower.

SPECIAL EVENT
Winter Festival of Lights
Queen Victoria Park, Murray St. and River Rd., Niagara Falls, 800-563-2557
Celebrate the start of the winter season with parades, fireworks, light displays and Disney shows. Late November-late January.

★
★
★
★
★
★

HOTELS

★★Aston Michael's Inn By The Falls
5599 River Rd., Niagara Falls,
905-354-2727, 800-263-9390;
www.michaelsinn.com
130 rooms. Restaurant, bar. Pool. $

★★Best Western Cairn Croft Hotel
6400 Lundy's Ln., Niagara Falls,
905-356-1161, 800-263-2551;
www.bestwestern.com
165 rooms. Restaurant, bar. Pool. $

★★★Doubletree Resort Lodge & Spa Fallsview Niagara Falls
6039 Fallsview Blvd., Niagara Falls,
905-358-3817, 800-222-8733;
www.niagarafallsdoubletree.com
Cathedral ceilings with wood beams, slate floors and freshly baked chocolate chip cookies welcome guests. The property is within walking distance to area attractions. The spacious guest rooms offer panoramic views of the upper Niagara River. Art lovers can check out the in-house gallery, Ochre Art Gallery. For pure relaxation, the Five Lakes AVEDA Day Spa is the place to go for relaxation. Buchanans Chophouse is the perfect spot to unwind.
224 rooms. Restaurant, two bars, children's activity center, spa. Pool. Busn. Center. $$

★★Embassy Suites Hotel Niagara Falls / Fallsview
6700 Fallsview Blvd., Niagara Falls,
905-356-3600, 800-420-6980;
www.embassysuitesniagara.com
512 rooms, 42 story, all suites. Complimentary full breakfast. Restaurant, bar. Pool. $

★★★Hilton Niagara Falls
6361 Fallsview Blvd., Niagara Falls,
905-357-3366, 888-370-0700;
www.hiltonniagarafalls.com
Located in the heart of the bustling Niagara Falls tourist area, this hotel is near all the area attractions. The dramatic lobby features lots of pale ochre marble and blond wood. Many of the elegant guest rooms offer outstanding views.
516 rooms. Restaurant, two bars. Pool. Busn. Center. $$

★★★Marriott Niagara Falls Fallsview
6740 Fallsview Blvd., Niagara Falls,
905-357-7300, 888-501-8916;
www.niagarafallsmarriott.com
Directly across from Horseshoe Falls, this is a prime Niagara Falls location. Area attractions, restaurants and shops are nearby. The interior of this elegant hotel has a light, sunny feel. The Falls can be viewed from many of the guest rpooms as well as right in the lobby.
427 rooms. Restaurant, bar. Pool. Busn. Center. $$

★Oakes Hotel Overlooking The Falls
6546 Fallsview Blvd., Niagara Falls,
905-356-4514;
www.niagarahospitalityhotels.com
256 rooms, 15 story. Pool. $

★★Old Stone Inn
5425 Robinson St., Niagara Falls,
905-357-1234;
www.oldstoneinn.on.ca
114 rooms. Restaurant, bar. Pool. $

★★★Renaissance Fallsview Hotel
6455 Fallsview Blvd., Niagara Falls,
905-357-5200, 800-363-3255;
www.renaissancefallsview.com
This hotel is very close to Niagara Falls and the Queen Victoria Park. The rooftop dining room provides views of the falls.
262 rooms. Two restaurants, bar. Pool. Busn. Center. $$

★★★Sheraton Fallsview Hotel And Conference Centre
6755 Fallsview Blvd., Niagara Falls,
905-374-1077, 800-267-0434;
www.fallsview.com
Guests can walk to the Falls and numerous area attractions, restaurants and shops. The large two-story lobby has a curved staircase with comfortable, casual seating. Guest rooms are attractive and feature deep blue bed coverings, luxurious linens and comfortable mattresses.

124

ONTARIO

402 rooms, 31 story. Three restaurants, two bars. Pets accepted, fee. Pool. Busn. Center. **$$**

SPECIALITY LODGING

Bedham Hall
4835 River Rd., Niagara Falls,
905-374-8515; www.bedhamhall.com
4 rooms, all suites. **$$**

Chestnut Inn
4983 River Rd., Niagara Falls,
905-374-7623; www.chestnutinnbb.com
4 rooms. Complimentary full breakfast. **$$**

Eastwood Lodge
5359 River Rd., Niagara Falls,
905-354-8686; www.theeastwood.com
6 rooms. Complimentary full breakfast. **$**

RESTAURANTS

★★Buchanan's Chophouse
6039 Fallsview Blvd., Niagara Falls,
905-353-4111.
Steak menu. Reservations recommended. Outdoor seating. **$$**

★★Capri
5438 Ferry St., Niagara Falls,
905-354-7519.
Italian menu. Reservations recommended. **$$**

★★Millery
5425 Robinson St., Niagara Falls,
905-357-1234, 800-263-6208;
www.oldstoneinn.on.ca
American menu. Reservations recommended. **$$**

★★Queenston Heights
14184 Niagara Pkwy., Niagara Falls,
905-262-4274, 877-642-7275
American menu. Reservations recommended. Outdoor seating. **$$**

★★Victoria Park
6342 Niagara Pkwy., Niagara Falls,
905-356-2217;
www.niagaraparks.com
American menu. Closed mid-October-mid-May. Outdoor seating. **$$$**

NIAGARA-ON-THE-LAKE

Often called the loveliest in Ontario, this picturesque town has a long and distinguished history that parallels the growth of the province. Once a busy shipping, shipbuilding and active commercial center, the beautiful old homes lining the tree-shaded streets testify to the area's prosperity. The town's attractions now include theater, historic sites, beautiful gardens and Queen Street, with its shops, hotels and restaurants. Delightful in any season, this is one of the best-preserved and prettiest remnants of the Georgian era.
Information: www.niagara-on-the-lake.com

WHAT TO SEE AND DO

Brock's Monument
14184 Niagara River Pkwy., Niagara,
905-468-4257.
Massive, 185-foot 56-meter. memorial to Sir Isaac Brock, who was felled by a sharpshooter while leading his troops against American forces at the Battle of Queenston Heights in October 1812. Narrow, winding staircase leads to tiny observation deck inside monument. Other memorial plaques in park; walking tour of important points on the Queenston Heights Battlefield begins at Brock Monument; brochure available here. Brock and his

aide-de-camp, Lieutenant-Colonel Macdonell, are buried here. Mid-May-Labour Day: daily.

Court House
Queen and Regent Sts.,
Niagara-on-the-Lake.
1847. Built on the site of the original government house, three-story building is now the home of Court House Theatre. First home of the Shaw Festival.

Fort George National Historic Site
26 Queen St., Niagara-on-the-Lake,
Niagara Pkwy., 905-468-4257.

1797. Once the principal British post on the frontier, this fort saw much action during the War of 1812. Eleven restored, refurnished buildings and massive ramparts. April-October: daily 10 a.m.-5 p.m.; rest of year by appointment.

Laura Secord Homestead
29 Queenston St., Queenston, 905-371-0254
Restored home of Canadian heroine is furnished with early Upper Canada furniture. After overhearing the plans of Americans billeted in her home, Laura Secord made an exhausting and difficult 19-mile 30-kilometer. walk to warn British troops, which resulted in a victory over the Americans at Beaverdams in 1813.

McFarland House
15927 Niagara Pkwy.,
Niagara-on-the-Lake, 905-356-2241
(1800). Georgian brick home used as a hospital in the War of 1812; furnished in the Loyalist tradition, 1835-1845. July-Labour Day: daily; mid-May-June and after Labour Day-September: weekends only.

Niagara Apothecary
5 Queen St., Niagara-on-the-Lake,
905-468-3845; www.niagaraapothecary.ca
(Circa 1820). Restoration of a pharmacy that operated on the premises from 1866-1964. Has a large golden mortar and pestle over door; original walnut and butternut fixtures, apothecary glass and interesting remedies of the past. May-Labour Day: Daily.

Niagara Historical Society Museum
43 Castlereagh St., Niagara-on-the-Lake,
905-468-3912
Opened in 1907, the earliest museum building in Ontario. Items from the time of the United Empire Loyalists, War of 1812, early Upper Canada and the Victorian era. March-December: daily; rest of year: weekends or by appointment.

St. Mark's Anglican Church
41 Byron St., Niagara-on-the-Lake,
905-468-3123.

(1805, 1843). Original church damaged by fire after being used as a hospital and barracks during the War of 1812. Rebuilt in 1822 and enlarged in 1843. Unusual three-layer stained-glass window. Churchyard dates from earliest British settlement. July-August: daily; rest of year by appointment.

St. Vincent de Paul Roman Catholic Church
73 Picton St., Niagara-on-the-Lake,
905-468-1383.
1835. First Roman Catholic parish in Upper Canada. Excellent example of Gothic Revival architecture; enlarged in 1965; older part largely preserved.

SPECIAL EVENTS
Days of Wine and Roses
Sunnybrook Farm Estate Winery,
1425 Lakeshore Rd., Niagara-on-the-Lake,
905-468-4263
Weekends during February.

Shaw Festival
Queen's Parade and Wellington St.,
Niagara-on-the-Lake, 905-468-2153,
800-657-1106; www.shawfest.com
Shaw Festival Theatre, specializing in the works of George Bernard Shaw and his contemporaries, presents 10 plays each year in repertory. Housed in three theaters, including the Court House Theatre. Staged by internationally acclaimed ensemble company. Also lunchtime theater featuring one-act plays by Shaw. Mid-April-October.

HOTELS
★★★Gate House Hotel
142 Queen St., Niagara-on-the-Lake,
905-468-3263;
www.gatehouse-niagara.com
This property has a contemporary Italian design and is located within walking distance of shops, historic sites, and the three theaters of the Shaw Festival.
10 rooms. Closed January-mid-Mar. Complimentary continental breakfast. Restaurant, bar. Pets accepted, fee. $$

★★Oban Inn
160 Front St., Niagara-on-the-Lake,
905-468-2165, 888-669-5566;
www.obaninn.ca

Once the home of a Scottish ship captain, today's guests find all the benefits of a modern hotel in a wonderfully quaint, historic property. The grounds, which overlook Lake Ontario, feature charming English-style gardens. Individually decorated guest rooms feature four-poster beds and antique furnishings with nice touches like complimentary turndown service. Take advantage of the complimentary in-town shuttle service when going sightseeing.
26 rooms. Complimentary full breakfast. Restaurant, bar. Pets accepted, fee. $$

★★★Pillar and Post
48 John St., Niagara-on-the-Lake,
905-468-1362, 888-669-5566;
www.vintageinns.com

This unique inn is located in a restored turn-of-the-century fruit canning factory. The lobby is full of plants and antique furniture. Don't miss a visit to the 100 Fountain Spa, where guests can relax and enjoy.
123 rooms. Restaurant, bar, spa. Pets accepted, fee. Pool. Busn. Center. $$

★★★Prince of Wales
6 Picton St., Niagara-on-the-Lake,
905-468-3246, 888-669-5566;
www.vintageinns.com

This historic treasure dates to 1864. Its unique character and formal charm make it one of Canada's most beloved hotels. A cozy day spa celebrates the English countryside in its treatment rooms and afternoon tea is a daily ritual. There is sophisticated dining at Escabeche restaurant, where a modern French menu tempts and delights.
112 rooms. Restaurant, bar, spa. Pet. Exercise. Swim. Busn. Center. $$$

★★★Queen's Landing
155 Byron St., Niagara-on-the-Lake,
905-468-2195, 888-669-5566;
www.vintageinns.com

Built with Victorian charm, this inn overlooks the Niagara River, opposite historic Fort Niagara.
144 rooms, 3 story. Restaurant, bar. Exercise. Swim. $$$

★★★White Oaks Conference Resort and Spa
253 Taylor Rd., SS4, Niagara-on-the-Lake,
905-688-2550, 800-263-5766;
www.whiteoaksresort.com

This large, modern resort has relaxation and comfort in mind. This is reflected in the guest room amenities such as Frette robes, nightly turndown service and pillow topped mattresses. The attitude is carried over to the full service spa and LIV, the resort's concept restaurant.
220 rooms, 7 story. Restaurant, bar, spa. Pool. Golf. Tennis. Busn. Center. $$

SPECIALITY LODGING
Moffat Inn
60 Picton St., Niagara-on-the-Lake,
905-468-4116; www.moffatinn.com
Historic inn 1835., 23 rooms. Restaurant, bar. $

RESTAURANTS
★★Buttery Theatre
19 Queen St., Niagara-on-the-Lake,
905-468-2564;
www.thebutteryrestaurant.com
American menu. Reservations recommended. Outdoor seating. $$

★★★Carriages
48 John St., Niagara-on-the-Lake,
905-468-2123, 888-669-5566;
www.vintageinns.com
This cozy, candlelit dining room of the Pillar and Post hotel features exposed beams, and a working brick oven.
American menu. Reservations recommended. Valet parking. Outdoor seating. $$$

★★★Escabéche
6 Picton St., Niagara-on-the-Lake,
905-468-3246, 888-669-5566;
www.vintageinns.com

ONTARIO

★
★
★
★
★

The formal dining room of the Prince of Wales hotel makes the Victorian experience truly memorable. International menu. Reservations recommended. Valet parking. $$$

★Fans Court
135 Queen St., Niagara-on-the-Lake, 905-468-4511.
Chinese menu. Closed Monday; also January. Reservations recommended. Outdoor seating. $$

OTTAWA

With its parks full of flowers and its universities, museums and diplomatic embassies, Ottawa is one of Canada's most beautiful cities. Ottawa is a city of waterways: the majestic Ottawa River, the fast-flowing Gatineau, the placid Rideau. But no waterway has defined Ottawa like the Rideau Canal, which is a playground for skaters in winter and for boaters in summer. The oldest continuously operated canal in North America, it celebrated its 175th anniversary in 2007. Filled with festivals, buskers, theater, music and dance, Ottawa also prides itself on a superb collection of museums—such as the Canadian Museum of Contemporary Photography, the Canadian Museum of Civilization and Ottawa's rowdy, lumberjack past as captured by the Bytown Museum. For everyone, the nation's capital showcases Canada's art, music, people and politics with grace and verve—in both English and French.

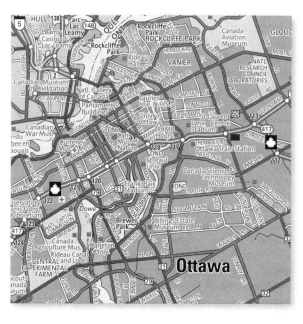

Information: www.ottawatourism.ca

WHAT TO SEE AND DO

BeaverTails

This popular Canadian pastry resembles the tail of a beaver and comes with a variety of sweet and salty toppings. The original kiosk serving this pastry is still operating in the ByWard Market district at the corner of George and William streets. The pastry is based on an ancient North American Voyageur recipe and is a descendant of the quick bread the Voyageurs baked.

Bytown Museum
540 Wellington St.,
613-234-4570

Artifacts, documents and pictures relating to Colonel By, Bytown and the history and social life of the region. Tours by appointment..

ByWard Market
55 ByWard Market Sq., Ottawa,
Bounded by Dalhousie and Sussex Dr.,
George and Clarence Sts.,
613-562-3325;
www.byward-market.com
Traditional farmers' market; building houses boutiques and art galleries; outdoor cafes. Exterior market daily.; interior market. April-December: daily; rest of year; Tuesday-Sunday..

128

ONTARIO

Canadian Museum of Contemporary Photography

1 Rideau Canal, Ottawa,
613-990-8527;
www.cmcp.gallery.ca
Showcases the work of Canada's preeminent photographers.

Canadian Museum of Nature

Metcalf and McLeod Sts., Ottawa,
613-566-4700, 800-263-4433;
www.nature.ca
Exhibits and displays focus on nature and the environment. Topics include dinosaurs, insects, gems and minerals, birds and mammals of Canada and the evolution of the planet.

Canadian Parliament Buildings

Wellington St. on Parliament Hill, Ottawa,
613-996-0896
Neo-Gothic architecture dominates this part of the city. House of Commons and Senate meet here; visitors may request free tickets to both chambers when Parliament is in session. Guided tour includes House of Commons, Senate Chamber, Parliamentary Library. Also here are the Centennial Flame, lit in 1967 as a symbol of Canada's 100th birthday, and Memorial Chapel, dedicated to Canadian servicemen who lost their lives in the Boer War, WWI, WWII and the Korean War. Observation Deck atop the Peace Tower.

Canadian Ski Museum

1960 Scott St., Ottawa,
613-722-3584;
www.skimuseum.ca
History of skiing; collection of old skis and ski equipment from Canada and around the world.

Central Experimental Farm

88 Prince of Wales Dr., Ottawa,
613-991-3044
Approximately 1,200 acres 486 hectares. of field crops, ornamental gardens, arboretum; showcase herds of beef and dairy cattle, sheep, swine, horses. Tropical greenhouse, agricultural museum, clydesdale horse-drawn wagon or sleigh rides.

Currency Museum

245 Sparks St., Ottawa,
613-782-8914;
www.currencymuseum.ca
Artifacts, maps and exhibits tell the story of money and its use throughout the world.

Double-decker bus tours

Capital Trolley Tours, Metcalfe and Sparks Sts., Ottawa,
613-729-6888
Buses seen in service in Britain visit various highlights of the city. April-mid-November: daily.

Laurier House National Historic Site of Canada

335 Laurier Ave. E., Ottawa,
613-992-8142;
www.parkscanada.gc.ca/laurierhouse
Former residence of two prime ministers: Sir Wilfrid Laurier and W. L. Mackenzie King. Re-created study of Prime Minister Lester B. Pearson. Books, furnishings and memorabilia.

Museum of Canadian Scouting

1345 Base Line Rd., Ottawa,
613-224-5131
Depicts the history of Canadian Scouting; exhibits on the life of Lord R.S.S. Baden-Powell, founder of the Boy Scouts; pertinent documents, photographs and artifacts.

National Archives of Canada

395 Wellington St., Ottawa,
613-995-5183
Collections of all types of material relating to Canadian history. Changing exhibits. Opposite is Garden of the Provinces. Flags representing all Canadian provinces and territories; fountain illuminated at night. May-November.

129

ONTARIO

National Arts Centre

53 Elgin St., Ottawa,
613-947-7000;
www.NAC-CNA.ca
Center for performing arts; houses a concert hall and two theaters for music, dance, variety and drama; home of the National Arts Centre Orchestra; more than 800 performances each year; canal-side cafe. Landscaped terraces with panoramic view of Ottawa.

National Aviation Museum

11 Aviation Pkwy., Ottawa,
Rockcliffe Airport, N.E. end of city,
613-990-1985, 800-463-2038;
www.aviation.nmstc.ca
More than 100 historic aircraft, 49 on display in a Walkway of Time. Displays demonstrate the development of aircraft in peace and war, emphasizing Canadian aviation.

National Gallery of Canada

380 Sussex Dr., Ottawa,
613-990-1985, 800-319-2787;
www.national.gallery.ca
Permanent exhibits include European paintings from the 14th century to the present; Canadian art from the 17th century to the present; contemporary and decorative arts, prints, drawings, photos and Inuit art; video and film. Reconstructed 19th-century Rideau convent chapel with Neo-Gothic fan-vaulted ceiling, only known example of its kind in North America. Changing exhibits fee., gallery talks, films; restaurants, bookstore.

National Museum of Science and Technology

1867 St. Laurent Blvd., Ottawa,
613-991-3044;
www.science-tech.nmstc.ca
More than 400 exhibits with many do-it-yourself experiments; Canada's role in science and technology shown through displays on Canada in space, transportation, agriculture, computers, communications, physics and astronomy. Unusual open restoration bay allows viewing of various stages of artifact repair and refurbishment.

Nepean Point

380 Sussex Dr., Ottawa,
Just W. of Sussex Dr. and St. Patrick,
613-239-5000
Lovely view of the area; Astrolabe Theatre, a 700-seat amphitheater, is the scene of musical, variety and dramatic shows in summer.

Ottawa Senators NHL.

Corel Centre, 1000 Palladium Dr., Kanata,
613-599-0200, 800-444-7367;
www.ottawasenators.com
Professional hockey team.

Paul's Boat Lines, Ltd.

Suffux and Rideau Sts., Ottawa,
613-225-6781
Rideau Canal sightseeing cruises depart from Conference Centre mid-May-mid-October: daily.. Ottawa River sightseeing cruises depart from foot of Rideau Canal Locks mid-May-mid-October: daily..

Rideau Canal

34A Beckwith St. S., Ottawa runs 125 miles 202 kilometers. between Kingston and Ottawa.,
613-992-8142, 800-230-0016
Constructed under the direction of Lieutenant-Colonel John By of the Royal Engineers between 1826 and 1832 as a safe supply route to Upper Canada. The purpose was to bypass the St. Lawrence River in case of an American attack. There are 24 lock stations where visitors can picnic, watch boats pass through the hand-operated locks and see wooden lock gates, cut stone walls and many historic structures. In summer there are interpretive programs and exhibits at various locations. Areas of special interest include Kingston Mills Locks, Jones Falls Locks off Hwy. 15., Smith Falls Museum off Hwy. 15., Merrickville Locks on Hwy. 43. and Ottawa Locks. Boating is popular (mid-May-mid-October: daily) and ice skating is available mid-December-late February: daily..

130

ONTARIO

Royal Canadian Mint
320 Sussex Dr., Ottawa,
613-993-8990, 800-276-7714;
www.rcmint.ca
Production of coins; collection of coins and medals. Guided tours and film; detailed process of minting coins and printing bank notes is shown.

Victoria Memorial Museum Building
240 McLeod St., Ottawa,
613-566-4700
Castle-like structure houses museum that interrelates man and his natural environment. Houses the Canadian Museum of Nature. Natural history exhibits from dinosaurs to present day plants and animals. Outstanding collection of minerals and gems.

SPECIAL EVENTS
Canada Day
90 Wellington St., Ottawa,
613-239-5000, 800-465-1867;
www.canadascapital.gc.ca
Celebration of Canada's birthday with many events throughout the city, including canoe and sailing regattas, concerts, music and dance, art and craft demonstrations, children's entertainment, fireworks. July 1.

Canadian Tulip Festival
90 Wellington, Ottawa, Capital Infocenter,
613-567-5757;
www.tulipfestival.ca
Part of a two-week celebration, culminated by the blooming of more than 3 million tulips presented to Ottawa by Queen Juliana of the Netherlands after she sought refuge here during WWII. Tours of flower beds; craft market and demonstrations, kite flying, boat parade. May.

Changing the Guard
Parliament Hill, 90 Wellington St., Ottawa,
613-993-1811
Late June-late August. 10:00 am-10:30 am

Ottawa International Jazz Festival
395 Wellington St., Ottawa,
613-993-1811;
www.ottawajazzfestival.com
Jazz artists from around the world perform at this week-long celebration. Ten days in mid-July.

Sound & Light Show on Parliament Hill
90 Wellington St., Ottawa,
613-239-5000, 800-465-1867;
www.canadascapital.gc.ca
Mid-May-Labour Day.

Winterlude
90 Wellington St., Ottawa,
613-239-5000;
www.canadascapital.gc.ca
Extravaganza devoted to outdoor concerts, fireworks, skating contests, dances, music, ice sculptures. Three weekends in February.

HOTELS
★★Albert At Bay Suite Hotel
435 Albert St., Ottawa,
613-238-8858, 800-267-6644;
www.albertatbay.com
197 rooms, all suites. Two restaurants, one bar. Renovated apartment building. $

★★Best Western Hotel Jacques Cartier
131 Laurier St., Hull,
819-770-8550;
www.bestwestern.com
144 rooms. Restaurant, bar. Opposite the Museum of Civilization. Pool. $

★Best Western Victoria Park Suites
377 O'Connor St., Ottawa,
613-567-7275, 800-465-7275;
www.victoriapark.com
123 rooms, 8 story. Complimentary continental breakfast. $

★★Delta Ottawa Hotel & Suites
361 Queen St., Ottawa,
613-238-6000, 888-890-3222;
www.deltahotels.com

131

ONTARIO

328 rooms. Two restaurants, one bar. Children's activity center. Pets accepted, fee. Pool. Busn. Center. **$**

★★Lord Elgin Hotel

100 Elgin St., Ottawa, 613-235-3333, 888-268-1113; www.lordelginhotel.ca

357 rooms. Restaurant, two bars. Originally opened in 1941; completely renovated. Pets accepted, fee. Pool. **$**

★★★Hilton Lac-Leamy

3 Blvd. Du Casino, Hull, 819-790-6444; www.hiltonlacleamy.com

Located on the shore of Lake Leamy and Des Carrieres Lake, connected to a casino, close to Gatineau's shopping district and right outside of an all-season walking/biking trail, this hotel has something for everyone. Various dining options abound with the french styled bistro, Le Cellier, or a fine dining experience at Le Baccara.

349 rooms, 20 story. Restaurant, bar. Pool. Busn. Center. **$$**

★★★Marriott Ottawa

100 Kent St., Ottawa, 613-238-1122, 800-853-8463; www.ottawamarriott.com

Located in the heart of downtown, the hotel is close to local attractions such as Canada's Parliament Buildings, the Rideau Canal, the Ottawa Congress Centre and the National Gallery of Canada. Enjoy a panoramic view of the city with your meal at the Merlot Rooftop Grill, a revolving restaurant.

480 rooms. Two restaurants, one bar. Children's activity center. Pets accepted, fee. Pool. Busn. Center. **$**

★★★Minto Place Suite Hotel.

433 Laurier Ave. W., Ottawa, 613-232-2200, 800-556-4638; www.mintohotel.com

The conveniences of this city hotel are enjoyed both onsite and off in Canada's capital city. Outside its doors, explore Parliament Hill, Casino Lac-Leamy and the Historic Byward Market. Inside, guests dine, shop, bank and pamper themselves.

417 rooms, all suites. Two restaurants, two bars. Swim. **$$$**

★★★The Fairmont Chateau Laurier

1 Rideau St., Ottawa, 613-241-1414, 800-441-1414; www.fairmont.com

This impressive castle enchants visitors with its setting overlooking Parliament Hill, the Rideau Canal and the Ottawa River. It is conveniently located in the city center. Enjoy elegant dining at Wilfrid's, while Zoe's Lounge is a more casual alternative. Guest services include a full-service fitness club with a stunning Art Deco pool.

429 rooms. Restaurant, bar. Pets accepted, fee. Pool. Busn. Center. **$$**

★★★The Westin Ottawa

11 Colonel By Dr., Ottawa, 613-560-7000, 800-937-8461; www.westin.com

Located only blocks from Parliament Hill and the historic Byward Market, this hotel is connected to the Rideau Center Shopping Complex and the Ottawa Congress Center.

487 rooms. Three restaurants, one bar. Pets accepted, fee. Pool. Busn. Center. **$$**

★★★The Fairmont Le Chateau Montebello

392 rue Notre Dame, Montebello, 819-423-6341, 800-441-1414; www.fairmont.com

Stretched out along the banks of the Ottawa River, this log cabin-style lodge charms with spectacular scenery. From hiking, biking and boating, the recreational pursuits offered here are endless. Sybaritic-minded visitors enjoy the pampering treatments at the spa, while gastronomes savor the cuisine at the resort's dining rooms.

210 rooms. Restaurant, bar. Children's activity center. Pets accepted, fee. Pool. Golf. Tennis. Busn. Center. **$$**

★★★Gasthaus Switzerland Inn

89 Daly Ave., Ottawa, 613-237-0335; www.ottawainn.com

This charming inn is located in a restored 1872 house. Enjoy traditional Swiss hospitality during a visit to Canada's capital. 22 rooms. Children over 12 years only. Complimentary full breakfast. Restaurant. $

RESTAURANTS

★★★Domus Cafe
87 Murray St., Ottawa, 613-241-6007; www.domuscafe.ca
For years, this was a simple cafe adjacent to the cooking store of the same name. It was recently bought by chef John Taylor. The cafe offers innovative combinations of local and international flavors.
French bistro menu. Reservations recommended. $$$

★★La Gondola
188 Bank St., Ottawa, 613-235-3733.
Italian menu. Reservations recommended. Outdoor seating. $$

★★Sitar
417 Rideau St., Ottawa, 613-789-7979.
Indian menu. Reservations recommended. $$

★★The Mill
555 Ottawa River Pkwy., Ottawa, 613-237-1311; www.the-mill.ca
Steak menu. Reservations recommended. Outdoor seating. $$$

SARNIA

Sarnia, located in the center of one of Canada's most popular recreation areas, is noted for its breathtaking sky blue water and beautiful waterfront parks. Lake Huron offers beaches from Canatara Park to nearby Lambton County beaches; the St. Clair River flows south of Sarnia into Lake St. Clair. Facilities for water sports and boating are excellent. The city and surrounding area have many golf courses, campsites and trailer parks. Easy access to the U.S. is provided by the International Blue Water Bridge (toll) spanning the St. Clair River between Sarnia and Port Huron, Mich.
Information: www.sarnia.com

WHAT TO SEE AND DO

Canatara Park
Cathcart Blvd. and N. Christina St., Sarnia, 800-265-0316
Information center housed in reconstructed 19th-century log cabin Victoria Day weekend-Labour Day weekend, Monday-Friday afternoons; rest of year, weekends.. Facilities for swimming, beach and bathhouse; picnicking, barbecuing, refreshments, lookout tower, fitness trail, natural area, toboggan hill, playground equipment and ball diamond.

Children's Animal Farm
Cathcart Blvd. and N. Cristina St., Sarnia, 519-332-0330; www.childrensanimalfarm.com
Farm buildings; animals, poultry and waterfowl.

Log Cabin
Cathcart Blvd. and N. Cristina St., Sarnia, Canatara Park
Two-floor cabin with natural wooden peg flooring, two fireplaces; interpretive programs featured in summer. Adjacent are carriage shed with farm implement artifacts from 1850 and a smokehouse.

Gardens
Germain Park, East St., Sarnia, 519-332-0330
Wide variety of plant life. The park also offers facilities for swimming fee.; tennis, lawn bowling, horseshoes, baseball and soccer.

Lambton Heritage Museum
10035 Museum Rd., Grand Bend, 519-243-2600
Features more than 400 Currier & Ives prints, Canada's largest collection of antique

★
★
★
☆
☆

pressed-glass water pitchers; two farm machinery barns; slaughterhouse, chapel and main exhibit center with a chronological natural and human history of Lambton County.

Moore Museum
94 Moore Line, Mooretown, 519-867-2020
Country store, early switchboard, late-1800s church organ in main building; Victorian cottage; log cabin; farm implements; one-room schoolhouse; 1890 lighthouse.

Oil Museum of Canada
2423 Kelly Rd., Sarnia, 519-834-2840
On the site of the first commercialized oil well in North America; historic items and data regarding the discovery. Six acres 2 1/2 hectares. of landscaped grounds with blacksmith shop, pioneer home and post office; train station, working oil field using 1860 methods.

Sombra Township Museum
3470 St. Clair Pkwy., Sarnia, 519-892-3982
Pioneer home with displays of household goods, clothes, books and deeds, marine artifacts, indigenous and military items, music boxes, photographic equipment and farming tools. June-September: afternoons; May: weekends; also by appointment.

SPECIAL EVENTS
Celebration of Lights
Front St. N. and Exmouth St., Sarnia, 800-265-0316; www.celebrationoflights.com
Seven-week festive season featuring 60,000 lights in waterfront park. Residential, commercial displays. Late November-December.

Sarnia Highland Games
Centennial Park, Front St. N. and Exmouth St., Sarnia, 519-542-5543; www.sarniahighlandgames.com
Caber and hammer tossing, stone throwing, haggis hurling, clan village, bands, dancers. Mid-August.

HOTELS
★Comfort Inn
815 Mara St., Sarnia, 519-383-6767, 800-228-5150; www.choicehotels.ca
100 rooms. Complimentary continental breakfast, children's activity center. Exercise. Busn. Center. **$**

★★Drawbridge Inn
283 N. Christina St., Sarnia, 519-337-7571, 800-663-0376.
95 rooms. Restaurant, bar. Pets accepted, fee. Exercise. Pool. **$**

★Holiday Inn
1498 Venetian Blvd., Sarnia, 519-336-4130; www.holiday-inn.com
151 rooms. Restaurant, bar. Pets accepted, fee. Pool. **$**

SAULT STE. MARIE
Founded and built on steel, Sault Ste. Marie is separated from its sister city in Michigan by the St. Mary's River. Lake and ocean freighters traverse the river, which links Lake Huron and Lake Superior. Activities are a testament both to a rowdy history and modern sensibility—enjoy canyon train tours, casinos, skiing, golf, canal lock tours, fantastic shopping, bushplane rides, art galleries, boisterous carnivals and relaxing boat cruises.
Information: www.ssmcoc.com

WHAT TO SEE AND DO
Agawa Canyon Train Excursion
Sault Ste. Marie, 705-946-7300, 800-242-9287; www.agawacanyontourtrain.com
A scenic day trip by Algoma Central Railway through a wilderness of hills and fjord like ravines. Two-hour stopover at the canyon. Dining car on train. June-mid-October: daily; January-March: weekends only.

Boat Cruises
65 Foster Dr., Sault Ste. Marie, 705-253-9850

Two-hour boat cruises from Norgoma dock, next to Holiday Inn on MV Chief Shingwauk and MV Bon Soo through American locks; also three-hour dinner cruises. June-mid-October.

Sault Ste. Marie Museum
690 Queen St., Sault Ste. Marie,
705-759-7278; www.saultmuseum.com
Local and national exhibits in a structure originally built as a post office. Skylight Gallery traces history of the region dating back 9,000 years; includes prehistoric artifacts, displays of early industries, re-creation of 1912 Queen Street house interiors. Durham Gallery displays traveling exhibits from the Royal Ontario Museum and locally curated displays. Discovery Gallery for children features hands-on exhibits.

SPECIAL EVENTS
Algoma Fall Festival
Algoma Festival Office, 224 Queen St. E., Sault Ste. Marie, 705-949-0822;
www.algomafallfestival.com
Visual and performing arts presentations by Canadian and international artists. Late September-late October.

Ontario Winter Carnival Bon Soo
269 Queen St. E., Sault Ste. Marie, 705-759-3000; www.bonsoo.on.ca

Features more than 100 events: fireworks, fiddle contest, winter sports, polar bear swim, winter playground sculptured from snow. Last weekend in January-first weekend in February.

HOTELS
★★Algoma's Water Tower Inn
360 Great Northern Rd., Sault Ste. Marie, 705-949-8111, 800-461-0800;
www.watertowerinn.com
180 rooms. Restaurant, bar. Pets accepted, fee. Pool. $

★★Holiday Inn
208 St. Mary's River Dr., Sault Ste. Marie, 705-949-0611, 888-713-8482;
www.holiday-inn.com
195 rooms, 9 story. Restaurant, bar. Pets accepted, fee. Exercise. Pool. $

RESTAURANTS
★Giovanni's
516 Great Northern Rd., Sault Ste. Marie, 705-942-3050;
www.giovannisfamilyrestaurant.com
Italian menu. $$

★★New Marconi
480 Albert St. W., Sault Ste. Marie, 705-759-8250.
American, Italian menu. $$$

135

ONTARIO

ST. CATHARINES
St. Catharines, "the Garden City of Canada," is located in the heart of the wine country and the Niagara fruit belt, which produces half of the province's output of fresh fruit. Originally a Loyalist settlement, it was also a depot of the Underground Railroad, which smuggled American slaves from southern plantations to freedom in Canada. Located on the Welland Ship Canal in North America St. Catharines was also the home of the first electric streetcar system in North America and is highlighted by a plethora of boats, beaches, world-class rowing, tree-lined streets and gardens and diverse festivals.
Information: www.stcatharines.ca/tourism/index.asp

WHAT TO SEE AND DO
Farmers' Market
50 Church St., St. Catharines,
905-688-5601
Large variety of fruit and vegetables from fruit belt farms of the surrounding area. Tuesday, Thursday, Saturday.

Happy Rolph Bird Sanctuary & Children's Farm
Reed Rd., St. Catharines,
905-937-7210
Feeding station for native fowl and farm animals; three ponds; nature trail,

picnicking, playground. Victoria Day-Thanksgiving.

Morningstar Mill
2710 DeCew Rd., St. Catharines.
at De Cew Falls, 905-688-6050.
Waterpowered, fine old mill containing rollers and millstones for grinding flour and feed. Picnic area. Victoria Day weekend-Thanksgiving weekend.

Old Port Dalhousie
Ontario St. and Lakeport Rd., St. Catharines,
Ontario St., N. of QEW to Lakeport Rd.,
905-935-7555
An 18th-century harbor front village, once the northern terminus of the first three Welland Ship Canals; now part of a larger recreation area with handcrafted wooden carousel, restaurants and shops.

Rodman Hall Arts Centre
109 St. Paul Crescent, St. Catharines,
905-684-2925
Art exhibitions, films, concerts, children's theater. Tuesday-Sunday; closed holidays.

Welland Canal Viewing Complex at Lock III
1932 Government Rd., St. Catharines,
via Queen Elizabeth Way exit at
Glendale Ave. to Canal Rd. then N.
905-688-5601
Unique view of lock operations from an elevated platform. Ships from more than 50 countries can be seen as they pass through the canal. Arrival times are posted.

St. Catharines Museum
1932 Government Rd., St. Catharines,
905-984-8880.
Illustrates development, construction and significance of Welland Canal; working scale model lock; displays on history of St. Catharines. Exhibitions on loan from major museums.

SPECIAL EVENTS
Can-Am Soapbox Derby
Jaycee Park, St. Catharines,
QEW N., exit Ontario St.,
More than 100 competitors from U.S. and Canada. June.

Folk Arts Festival
85 Church St., St. Catharines,
905-685-6589
Folk Art Multicultural Centre. Open houses at ethnic clubs, concerts, ethnic dancing and singing. Art and craft exhibits; big parade. Two weeks in late May.

Niagara Grape and Wine Festival
8 Church St. #100, St. Catharines,
905-688-2570
Wine and cheese parties, athletic events, grape stomping, arts and crafts, ethnic concerts and parade with bands and floats to honor ripening of the grapes. Grand Parade last Saturday of festival. Ten days in late September.

Niagara Symphony Association
73 Ontario St., Unit 104, St. Catharines,
905-687-4993
Professional symphony orchestra; amateur chorus; summer music camp. September-May.

Royal Canadian Henley Regatta
Henley Rowing Course, 61 Main,
St. Catharines, 905-935-9771;
www.henleyregatta.ca
Champion rowers from all parts of the world. Second in size only to the famous English regatta. Several nation- and continent-wide regattas take place on this world-famous course. April-October.

Salmon Derby
Lighthouse and Lake Shore Roads,
St. Catharines, 905-935-6700
Open season on Lake Ontario for coho and chinook salmon; rainbow, brown and lake trout. Prizes for all categories. Mid-April-mid-May.

ONTARIO

HOTELS

★★Four Points by Sheraton
3530 Schmon Pkwy., Thorold,
905-984-8484, 877-848-3782;
www.fourpointsuites.com
129 rooms. Restaurant, bar. Pets accepted, fee. Pool. Busn. Center. **$**

★★Holiday Inn
2 N. Service Rd., St. Catharines,
905-934-8000, 877-688-2324;
www.stcatharines.holiday-inn.com
140 rooms. Restaurant, bar. Pets accepted, fee. Pool. **$**

★★Quality Inn
327 Ontario St., St. Catharines,
905-688-2324;
www.qualityparkway.com
125 rooms. Restaurant, bar. Pets accepted, fee. Pool. **$**

STRATFORD

The names Stratford and Avon River can conjure up only one name—Shakespeare. And that is exactly what you will find in this lovely city. World-renowned, this festival of fine theater takes place here every year. For a relatively small town, Stratford offers up a wonderful variety of shows, concerts, plays, art galleries and spas—ideal for a weekend escape, and sealed with plentiful gardens and a Victorian city core.
Information: www.welcometostratford.com

WHAT TO SEE AND DO

Confederation Park
52 Romeo St. N., Stratford,
519-273-3352.
Features rock hill, waterfall, fountain, Japanese garden and commemorative court.

Gallery of Stratford
54 Romeo St. N., Stratford,
519-271-5271
Public gallery in parkland setting; historical and contemporary works. Guided tours on request.

Shakespearean Gardens
Huron St., Stratford,
519-271-5140
Fragrant herbs, shrubs and flowering plants common to William Shakespeare's time.

SPECIAL EVENTS

Kinsmen Antique Show
Stratford Arena, 15 Morenz, Stratford,
519-271-2161
Late July-August.

Stratford Festival
55 Queen St., Stratford,
519-273-1600, 800-567-1600
Contemporary, classical and Shakespearean dramas and modern musicals. Performances at Festival, Avon and Tom Patterson theaters. May-November, matinees and evenings.

HOTELS

★★Festival Inn
1144 Ontario St., Stratford,
519-273-1150, 800-463-3581;
www.festivalinnstratford.com
182 rooms. Restaurant, bar. Pool. **$**

★★★Queen's Inn
161 Ontario St., Stratford,
519-271-1400; www.queensinnstratford.ca
This lovely Victorian inn is located on the main street of downtown, close to a variety of shops and restaurants. It features uniquely decorated rooms that give the guest a home-away-from-home feel.
32 rooms. Two restaurants. Pets accepted, fee. **$**

★Stratford Suburban
2808 Ontario St. E., Stratford,
519-271-9650;
www.suburbanmotel.com
25 rooms. Pool. Tennis. **$**

ONTARIO

★
★
★
★
★

★★★Touchstone Manor

325 St. David St., Stratford,
519-273-5820;
www.touchstone-manor.com

This 1938 inn is located in a quiet, residential neighborhood within walking distance of downtown and about a 1/2 hour walk to the Shakespeare Festival area.
4 rooms. Closed late December-late January. Children over 12 years only. Complimentary full breakfast. **$$$**

★★Victorian Inn

10 Romeo St. N., Stratford,
519-271-4650, 800-741-2135;
www.victorian-inn.on.ca
115 rooms. Restaurant. Pool. **$**

RESTAURANTS
★★★Carters

116 Downie St., Stratford, 519-271-9200 ;
www.carters-on-downie.com/restaurant/
This restaurant is located in downtown Stratford, just a few blocks off the square, so it's a great place to stop for a bite while shopping. The cuisine is French with a contemporary twist. There is a warm, intimate feel with fireplaces.
French menu. Lunch, dinner. Closed Monday; also January. Business casual attire. Reservations recommended.

★★★Church Restaurant and the Belfry

70 Brunswick St., Stratford, 519-273-3424;
www.churchrestaurant.com
Housed in a 19th-century 1874. Gothic church, the facade and the interior decor painted walls, wooden arches and stained glass windows. showcase opulent French meals. The restaurant is located behind several of the festival theaters. For three weeks in summer, the restaurant offers cabaret performances.
French menu. Reservations recommended. **$$$**

★★Keystone Alley Cafe

34 Brunswick St., Stratford,
519-271-5645;
www.keystonealley.com
Closed Sunday-Monday; two weeks in March. Reservations recommended. Outdoor seating. **$$$**

★House of Gene

108 Downie St., Stratford,
519-271-3080
Chinese menu. **$$**

★Madelyn's Diner

377 Huron St., Stratford,
519-273-5296
American diner. **$$**

★★Old Prune

151 Albert St., Stratford, 519-271-5052;
www.cyg.net/~oldprune
Restored Edwardian residence; enclosed garden terrace. Closed Monday; November-mid-April. **$$$**

★★★Rundle's

9 Cobourg St., Stratford,
519-271-6442;
www.rundlesrestaurant.com
Located on the river at ground zero for the Stratford Festival, this longtime favorite affords the most elegant dining in the area. Like the environment, the chef's food is simple, elegant and thoroughly enjoyable.
American menu. Outdoor seating. **$$$$**

THUNDER BAY

Thanks to its prime location on Lake Superior, Thunder Bay is a major grain shipping port with a colorful history tied to the fur trade of the early 19th century. The town's Fort William, inland headquarters for the trade, relives the glory of Canada's wilder days. History aside, Thunder Bay offers skiing, parks and a home base for explorations around Lake Superior.
Information: www.visitthunderbay.com

138

ONTARIO

WHAT TO SEE AND DO

Amethyst Mine Panorama
400 Victoria Ave., Thunder Bay. 35 miles/56 kilometers N.E., 5 miles/8 kilometers off Hwy. 11/17 on E. Loon Rd.,
807-622-6908
Open-pit quarry adjacent to Elbow Lake. The quarrying operation, geological faults, Canadian Pre-Cambrian shield and sample gem pockets are readily visible. Gem picking.

Centennial Conservatory
1101 Dease St., Thunder Bay,
807-622-7036
Wide variety of plant life, including banana plants, palm trees and cacti.

Centennial Park
Centennial Park Rd. and Hudson Ave., Thunder Bay, Near Boulevard Lake,
807-683-6511
Summer features include a reconstructed 1910 logging camp; logging camp museum. Playground. Cross-country skiing; sleigh rides in winter.

International Friendship Gardens
2000 Victoria Ave., Thunder Bay,
807-625-3166
Park is composed of individual gardens designed and constructed by various ethnic groups including Slovakian, Polish, German, Italian, Finnish, Danish, Ukranian, Hungarian and Chinese.

Kakabeka Falls Provincial Park
Thunder Bay,
20 miles/32 kilometers W. via Hwy. 11/17,
807-473-9231
A spectacular waterfall on the historic Kaministiquia River, formerly a voyageur route from Montréal to the West. The 128-foot 39-meter. falls can be seen from highway stop. The flow of water is best in spring and on weekends; the flow is reduced during the week. There's a sand beach in the park, plus hiking and interpretive trails, areas for camping, a playground and a visitor service center.

Old Fort William
1 King Rd., Thunder Bay, Off Hwy. 61 S,
807-577-8461
Authentic reconstruction of the original Fort William as it was from 1803 to 1821. Visitors experience the adventure of the Nor'westers convergence for the Rendezvous re-creation staged 10 days in mid-July.. Costumed staff populate 42 buildings on the site, featuring trademens' shops, farm, apothecary, fur stores, warehouses, Great Hall, voyageur encampment, indigenous encampment; historic restaurant.

Quetico Provincial Park
Thunder Bay, 27 miles W. on Hwy. 11/17,
218-387-2075;
www.ontarioparks.com
Quetico is a wilderness park composed largely of rugged landscape. There are no roads in the park, but its vast network of connecting waterways allows for some of the best canoeing in North America. Fishing and swimming are the primary activities in the park. Appropriate fishing licenses are required. Car camping is permitted at 107 sites in two areas of the Dawson Trail Campgrounds. Permits can be obtained at park ranger stations. Picnic facilities, trails and a large assortment of pictographs may be enjoyed. In winter, vacationers can ice fish and cross-country ski, although there are no maintained facilities. Victoria Day weekend-Thanksgiving weekend: daily.

Thunder Bay Art Gallery
1080 Keewatin St., Thunder Bay,
on Confederation College Campus, use Harbor Expy. from Hwy. 11/17,
807-577-6427
Changing exhibitions from major national and international museums; regional art; contemporary native art. Tours, films, lectures, concerts.

ONTARIO

HOTELS

★Comfort Inn
660 W. Arthur St., Thunder Bay,
807-475-3155;
www.comfortinn.com
80 rooms. Pets accepted, fee. **$**

★★Golden Tulip Valhalla Inn Thunder Bay
1 Valhalla Inn Rd., Thunder Bay,
807-577-1121, 800-964-1121;
www.valhallainn.com
267 rooms. Restaurant, bar. Pets accepted, fee. Pool. **$$**

★★Prince Arthur
17 N. Cumberland, Thunder Bay,
807-345-5411;
www.princearthur.on.ca
121 rooms, 6 story. Restaurant, bar. Overlooks the harbor. Pets accepted, fee. Pool. **$**

★★Victoria Inn
555 W. Arthur St., Thunder Bay,
807-577-8481, 800-387-3331;
www.tbaytel.net/vicinn
182 rooms. Restaurant, bar. Indoor water slide. Pets accepted, fee. Pool. **$**

RESTAURANT

★★The Keg
735 Hewitson St., Thunder Bay,
807-623-1960;
www.kegsteakhouse.com
Seafood, steak menu. **$$$**

★
★
★
★
★

TORONTO

Toronto is one of Canada's leading industrial, commercial and cultural centers. Having earned its name from the native word for "meeting place," Toronto is an awesome cosmopolitan city—the United Nations recently deemed it the world's most ethnically diverse city. A performing arts powerhouse, the city presents everything from Broadway musicals to stand-up comedy and opera to dance. Good shopping can be found throughout the city, but Torontonians are most proud of their Underground City, a series of subterranean malls linking more than 300 shops

and restaurants in the downtown area. For professional sports fans, Toronto offers the Maple Leafs (hockey), Blue Jays (baseball), Raptors (basketball) and Argonauts (football). A visit to the harbor front, a boat tour to the islands, or enjoying an evening on the town should round out your stay.

Information: www.torontotourism.com

WHAT TO SEE AND DO

Allan Gardens
19 Horticultural Ave., Toronto,
416-392-7288.
Indoor/outdoor botanical displays, wading pool, picnicking, concerts.

Bata Shoe Museum
327 Bloor St. W., Toronto,
416-979-7799; www.batashoemuseum.ca
When Mrs. Sonja Bata's passion for collecting historical shoes began to surpass her personal storage space, the Bata family established The Bata Shoe Museum Foundation. Architect Raymond Moriyama's award-winning five-story, 3,900-square-foot 362-square-meter. building now holds more than 10,000 shoes, artfully arranged in four galleries to celebrate the style and function of footwear throughout 4,500 years of history. One permanent exhibition, "All About Shoes," showcases a collection of 20th-century celebrity shoes; artifacts on exhibit range from Chinese bound-foot shoes and ancient Egyptian sandals to chestnut-crushing clogs and Elton John's platforms.

Black Creek Pioneer Village
1000 Murray Ross Pkwy., Downsview,
2 miles/3 kilometers N. on Hwy. 400,
E. on Steeles, then 1/2 mile/1 kilometer
to Jane St., 416-736-1733
Step back in time with a visit to this village. Workers wearing period costumes welcome you into 35 authentically restored homes, workshops, public buildings and farms and demonstrate skills such as open-hearth cooking, bread-making, looming, milling, blacksmithing, sewing and printing.

Bloor/Yorkville area
Bounded by Bloor St. W. Ave. Rd.,
Davenport Rd. and Yonge St., Toronto;
www.bloor-yorkville.com
The Bloor/Yorkville area is one of Toronto's most elegant shopping and dining sections, with art galleries, nightclubs, music, designer couture boutiques and first-rate art galleries. The area itself is fun to walk around, with a cluster of courtyards and alleyways. There's also a contemporary park in the heart of the neighborhood with a huge piece of granite called The Rock. It was brought here from the Canadian Shield, a U-shaped region of ancient rock covering about half of Canada.

Bruce Trail/Toronto Bruce Trail Club
416-763-9061
Canada's first and longest footpath, the Bruce Trail runs 437 miles 703 kilometers. along the Niagara Escarpment from Niagara to the Bruce Peninsula. It provides the only public access to the Escarpment, a UNESCO World Biosphere Reserve.

Canada's Sports Hall of Fame
160 Princes' Blvd., Toronto, 416-260-6789;
www.cshof.ca
Erected to honor the country's greatest athletes in all major sports, Canada's Sports Hall of Fame features exhibit galleries, a theater, library, archives and kiosks that show videos of Canada's greatest moments in sports. Don't miss the Heritage Gallery lower level., which contains artifacts showcasing the development of 125 years of sport. Also stop in at the 50-seat Red Foster Theatre, which projects films clips that highlight Canadian sports, such as The Terry Fox Story.

Canadian Trophy Fishing
80 The Boardwalk Way, Suite 320,
Markham, 905-472-8000;
www.cdntrophyfishing.com
Canadian Trophy Fishing supplies the equipment, facilities, and fishing license for Chinook salmon which can weigh as much as 40 pounds., coho salmon, Atlantic salmon, rainbow trout, brown trout, lake trout or whitefish. They suggest you bring a large cooler to take home all of your catches, but for an extra fee they will smoke, fillet, freeze and ship. Ice fishing season is January-mid-March.

Casa Loma
1 Austin Terrace, Toronto,
416-923-1171; www.casaloma.org
Grab an audio cassette and a floor plan and take a self-guided tour of this domes-

141

ONTARIO

★
★
★
★
☆

tic castle, built in 1911 over three years at a cost of $3.5 million. As romantic as he was a shrewd businessman, Sir Henry Pellatt, who founded the Toronto Electric Light Company, had an architect create this medieval castle. Soaring battlements, secret passageways, flowerbeds warmed by steam pipes, secret doors, servants' rooms and an 800-foot 244-meter. tunnel are just some of the treats you'll discover.

Colborne Lodge

Colborne Lodge Dr. and The Queensway, Toronto, 416-392-6916;
www.city.toronto.on.ca/culture/colborne.htm
The successful 19th-century architect John Howard was just 34 when he completed this magnificent manor, named for the architect's first patron, Upper Canada Lieutenant Governor Sir John Colborne. It stands today as an excellent example of Regency-style architecture, with its stately verandas and lovely placement in a beautiful setting.

CN Tower

301 Front St. W., Toronto, 416-868-6937;
www.cntower.ca
Toronto's CN Tower is the tallest freestanding structure in the world. At 1,815 feet (553 meters). from the ground to the tip of its communications aerial, it towers over the rest of the city. Take the elevator to the top, where on a clear day it's said you can see the spray coming off Niagara Falls 62 miles (100 kilometers) away. Any level provides spectacular views.

Discovery Harbour

93 Jury Dr., Penetanguishene,
705-549-8064
Marine heritage center and reconstructed 19th-century British Naval dockyard. Established in 1817, the site includes a 19th-century military base. Now rebuilt, the site features eight furnished buildings and an orientation center. Replica of 49-foot 15-meter. British naval schooner, H.M.S. Bee; also H.M.S. Tecumseth and Perseverance. Costumed interpreters bring the base to life, circa 1830. Sail training and excursions.

Dragon City Shopping Mall

280 Spadina Ave., Toronto,
416-596-8885
Located in the heart of Chinatown, the Dragon City Shopping Mall consists of more than 30 stores and services. Buy Chinese herbs, look at Asian jewelry, browse chic Chinese housewares and gifts, or admire Oriental arts and crafts. Afterwards treat yourself to a meal at Sky Dragon Cuisine in the Dragon City tower, an upscale Chinese restaurant with a beautiful view of the Toronto skyline.

Easy and The Fifth

225 Richmond W., Toronto,
416-979-3000.
A dance club for the over-25 crowd, the music is tango to Top 40, the dress code is upscale casual and the atmosphere is loft-apartment-open, with two bars and several specialty bars such as The Green Room, where you can shoot pool, play craps and smoke a cigar to the accompaniment of live jazz.. On Thursday from 6-10 p.m., enjoy cocktail hour with a complimentary buffet. Thursday 6 p.m.-2 a.m.; Friday-Saturday from 9 p.m.

Eaton Centre

220 Yonge St., Toronto, 416-598-8560;
www.torontoeatoncentre.com
This 3 million-square-foot 278,709-square-meter. building is a masterpiece of architecture and environment. Its glass roof rises 127 feet 39 meters. above the mall's lowest level. The large, open space contains glass-enclosed elevators, dozens of long, graceful escalators and porthole windows. A flock of fiberglass Canadian geese floats through the air. Even if shopping isn't a favorite vacation activity, Eaton Centre is worth a trip.

Edwards Gardens

777 Lawrence Ave. E., Toronto,
416-392-8186.
Civic garden center; rock gardens, pools, pond, rustic bridges.

Elgin & Winter Garden Theatre Centre

189 Yonge St., Toronto, 416-872-5555

The 80-year history of the two theaters speaks more volumes than one of its excellent productions. Built in 1913, each theater was a masterpiece in its own right: The Elgin was ornate, with gold leaf, plaster cherubs and elegant opera boxes; the walls of the Winter Garden were hand-painted to resemble a garden and its ceiling was a mass of beech bows and twinkling lanterns. Through the years, the stages saw the likes of George Burns and Gracie Allen, Edger Bergen and Charlie McCarthy, Milton Berle and Sophie Tucker. The Ontario Heritage Foundation offers year-round guided tours on Thursdays at 5 p.m. and Saturdays at 11 a.m.

Exhibition Place
Lakeshore St., Toronto. S, off Gardener Expy, 416-393-6000
Designed to accommodate the Canadian National Exhibition, this 350-acre/141-hectare park has events year-round, as well as the Marine Museum of Upper Canada. August-September: daily.

George R. Gardiner Museum of Ceramic Art
111 Queen's Park, Toronto, 416-586-8080; www.gardinermuseum.on.ca
One of the world's finest collections of Italian majolica, English Delftware and 18th-century continental porcelain.

Gibson House
5172 Yonge St., North York, 416-395-7432
Home of land surveyor and local politician David Gibson; restored and furnished to 1850s style. Costumed interpreters conduct demonstrations.

Grange Park
Dundas and Beverly Sts., Toronto
Wading pool, playground. Ice rink winter, weather permitting..

Harbourfront Centre
235 Queens Quay W., Toronto, 416-973-3000; www.harbourfront.on.ca

This 10-acre 4-hectare. waterfront community is alive with theater, dance, films, art shows, music, crafts and children's programs. Most events are free. Daily.

High Park
1873 Bloor St. W. and Keele St., Toronto, 416-392-1111
High Park is an urban oasis with expansive fields for sports, picnicking and cycling; a large lake that freezes in the winter; a small zoo, swimming pool, tennis courts and bowling greens.

Historic Fort York
100 Garrison Rd., Toronto, 416-392-6907; www.city.toronto.on.ca/culture/fort_york.htm
It may not have seen a lot of action—just one battle during the War of 1812—but Fort York's place in Toronto's history is secure. It is the birthplace of modern Toronto, having played a major role in saving York now Toronto. from being invaded by 1,700 American soldiers. Today's Fort York has Canada's largest collection of original War of 1812 buildings and is a designated National Historic Site.

Hummingbird Centre for the Performing Arts
1 Front St. E., Toronto, 416-393-7469; www.hummingbirdcentre.com
Stage presentations of Broadway musicals, dramas and concerts by international artists. Home of the Canadian Opera Company and National Ballet of Canada. Pre-performance dining.

Huronia Historical Parks
Toronto, 705-526-7838.
Two living history sites animated by costumed interpreters.

Ice Skating at Grenadier Pond
1873 Bloor St., 416-392-6916.
One of the most romantic ice skating spots you'll find is Grenadier Pond in High Park, one of 25 parks offering free artificial rinks throughout the city. In addition to vendors selling roasted chestnuts,

143

ONTARIO

★
★
★
★

there's a bonfire to keep toasty. Other free ice rinks include Nathan Phillips Square in front of City Hall and an area at Harbor front Centre. Equipment rentals are available on site.

Kensington Market
College St. and Spadina Ave., Toronto,
This maze of narrow streets is lined with food shops, vintage clothing stores, restaurants and jewelry vendors. There are bargain hunters haggling, Cafe owners enticing diners and little stores brimming with items from Asia, South America, the Middle East and Europe.

Kortright Centre for Conservation
9550 Pine Valley Dr., Woodbridge,
905-832-2289
Environmental center with trails, beehouse, maple syrup shack, wildlife pond and plantings. Naturalist-guided hikes. Cross-country skiing no rentals.; picnic area, Cafe; indoor exhibits and theater.

Little Italy
W. of Bathurst St. between Euclid Ave. and Shaw St., Toronto;
www.torontotourism.com
After the British, Italians make up the largest cultural group in Toronto. Though the Italian community moved north as it grew, the atmosphere of Little Italy remains. Restaurants and bars open onto the sidewalks.

Lorraine Kimsa Theatre for Young People
165 Front St. E., Toronto, 416-862-2222;
www.lktyp.ca
Professional productions for the entire family. October-May: Saturday-Sunday.

Mackenzie House
82 Bond St., Toronto, 416-392-6915
Restored 19th-century home of William Lyon Mackenzie, first mayor of Toronto; furnishings and artifacts of the 1850s; 1840s print shop.

Market Gallery
95 Front St. E., Toronto, 416-392-7604
Exhibition center for Toronto Archives; displays on city's historical, social and cultural heritage; art, photographs, maps, documents and artifacts. Wednesday-Saturday, Sunday afternoons.

Martin Goodman Trail
Toronto, 416-392-8186;
www.city.toronto.on.ca/parks
Leave it to fitness-conscious Toronto not just to have a beautifully maintained waterfront, but to build a trail that takes you from one end to the other. The Martin Goodman Trail is a public jogging, biking, walking and in-line skating path that connects all the elements of the waterfront, traversing 13 miles (21 kilometers). It also runs past several spots for bike and skate rentals.

McMichael Canadian Art Collection
10365 Islington Ave., Kleinburg,
905-893-1121; www.mcmichael.com
Works by Canada's most famous artists— the Group of Seven, Tom Thomson, Emily Carr, David Milne, Clarence Gagnon and others. Also Inuit and contemporary indigenous art and sculpture. Restaurant, book, gift shop. Constructed from hand-hewn timbers and native stone, the gallery stands in 100 acres 40 hectares. on the crest of Humber Valley; nature trail.

Medieval Times
Exhibition Place, Dufferin Gate, Toronto,
416-260-1234; www.medievaltimes.com
This 11th-century castle was created to replicate an 11th-century experience, complete with knightly competitions and equestrian displays.

Mount Pleasant Cemetery
375 Mount Pleasant Rd., Toronto,
416-485-9129;
www.mountpleasantgroupofcemeteries.ca
One of the oldest cemeteries in North America, the Mount Pleasant Cemetery is the final resting place of many well-known Canadians, including Sir Frederic Banting and Charles Best, the discoverers of insulin; renowned classical pianist Glenn Gould; and Prime Minister William Lyon Mackenzie King, who led Canada through World

★
★
★
★
★

War II. The grounds hold rare plants and shrubs as well as a Memorial Peony Garden. Its many paths are used frequently by walkers and cyclists and who want a few quiet moments.

Ontario Parliament Buildings
Queen's Park, 111 Wellesley St. W., Toronto, 416-325-7500
Guided tours of the Legislature Building and walking tour of grounds. Gardens; art collection; historic displays.

Ontario Place
955 Lakeshore Blvd. W., Toronto, 416-314-9811; www.ontarioplace.com
A 96-acre 39-hectare. cultural, recreational and entertainment complex on three artificial islands in Lake Ontario. Includes an outdoor amphitheater for concerts, two pavilions with multimedia presentations, Cinesphere theater with IMAX films year-round; fee.; children's village. Three villages of snack bars, restaurants and pubs; miniature golf; lagoons, canals, two marinas; 370-foot (113-meter). water slide, showboat, pedal and bumper boats; Wilderness Adventure Ride. Mid-May-early September.

Ontario Science Centre
770 Don Mills Rd., Toronto, 416-696-1000; www.ontariosciencecentre.ca
Ten huge exhibition halls in three linked pavilions are filled with exhibits on space and technology. Stand at the edge of a black hole, watch bees making honey, test your reflexes, heart rate or grip strength, use pedal power to light lights or raise a balloon, hold hands with a robot, or land a spaceship on the moon. Throughout the museum there are slide shows and films that demonstrate various aspects of science and two Omnimax theaters show larger-than-life films.

Parachute School of Toronto
Baldwin Airport, 5714 Smith Blvd., 800-361-5867; www.parachuteschool.com
For the ultimate in memorable vacation experiences, morning instruction is followed by an afternoon jump.

Paramount Canada's Wonderland
9580 Jane St., Vaughan, 905-832-8131; www.canadaswonderland.com
This 300-acre (121-hectare) theme park is situated 30 minutes outside Toronto and features more than 140 attractions including a 20-acre 8-hectare. water park, live shows and more than 50 rides. Specialties among the rides are the parks roller coasters, from creaky old-fashioned wooden ones to "The Fly," a roller coaster designed to make every seat feel as if it's the front car.

Pier: Toronto's Waterfront Museum
245 Queen's Quay W., Toronto.
Original 1930s pier building on Toronto's celebrated waterfront includes two floors of hands-on interactive displays, rare historical artifacts, re-creations of marine history stories, art gallery, boat-building center, narrated walking excursions, children's programs. March-October: daily.

Queen's Park
College and University, Toronto, Queen's Park Crescent, 416-325-7500
Ontario Parliament Buildings are located in this park.

Queen Street West
From University Ave. to Bathurst St., Toronto
Come to Queen West for vintage clothing stores, trendy home furnishings, hip styles that used to be original grunge and street vendor bohemia, as well as the handiwork of many up-and-coming fashion designers. In between the boutiques are antique stores, used bookstores and terrific bistros and cafes.

Riverdale Park
Broadway Ave., Toronto, 416-392-1111
Summer: swimming, wading pools; tennis, playgrounds, picnicking, band concerts. Winter: skating; 19th-century farm.

Rivoli
334 Queen St. W., Toronto, 416-596-1908; www.rivoli.ca

★
★
★
★

This offbeat, artsy performance club opened in 1982 on the site of Toronto's 1920s Rivoli Vaudeville Theatre. The focus is on eclectic and cutting-edge music and performances and includes everything from grunge and rock to poetry readings and comedy. The Indigo Girls, Tory Amos and Michelle Shocked all made their Toronto debuts here. Don't forget to check out the 5,000-square-foot 465-square-meter. pool hall with 13 vintage tables, including an 1870s Brunswick Aviator and a 1960s futuristic AMF seen in the Elvis movie "Viva Las Vegas."

Rogers Centre

1 Blue Jays Way, Toronto,
416-341-2770; www.rogerscentre.com
Home of Toronto Blue Jays MLB. and Argonauts CFL..

Royal Ontario Museum

100 Queen's Park, Toronto,
416-586-5549; www.rom.on.ca
When the ROM opened its doors to the public in 1914, its mission was to inspire wonder and build understanding of human cultures and the natural world. And its collections in archaeology, geology, genealogy, paleontology and sociology have moved in that direction ever since. One of the most-visited galleries is the Nubia Gallery, built in 1998 after a ROM team discovered a new archaeological culture in the Upper Nubia region of Northern Sudan, unearthing the remains of a settlement dating to 1000-800 B.C. The discovery has been officially recognized by UNESCO as "Canada's contribution to the United Nations' Decade for Cultural Development."

Second City

51 Mercer St., Toronto, 416-343-0011;
www.secondcity.com
The Toronto branch of the famous Improv Club has turned out its own respectable list of veterans. Among those who have trained here are Gilda Radner, Mike Meyers, Martin Short, Ryan Stiles and dozens of others.

St. Lawrence Centre for the Arts

27 Front St. E., Toronto, 416-366-7723;
www.stlc.com
Performing arts complex features theater, music, dance, films and other public events.

St. Lawrence Market

92 Front St. E., Toronto, 416-329-7120;
www.stlawrencemarket.com
In 1803, Governor Peter Hunt designated an area of land to be market block. Today, the St. Lawrence Market provides a good snippet of the way Toronto used to be, with enough of the character of the original architecture to make you feel as though the old city were alive and well. The market itself, Toronto's largest indoor market, sells 14 different categories of foods, which include incredibly fresh seafood, poultry, meat, organic produce, baked goods, gourmet teas and coffees, plus fruit and flowers.

Spadina Historic House and Garden

285 Spadina Rd., Toronto, 416-392-6910
Built for financier James Austin and his family, this 50-room house has been restored to its 1866 Victorian glory and is open to those who want to see how the upper crust spent quiet evenings at home. It's filled with the family's art, artifacts and furniture and until 1982 it was filled with the family itself; that's when the last generation of Austins left and the house was turned over to public ownership. Docents tend to the glorious gardens and orchard, which are open to the public in the summer.

Ste.-Marie among the Hurons

E. of Midland on Hwy. 12
(1639-1649). Reconstruction of 17th-century Jesuit mission that was Ontario's first European community. Twenty-two furnished buildings include native dwellings, workshops, barn, church, cookhouse, hospital. Candlelight tours, canoe excursions. Cafe features period-inspired meals and snacks. Orientation center, interpretive museum. World-famous Martyrs' Shrine site of papal visit. is located across the highway. Other area highlights include pioneer museum, replica indigenous village, Wye Marsh Wildlife Centre.

146

ONTARIO

Taste of the World Neighborhood Bicycle Tours and Walks
416-923-6813;
www.torontowalksbikes.com
Equal parts fact and food, the tour walks visitors through a forgotten hanging square, a hidden gallery and a lost pillory site. The eats include East Indian treats with new twists, decadent offerings with Belgian chocolate, sandwich samples at Carousel Bakery and a spread at St. Urbain Bagel. On Sundays, a different tour focuses on the contributions of 200 years of immigrant activity in the Kensington market, exploring Jewish and East Indian snacks, Lebanese treats and, of course, chocolate truffles. The tour company suggests a light breakfast with the St. Lawrence Tour and no breakfast with the Kensington tour. Daily 9:30 a.m.-1 p.m..

Todmorden Mills Heritage Museum & Arts Centre
67 Pottery Rd., Toronto,
416-396-2819
Restored historic houses; Parshall Terry House 1797. and William Helliwell House 1820.. Also museum; restored 1899 train station.

Toronto Blue Jays MLB.
Rogers Centre, 1 Blue Jays Way, Toronto,
416-341-1000; www.bluejays.mlb.com
Professional baseball team.

Toronto Maple Leafs NHL.
Air Canada Centre, 40 Bay St., Toronto,
416-815-5700;
www.mapleleafs.com
Professional hockey team.

Toronto Music Garden
475 Queen's Quay W., Toronto,
416-973-3000;
www.city.toronto.on.ca/parks/
music_index.htm
In the mid-1990s, internationally renowned cellist Yo-Yo Ma worked with several other artists to produce a six-part film series inspired by the work of Johann Sebastian Bach's "Suites for Unaccompanied Cello." The first film was entitled The Music Garden and used nature to interpret the music of Bach's first suite. Toronto was approached to create an actual garden based on The Music Garden and the result—Toronto Music Garden—now graces the waterfront, a symphony of swirls and curves and wandering trails. In the summertime, free concerts are given. Tours are offered, with a guide or self-guided with a hand-held audiotape.

Toronto Island Park
9 Queens Quay, Toronto, S. across Inner Harbor, 416-392-8186
Just seven minutes by ferry from Toronto lie 14 beautiful islands ripe for exploration. Centre Island is the busiest, and home to Centreville, an old-fashioned amusement park with an authentic 1890s carousel, flume ride, turn-of-the-century village complete with a Main Street, tiny shops, firehouse and even a small, working farm. Alternately, all the islands are great for bike-based exploration rentals available. with 612 acres/248 hectares of park and shaded paths.

Toronto Raptors NBA.
Air Canada Centre, 40 Bay St., Ste. 400, Toronto,
416-366-3865;
www.raptors.com
Professional basketball team.

Toronto Stock Exchange
130 King St. W., Toronto,
416-947-4676; www.tsx.com
The Stock Market Place visitor center has multimedia displays, interactive games and archival exhibits to aid visitors in understanding the market.

Toronto Symphony
60 Simcoe St., Toronto,
416-593-4828; www.tso.ca
Classical, pops and children's programs; Great Performers series. Wheelchair seating, audio enhancement for the hearing impaired.

Toronto Tours Ltd.
145 Queens Quay W., Toronto,
416-869-1372;

147

ONTARIO

★
★
★
★
★

www.torontotours.com

Four different boat tours of Toronto Harbor.

Toronto Zoo

361A Old Finch Ave., Scarborough,
N. of Hwy. 401 on Meadowvale Rd.,
416-392-5900;
www.torontozoo.com

There are more than 5,000 animals representing over 450 species at the Toronto Zoo. Well-designed and laid out, four large tropical indoor pavilions and several smaller indoor viewing areas, plus numerous outdoor exhibits compose 710 acres 287 hectares. of zoo geographic regions, which can be explored on six miles 9.6 kilometers. of walking trails. When you're tired of walking, sit down for a refreshment, or take a ride on a pony, camel, or a safari simulator.

Waddington McLean & Company

111 Bathurst St., Toronto,
416-504-9100

The largest and oldest auction house in Canada, Waddington's professional services have stayed the same for more than 150 years. They do appraisals, consultation and valuation. But the real fun comes every Wednesday, when the Canadian-owned house holds weekly estate/household auctions. Twice a year, in spring and fall, they host a fine art auction with catalogued items up for bid.

Woodbine Racetrack

555 Rexdale Blvd., Rexdale, 416-675-7223;
www.woodbineentertainment.com

The only track in North America that can offer both standard-bred and thoroughbred racing on the same day, Woodbine is home to Canada's most important race course events. It hosts the $1 million Queens Plate, North Americas oldest continuously run stakes race; the $1 million ATTO; the $1.5 million Canadian International and the $1 million North America Cup for Standard-breds. It also has an outstanding grass course; it was here, in 1973, that Secretariat bid farewell to racing with his win of the grass championship. Woodbine has 1,700

slot machines and many different dining options for those times when you might need intake instead of outgo.

SPECIAL EVENTS

Beaches International Jazz Festival

Queen St. E., Toronto, 416-698-2152;
www.beachesjazz.com

For four days every summer since 1989, the Beaches community of Toronto has resonated with the sound of world-class jazz at the Beaches International Jazz Festival, a musical wonder that attracts nearly 1 million people to the water's edge. More than 40 bands play nightly, with over 700 musicians casting their spell over a crowd that includes children waving glow sticks, toe-tapping seniors and just about everyone in between. In addition to international artists with a focus on Canadians., the Festival also serves as a springboard for talented amateurs. Mid-late July.

Bloor Yorkville Wine Festival

Events held throughout the city;
www.santewinefestival.net

In the late 1990s, three separate organizations, among them the Wine Council of Ontario, began a festival that has grown to include more than 70 wineries from 11 countries. Activities include five days of international wine tasting, dinners, parties and discussions that are held at various restaurants, bars and hotels all over town. There is a strong educational element to the festival, with seminars held throughout the week. If you're truly a wine aficionado you'll definitely want to wait until Saturday, the last day of the festival, which includes eight specially designed wine- and food-related seminars. And if you're a novice, sign up for the Pre-Tasting Seminar to learn how to swish, sip and savor like the pros.

Canadian International

Woodbine Racetrack, 555 Rexdale Blvd.,
Rexdale, 416-675-7223;
www.woodbineentertainment.com

World-class thoroughbreds compete in one of Canada's most important races. Mid-late October.

Canadian National Exhibition

Exhibition Place, Lake Shore Blvd. and
Strachan Ave., Toronto,
416-393-6300; www.theex.com

This gala celebration originated in 1879 as the Toronto Industrial Exhibition for the encouragement of agriculture, industry and the arts, though agricultural events dominated the show. Today sports, industry, labor and the arts are of equal importance to CNE. The "Ex," as it is locally known, is so inclusive of the nation's activities that it is a condensed Canada. A special 350-acre 141-hectare. park has been built to accommodate the exhibition. Hundreds of events include animal shows, parades, exhibits, a midway and water and air shows. Virtually every kind of sporting event is represented, from frisbee-throwing to the National Horse Show. Mid-August-Labour Day.

Caribana

Exhibition Place, Lake Shore Blvd. and
Strachan Ave., Toronto;
www.caribana.com

Caribbean music, grand parade, floating nightclubs, dancing, costumes and food at various locations throughout city. Late July-early August.

Celebrate Toronto Street Festival

Yonge St., between Lawrence Ave. and
Dundas St., Toronto, 416-395-0490;
www.city.toronto.on.ca/special_events/
streetfest

Each July, on the first weekend after Canada Day, Toronto's Yonge Street—the longest street in the world—is transformed into more than 500,000 square feet 46,452 square meters. of free entertainment, with something for people of all ages and tastes. Each of five intersections along Yonge Street runs its own distinctive programming mix; one has nothing but family entertainment, another has world music, a third has classic rock and so forth. Jugglers, stilt-walkers and buskers enliven street corners; spectacular thrill shows captivate pedestrians. Call for schedule. Early July.

CHIN International Picnic

Exhibition Place, Lake Shore Blvd. and
Strachan Ave., Toronto,
416-531-9991; www.chinradio.com

Contests, sports, picnicking. First weekend in July.

Designs on Ice

100 Queen St. W., Toronto,
416-395-0490; www.city.toronto.on.ca

This ice sculpture competition gives contestants exactly 48 hours to chisel a block of ice into a winter work of art. Each year brings a different theme. A recent one, for example, was J.R.R. Tolkien's epic *The Lord of the Rings*, which brought forth a wonderland of hobbits, dwarves, trolls, orcs, wizards and elves. The public chooses the winners and the awards ceremony is part of a family skating party with live music. The sculptures stay up as long as the weather cooperates. Last weekend in December.

Outdoor Art Show

Nathan Phillips Square, Queen and
Bay Sts., Toronto, 416-408-2754;
www.torontooutdoorart.org

Mid-July.

Royal Agricultural Winter Fair

Coliseum Building, Exhibition Place, Lake
Shore Blvd. and Strachan Ave., Toronto,
416-263-3400;
www.royalfair.org

World's largest indoor agricultural fair exhibits the finest livestock. Food shows. Royal Horse Show features international competitions in several categories. Early November.

Sunday Serenades

5100 Yonge St., Toronto,
416-338-0338; www.city.toronto.on.ca

See if moonlight becomes you and play Fred and Ginger under the stars at Mel Lastman Square. Each Sunday evening in June and July you can Lindy Hop, Big Apple and Swing to live big band and swing music. It's free and easy and lots of fun. Mid-July-mid-August.

149

ONTARIO

Toronto International Film Festival

Eaton Centre, 220 Yonge St., Toronto, 416-968-3456

Celebration of world cinema in downtown theaters; Canadian and foreign films, international moviemakers and stars. Early September.

Toronto Kids Tuesday

100 Queen St. W., Toronto; www.city.toronto.on.ca

For four consecutive Tuesdays in July and August, Nathan Philips Square is turned into a kid's fantasyland. There's entertainment, face painting, coloring, chalk art, make-and-take crafts, make your own t-shirts, build-a-kite; it depends on who is entertaining and what the theme of the day is. The Stylamanders bring zany choreography and championship yo-yo tricks, which was followed by a high-energy day of play, including interactive games with the Toronto Maple Leafs. July-August.

Toronto Wine and Cheese Show

6900 Airport Rd., Mississauga, 800-265-3673; www.towineandcheese.com

A mainstay since 1983, the Toronto Wine and Cheese show brings a world of top-tier wines, beers, lagers, ales, single malt whiskies, cheeses and specialty food to town. Learn from famous chefs, sample an exquisite collection of cigars, find out how to buy the perfect bottle of wine and enjoy free seminars by well-known food and wine experts. Ages 19 and up only. Mid-April.

HOTELS

★★★Delta Chelsea

33 Gerrard St. W., Toronto, 416-595-1975, 800-268-1133; www.deltachelsea.com

Located in the heart of downtown Toronto, guests are within minutes of the city's best theatre, shopping and attractions. After a long day, unwind in an elegant guest room with choice amenities.

1,590 rooms. Two restaurants, two bars. Pet. Swim. Busn. Center. **$$$**

★★Delta Toronto East

2035 Kennedy Rd., Scarborough, 416-299-1500; www.deltahotels.ca

368 rooms. Restaurant, bar. Children's activity center. Pets accepted, fee. Pool. **$$**

★★★Fairmont Royal York

100 Front St. W., Toronto, 416-368-2511, 800-527-4727; www.fairmont.com

The Royal York became known as a city within a city, with its 1.5 acres (6 hectares) of public rooms including a 12,000-book library, a concert hall with a 50-ton pipe organ and 10 ornate passenger elevators. A $100 million project restored the guest rooms and public spaces to their original elegance and added a health club.

1,365 rooms. Five restaurants, four bars. Pet. Swim. Busn. Center. **$$$**

★★★★Four Seasons Hotel Toronto

21 Avenue Rd., Toronto, 416-964-0411; www.fourseasons.com/toronto

The Four Seasons Hotel Toronto is in a prime location in the upscale neighborhood of Yorkville. Guest rooms feature elegant colonial décor, plush furnishings and charming views of Yorkville, or stunning views of the city's downtown. Not forgotten are busineess travels who are pampered with the in-house business center and complimentary limousine service. Guests can relax by the heated indoor and outdoor pool, sauna, whirlpool and fitness center. Dinner should not be missed at with classic French cuisine served in the hotel's restaurant, Truffles.

380 rooms, 32 story. Pets accepted, some restrictions. High-speed Internet access. Two restaurants, two bars. Fitness room. Indoor pool, outdoor pool, whirlpool. Business center.

★★★Hilton Toronto

145 Richmond St. W., Toronto, 416-869-3456, 800-445-8667; www.toronto.hilton.com

Guests will enjoy the location of this hotel in Toronto's financial and entertainment districts.
601 rooms. Two restaurants, two bars. Pets accepted, fee. Pool. Busn. Center. **$$**

★Holiday Inn Express
50 Estates Dr., Scarborough, 416-439-9666, 800-465-4329; www.holiday-inn.com
138 rooms. Complimentary continental breakfast. **$**

★★★Hotel Le Germain
30 Mercer St., Toronto,
416-345-9500, 800-858-8471;
www.germaintoronto.com
Sleek lines, modern architectureand a two-level lobby define this new hotel. Facilities such as a massage room, two rooftop terraces and a library with an open-hearth fireplace enhance guests' stays. Four suites have fireplaces and private terraces.
122 rooms. Restaurant, bar. Pets accepted, fee. Exercise. **$$**

★★★InterContinental Toronto
220 Bloor St. W., Toronto,
416-960-5200, 888-567-8725;
www.intercontinental.com
Located in the exclusive Yorkville neighborhood, this modern hotel has guest rooms designed to be both inviting and efficient. Thoughtful details are offered through out the hotel, such as an international newspaper service and will print a copy of any major newspaper upon request.
210 rooms. Restaurant, bar. Pets accepted, fee. Exercise. Pool. Busn. Center. **$$**

★★★InterContinental Hotel Toronto Centre
225 Front St. W., Toronto,
416-597-1400, 800-422-7969;
www.intercontinental.com
The downtown InterContinental caters to business travelers who need meeting space, business support and proximity to the adjacent Metro Toronto Convention Centre. The hotel is great for leisure travelers who want to stay close to theater, dining and shopping venues.

586 rooms. Restaurant, bar. Exercise. Swim. Busn. Center. **$$$$**

★Inn on the Park
1100 Eglinton Ave E, 416- 444-2561
269 rooms. Restaurant, bar. Children's activity center. Fitness room. Indoor pool, whirlpool. Business center. **$$**

★★★Le Royal Meridien King Edward
37 King St. E., Toronto,
416-863-9700, 800-543-4300;
www.lemeridien-kingedward.com
Le Royal Meridien King Edward is the grande dame of Toronto. This historic landmark opened to the public in 1903 and has been hosting the world's elite ever since. Sharing the hotel's affinity for England in their decor, the Cafe Victoria and Consort Bar are essential elements of the superb King Edward experience.
292 rooms, 16 story. Two restaurants, bar. Pet. Busn. Center. **$$$**

★★★Marriott Toronto Airport
901 Dixon Rd., Toronto,
416-674-9400, 800-905-2811;
www.marriott.com
Both business and leisure travelers will like this property's proximity to Pearson International Airport and many of the city's other top attractions. The property offers a variety of dining options. Mikada servers traditional Japanese dishes while the Terrace's menu is Continental. Toucan's Lounge & Patio is a nice place to meet up with friends for a quick drink.
424 rooms. Three restaurants, bar. Pets accepted, fee. Pool. Busn. Center. **$$**

★★★Marriott Bloor Yorkville
90 Bloor St. E., Toronto,
416-961-8000, 800-859-7180;
www.marriott.com
Situated in the fashionable Yorkville neighborhood, this hotel's creative and artistic decor makes it fit right in. Although it's located at perhaps the city's busiest intersection, the hotel feels tucked away. Plentiful amenities plus the attractions of

151

ONTARIO

★

★

★

★

★

a tourist-friendly neighborhood, close to the business district and with state-of-the-art facilities.
258 rooms. Restaurant, bar. Busn. Center. **$$$**

★★★Marriott Toronto Eaton Centre
525 Bay St., Toronto,
416-597-9200, 800-905-0667;
www.marriotteatoncentre.com
In the financial district and near the theater district, this property attracts all types of visitors with its extensive offerings. There is a top-floor pool overlooking the city.
459 rooms. Restaurant, bar. Pool. Busn. Center. **$$**

★★★Metropolitan Hotel Toronto
108 Chestnut St, Toronto,
416-977-5000;
www.metropolitan.com
All of Toronto is within easy reach from the Metropolitan Hotel, close proximity to world-renowned shopping, art galleries and museums, the hotel has the services of a large property and the intimacy of a private residence. Fully-staffed fitness and business centers are also on hand to assist all guests. The Lai Wah Heen s a serene setting for its luscious Cantonese cuisine which is considered an excellent example of authentic dim sum.
422 rooms. Pets accepted, some restrictions. Two restaurants, bar. Fitness room. Indoor pool, whirlpool. Business center. **$$$$**

★★Novotel Toronto Center
45 The Esplanade, Toronto, 416-367-8900.
262 rooms. Restaurant, bar. Pets accepted, fee. Pool. **$$**

★★★Pantages Suites Hotel And Spa
210 Victoria St., Toronto,
416-362-1777, 866-852-1777;
www.pantageshotel.com
Unique amenities and services such as a complimentary meditation channel, yoga mats, 400-thread-count Egyptian cotton linens, 27-inch flat-screen TVs and in-room European kitchens. Guests are close to The Eaton Centre mall and other Toronto attrac-

tions and just two minutes from the subway and Toronto's underground walkway.
111 rooms, all suites. Complimentary continental breakfast. Exercise. Swim. Busn. Center. **$$$**

★★★Old Mill Inn and Spa
21 Old Mill Rd., Toronto,
416-236-2641, 866-653-6455;
www.oldmilltoronto.com
This Tudor-style inn and the adjacent meeting and conference facility exude old-world charm. In summer and winter, the setting is spectacular. The inn sits 15 minutes northwest of downtown Toronto in the Humber River Valley, which offers opportunities for hiking, biking and in-line skating.
60 rooms. Complimentary continental breakfast. Two restaurants, bar. Exercise. Busn. Center. **$$$**

★★★★Park Hyatt Toronto
4 Avenue Rd., Toronto,
416-925-1234, 800-977-4197;
www.parktoronto.hyatt.com
The Park Hyatt Toronto calls the stylish Yorkville area home. Located at the intersection of Avenue Road and Bloor Street, this hotel has some of the world's leading stores just outside its doors. Public and private spaces have a rich feeling completed with handsome furnishings and a clean, modern look dominates the rooms and suites. The demands of the world dissipate at the Stillwater Spa. International dishes are the specialty at Annona, while the grilled steaks and seafood of Morton's of Chicago are always a treat.
346 rooms. Restaurant, bar. Busn. Center. **$$$**

★★Quality Suites Toronto Airport
262 Carlingview Dr., Etobicoke,
416-674-8442, 800-424-6423;
www.qualityinn.com
254 rooms. Restaurant, bar. Pets accepted, fee. **$**

★★Radisson Hotel Toronto East
55 Hallcrown Pl., North York,
416-493-7000, 800-333-3333;

ONTARIO

www.radisson.com
228 rooms. Restaurant, bar. Pool. **$**

★★Radisson Plaza Hotel Admiral
249 Queens Quay W., Toronto,
416-203-3333, 800-333-3333;
www.radisson.com
157 rooms. Two restaurants, bar. Pool.
Busn. Center. **$$**

★★Renaissance Toronto Hotel Downtown
1 Blue Jays Way, Toronto,
416-341-7100, 800-237-1512;
www.renaissancehotels.com
348 rooms. Restaurant, bar. Exercise.
Swim. Busn. Center. **$$$**

★★★Sheraton Centre Hotel
123 Queen St. W., Toronto,
416-361-1000, 800-325-3535;
www.sheratoncentretoronto.com
This towering edifice in the heart of downtown does everything on a grand scale. Possibly the most impressive feature, though, would be the waterfall gardens bursting with flowers and greenery. The indoor/outdoor pool bridges the gap between hotel and garden, with deck and terrace options in relaxation.
1,382 rooms. Restaurant, bar. Pets accepted, fee. Pool. Busn. Center. **$$**

★★★Sheraton Gateway Hotel
Toronto International Airport, Terminal 3,
Toronto, 905-672-7000, 800-325-3535;
www.sheraton.com
The hotel is connected to Terminal 3 at Toronto International Airport. First-class soundproofing and Sheraton Sweet Sleeper beds help ensure a good night's sleep before an early flight. This glass-walled hotel is thoroughly modern, with every facility for the business traveler and comfort and convenience for the leisure traveler.
474 rooms. Restaurant, bar. Airport. Pets accepted, fee. Pool. Busn. Center. **$$**

★★★SOHO Metropolitan Hotel
318 Wellington St. W., Toronto,
416-599-8800

This boutique hotel earns high marks for its urban chic interiors, stylish food, central location and smart technology. The accommodations appeal with clean, simple lines and light wood furnishings. The SoHo Metropolitan's Senses Bakery & Restaurant offers the contemporary gourmet experience with its artfully designed and creatively prepared cuisine.
366 rooms. Two restaurants, bar. Pet. Swim. Busn. Center. **$$$**

★★★The Millcroft Inn & Spa
55 John St., Alton, 519-941-8111,
800-383-3976; www.millcroft.com
This former knitting mill (1881) is situated on 100 acres (40 hectares) on the Credit River.
52 rooms. Complimentary continental breakfast. Restaurant, bar. Pool. Tennis. **$$**

★★★The Sutton Place
955 Bay St., Toronto, 416-924-9221;
www.suttonplace.com
You get an old Europe feel from the rich surroundings, including mahogany trim in the meeting rooms and crystal chandeliers. Original art and antiques grace the guest rooms and suites.
292 rooms. Restaurant, bar, spa. Pets accepted, fee. Pool. Busn. Center. **$$**

★★★The Westin Prince Toronto
900 York Mills Rd., Toronto,
416-444-2511, 800-228-3000;
www.westin.com
Located in the center of downtown Toronto, this hotel is just minutes from both the Ontario Science Centre and the Ford Centre for the Performing Arts.
381 rooms. Restaurant, bar. Exercise. Pool. Tennis. Busn. Center. **$$**

★★★Westin Harbour Castle
1 Harbour Sq., Toronto,
416-869-1600, 800-228-3000;
www.westin.com/harbourcastle
The striking towers of this hotel are among the most recognized landmarks in the city. The glass-walled foyer offers a wide, clear view of Lake Ontario. Close to a host of

ONTARIO

★
★
★
★
★

tourist attractions, including the Air Canada Centre, the CN Tower, the Eaton Centre and the theater district.

977 rooms. Two restaurants, two bars, children's activity center. Pet. Swim. Tennis. Busn. Center. **$$$$**

★★★Windsor Arms Hotel
18 St. Thomas St., Toronto,
416-971-9666, 877-999-2767;
www.windsorarmshotel.com

The accommodations in this intimate and stylish hotel are sleek, modern and sublime. The Tea Room serves a traditional tea by day and at night is transformed into Toronto's only champagne and caviar bar. Club 22 entertains with piano entertainment and live bands; and the Cigar Lounge offers decadent treats.

28 rooms, all suites. Complimentary continental breakfast. Restaurant, bar. Pet. Swim. **$$$**

★★★Wyndham Bristol Place Hotel
950 Dixon Rd., Etobicoke,
416-675-9444, 877-999-3223;
www.wyndham.com

287 rooms. Restaurant. Pool. Busn. Center. **$$**

RESTAURANTS

★★★360
301 Front St. W., Toronto,
416-362-5411; www.cntower.ca

As the name suggests, this restaurant completes a 360-degree rotation, offering a breathtaking view from the CN Tower. The scenery inside is attractive as well, with colorful decor and a fresh, seasonal menu. International menu. Reservations recommended. **$$$**

★★★Auberge du Pommier
4150 Yonge St., Toronto,
416-222-2220;
www.aubergedupommier.com

Located north of the city, this restaurant in an industrial park manages to feel like it is actually in rural France. The attentive service and comfortable décor are pleasing.

French, American menu. Reservations recommended. **$$$**

★★Barootes
220 King St. W., Toronto, 416-979-7717;
www.barootes.com

International menu. Reservations recommended. **$$**

★★★Biagio
155 King St. E., Toronto,
416-366-4040.

Located in the historic St. Lawrence Hall near the theater district, this modern Italian restaurant serves specialties from the north. An ornate ceiling and a lovely patio with a fountain add to the ambience. Italian menu. Outdoor seating. **$$$**

★Bumpkins
21 Gloucester St., Toronto, 416-922-8655;
www.bumpkins.ca

French menu. Reservations recommended. Outdoor seating. **$$**

★★★★Canoe
66 Wellington St. W., Toronto
416-364-0054.

Canoe is a stunning venue in which to experience creative, satisfying regional Canadian cuisine. While dazzling ingredients tend to be sourced from wonderful local producers, many organic, the kitchen borrows flavors and techniques from the world at large, including Asia, France and the American South. The end product is inventive food and an equally original room. Canadian menu. Reservations recommended. **$$$**

★★Carman's Club
26 Alexander St., Toronto, 416-924-8558.
Steak, seafood menu. **$$$**

★★★Centro Grill & Wine Bar
2472 Yonge St., Toronto, 416-483-2211;
www.centro.ca

A lot of tastes are rolled into one destination at this contemporary European restaurant with a downstairs sushi and oyster bar. Colorful, New Age-style dining room and

the worldly menu is never a bore with novelties like caribou chop with juniper berry oil, Alsatian spatzle and Arctic cloudberry sauce.
International menu. Reservations recommended. $$$

★★★★Chiado
864 College St., Toronto, 416-538-1910; www.chiadorestaurant.ca
Paying homage to the old seaside town but updating dishes for a more modern sensibility, Chiado features what might best be described as "nouvelle Portuguese cuisine." The food is first-rate and fabulous, featuring an ocean's worth of fresh fish simply prepared with olive oil and herbs, as well as innovative takes on pheasant, game and poultry. To add to the authenticity of the experience, Chiado has the largest collection of fine Portuguese wines in North America and a superb selection of vintage ports.
Spanish menu. Reservations recommended. $$$

★★Dynasty Chinese
131 Bloor St. W., Toronto, 416-923-3323.
Chinese menu. Reservations recommended. $$$

★Grano
2035 Yonge St., Toronto, 416-440-1986; www.grano.ca
Italian menu. Outdoor seating. $$

★★Grazie
2373 Yonge St., Toronto, 416-488-0822; www.grazie.ca
Italian menu. $$

★★★Hemispheres
108 Chestnut St., Toronto, 416-599-8000; www.metropolitan.com/hemis
Hemispheres elevates hotel dining to a whole new level with its stylish interior and international fusion cuisine. The menu includes European and Continental classics, many with an Asian bent. Wine lovers will appreciate the well-rounded and extensive cellar.
International menu. Reservations recommended. $$

★★Il Posto Nuovo
148 Yorkville Ave., Toronto, 416-968-0469; www.ilposto.ca
Italian menu. Reservations recommended. Outdoor seating. $$$

★★★Joso's
202 Davenport Rd., Toronto, 416-925-1903.
The walls are covered with the chef's racy art and celebrity pictures at this popular restaurant, which offers unique but excellent Mediterranean cuisine. Outdoor seating. $$$

★★★La Fenice
319 King St. W., Toronto, 416-585-2377.
The stark, modern dining room of this downtown restaurant recalls the chic design aesthetic of Milan.
Italian menu. Reservations recommended. $$$

★★★Lai Wah Heen
108 Chestnut St., Toronto, 416-977-9899; www.laiwahheen.com
Lai Wah Heen, meaning "luxurious meeting place," is truly luxurious with its two-level dining room featuring black granite, 12-foot (3.6-meter) ceilings and solarium-style glass wall. Exotic herbs and spices, skillful use of tropical fruits and seafood dishes make for a Cantonese menu rich with Pacific Rim flair.
Cantonese, Chinese menu. Reservations recommended. Valet parking. $$

★Matignon
51 Ste. Nicholas St., Toronto, 416-921-9226; www.matignon.ca
French menu. Reservations recommended. $$

★★Millcroft Inn
55 John St., N. Alton, 519-941-8111; www.millcroft.com
A restaurant with a reputation for fine dining makes any occasion a time to celebrate, especially during the holidays when special

155

ONTARIO

★
★
★
★
★

menus are offered. Be sure to sample their vintage wines.
French menu. **$$$**

★★★Mistura
265 Davenport Rd., Toronto,
416-515-0009; www.mistura.ca
Contemporary, seasonal Italian cuisine and a stylish, upscale environment are the hallmarks of this elegant Toronto restaurant. Past menu items like wild boar filled pasta with dried cherries have delighted guests along with fresh ingredients and artful presentation. Desserts are just as inventive.
Italian menu. **$$**

★★★★North 44
2537 Yonge St., Toronto, 416-487-4897;
www.north44restaurant.com
Style, serenity and elegance infuse every aspect of North 44 Degrees. From the recently renovated loft-like dining room to the world-class New Continental cuisine, North 44 Degrees is a sublime and sexy dining experience. A sophisticated crowd fills the restaurant, named for the city's latitude, on most nights. Chef/owner Mark McEwan expertly blends the bright flavors of Asia with those of Italy, France and Canada. The service is smooth, refined and in perfect harmony with the cool space and stellar cuisine.
International menu. Reservations recommended. **$$$$**

★★★Old Mill
21 Old Mill Rd., Toronto, 416-236-2641,
866-653-6455; www.oldmilltoronto.com
The main dining room of the Old Mill Inn & Spa, a charming, English-style inn along the Humber River, the Old Mill features a warm and romantic atmosphere with beamed ceilings, a roaring fireplace, brick walls and soft lighting.
International menu. Jacket required (weekend dinner). Reservations recommended. Outdoor seating. Cover charge (Friday-Saturday from 8 p.m.) **$$$**

★★★Opus Restaurant
37 Prince Arthur Ave., Toronto,
416-921-3105;
www.opusrestaurant.com
This plush Yorkville restaurant is elegant, romantic and filled with the energy of Toronto's powerful and moneyed elite.
International menu. Reservations recommended. Outdoor seating. **$$$**

★★★Oro
45 Elm St., Toronto, 416-597-0155;
www.ororestaurant.com
This restaurant has changed hands and names many times since it opened in 1922 and is famous for its patrons, who have included Ernest Hemingway and Prime Minister Jean Chrétien. The decor is contemporary and elegant, as is the food.
International menu. **$$$**

★★★Pangaea
1221 Bay St., Toronto, 416-920-2323;
www.pangaearestaurant.com
Vaulted ceiling and exotic floral arrangements set the stage for sophisticated continental cuisine using the wealth of each season's harvest. Tired Bloor Street shoppers will find this a great place to break for lunch or tea.
International menu. Reservations recommended. **$$$**

★★Pastis
1158 Yonge St., Toronto, 416-928-2212;
French menu. **$$**

★★Pier 4 Storehouse
245 Queen's Quay W., Toronto,
416-203-1440; www.pier4rest.com
Seafood menu. Reservations recommended. Outdoor seating. **$$$**

★★Provence
12 Amelia St., Toronto,
416-924-9901;
www.provencerestaurant.com
French menu. Outdoor seating. **$$$**

★★Quartier
2112 Yonge St, Toronto, 416-545-0505
Thai menu. Lunch, dinner. Reservations recommended. **$$**

★
★
★
★
★

★★Rodney's Oyster House
469 King St. W., Toronto,
416-363-8105;
www.rodneysoysterhouse.com
Seafood menu. Reservations recommended.
Outdoor seating. **$$**

★★Rosewater Supper Club
19 Toronto St., Toronto, 416-214-5888;
www.libertygroup.com
French menu. Reservations recommended.
Outdoor seating. **$$$**

★★★★Scaramouche
1 Benvenuto Pl., Toronto, 416-961-8011;
www.scaramoucherestaurant.com
Up on a hillside overlooking the dazzling
downtown lights, Scaramouche is the
perfect hideaway for falling in love with
food or your dining companion.. This modern, bi-level space is known for its fantastic contemporary French fare and is often
jammed with dressed-up, savvy locals. The
restaurant is divided between a formal dining room upstairs and a modestly priced
pasta bar downstairs.
French menu. Reservations recommended.
$$$$

★★Senator
249 Victoria St., Toronto, 416-364-7517;
www.thesenator.com
Seafood, steak menu. **$$$**

★★★★Splendido
88 Harbord St., Toronto, 416-929-7788;
www.splendido.ca
Splendido has hit its stride and has become
one of Toronto's best restaurants, with
interpretations of international cuisines
and a focus on clean, flavorful sauces and
local Canadian ingredients. Several charm-
ing details like the Champagne cart and the
selection of petit fours make this a fun and
enjoyable dining experience.
International menu. Closed Monday; July-
August: Sunday. Reservations recom-
mended. **$$$**

★★★Susur
601 King St. W., Toronto, 416-603-2205;

www.susur.com
This internationally acclaimed restaurant
blends flavors of the East and West to create
innovative, eclectic dishes. Tasting menus,
available in five or seven courses, change
on a daily basis to reflect the fresh ingredients available at local markets, so you'll
be treated to a new dining experience with
each visit.
International menu. Reservations recom-
mended. **$$$**

★★Ta Ke Sushi
22 Front St. W., Toronto, 416-862-1891.
Japanese, sushi menu. Reservations recom-
mended. **$$**

★Thai Flavor
1554 Avenue Rd., Toronto, 416-782-3288.
Thai menu. **$**

★★★★The Fifth
225 Richmond St. W., Toronto,
416-979-3005;
www.thefifthgrill.com
It takes work to make it to The Fifth.
First, an alley entrance leads you to The
Easy, an upscale nightclub and former
speakeasy. Once inside The Easy, you are
directed onto a Persian rug-lined vintage
freight elevator. There, an attendant takes
you to floor number five. Exit and you
have finally arrived at The Fifth, a trea-
sured contemporary French restaurant and
supper club. The food is of the delicious
updated French variety and the dishes are
perfectly prepared, beautifully presented
and easily devoured.
French menu. Closed Sunday-Wednesday.
Bar. Reservations recommended. Outdoor
seating. **$$$$**

★★★★Truffles
21 Avenue Rd., Toronto, 416-964-0411;
www.fourseasons.com
Filled with light and luxury, Truffles' dining room feels like the parlor room of a
fabulous art collector with impeccable
taste. Located in the Four Seasons Hotel
Toronto, Truffles is known for its distinct,
stylized brand of modern Provencal-style

ONTARIO

★
★
★
★
★

cuisine. Smooth service and an extensive wine list make Truffles a truly inspired dining event.

French menu. Jacket required. Reservations recommended. **$$$$**

★United Baker's Dairy Restaurant
506 Lawrence Ave. W., Toronto,
416-789-0519
Jewish menu. **$**

★★Zachary's Restaurant
950 Dixon Road, Etobicoke,
416-679-4394
Continental menu. Dinner. Reservations recommended. **$ $**

SPAS

★★★★Stillwater Spa at Park Hyatt Toronto
4 Avenue Rd, Toronto, 416-926-2389;
parktoronto.hyatt.com/hyatt/pure/spas
With its cool, crisp interiors—complete with a fireplace in the Tea Lounge and waterfalls and streams throughout the facility—and fabulous mind and body relaxation therapies, Park Hyatt Toronto's Stillwater Spa offers you an escape. The signature Stillwater massage customizes an aromatherapy blend to accompany a relaxing bodywork combination of Swedish massage, triggerpoints pressure and stretching techniques. **$$$**

WINDSOR

Windsor is located at the tip of a peninsula and is linked to Detroit by the Ambassador Bridge and the Detroit-Windsor Tunnel. Aside from its status as the Ambassador City, thanks to its proximity to the United States, Windsor is also known as the City of Roses for its many beautiful parks. The Sunken Gardens and Rose Gardens in Jackson Park boast more than 500 varieties of roses, while Coventry Garden and Peace Fountain has the only fountain floating in international waters. A cosmopolitan and determinedly bilingual city with many French influences, Windsor enjoys a symphony orchestra, theaters, a light opera company, art galleries, nightlife and all the amenities of a large city.
Information: www.city.windsor.on.ca

WHAT TO SEE AND DO

Art Gallery of Windsor
401 Riverside Dr. W., Windsor,
519-977-0013;
www.artgalleryofwindsor.com
Collections consist of Canadian art, including Inuit prints and carvings, with emphasis on Canadian artists from the late to the present. Children's gallery; gift shop.

Casino Windsor
377 Riverside Dr. E., Windsor,
519-258-7878, 800-991-7777;
www.casinowindsor.com
The casino overlooks the Detroit skyline and is easily accessible from a number of hotels.

Colasanti Farms, Ltd
1550 Rd. 3 E., Kingsville,
28 miles/45 kilometers S.E., on Hwy. 3 near Ruthven, 519-326-3287;
www.colasanti.com
More than 25 greenhouses with acres of exotic plants; large collection of cacti; farm animals, parrots and tropical birds; crafts; mini-putt; restaurant.

Coventry Gardens and Peace Fountain
Riverside Dr. E. and Pillette Rd., Windsor,
519-253-2300
Riverfront park and floral gardens with a 75-foot-high 23-meter. floating fountain; myriad 3-D water displays with spectacular night illumination. May-September: daily..

Fort Malden National Historic Park
100 Laird Ave., Amherstburg,
18 miles/29 kilometers S. via City Rd. 20,
519-736-5416;
www.parkscanada.gc.ca/malden
Ten-acre (4-hectare) park with remains of fortification, original 1838 barracks and

1851 pensioner's cottage; visitor and interpretation centers with exhibits.

Heritage Village
Windsor, 519-776-6909.
Historical artifacts and structures on 54 acres (22 hectares). Log cabins (1826 and 1835), railway station (1854), house (1869), church (1885), schoolhouse (1907), barber shop circa (1920), general store (1847); transportation museum. Special events. Picnic facilities.

Jack Miner Bird Sanctuary
332 Rd. 3 W., Kingsville, 519-733-4034, 877-289-8328; www.jackminer.com
Canada geese and other migratory waterfowl; ponds, picnicking, museum. Canada geese "air shows" during peak season.

John Freeman Walls Historic Site and Underground Railroad Museum
859 Puce Rd., 519-727-6555; www.undergroundrailroadmuseum.com
John Freeman Walls, a fugitive slave from North Carolina, built this log cabin in 1846. It subsequently served as a terminal of the Underground Railroad and the first meeting place of the Puce Baptist Church. It has remained in the possession of Walls's descendants. May-October, by appointment only.

North American Black Historical Museum
277 King St., Amherstburg, 519-736-5433, 800-713-6336; www.blackhistoricalmuseum.com
Chronicles achievements of black North Americans, many of whom fled the United States for freedom in Canada. Permanent exhibits on Underground Railroad; artifacts, archives, genealogical library. April-November.

Odette Sculpture Park
Between Church St. and Huron along the Detroit River, 519-253-2300, 888-519-3333; www.windsorsculpturepark.com
Walk or cycle the paths through this 2-mile (3.5-kilometer) park past large sculptures by Canadian and international artists.

Park House Museum
214 Dalhousie St., Amherstburg, 519-736-2511
Solid log, clapboard-sided house circa 1795, considered to be oldest house in area. Built in Detroit, moved here in 1799. Restored and furnished as in the 1850s. Demonstrations of tinsmithing; pieces for sale.

Point Pelee National Park
407 monarch Ln., 519-322-2365; www.parkscanada.gc.ca/pelee
The park is a 6-square-mile (16-square-kilometer) tip of the Point Pelee peninsula. Combination dry land and marshland, the park also has a deciduous forest and is situated on two major bird migration flyways. More than 350 species have been sighted in the park. A boardwalk winds through the 2,500 acres (1,011) hectares. of marshland. Fishing, swimming, canoeing; picnicking, trails and interpretive center, biking (rentals).

University of Windsor - University Players
401 Sunset Ave., Windsor, 519-253-4232; www.universityplayers.com
On campus is Essex Hall Theatre, featuring several productions per season. September-March.

Willistead Manor
1899 Niagara St., Windsor, 519-253-2365.
(1906) Restored English Tudor mansion built for Edward Chandler Walker, son of famous distiller Hiram Walker, on 15 acres 6 hectares. of wooded parkland; elegant interiors with hand-carved woodwork; furnished in turn-of-the-century style. July-August: Sunday and Wednesday; September-June: first and third Sunday of each month.

Windsor's Community Museum
254 Pitt St. W., Windsor, 519-253-1812; www.windsorpubliclibrary.com/hours/museum
Exhibits and collections interpret the history of Windsor and southwestern Ontario. Located in the historic Francois Baby House.

159

ONTARIO

★
★
★
★
★

Wreck Exploration Tours
9 Robson Rd., Leamington,
519-326-1566, 888-229-7325.
Exploration of a 130-year-old wreck site. Shoreline cruise; artifact orientation. May-October, reservations required.

SPECIAL EVENTS
Carrousel of the Nations
519-255-1127; www.themcc.com
This family event features villages showcasing food, music traditions and dancing from all over the world. Three weekends in June.

Festival Epicure: A Celebration of Food, Wine and Music
Riverside Festival Plaza, Windsor,
519-971-5005; www.festivalepicure.com
Sample food from local eateries and wine from regional wineries. Performances ranging from pop to bluegrass by Detroit and Windsor musicians. Mid-July.

International Freedom Festival
Riverside Dr. and Ouelette Ave., Windsor, 519-252-7264.
Two-week joint celebration by Detroit and Windsor with many events, culminating in fireworks display over the river. Late June-early July.

HOTELS
★★Best Western Continental Inn
3345 Huron Church Rd., Windsor,
519-966-5541, 800-780-7234;
www.bestwestern.com
71 rooms. Complimentary continental breakfast. Restaurant, bar. Pool. $

★Comfort Inn
1100 Richmond St., Chatham,
519-352-5500, 800-228-5150;
www.comfortinn.com
81 rooms. Pets accepted, fee. $

★★Radisson Riverfront Hotel Windsor
333 Riverside Dr. W., Windsor,
519-977-9777, 800-267-9777;
www.radisson.com

207 rooms, 19 story. Restaurant, bar. Pets accepted, fee. Pool. $$

★★Wheels Inn
615 Richmond St., Chatham,
519-351-1100; www.wheelsinn.com
350 rooms, 10 story. Four restaurants, bar. Pool. Busn. Center. $

★★★Casino Windsor Hotel
377 Riverside Dr. E., Windsor,
519-258-7878, 800-991-7777;
www.casinowindsor.com
An oasis from the frenetic casino activity, this hotel's guest rooms feature views of the Detroit skyline or the city of Windsor.
389 rooms. Five restaurants, three bars. Casino. Swim. $$$

★★★Hilton Windsor
277 Riverside Dr. W., Windsor,
519-973-5555, 800-774-1500;
www.hilton.com
The waterfront location is key for both business and leisure travelers. The hotel is also conveniently interconnected to the Cleary International Convention Centre and close to other local attractions. The casual Park Terrace Restaurant serves breakfast, lunch and dinner. The River Runner Bar is a great place to catch the game.
305 rooms, 25 story. Restaurant, bar. Pool. Busn. Center. $$

RESTAURANTS
★★Chatham Street Grill
149 Chatham St. W., Windsor,
519-256-2555
Continental menu. Reservations recommended. Outdoor seating. $$

★★Cook Shop
683 Ouellette Ave., Windsor, 519-254-3377
Italian menu. Closed Monday; also two weeks in August. Reservations recommended. $$

★Tunnel Bar-B-Q
58 Park St. E., Windsor, 519-258-3663;
www.tunnel-bar-b-q.com
American, steak menu. $$

PRINCE EDWARD ISLAND

CANADA'S SMALLEST PROVINCE RESTS IN THE GULF OF ST. LAWRENCE ON THE EAST COAST, between Nova Scotia and New Brunswick. The island is just 40 miles (64 kilometers) wide at its broadest point, narrowing to only four miles (six kilometers) wide near Summerside and only 140 miles (224 kilometers) long. Charlottetown and Summerside are the only cities in the province. As charming as they are, it's no wonder this idyllic getaway, with its red soil, warm waters, fine white beaches and deep-cut coves, is more famed for its pastoral views and its promise of unspoiled, pristine relaxation.

Explore the Hillsborough River, one of the Canadian Heritage Rivers; scenic, red clay Heritage Roads; about 50 lighthouses (seven open to the public in the summer); three scenic routes—Lady Slipper Drive, Blue Heron Drive and Kings Byway—that travel around the islands coastline; 30 nine- and 18-hole golf courses; and a wealth of shops selling everything from traditional crafts to handmade soaps and Mikmaq figurines. Deep-sea fish, dig for clams, watch for more than 330 species of birds and sea kayak the coastline. Or simply unwind on one of many beaches.

Prince Edward Island is divided into six day-tour regions. "North by Northwest" encompasses the area from North Cape to Cedar Dunes Provincial Park, an area of unspoiled beauty with secluded beaches, picturesque fishing and farming communities and quaint churches. "Ship to Shore" covers the southwest, which proudly stewards a prosperous shipbuilding heritage, fox farming and world-famous Malpeque oysters. Also here is the city of Summerside, located on the Bedeque Bay. "Anne's Land," the white sand beaches and central north shore of the province, brings literary fans to the real-life paradise of the beloved Anne of Green Gables, heroine of books written by Lucy Maud Montgomery.

"Charlotte's Shore" encompasses the south central region, highlighted by Charlottetown, the provincial capital, as well as scenic red cliffs and warm waters. "Bays & Dunes," in the northeast corner, offers the island's best coastline views, with miles of white sand beaches and spectacular dunes bordering the scenic countryside. "Hills & Harbors," through the southeast, is home to some of the most pleasing vistas and peaceful fishing villages in the province.

The 80-minute ferry ride to and from the island is a relaxing, scenic journey that is popular with visitors and locals alike.

★ SPOTLIGHT

★ The Confederation Bridge is the longest bridge over ice-covered waters in the world and one of the most significant Canadian engineering feats of the 20th century. It took the more than 6,000 people employed by the Strait Crossing organization four years to construct the bridge—from October 1993 to May 1997.

161

Northumberland ferries (888-249-7245; www.nfl-bay.com) operate between Caribou, Nova Scotia and Wood Islands, Prince Edward Island about every 90 minutes from May through late December, weather permitting. A second ferry link, Corporation Transport Maritime Arien (CTMA), offers regular ferry service (about a five-hour trip) from Souris, P.E.I. to Cap-aux-Meules, les-de-la-Madeliene, Quebec except during February and March. Or for an equally interesting passage to Canada's beach-ridden gem, drive from New Brunswick to P.E.I. across the Confederation Bridge, the longest of its kind in the world.

Provincial Capital: Charlottetown
Information: www.peiplay.com

CONFEDERATION BRIDGE

Not too long ago, the only way to get to Prince Edward Island was by air or water. That changed a decade ago when construction of the Confederation Bridge was completed. The bridge allows travel from New Brunswick to the town of Borden-Carleton on P.E.I. Built with more than 3.5 million tons of concrete and two million cubic yards of aggregate, the bridge has 44 main bridge spans, two traveling lanes and one emergency lane in either direction. There are 310 streetlights and 34 traffic lights (which remain green under normal conditions). The bridge is open only to motor vehicles; cyclists and pedestrians must use a shuttle to get across.

Information: www.confederationbridge.com

CONFEDERATION TRAIL

Those with enough pedal or foot power can travel the island from tip to tip on the Confederation Trail—a unique hiking, biking and snowmobile path that travels from Tignish on the west side of the island to Elmira on the east. The route totals more than 169 miles (270 kilometers), with branch trails extending into Charlottetown, Souris, Georgetown and Montague. There is also a link to the Confederation Bridge in Borden-Carleton. The easily traveled stone dust surface took the place of the Prince Edward Island railway, abandoned in 1989. Travelers pass woods, rivers and pastoral scenes along the route, in between small island communities. There are many places to stop for refreshments and a well-earned break. Prince Edward Island is the first province in Canada to complete its section (the Confederate Trail) of the TransCanada Trail.

CAVENDISH

Located near the western end of Prince Edward Island National Park, Cavendish is more than 15 miles (24 kilometers) of world-famous beaches, and is the heart and soul of Anne of Green Gables. Silky-white dunes, red sandstone cliffs and crystal blue water are all warmed by the Gulf stream. Together with the allure of Canada's red-haired darling, Cavendish attracts thousands of visitors from around the world.

Information: www.cavendishbeachresort.com

WHAT TO SEE AND DO

Avonlea-Village of Anne of Green Gables

Rte. 6, Cavendish,
902-963-3050;
www.avonlea.ca

Families can spend a delightful day exploring Anne's world, meeting the novel's characters, visiting the barnyard, riding ponies and milking cows. Three music shows daily include children's shows; heritage buildings; museums; Avonlea Gardens. June-

August: daily 9 a.m.-5 p.m.; September: Daily 10 a.m.-4 p.m.

Birthplace of Lucy Maud Montgomery
Junction Hwys. 6 and 20, New London, 902-886-2099; www.gov.pe.ca/visitorsguide/search/display.php3?number=31
A replica of the "Blue Chest," the writer's personal scrapbooks containing copies of her many stories and poems, as well as her wedding dress and veil, are stored here. May-Thanksgiving: daily

Lucy Maud Montgomery's Cavendish Home
Rte. 6, Cavendish, 902-963-2231; www.peisland.com/lmm
The site where Montgomery, author of Anne of Green Gables and 22 other novels, was raised by her grandparents from 1876 to 1911. The bookstore and museum houses the original desk, scales and crown stamp used in the post office. June-September: daily.

Green Gables
Prince Edward Island National Park, Rtes. 6 and 13, Cavendish, 902-672-6350; www.gov.pe.ca/greengables
Famous as the setting for Lucy Maud Montgomery's "Anne of Green Gables." Surroundings portray the Victorian setting described in the novel. Tours available off-season. May-October: Daily.

Prince Edward Island National Park
Cavendish, 902-672-6350; www.canadianparks.com/prince_edward/peislnp/index.htm
Prince Edward Island National Park, 25 square miles (40 square kilometers), is one of eastern Canada's most popular vacation destinations. Warm salt waters and sandy beaches abound. There are several supervised beach areas for swimmers and miles of secluded shoreline to explore. In addition to golf, tennis, bicycling and pic-nicking, the park offers campfires, beach walks, an interpretation program high-lighting the natural and cultural features and stories of the area and more. Green Gables and its association with Lucy Maud Montgomery's "Anne of Green Gables" is a major attraction, with daily walks offered around the house and grounds. Many private cabins, hotels and campgrounds border the park.

Rainbow Valley Family Fun Park
1 Ave. Wolfe, Montcalm, Cavendish, 902-963-2221; www.rainbowvalley.pe.ca
Approximately 40 acres of woodland, lakes and landscaped areas; children's farm with petting areas; playground, swan boats, flumes, water slides; entertainment; pic-nicking, cafe. Monorail ride. June-Labour Day.

Woodleigh Replicas & Gardens
Burlington, 902-836-3401; www.woodleighreplicas.com
An extensive outdoor display of large-scale models of famous castles and buildings of legendary, historic and lit-erary interest. Included are the Tower of London, Dunvegan Castle and Anne Hathaway Cottage. Several models are large enough to enter and are furnished. Flower, shrub garden; children's play-ground; food service.

HOTEL

★Cavendish Corner
29 Pownal St., Charlottetown, PE, 902-367-3205, 877-963-2251; www.resortatcavendishcorner.com
46 rooms. Closed mid-October-mid-May. Complimentary full breakfast (off-season only). Restaurant, children's activity cen-ter. Swim. $

★Silverwood Motel
Green Gables Post Office, Cavendish Beach, 902-963-2439; www.silverwoodmotel.com

★
★
★
★
★
★

76 rooms. Restaurant. Pool. **$**

RESTAURANT
★★New Glasgow Lobster Suppers

Rte. 258 New Glasgow, Cavendish,
902-964-2870;
www.peilobstersuppers.com
Seafood menu.Closed November-May. **$$**

CHARLOTTETOWN

Having hosted the conference that led to the formation of Canada in 1864, Charlottetown today is a walkable, charm-filled heritage city with a scenic natural harbor, boating, yachting, swimming and plentiful seafood. Bistros, museums and artisan shopping, as well as a plethora of amenities, make this the P.E.I. traveler's headquarters.
Information: www.city.charlottetown.pe.ca

WHAT TO SEE AND DO

Abegweit Sightseeing Tours
157 Nassau, Charlottetown,
902-894-9966.
Charlottetown tours on authentic London double-decker buses; also north and south tours. Bilingual guide service available.

Basin Head Fisheries Museum
RR 2, Souris PEI,
902-357-7233;
www.gov.pe.ca/peimhf/
index.php3?number=1015692
Depicts the history of fishing in the province. Fishing equipment, scale models showing methods; old photographs, fish charts and other marine articles. Film and slide projections. Mid-June-late September: daily.

Beaconsfield
2 Kent St., Charlottetown,
902-368-6603
(1877) Mansard-style house built for shipbuilder is architecturally intact; guided tours. Headquarters of Prince Edward Island Museum & Heritage Foundation; bookstore. Regular and annual events.

Confederation Centre of the Arts
145 Richmond St., Charlottetown,
902-628-1864, 800-565-0278;
www.confederationcentre.com
(1964) Canada's National Memorial to the Fathers of Confederation; opened by Queen Elizabeth II to honor the centennial of the 1864 Confederation Conference. Contains provincial library, Confederation Centre

Museum and Art Gallery, theaters and the Robert Harris Collection of portraiture. Courtyard restaurant, gift shop. Home of the Charlottetown Festival. Gallery and museum.

Fort Amherst/Port La Joye National Historic Park
2 Palmers Ln.,
Near Rocky Point. Hwy. 19 across the harbor mouth, Charlottetown,
902-566-8295
Only earthworks of the former French fort Port la Joye (built in 1720) are still visible. Captured by the British in 1758, it was abandoned in 1768. Cafe, boutique. Interpretive center. Mid-June-Labour Day: daily.

Founder's Hall-Canada's Birthplace Pavilion
6 Prince St., Charlottetown,
902-368-1964;
www.foundershall.ca
Learn about the nation's history beginning in 1864 in this 21,000-square-foot (1,951-square-meter) waterfront attraction, with state-of-the-art displays and multimedia presentations. Restaurant; boutique.

Government House
Charlottetown,
902-368-5480;
www.gov.pe.ca
Tour the lieutenant governor's official residence. The Victorian Fanningbank Historic House was built in 1832. Tours explain the history of the house and the room furnishings. Visitors are free to

★
★
★
★

explore the lovely flower gardens around the property after the tour. July-August, Monday-Friday 10 a.m.-4 p.m.

Green Park Shipbuilding Museum
Port Hill, 902-831-7947;
www.gov.pe.ca/peimhf/
index.php3?number=1015695
Former estate of James Yeo, Jr., whose family members were leading shipbuilders of the 19th century. House (1865) restored to reflect life during the prosperous shipbuilding era. Photos of famous ships and artifacts in interpretive center; audiovisual presentation in museum theater. Lecture series and concerts. Annual events. Swimming; camping at Malpeque Bay. Mid-June-Labour Day: daily

Orwell Corner Historic Village
Charlottetown, 902-651-8515.
Reconstructed rural crossroads community of late 19th century. Combined store, post office and farmhouse; school, church, cemetery and barns. Farming activities as they were practiced 100 years ago. Annual events. Ceilidhs (Wednesday evenings).

Province House
165 Richmond St., Charlottetown,
902-566-7626.
(1847) Birthplace of the Canadian nation and a national historic site. Confederation room where delegates met in 1864 to discuss confederation. National memorial, seat of Provincial Legislature. Tours.

St. Dunstan's Basilica
Charlottetown, 902-894-3486.
Largest church on the island. Gothic cathedral with distinctive triple towers contains beautiful stained-glass windows and an impressive altar: It is 37 feet (11 meters) high, made of many types of marble and crowned with a beautiful rose window. Audio loop for hearing impaired.

SPECIAL EVENTS
Charlottetown Festival
Confederation Centre of the Arts,
145 Richmond St., Charlottetown,
902-566-1267;
www.conferderationcentre.com
During this festival, you'll find original Canadian musicals, including "Anne of Green Gables" and other productions, as well as special gallery presentations and theater. Late May-mid-October.

Festival of Lights
Charlottetown Waterfront, Confederation Landing Park. Water and Great George Sts., Charlottetown, 902-629-1864.
Buskers, children's concerts, Waterfront Magic, children's midway. Fireworks display over Charlottetown Harbor on July 1 (Canada Day). Late June-early July.

Prince Edward Island Studio Tour
902-368-6300.
Shoppers delight at this annual weekend-long event. Purchase island-made crafts and giftware at more than 140 participating craft studios, galleries, shops and museums across the island, without paying the provincial sales tax. Pick up the official directory and map at any P.E.I. visitor information center. Late September.

HOTELS
★★Best Western Charlottetown
238 Grafton St., Charlottetown,
902-892-2461, 800-528-1234;
www.bestwestern.com
146 rooms. Restaurant, bar. Pet. Exercise. Swim. $

★★The Charlottetown
75 Kent St., Charlottetown,
902-894-7371, 800-565-7633;
www.rodd-hotels.ca
115 rooms, 5 story. Restaurant, bar. Pets accepted, fee. Swim. $$$

165

PRINCE EDWARD ISLAND

★★★Delta Prince Edward
18 Queen St., Charlottetown,
902-566-2222, 800-268-1133;
www.deltahotels.com

Overlooking Charlottetown Harbor in an area of shops and restaurants, this large red brick hotel is located at the foot of Queen Street at Peake's Wharf. Renovated guest rooms have a modern flair and are comfortable and well-appointed. The hotel features its own marina and guests can walk along the waterfront or take a harbor cruise from the hotel.

211 rooms, 10 story. Two restaurants, bar. Pets accepted, fee. Pool. Busn. Center. **$$$**

★★Rodd Royalty Inn
Hwy. 1 and Hwy. 2, Charlottetown,
902-894-8566, 800-565-7633;
www.rodd-hotels.ca

122 rooms, 3 story. Restaurant, bar. Swim. **$$**

166

QUÉBEC

AN ENCLAVE OF EUROPE IN THE HEART OF NORTH AMERICA, QUÉBEC IS A DIVERSE AND COLORFUL province that is fiercely proud of its French heritage. Delightfully blending old and new world, and passionate politics with a unique joie de vivre, this nation within a nation hums with incredible cuisine and an unmatched nightlife alongside glorious mountains, charming villages, First Nations culture and an untamed wilderness. French is the language used by the majority of Québecers, though English is spoken or understood almost everywhere in the province.

By reason of its history and culture, Québec has forged a unique personality. Québecers enjoy fine dining and entertainment as evidenced by the busy calendar of festivals and other events—but they also maintain a classic Canadian hardiness and sense of adventure in a magnificent landscape. As a place where both European and North American cultural influences play out, Québec has always produced an incredibly fertile creative energy and cultural vitality. The result is a thriving literature, theatrical, art, sculpture and crafts scene.

Historic yet resolutely modern, vibrant and festive, the cities of Montréal, Québec and Gatineau embody urban Québec with their rich architectural heritage, dynamic cultural melting pot and splendid surroundings that respect nature. The wider river region, centered around the historic St. Lawrence river (one of the largest in the world), is home to old coastal villages, islands, bird sanctuaries, marine mammals and lighthouses, all bound by rural and rugged coastline.

Further afield, Québecers have mastered the art of resort living and eco-tourism. Québec's vast natural heritage comprises 27 national parks, numerous wildlife reserves and three biosphere reserves recognized by UNESCO. Ecotourism and adventure tour guides can support your discovery of the most beautiful sites in Québec on foot, by canoe or by kayak. During the summer enjoy golf, biking, tennis, hiking, swimming and water sports, and in winter get outside to snowmobile, ski, skate and even dogsled. Whatever the day holds, fine cuisine will await you on the patio or by the hearth. For the more independent wanderer, Québec has pushed the boundaries of adventure since the days of the fur traders. In this vast territory, bears, deer and caribou are often the only inhabitants. Explore the province's length and breadth by canoe, snowmobile or seaplane, with nature as your travel companion.

Provincial Capital: Québec City
Information: www.bonjourquebec.com

 SPOTLIGHT

★ The old quarter of Québec City is the only fortified city in North America, with ramparts that look down into the maze of cobblestoned streets below. There's a funicular (like an outside elevator) a few blocks away that descends to Lower Town, not far from the docks, a very steep (but very short) ride that delights children.

167

QUÉBEC

DRUMMONDVILLE

This industrial and commercial town, advantageously located at the junction of the St. Laurent plains and at the beginning of the Eastern Townships, nests in an ideal position to Montreal, Trois-Rivières and Sherbrooke—and is one of the province's gathering cities. Long known as an industry gorilla, Drummondville has gained popularity among travelers for its shows and major events, mountain biking, wineries, golf and plentiful sugar shacks that reward visitors with fresh maple syrup throughout the festive winter.
Information: www.tourisme-drummond.com

WHAT TO SEE AND DO

Le Village Québecois d'Antan
1425 Montplasir St., Drummondville, N. via Hwy. 20, exit 181,
819-478-1441, 877-710-0267;
www.villagequébecois.com
Le Village Québecois d'Antan re-creates a rural French-Canadian village typical of the period from 1810-1910. Forty of the 60 buildings are authentic and the remaining are replicas built by craftsmen. Some of these structures include a baker's house, an apothecary, a blacksmith's house and a doughnut shop. June-September: daily 10 a.m.-6 p.m.

Manoir et Domaine Trent
Drummondville, Parc des Voltigeurs, 819-472-3662.
Period home 1836. restored by artisans; restaurant. Camping. Late June-August.

SPECIAL EVENT

World Folklore Festival
Heriot and Du Pont, Drummondville,
819-472-1184, 800-265-5412;
www.mondialdescultures.com
One of the major folklore events in North America. International singers, dancers and musicians participate at four different sites. Ten days in July.

HOTEL

★★Best Western Universel
915 rue Hains, Drummondville,
819-478-4971, 800-668-3521;
www.bestwestern.com
115 rooms. Restaurant, bar. Pets accepted, fees. Pool. $

RESTAURANT

★★Restaurant du Bois-Joli
505 St. Joseph Blvd. Ouest, Drummondville,
819-472-4366.
French menu. $$

GRANBY

On the eastern doorstep of Montreal, the town is a favorite excursion spot for the city's folk. Eighteen beautiful parks boast an array of old European fountains as well as a positively European devotion to decadent food. An abundance of maple groves makes sugaring-off parties a popular activity, and beautiful natural surroundings make this town a jumping-off point for mountain biking, horseback riding and water sports enthusiasts.
Information: www.granby-bromont.com

WHAT TO SEE AND DO

Granby Zoo
Pavilion Horace-Boivin,
525 St. Hubert St., Granby,
450-372-9113, 877-472-6299;
www.zoogranby.ca

This zoo houses more than 1,000 animals of 225 species from America, Asia, Africa and Oceania/South Sea Islands. An amusement park, the Parc Aquaique Amazoo, features the largest heated wave pool in Québec and an Amazonian village. Mid-May-late August: daily 10 a.m.-7 p.m..

Nature Interpretation Centre of Lake Boivin
700 rue Drummond, Granby,
450-375-3861
Guided walking tours through woodland and marsh; concentrations of waterfowl and nature exhibits.

Yamaska Provincial Park
1780 boul. David-Bouchard, Boucherville,
3 miles/4.8 kilometers E.,
450-776-7182;
www.sepaq.com
Visitors can enjoy many activities at this park, from hiking, kayaking and swimming in the summer to ice fishing and snowshoeing in the winter. Picnic areas and a snack bar are located here and there are a variety of restaurants nearby.

SPECIAL EVENT
Granby International
Drummond and Leclerc, Granby,
450-777-1330;
www.vagi.qc.ca
This antique car show takes place in Daniel-Johnson Park, on the banks of Lake Boivin. More than 30,000 car collectors and enthusiasts come to look and in some cases, bid on cars that are up for auction. Last weekend in July.

HOTEL
★★Auberge Bromont
95 rue Montmorency, Bromont,
450-534-1199, 888-276-6668;
www.aubergebromont.com
50 rooms. Restaurant. Exercise room. Pool. Golf. Tennis. $

MONT TREMBLANT
In 1894, the provincial government of Québec established this 482-square-mile 1,248-square-kilometer. wilderness reserve as a park in order to protect its abundant wildlife, 300 lakes, three rivers, three major hydrographical basins, innumerable streams, waterfalls and mountains that reach as high as 3,120 feet 960 meters.. Today it is a mecca of fishing, hiking, canoeing, biking, swimming, sailing, snowmobiling, snowshoeing and cross-country and downhill skiing—and in the fall, people come here in droves for the foliage alone. Entrances are at St. Donat, on Hwy. 125, St. Faustin on Hwy. 117 North, or St. Cme on Hwy. 343.
Information: www.tremblant.ca

SPECIAL EVENTS
Music in the Mountains
Mont Tremblant Provincial Park,
888-736-2526;
www.tremblant.com
Special music performances, workshops and activities. Late August-early September.

Tremblant International Blues Festival
Mont Tremblant Provincial Park,
888-736-2526;
www.tremblant.com
Ten days of the biggest blues festival in Canada, featuring more than 400 artists in almost 200 performances on indoor and outdoor stages. Internationally known artists; blues-themed painting and photography exhibits; workshops

and music courses; Louisiana-inspired cuisine. Mid-July.

HOTELS
★★Club Tremblant
121 rue Cuttle, Ville de Mont-Tremblant,
819-425-2731, 800-567-8341;
www.clubtremblant.com
100 rooms. Restaurant, bar. Children's activity center. Pool. Tennis. $$

★★★Fairmont Tremblant
3045 Chemin de la Chapelle,
Mont Tremblant,
819-681-7000;
www.fairmont.com
The Fairmont's location at the base of the Laurentian Mountains makes it a skier's paradise, with ski-in, ski-out access to the slopes, yet its

★
★
★
★
★

plentiful menu of activities ensures that non-skiers are also cosseted. The guest rooms and suites offer a sophisticated twist on traditional ski lodge décor while incorporating creature comforts. The region's rich culinary history is celebrated where guests are treated to some of the best meals in town.

316 rooms, 10 story. Restaurant, bar. Pool. Busn. Center. **$$**

★★★Le Westin Resort, Tremblant
100 Chemin Kandahar, Mont Tremblant, 819-681-8000, 888-736-2526; www.westin.com

A resort for all seasons, The Westing has luxurious guest rooms, many with balconies and fireplaces, a separate entrance for skiers and an outdoor heated saltwater pool Twenty outdoor tennis courts and two 18-hole golf courses challenge all comers. After an activity-filled day, savor Soto's Japanese cuisine or the American fare at Panache.

126 rooms. Complimentary continental breakfast. Restaurant, bar. Children's activity center, spa, beach. Pool. Golf. Tennis. Busn. Center. **$$**

★★Gray Rocks Resort And Convention Centre
2322 rue Labelle, Mont Tremblant, 819-425-2771, 800-567-6762; www.grayrocks.com

164 rooms. Restaurant, bar. Children's activity center. Beach. Seaplane base. Pool. Golf. Tennis. **$**

RESTAURANTS
★Auberge Sauvignon
2723 Chemin Principal, Mont Tremblant, 819-425-5466, 866-665-5466; www.aubergesauvignon.com

French menu. Dinner. No Handicpped. **$$$**

★Le Shack
3035 De La Chatelle, Mont Tremblant, 819-681-4700; www.leshack.com

Lunch, dinner. **$$**

★Pizzateria
118 Ch. Kandahar Village Center, Mont Tremblant, 819-681-4522.

Lunch, dinner. **$**

170

★
★
★
★
★

MONTREAL
Blessed by its location on an island at the junction of the St. Lawrence and Ottawa rivers, Montreal has served for more than three centuries as a gigantic trading post. However, despite its status as a commercial, financial and industrial center, Montreal has an unconventional, eclectic heart. An internationally recognized patron of the fine arts, the city hosts several acclaimed festivals attended by the international elite, and its cosmopolitan flavor is enhanced by its two-thirds French-speaking population, as well as more than 80 ethnic communities that welcome visitors to colorful neighborhoods, attractions and markets.

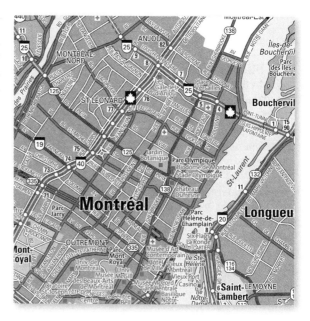

Montreal is made up of two parts: the Old City, which is a maze of narrow streets, restored buildings and old houses, best seen on foot and the modern Montreal, with its many skyscrapers, museums, theaters, restaurants and glittering nightlife. The boutiques and department stores of Sainte-Catherine Street are a shopper's paradise, while the cafe-terraces of Crescent Street encourage people-watching while sipping coffee in the sunshine. In the brisk winter, locals and visitors alike take refuge in Montreal's underground city, an impressive pedestrian network more than 19 miles (30 kilometers) long with hundreds of shops, restaurants, attractions and one of the most unique subway systems anywhere—in which each station has been decorated by a different architect for what's been called "the largest underground art gallery in the world."
Information: www.tourisme-montreal.org

WHAT TO SEE AND DO

Angrignon Park
7503 boul. de la Vérendrye, Montreal,
514-872-2816
On 262 acres 106 hectares. with more than 21,600 trees; lagoons, river; playground, picnicking, bicycling, ice skating, cross-country skiing.

Biodome de Montreal
4777 Pierre-De Coubertin Ave., Montreal,
514-868-3000;
www.biodome.qc.ca
The former Olympic Velodrome has been transformed into an environmental museum that combines elements of a botanical garden, aquarium, zoo and nature center. Four eco-systems—Laurentian Forest, Tropical Forest, Polar World and St. Laurent Marine—sustain thousands of plants and small animals. The Biodome also features a 1,640 feet 500-meter. Nature Path with text panels and maps and Naturalia, a discovery room.

Caleche Tours
Horse-drawn carriages depart from Place d' Armes, Mount Royal Park or the Old Port of Montreal.

Casino Montreal
1 Ave. du Casino, Montreal,
Expo 67's famous French Pavilion,
514-392-2746, 800-665-2274;
www.casinos-quebec.com
The Casino de Montreal offers guests a variety of games, with more than 120 gaming tables as well as 3,060 slot machines. Open 24 hours.

Château Ramezay
280 rue Notre-Dame Est., Montreal,
In front of City Hall,
514-861-3708;
www.chateauramezay.qc.ca
This historic building was constructed in the 18th century and was once the home of the governors of Montreal, the West Indies Company of France and the Governors-General of British North America. It opened as a museum in 1895 and today is the oldest private museum in Québec. Collections include furniture, paintings, costumes, porcelain, manuscripts and art objects of the 17th-19th centuries.

David M. Stewart Museum
20 Chemin Tour L'le, St. Helen Island,
514-861-6701;
www.stewart-museum.org
The Stewart Museum houses artifacts such as maps, firearms, kitchen utensils, engravings and navigational and scientific instruments that trace Canadian history from the 16th to 19th centuries.

Dorchester Square
1555 Peel St., Montreal.
In the center of Montreal, this park is a popular meeting place. Also here is Mary Queen of the World Cathedral, a 1/3-scale replica of St. Peter's in Rome, as well as the information center of Montreal and Tourisme Québec.

Floral Park
le Notre-Dame, Montreal.
Site of Les Floralies Internationales 1980; now permanent, it displays a collection

★
★
★
★
★

of worldwide flowers and plants. Walking trails; pedal boats, canoeing; picnic area, restaurant. Third week in June-mid-September: daily.

The Laurentians
www.laurentides.com

The Laurentian region, just 45 miles 72 kilometers. from Montreal, is a rich tourist destination. Surrounded by forests, lakes, rivers and the Laurentian Mountains, this area provides ample settings for open-air activities year-round. Water sports abound in summer, including canoeing, kayaking, swimming, rafting, scuba diving and excellent fishing. Hunting, golfing, horseback riding and mountain climbing are also popular in warmer months, as is bicycling along the 125-mile 201-kilometer. P'tit train du Nord trail. Brilliant fall colors lead into a winter ideal for snow lovers. The Laurentian region boasts a huge number of downhill ski centers, 600 miles 966 kilometers. of cross-country trails and thousands of miles of snowmobiling trails. The territory of the Laurentian tourist zone is formed on the south by the Outaouais River, des Deux-Montagnes Lake and the Milles-les River. On the east, its limits stretch from the limit of Terrebonne to Entrelacs. It is bounded on the north by Ste.-Anne du Lac and Baskatong Reservoir and on the west by the towns of Des Ruisseaux, Notre-Dame de Pontmain and Notre Dame du Laus. Places listed are Mont Tremblant Provincial Park, St. Jrme and Saint-Jovite.

Fort Lennox
Saint-Paul-de-l'ile-aux-Noix, 1 61st Ave., Montreal, off Hwy. 223, 450-291-5700; www.parcscanada.gc.ca

Located on le-aux-Noix, Fort Lennox was designed to protect against an American invasion. Costumed guides provide visitors with insight into the history of these fortifications.

Insectarium de Montreal
4101 rue Sherbrooke Est., Montreal, 514-872-1400

The Insectarium features a collection of more than 350,000 insects in a building designed to resemble a stylized insect. Interactive and participatory exhibits take visitors through aviaries and living displays in six geographically themed areas. Includes a butterfly aviary summer. and a children's amusement center.

La Fontaine Park
Sherbrooke and Ave., du Parc Lafontaine, Montreal, 514-872-2644

Outdoor enthusiasts delight in this park for its many recreational opportunities. Along with paddle boating on two manmade lakes, visitors may enjoy foot paths and bicycle trails and, in the winter, cross-country skiing, ice skating and snowshoeing.

La Ronde
le Sainte-Hlne, 22 Chemin Macdonald, Montreal, 514-397-2000; www.laronde.com

A 135-acre amusement park with 35 rides, including a 132-foot 40-meter. high wooden roller coaster; arcades, entertainment on a floating stage; water-skiing; live cartoon characters, children's village; circus, boutiques and restaurants. Mid-May-late October.

Maison St. Gabriel
Pointe-Saint-Charles, 2146 place de Dublin, Montreal, 514-935-8136; www.maisonsaint-gabriel.qc.ca

Built in the late 17th century as a farm; also served as school for Marguerite Bourgeoys, founder of the Sisters of the Congregation de Notre-Dame, who looked after young French girls who were to marry the early colonists. The site includes vegetable, herb and flower gardens. The house itself has period furnishings and tools and items of French-Canadian heritage, including woodcuts from ancient churches and chapels. mid-April-late June, September-mid-December: Tuesday-Sunday 1 p.m.-5p.m., late June-early September: Tuesday-Sunday 11 a.m.-6 p.m..

McCord Museum of Canadian History
690 rue Sherbrooke Ouest, Montreal,

514-398-7100;
www.mccord-museum.qc.ca
Extensive and diverse collections including the most important First Nations collection in Québec, Canadian costumes and textiles and the Notman photographic archives.

Montreal Botanical Garden
4101 rue Sherbrooke Est., Montreal,
514-872-1400;
www.ville.montreal.qc.ca/jardin
Within 180 acres 73 hectares. grow more than 26,000 species and varieties of plants; 30 specialized sections include roses, perennial plants, heath gardens, flowery brooks, bonsai, carnivorous plants and an arboretum; one of the world's largest orchid collections; seasonal flower shows. The bonsai and penjing collections are two of the most diversified in North America. Chinese and Japanese gardens; restaurant, tea room.

Montreal Canadiens (NHL)
1260 de La Gauchetière S.W., Montreal,
514-790-1245;
www.canadiens.com
Professional hockey team.

Montreal Harbor Cruises
Depart from Quai King Edward in Old Montreal,
514-842-3871, 800-563-4643;
www.croisieresaml.com
Various guided cruises and dinner excursions 1-4 hours.; bar service. Reservations are advised. May-mid-October.

Montreal Museum of Fine Arts
1379-80 rue Sherbrooke Ouest, Montreal,
514-285-2000, 800-899-6873;
www.mmfa.qc.ca
Museé des beaux-arts de Montreal. Canada's oldest art museum, founded in 1860, has a wide variety of displays ranging from Egyptian statues to 20th-century abstracts. Canadian section features old Québec furniture, silver and paintings.

Montreal Planetarium
1000 rue Saint-Jacques Ouest, Montreal,
514-872-4530;

www.planetarium.montreal.qc.ca
See the stars at the Montreal Planetarium, where its 385-seat theater holds multimedia astronomy shows, with projectors creating all features of the night sky. Just outside the theater are temporary and permanent exhibits on the solar system, meteorites, fossils and other astronomy-related topics.

Museé d'art contemporain de Montreal
185 rue Sainte-Catherine Ouest, Montreal,
514-847-6226;
www.macm.org
The only museum in Canada that is devoted exclusively to modern art. Gift shop, bookstore, garden, restaurant.

Museum of Decorative Arts
2200 rue Crescent, Montreal,
514-284-1252
Historic mansion Chateau Dufresne 1918., partially restored and refurnished, now houses international exhibitions of glass, textiles and ceramic art; changing exhibits.

The Montreal Science Centre
King-Edward Pier, 333 rue de la Commune Ouest, Montreal,
514-496-4724, 877-496-4724;
www.centredesciencesdemontreal.com/en
Uncover the mysteries of science and technology through multimedia and hands-on exhibits, an IMAX theater and more.

Notre-Dame Basilica
110 rue Notre-Dame Ouest, Montreal,
514-842-2925, 866-842-2925;
www.basiliquenddm.org
In 1672, one of the most beautiful churches in North America was erected on the present Notre-Dame street. When this became inadequate for the growing parish, a new church designed by New Yorker James O'Donnell was built. It was completed in 1829 and two towers and interior decorations were added later. Le Gros Bourdon, a bell cast in 1847 and weighing 24,780 pounds 11,240 kilograms., is in Perseverance Tower; there is a 10-bell chime in Temperance Tower. Built of Montreal limestone, the basilica is neo-Gothic in design with

QUÉBEC

a beautiful main altar, pulpit and numerous statues, paintings and stained-glass windows.

Notre-Dame-de-Bon-Secours Church
400 rue St. Paul Est., Montreal,
514-282-8670
Founded in 1657 by teacher Marguerite Bourgeoys and rebuilt 115 years later, this is one of the oldest churches still standing in the city. With its location near the Port of Montreal, parishioners often prayed here for the safety of the community's sailors. In recognition of this, many fishermen and other mariners presented the church with miniature wooden ships, which hang from the vaulted ceiling today. The tower offers views of the river and city. Housed here is the Marguerite Bourgeois museum, which features objects pertaining to early settlers.

The Old Fort
1820-1824. Oldest remaining fortification of Montreal; only the arsenal, powder magazine and barracks building still stand. Two military companies dating to the 18th century, La Compagnie Franche de la Marine and the 78th Fraser Highlanders, perform colorful military drills and parades. late June-August, Wednesday-Sunday.

Old (Vieux) Montreal
Bounded by McGill, Berri,
Notre-Dame Sts. and the St. Lawrence River;
www.old.montreal.qc.ca
The city of Montreal evolved from the small settlement of Ville-Marie founded by de Maisonneuve in 1642. The largest concentration of 19th-century buildings in North America is found here; several original dwellings remain, while many other locations are marked by bronze plaques throughout the area. The expansion of this settlement led to what is now known as Old Montreal. The area roughly forms a 100-acre 40-hectare. quadrangle which corresponds approximately to the area enclosed within the original fortifications.

Old Port of Montreal
de la Commune St., Montreal,
514-496-7678, 800-971-7678;

www.oldportofmontreal.com
A departure point for boat cruises, and a recreation and tourist park hosting exhibitions, special events and entertainment.

Olympic Park
4141 Pierre de Coubertin Ave., Montreal,
514-252-4141, 877-997-0919;
www.rio.gouv.qc.ca
The stadium was the site of the 1976 Summer Olympic Games and is now home to les Alouettes de Montreal football team. The world's tallest inclined tower(626 feet or 191 meters, leaning and at a 45-degree angle.) Cafeteria. Souvenir shop. Tours of the stadium are given daily.

Place d'Armes
rue St. Jacques, Montreal,
514-877-6810
A square of great historical importance and center of Old Montreal. The founders of Ville-Marie encountered the Iroquois here in 1644 and rebuffed them. In the square's center is a statue of de Maisonneuve, first governor of Montreal and at one end is the St. Sulpice seminary 1685. with an old wooden clock 1710. At 119 St. Jacques St. is the Bank of Montreal. This magnificent building contains a museum with collection of currency, mechanical savings banks, photographs and a reproduction of old-fashioned teller's cage. (Monday-Friday.) Some of the most important financial houses of the city are grouped around the square.

Place des Arts
260 Boul. de Maisonneuve Oeste,
514-842-2112; www.pdarts.com
This four-theater complex is the heart of Montreal's artistic life. L'Opra de Montreal, the Montreal Symphony Orchestra, les Grands Ballets Canadiens and La Compagnie Jean-Duceppe theatrical troupe have their permanent homes here. Other entertainment includes chamber music, recitals, jazz, folk singers, variety shows, music hall, theater, musicals and modern and classical dance.

Place Jacques-Cartier
Between rue Notre-Dame and rue de la

Commune, Montreal

Named for the discoverer of Canada, this was once a busy marketplace. Today, restaurants, cafes, bars, cyclists, in-line skaters and street performers are found around the plaza, which is closed to traffic. The oldest monument in the city, the Nelson Column, is in the square's upper section.

Parc Jean-Drapeau

1 Circuit Gilles-Villeneuve, Montreal,
514-872-6120;
www.parcjeandrapeau.com

Two islands in the middle of the St. Lawrence River; access via Jacques-Cartier Bridge or Metro subway. le Ste. Hlne St. Helen's Island. was the main anchor site for Expo '67; now a 342-acre 138-hectare. multipurpose park with three swimming pools; picnicking; cross-country skiing, snowshoeing. le Notre-Dame Notre Dame Island., to the south, was partly built up from the river bed and was an important activity site for Expo '67. Here is Gilles-Villeneuve Formula 1 racetrack; also beach, paddleboats, windsurfing and sailing.

Parc du Mont-Royal

Cote des Neiges and Remembrance rds.,
1260 Ch. Rememberance Montreal,
514-843-8240;
www.lemontroyal.qc.ca

Designed by Frederick Law Olmsted the creator of Central Park in New York City, Parc du Mont-Royal is also a park located in the heart of a city. Popular with visitors to Montreal, there is something for everyone here: cycling, hiking, picnicking, paddle boating, cross-country skiing and snowshoeing. Bikes, paddleboats, skis and snowshoes may be rented at the park.. Daily 6 a.m.-midnight.

Parc Safari

850 Rte. 202, Hemmingford,
33 miles/56 kilometers S. of Montreal on
Hwy. 15 to exit 6, then follow zoo signs,
450-247-2727;
www.parcsafari.com

Features 750 animals, rides and shows, children's theater and play area, swimming beach; drive-through wild animal reserve;

picnicking, restaurants, boutiques. Mid-May-mid-September: daily.

Pointe-à-Callière, the Montreal Museum of Archaeology and History

350 Place Royale, Montreal, corner of
Place Youville in Old Montreal,
514-872-9150;
www.pacmuseum.qc.ca/indexan.html

Built in 1992 over the site of the founding of Montreal, the main museum building, the Eperon, actually rests on pillars built around ruins dating from the town's first cemetery and its earliest fortifications, which are now in its basement. Two balconies overlook this archaeological site and a 16-minute multimedia show is presented using the actual remnants as a backdrop. From here, visitors continue underground, amid still more remnants, to the Archaeological Crypt, a structure that allows access to many more artifacts and remains; architectural models beneath a transparent floor illustrate five different periods in the history of Place Royale. The Old Customs House Ancienne-Douane. houses thematic exhibits on Montreal in the 19th and 20th centuries. Permanent and changing exhibits.

Rue Saint-Paul

The oldest street in Montreal. The mansions of Ville-Marie once stood here, but they have been replaced by commercial houses and office buildings.

St. Joseph's Oratory of Mont Royal

3800 Chemin Queen Mary, Montreal,
514-733-8211;
www.saint-joseph.org

The chapel was built in 1904 as a tribute to St. Joseph by Brother Andre, a member of the Congregation of Holy Cross. A larger crypt church was completed in 1917, when crowds coming to see Brother Andre and pray to St. Joseph were getting too large for the chapel. Today, the main church is a famous shrine attracting more than two million pilgrims yearly. A basilica with a seating capacity of 2,200 was founded in 1924; the dome towers over the city and a 56-bell carillon made in France is outstanding. The

175

QUÉBEC

Oratory's museum features 200 nativity scenes from 100 different countries.

SPECIAL EVENTS

Canadian Grand Prix

Parc Jean-Drapeau, Montreal,
514-350-0000; www.grandprix.ca
Held annually since 1967, this Formula 1 race took place on the Mont-Tremblant Circuit until 1977. At that time, the track was considered too dangerous and the then-named le-Notre-Dame Track was built. The first race at the new track was held in 1978 and was won by Gilles Villeneuve, Canada's first F1 driver. In 1982, when Villeneuve was tragically killed during practice laps at the Belgian Grand Prix, the track was re-named in his honor. If you wish to attend this event, make sure to purchase tickets well in advance; they can be extremely hard to come by, as this event is quite popular. Mid-June.

Fete Nationale

82 rue Sherbrooke Ouest, Montreal,
514-849-2560; www.fetenationale.qc.ca
St. Jean-Baptiste, patron saint of the French Canadians, is honored with three days of festivities surrounding the provincial holiday. The celebration includes street festivals, a bonfire, fireworks, musical events and parades. Mid-June.

International Fireworks Competition

le Sainte-Hlne, 22 Chemin Macdonald, Montreal, 514-397-2000;
www.montrealfireworks.com
Held in Montmorency Falls Park, this musical fireworks competition attracts master fireworks handlers from around the world. Fireworks start at 10 p.m., rain or shine. Late June-late July.

Just for Laughs Festival

2095 boul. St. Laurent, Montreal,
514-845-2322, 888-244-3155;
www.hahaha.com
This comedy festival features comic talent from all over the world. Shows are performed in more than 25 venues along St. Denis Street and are broadcast to millions of viewers worldwide. Artists who have performed at past festivals include Jerry Seinfeld, Jay Leno, Rowan Atkinson, Jon Stewart, Lily Tomlin and the cast of "The Simpsons." Mid-July.

Montreal Bike Fest

1251 rue Rachel Est., Montreal,
514-521-8356, 800-567-8356;
www.velo.qc.ca/feria/index_e.lasso
An entire week of events celebrating the bicycle, ending when 40,000 cyclists ride through the streets of Montreal. Includes a 16-mile 26-kilometers. outing for up to 10,000 children. Late May-early June.

Montreal High Lights Festival

822 rue Sherbrooke Est., Montreal,
514-288-9955, 888-477-9955
Spotlights the city's cultural and artistic diversity. Mid-February-early March.

Montreal International Jazz Festival

822 rue Sherbrooke Est., Montreal,
514-871-1881, 888-515-0515;
www.montrealjazzfest.com
More than 1,200 musicians and one million music lovers from around the world gather to celebrate jazz and other types of music. The 10-day fest includes more than 350 indoor and outdoor concerts. Late June-early July.

World Film Festival

1432 de Bleury St., Montreal,
514-848-3883;
www.ffm-montreal.org
Montreal's World Film Festival was organized to celebrate all types of cinema, from documentaries and drama to comedy and science fiction. Amateur and well-known filmmakers alike participate in the event, which screens films from nearly 70 countries. Late August-early September.

HOTELS

★★★Auberge du Vieux-Port

97 rue de la Commune Est., Montreal,
514-876-0081, 888-660-7678;
www.aubergeduvieuxport.com

QUÉBEC

This historic landmark building served several functions before becoming a full-service inn. It was transformed into an inn in 1995, with Les Ramparts restaurant serving up fine, French cuisine, and a rooftop terrace affording a panoramic view of the St. Lawrence River. Guests are pampered with a full breakfast, afternoon wine and cheese and more.

27 rooms. Complimentary full breakfast. Restaurant, bar. **$$**

★★★Auberge Handfield
555 boul. Richelieu, St. Marc-Sur-Richelieu,
450-584-2226;
www.aubergehandfield.com

Guests can chose between a room with a view of the garden or river. Small shops and boutiques are nearby with a larger shopping mall only a ten-minute drive away.

56 rooms. Restaurant, bar. Exercise room. Pool. **$**

★★★Chateau Versailles Hotel
1659 rue Sherbrooke Ouest, Montreal,
888-933-8111, 514-933-8111;
www.versailleshotels.com

Located at the start of Montréal's famous Miracle Mile shopping district and the foot of Mont Royal, this 1800s hotel features distinctly unique rooms in four renovated Victorian townhouses. The property is also just minutes by metro to the Molson Centre, and the Place des Arts.

65 rooms, 15 story. Complimentary continental breakfast. Restaurant, bar. Pets accepted, fees. Exercise room. Busn. Center. **$$**

★★Courtyard By Marriott Montreal Downtown
410 rue Sherbrooke Ouest, Montreal,
514-844-8855, 800-449-6654;
www.marriott.com

157 rooms. Complimentary continental breakfast. Restaurant, bar. Pool. **$**

★★★Delta Montreal
475 President Kennedy Ave., Montreal,
514-286-1986, 877-286-1986;
www.deltamontreal.com

This modern, inviting hotel is located in the heart of downtown, near the Convention Centre and the Place des Arts. Have a game on the squash courts at Delta's elaborate spa and sports center. And then enjoy French cuisine at Le Bouquet or relax at Le Cordial, the hotel's full-service bar.

456 rooms. Restaurant, bar. Children's activity center. Pets accepted, fees. Exercise room. Pool. Busn. Center. **$**

★★★Fairmont The Queen Elizabeth
900 boul. Rene Levesque Ouest, Montreal,
514-861-3511, 800-441-1414;
www.fairmont.com

This contemporary hotel is in the city center, located above the train station and linked to the underground system of shops and restaurants. Dining is an event savored by hotel guests and locals alike, who frequent the renowned Beaver Club for its gourmet meals or the convivial, Mediterranean-inspired Le Montrealais Bistrot-Bar-Restaurant.

1,039 rooms, 21 story. Two restaurants, bar. Pets accepted, fees. Exercise room. Pool. Busn. Center. **$$**

★★★Hilton Montreal, Bonaventure
900 de la Gauchetiere Ouest, Montreal,
514-878-2332, 800-267-2575;
www.hiltonmontreal.com

This hotel is perched on top of the Place Bonaventure Exhibition Hall. There are rooftop gardens to explore and a year-round outdoor pool. The central city location is perfect for sightseeing in Old Montréal, gambling at the casino or shopping the underground boutiques.

395 rooms. Restaurant, bar. Pets accepted, fees. Exercise room. Pool. Busn. Center. **$$**

★★★Hilton Montreal Dorval Airport
12505 Cote de Liesse, Dorval,
514-631-2411; www.dorval.hilton.com

Perfect for the business or leisure traveler, with its location only a two minute drive to the airport. Guests can relax in either by the pool or jacuzzi and then enjoy their open and airy room. Dine at Au Coin du Feu and

QUÉBEC

enjoy the seafood and steak cuisine, and then have a cocktail at Eclipse.

494 rooms, 10 story. Restaurant, bar. Pets accepted, fees. Exercise room. Pool. Busn. Center. **$**

★★★Hilton Montreal/Laval
2225, autoroute des Laurentides, Laval, 450-682-2225; www.hilton.com
Situated on 30 minutes from downtown Montreal, this hotel offers something for everyone. A heated indoor swimming pool, a steam room and a waterfall jacuzzi are just some of the amenities here. La Grigliata offers Mediterranean cuisine for breakfast, lunch and dinner.
170 rooms. Restaurant, bar. Exercise room. Pool. Busn. Center. **$$**

★★Holiday Inn Select Montreal
99 Viger Ave., Ouest, Montreal, 514-878-9888, 888-878-9888; www.yul-downtown.hiselect.com
235 rooms. One restaurant, two bars. Exercise room. Pool. Busn. Center. **$$**

★★★Hostellerie Les Trois Tilleuls
290 rue Richelieu, St. Marc-Sur-Richelieu, 514-856-7787; www.lestroistilleuls.com
This 1880s farmhouse is tucked away to give visitors a quiet and relaxing stay. Located an hour's drive from town, this hotel offers rooms with a view of the Richelieu River.
59 rooms. Restaurant, bar. Pool. Tennis. Busn. Center .**$**

★★★Hotel InterContinental Montreal
360 rue Ste Antoine Ouest, Montreal, 514-987-9900 ; www.montreal.intercontinental.com
This sophisticated, elegant hotel is located across from the Convention Center in downtown Montréal. It's only a short walk from the popular Old Town. The hotel's building houses shops and businesses, with the guest rooms starting on the tenth floor.
357 rooms. Pets accepted, some restrictions; fee. 2 restaurants, bar. Fitness room. Indoor pool. Business center. **$**

★★★Hostellerie Rive Gauche
1810 Richelieu Blvd., Beloeil, 450-467-4477; www.hostellerierivegauche.com
Just 20 minutes from downtown Montréal, this hotel offers year-round recreation. All rooms have views of the Richelieu River or Mont St.-Hilaire.
22 rooms. Restaurant, bar. Pool. Tennis. **$**

★★Hotel Chéribourg
2603 Chemin du Parc, Orford, 819-843-3308, 800-567-6132; www.cheribourg.com
97 rooms. Restaurant, bar. Exercise room. Pool. Tennis. **$**

★★★Hotel du Fort
1390 rue du Fort, Montreal, 514-938-8333, 800-565-6333; www.hoteldufort.com
Located just steps from rue Ste. Catherine, this property is near attractions, shops and restaurants. The hotel puts its emphasis on providing upscale service and the comforts of home. Understated guest rooms offer city views. Room service options include menus from area restaurants.
124 rooms. Complimentary continental breakfast. Restaurant, bar. Busn. Center. **$**

★★★Hotel Gault
449 rue Ste. Hlne, Montreal, 514-904-1616, 866-904-1616; www.hotelgault.com
You might not expect to find an ultramodern hotel in a historic neighborhood, but the Hotel Gault is exactly that. Inside, you'll find interiors of glass, concrete and steel, balanced with warm woods. Soundproofed guest rooms feature flat-screen TVs, CD and DVD players, and comfortable workstations, while some have private terraces. A variety of living spaces are available,
30 rooms. Restaurant, bar. Exercise room. Busn. Center. **$$**

★★Hotel Le Cantlie Suites
1110 rue Sherbrooke Ouest, Montreal, 514-842-2000, 800-567-1110;

www.hotelcantlie.com
250 rooms, all suites. Restaurant, bar. Pool. Busn. Center. **$$**

★★★Hotel L'eau A La Bouche
3003 Bd Ste. Adele, Sainte Adèle,
450-229-2991;
www.leaualabouche.com
Located just 45 minutes from Montreal, Hotel L'eau a la Bouche is amid the greenery of the Laurentian Mountains. Rooms offer mountain views. A state of relaxation is achievable, whether its the heated outdoor pool, enjoying nearby activities or a visit the hotel's spa. Having a meal at the hotel's restaurant is a must, where the award-winning cuisine of chef Anne Desjardins lives up to the L'Eau A La Bouche name.
25 rooms. Restaurant, bar, spa. Exercise room. **$$**

★★★Hotel Le Germain
2050 rue Mansfield, Montreal,
514-849-2050, 877-333-2050;
www.hotelgermain.com
This distinctive boutique hotel offers hospitality, comfort and relaxation in an elegant setting. The convenient downtown location makes it close to shopping, museums, concert halls and movie theaters. Guest rooms feature original photos by Louis Ducharm.
101 rooms, 13 story. Complimentary full breakfast. Restaurant, bar. Pets accepted, fees. Exercise room. **$$**

★★★★Hotel Le St. James
355 Saint Jacques St., Montreal,
514-841-3111, 866-841-3111;
www.hotellestjames.com
At the majestic Hotel Le St. James, each room and suite is individually decorated with antiques and art. A former bank, the building's imposing facade features ornate moldings and details fully restored to their 1870s grandeur. The convention center, downtown business area, Old Port area and the St. Lawrence River are the main sights of Old Montreal that are just a short stroll away from the hotel. Lunch and dinner feature regional, market-driven fare and afternoon tea is served as well.

61 rooms. Restaurant, bar, spa. Pet. Exercise. Busn. Center. **$$$$**

★★★Hotel Nelligan
106 rue St. Paul Ouest, Montreal,
514-788-2040, 877-788-2040;
www.hotelnelligan.com
This boutique hotel consists of two connected buildings. The exposed-brick and stone walls hint at its lengthy history, but the hotel provides all the modern touches that guests expect in an urban hotel. A wine and cheese reception is offered daily. Verses, the hotel's restaurant, serves French fare in a hip and trendy setting.
63 rooms. Complimentary continental breakfast. Restaurant, bar. Exercise room. Busn. Center. **$$**

★★Novotel
1180 rue de la Montagne, Montreal,
514-861-6000, 800-668-6835;
www.novotelmontreal.com
228 rooms. Restaurant, bar. Pets accepted, fees. Exercise room. Busn. Center. **$**

★★★Hotel Omni Mont-Royal
1050 rue Sherbrooke Ouest, Montreal,
514-284-1110, 800-843-6664;
www.omnihotels.com
This elegant property is centrally located in the historic Golden Square Mile area in the heart of downtown and at the foot of Mont Royal. Shops, museums, nightlife and fine dining are within walking distance. And don't let your pooch miss out on this sophisticated hotel. Pets receive specially designed treats.
300 rooms, 31 story. Two restaurants, bar, spa. Pets accepted. Exercise room. Pool. Busn. Center. **$$**

★★★Hotel Place d'Armes
55 Saint-Jacques Ouest, Montreal,
514-842-1887, 888-450-1887;
www.hotelplacedarmes.com
Step from Old Montreal's centuries-old charm into new millennium modishness at Le Place d'Armes Hotel and Suites. The boutique hotel's ultramodern decor will delight the most sophisticated travelers.

QUÉBEC

135 rooms, 6 story. Complimentary continental breakfast. Restaurant, bar, spa. **$$$**

★★★Hotel St. Paul
355 rue McGill, Montreal,
493-062-9011, 866-380-2202;
www.hotelstpaul.com
Set in a restored Beaux Arts building, the Hotel St. Paul is all about contemporary cool. Lighting above guest room doors revolve around two themes: earth (lit in red) and sky (lit in blue). The spare accommodations feature large windows, modern furnishings and animal-skin accents. The on-site restaurant, Cube, serves fresh seasonal cuisine.
120 rooms. Complimentary continental breakfast. Restaurant, bar. Pets accepted, fees. Exercise room. Busn. Center. **$$**

★★★Hyatt Regency Montreal
1255 Jeanne-Mance, Montreal,
514-982-1234, 866-816-3871;
www.montreal.hyatt.com
Enjoy a lively urban retreat at the Hyatt Regency Montréal. Located in the Cultural District, the Hyatt is part of the elaborate shopping, dining, and entertainment center Complexe des Jardins and adjacent to Place des Arts. The hotel also has underground access to the Montréal Convention Center.
605 rooms, 12 story. Restaurant, bar. Exercise room. Pool. Busn. Center. **$$**

★★★Le Saint Sulpice Hotel Montreal
414 rue Saint Sulpice,
Montreal,
514-288-1000, 877-785-7423;
www.lesaintsulpice.com
Step back in time at this luxury hotel, located in the historic part of Montreal, just steps from the Notre-Dame Basilica and the Old Port. Sample steaks and seafood as well as regional specialties in S Le Restaurant. The Essence Health Center features beautifying treatments in addition to modern exercise equipment.
108 rooms, all suites. Complimentary continental breakfast. Restaurant, bar, spa. Exercise. **$$$**

★★★Loews Hotel Vogue
1425 rue de la Montagne, Montreal,
514-285-5555, 800-465-6654;
www.loewshotels.com
The fresh spirit and chic modernity of the Loews Hotel Vogue breathes new life into old-world Montréal. The accommodations provide sleek shelter with silk upholstered furnishings, while creature comforts like oversized bathrooms appeal to every guest. Don't miss L'Opéra Bar, the place be seen.
142 rooms. Restaurant, bar. Pets accepted, fees. Busn. Center. **$$**

★★★Marriott Montreal Chateau Champlain
1050 de la Gauchetiere Ouest, Montreal,
514-878-9000, 800-200-5909;
www.marriott.com
Charming Art Nouveau décor adorns the guest rooms with views of the Cathedral, Parc Mont Royal, and Old Montréal. And hospitality rules at the Mediterranean-flavored Le Samuel de Champlain restaurant, while Le Senateur Bar satisfies discriminating tastes.
611 rooms. Restaurant, bar. Exercise room. Pool. **$$**

★★★Petite Auberge Les Bons Matins
1401 Argyle Ave., Montreal,
514-931-9167, 800-588-5280;
www.bonsmatins.com
Guests stay in rooms in adjoining restored century-old row townhomes in the heart of Montréal, close to main thoroughfares Sainte-Catherine Street and Crescent Street and just steps away from the Lucien L'Allier metro stop. Antiques and paintings by a family artist decorate rooms, all with private baths with bathrobes and natural bath products. A full gourmet breakfast is served daily in the dining room.
27 rooms. Pets accepted, some restrictions. Complimentary full breakfast. **$$**

★★Quality Inn
6680 Taschereau Blvd., Brossard,
450-671-7213, 800-267-3837;
www.qualityinn.com

91 rooms. Complimentary continental breakfast. Check-out noon. Restaurant, bar. Outdoor pool. Pool. **$**

★★★The Ritz-Carlton, Montreal
1228 rue Sherbrooke Ouest, Montreal, 514-842-4212, 800-363-0366; www.ritzmontreal.com

This classic hotel is a leisure traveler's dream, with the quaint Old Town, Olympic Center, and renowned museums located just a short distance from the hotel. The sumptuously appointed rooms and suites, the mood here is resolutely distinguished. Gastronomic pleasures abound here at the elegant Le Café de Paris and the romantic garden setting of Le Jardin du Ritz.

229 rooms. Restaurant, bar. Pets accepted, fees. Exercise room. Busn. Center. **$$**

★★★Sofitel Montreal
1155 Rue Sherbrooke Ouest, Montreal, 514-285-9000; www.sofitel.com

Modern and elegant, this hotel is set at the foot of Parc Mont Royal on Sherbrooke Street and close to galleries, boutiques and the historic center of the city. Enjoy morning croissants and evening cocktails in Le Bar and dine on Provencal-inspired cuisine in Renoir.

258 rooms. Restaurant, bar. Pets accepted, fee. Exercise room. Busn. Center. **$$$**

★★★Super 8 Montreal - West/Vaudreuil
21700 Trans-Canada Hwy., Vaudreuil, 450-424-8898.

This European-inspired property sits along the shore of Lac des Deux Montagnes. 117 rooms. Restaurant, bar. Exercise room. Pool. Tennis. **$$**

SPECIALITY LODGINGS
Angelica Blue B&B
1213 Ste., Elizabeth, Montreal, 514-844-5048, 800-878-5048; www.angelicablue.com
6 rooms. Complimentary full breakfast. **$**

Auberge de la Fontaine
1301 rue Rachel Est., Montreal, 514-597-0166, 800-597-0597;

www.aubergedelafontaine.com
21 rooms. Complimentary full breakfast. **$$**

Le Petit Prince B&B
1384 Overdale Ave., Montreal, 514-938-2277, 877-938-9750; www.montrealbandb.com
4 rooms. Complimentary full breakfast. **$$**

Le Traversin B&B
4124 St-Hubert St., Montreal, 514-597-1546; www.letraversin.com
4 rooms. **$$**

Manoir Harvard
4805 Harvard Ave., Montreal, 514-488-3570, 888-373-3570; www.manoirharvard.com
5 rooms. Complimentary full breakfast. **$$**

RESTAURANTS
★★★Au Pied De Cochon
536 rue Duluth Est., Montreal, 514-281-1114

The "Pig's Foot" has regional cuisine with an emphasis on beef, lamb, venison, duck and yes, pork. There are several varieties of foie gras and fish. Take the Au Pied De Cochon-The Album home as a souvenir. Closed Monday. Reservations recommended. **$$$**

★Au Tournant de la Riviere
5070 Salaberry, Carignan, 450-658-7372
French menu. **$$$**

★★Auberge Handfield
555 boul. Richelieu, St. Marc-Sur-Richelieu, 450-584-2226; www.aubergehandfield.com
French menu. Closed Monday; also mid-January-early May. Reservations recommended. Outdoor seating. **$$$**

★★Biddle's Jazz and Ribs
2060 rue Aylmer, Montreal, 514-842-8656

181

American menu, Steak menu. Reservations recommended. Outdoor seating. **$$**

★★★Bistro à Champlain
75 Chemin Masson, Ste., Marguerite, 450-228-4988; www.bistroachamplain.com
Located on the edge of Lake Masson in the Laurentian Mountains, this elegant, rustic restaurant draws an international clientele. French menu. Closed Monday-Tuesday. **$$$**

★★★Cafe de Paris
1228 rue Sherbrooke Ouest, Montreal, 514-842-4212; www.ritzcarlton.com
This premier dining room, featuring regional French Québecois cuisine, is located on the ground floor of the Ritz Carlton with views of rue Sherbrooke and Le Jardin du Ritz the garden. The elegant presentations and smooth service are the hallmarks of this sophisticated room. In season, reservations are essential and the outdoor seating area is booked solid.
French menu. **$$$**

★★★Cafe Ferreira
1446 rue Peel, Montreal, 514-848-0988; www.ferreiracafe.com
This restaurant is one of the most stylish dining rooms in Montreal. The friendly staff serves up wonderful Portuguese cuisine, with an emphasis on fresh fish and a comprehensive selection of Portuguese wines and ports. Closed Sunday. Bar. Reservations recommended. Outdoor seating. **$$$**

★Cafe Ste. Alexandre
518 rue Duluth Est., Montreal, 514-849-4251.
Italian, Greek, Seafood menu. Reservations recommended. Outdoor seating. **$$**

★★★Chez L'Epicier
311 rue Saint-Paul Est., Montreal, 514-878-2232; www.chezlepicier.com
This cozy and informal French restaurant is located in a building in Old Montreal that dates to the late 1800s. The restaurant uses fresh, local products for its daily-changing menu and its food products are available for sale in a neighborhood market setting.
French menu. Closed for two weeks in January. Reservations recommended. **$$$**

★★★Chez la Mere Michel
1209 rue Guy, Montreal, 514-934-0473; www.chezlameremichel.com
In a city with volumes of competition, this fine French restaurant has succeeded in its downtown historic-home location since 1965. The menu is classic and well prepared and includes a fantastic strawberry Napoleon for dessert.
French menu. Closed Sunday. **$$$**

★★★Cube
355 rue McGill, Montreal, 514-876-2823;
This contemporary French restaurant is located in the Hotel St. Paul, close to Old Montreal. Its crisp and minimalist décor and cube serveware add to the coolness of the place. Although Cube is a hot spot, it has a down-to-earth staff who makes dining here enjoyable.
French regional menu. Lunch, dinner, brunch. Bar. Business casual attire. Reservations recommended. Valet parking. **$$$**

★★Globe
3455 St. Laurent, Montreal, 514-284-3823; www.restaurantglobe.com
French menu. Reservations recommended. **$$$**

★★Il Cortile
1442 rue Sherbrooke Ouest, Montreal, 514-843-8230
Italian menu. Reservations recommended. Outdoor seating. **$$$**

★★Jardin Nelson
407 Place Jacques-Cartier, Montreal, 514-861-5731; www.jardinnelson.com
American, Italian menu. Closed November-March. Reservations recommended. Outdoor seating. **$$**

QUÉBEC

★★★★L'eau a la Bouche
3003 Ste. Adele Blvd, Ste. Adele,
450- 229-2991; www.leaualabouche.com
Tucked into a forests surrounding the Laurentian Mountains, near the village of Sainte-Adèle, you will find L'eau a la Bouche, a charming little restaurant located on the property of the Hotel L'eau a la Bouche. The gourmet menu is built around local produce, fish, meat and homegrown herbs and vegetables, woven together and dressed up with a perfect dose of French technique and modern flair. Attentive, thoughtful service and a vast wine list make this luxurious dining experience unforgettable.
French menu. Breakfast, dinner. Bar.**$$$**

★★L'Express
3927 Ste., Denis, Montreal,
514-845-5333
French menu. Reservations recommended. **$$**

★★La Gaudriole
825 rue Laurier Est., Montreal,
514-276-1580; www.lagaudriole.com
French menu. Closed first week in January, mid-July-early August. Reservations recommended. **$$$**

★ La Louisiane
5850 rue Sherbrooke Ouest, Montreal,
514-369-3073
Cajun menu. Closed Monday. **$$**

★★★La Maree
404 Place Jacques Cartier, Montreal,
514-861-9794
Situated in Old Montreal, this romantic dining room offers classic French cuisine in an ornate, Louis XIII atmosphere. The historic 1808 building is just the place to enjoy old-fashioned, formal service and a great bottle of wine from the cellar.
French menu. Reservations recommended. Outdoor seating. **$$$**

★★★La Rapiere
1155 rue Metcalfe, Montreal, 514-871-8920.
Southwestern French cooking with a personal touch is the draw at this sophisticated restaurant in downtown Montreal. Cassoulet, foie gras and other specialties from southwest France are served in a typical country-French setting.
Closed Sunday; also mid-July-mid-August, 15 days in December. Bar. Jacket required. Reservations recommended. **$$$**

★La Sauvagine
1592 Rte. 329 Nord, Ste. Agathe,
819-326-7673; www.lasauvagine.com
French menu. Closed Monday-Tuesday off-season. **$**

★★★Laloux
250 Pine Ave. Est., Montreal,
514-287-9127; www.laloux.com
One of the few "bistro parisiens" in Montreal, this local favorite features excellent cuisine du marche served in a sober but refined environment.
French menu. Reservations recommended. Outdoor seating. **$$$**

★★Le Cafe Fleuri
1255 rue Jeanne Mance, Montreal,
514-841-2010; www.montreal.hyatt.com
French menu. Outdoor seating. **$$**

★★Le Chrysantheme
1208 rue Crescent, Montreal,
514-397-1408
Chinese menu. Closed Monday; last week in July. **$$**

★Le Jardin de Panos
521 rue Duluth Est., Montreal,
514-521-4206
Greek menu. Outdoor seating. **$$**

★★The Keg
25 rue St. Paul Est., Montreal,
514-871-9093; www.kegsteakhouse.com
Steak menu. **$$$**

★★★Le Lutetia
1430 rue de la Montagne, Montreal,
514-288-5656;
www.hoteldelamontagne.com
Located in the popular l'Hotel de la Montagne, this restaurant serves cuisine in a

QUÉBEC

comfortable rococo setting. The service is gracious and accommodating, the decor pleasant and interesting.
French menu. Reservations recommended. **$$$**

★★★Le Mas des Oliviers
1216 rue Bishop, Montreal,
514-861-6733;
www.lemasdeoliviers.ca
This small, traditional French restaurant has been offering rich cuisine in a Provencal setting for more than 30 years.
French menu. Reservations recommended. **$$$**

★★★Le Mitoyen
652 rue de la Place Publique, Montreal,
450-689-2977;
www.restaurantlemitoyen.com
Quietly elegant dining rooms, cozily sized for intimate dining for individuals, couples, or groups, present the freshest of local ingredients. Gracious servers in time-honored country tradition welcome guests as honored friends. Both native Montrealers and out-of-towners enjoy the exquisite fare and homey atmosphere.
Regional cuisine. Closed Monday. Outdoor seating. **$$$**

★★Le Parchemin
1333 rue University, Montreal,
514-844-1619;
www.leparchemin.com
French menu. Closed Sunday. **$$$**

★★Le Paris
1812 Ste., Catherine Ouest, Montreal,
514-937-4898.
French menu. Reservations recommended. **$$**

★★★Le Piémontais
1145-A rue de Bullion, Montreal,
514-861-8122
Experience authentic, Piedmont-region cuisine at this comfortable Italian restaurant. Simple but artfully prepared dishes are presented with professional and attentive service.

Italian menu. Closed Sunday; third week in July-August 15. Reservations recommended. **$$$**

★★★Le Piment Rouge
1170 Peel St., Montreal,
514-866-7816;
www.lepimentrouge.com
The bold cuisine of China's Szechwan province is is set in an airy, contemporary restaurant located in the former Windsor Hotel. A signature dish include spicy peanut butter dumplings, a recipe the restaurant is credited with inventing in Montréal. Le Piment Rouge also stocks more than 3,000 wines.
Chinese menu. **$$**

★★★Les Caprices de Nicolas
2072 rue Drummond, Montreal,
514-282-9790; www.lescaprices.com
The intimate candlelight and romantic indoor/outdoor garden combine to make this restaurant a true special-occasion destination. Given the classic, formal service, it is a pleasant surprise to find the French dishes on the menu refreshingly updated with light, vibrant flavors and seasonal market produce. A wine list of 500 labels adds to the excitement.
French menu. Closed December 24-January 10. Jacket required. Reservations recommended. **$$$**

★★★Les Continents
360 rue St. Antoine Ouest, Montreal,
514-847-8729, 800-361-3600;
www.intercontinental.com
Located on the second floor of the Hotel InterContinental Montreal, Les Continents has beautiful views of Jean-Paul Riopelle Park and the colorful Convention Centre. The menu features contemporary French cuisine with Canadian influences.
French Canadian menu. Closed Easter weekend. **$$$**

★★★Les Remparts
93 rue de la Commune Est., Montreal,
514-392-1649;
www.restaurantlesremparts.com
Located in the basement of the Auberge du Vieux-Port, on the site of Montreal's origi-

nal fortress, this French restaurant offers a comfortable, cozy atmosphere with professional, attentive service. The restaurant is decorated with candles on each table, stone floors and exposed brick walls with parts of the old fort's stonework on display.
French menu. Reservations recommended. Outdoor seating. **$$$**

★★★Les Trois Tilleuls
290 rue Richelieu, Montreal,
514-856-7787, 800-263-2230;
www.lestroistilleuls.com
Modern interpretations of classic French cuisine, complemented by home baking, is the focus at this 1880s farmhouse. Gardens and terrace offer views of the St. Lawrence River. Located on the South Shore, 35 minutes from downtown Montreal.
French menu. Reservations recommended. Outdoor seating. **$$$$**

★★★Med Bar and Grill
3500 boul. St. Laurent, Montreal,
514-844-0027; www.medgrill.com
If you're seeking a spot to see and be seen, or a chic place to linger over luscious cocktails while perched amidst Montreal's most stylish set, Med Bar and Grill is an excellent option. The food is upscale but remains fun and inviting. Classic dishes of the Mediterranean are given a modern spin here, reflecting the seasons and incorporating the regions bountiful produce.
Closed Sunday. Reservations recommended. **$$$**

★★Mikado
368 rue Laurier Ouest, Montreal,
514-279-4809; www.mikadomontreal.com
Japanese menu. Lunch, dinner. Bar. Reservations recommended. **$$**

★★Moishe's
3961 boul. St. Laurent, Montreal,
514-845-3509; www.moishes.ca
Steak menu. Lunch weekdays only. Reservations recommended. **$$$**

★★★Nuances
1 Ave. de Casino, Montreal,

514-392-2708, 800-665-2274;
www.casinos-quebec.com
This stylish, modern bistro, located within the Montreal Casino, is swathed in soothing earth tones and decorated with original works by local artists custom-designed for the space. The upscale menu stars exquisitely updated French cuisine assembled from a cast of natures best seasonal products.
French menu. Jacket required. Reservations recommended. **$$$**

★★Primadonna
3479 boul. St. Laurent, Montreal,
514-282-6644;
www.primadonnaonline.com
Italian menu, sushi. Reservations recommended. **$$$$**

★★Quelli Della Notte
6834 boul. St. Laurent, Montreal,
514-271-3929; www.quelli.ca
Italian menu. **$$$**

★★★Queue de Cheval
1221 boul. Rene-Levesque Ouest,
Montreal, 514-390-0090;
www.queuedecheval.com
Prime, dry-aged meats are the showstoppers at Queue de Cheval, a rustic, chateaustyled steakhouse accented with rich maple wood and tall, vaulted ceilings in the heart of Montreal. The menu also has a generous raw bar, a terrific selection of salads and vegetarian appetizers and a shimmering Fresh Fish Market.
Steak menu. Reservations recommended. Outdoor seating. **$$$**

★★Restaurant Chang Thai
2100 Crescent St., Montreal,
514-286-9994.
Thai menu. **$$**

★★Restaurant Chez Lévèque
1030 rue Laurier Ouest, Montreal,
514-279-7355.
French menu. Reservations recommended. **$$**

185

QUÉBEC

★Restaurant Daou

519 Faillon Est., Montreal,
514-276-8310.
Lebanese menu. Closed Monday. **$$**

★★Restaurant Sho-Dan

2020 rue Metcalfe, Montreal,
514-987-9987; www.sho-dan.com
Japanese menu. Lunch weekdays only. **$$**

★★★Ristorante Da Vinci

1180 rue Bishop, Montreal,
514-874-2001;
www.davinci.qc.ca
This charming restaurant offers an authentic atmosphere, warm, attentive service and well-prepared traditional dishes made with fresh ingredients.
Italian menu. Closed Sunday. Reservations recommended. Outdoor seating. **$$$**

★★Rosalie Restaurant

1232 rue de la Montagne, Montreal,
514-392-1970;
www.rosalierestaurant.com
French bistro menu. Lunch weekdays only. Reservations recommended. Outdoor seating. **$$**

★★★★Toque!

900 place Jean-Paul Riopelle, Montreal,
514-499-2084;
www.restaurant-toque.com
Toque! is a graceful, luxurious, contemporary French restaurant located across from the Convention Centre and Jean-Paul Riopelle Park. Plates are garnished with such impeccable attention to detail that you may spend several minutes debating whether or not to ruin it. The talented and hospitable chef, Norman Laprise wields magic with a whisk and uses locally farmed ingredients to create a miraculous menu of sophisticated, avant-garde French fare.
French menu. Closed Sunday-Monday; also two weeks in late December-early January. Reservations recommended. **$$$**

★★Zen

1050 rue Sherbrooke Ouest, Montreal,
514-284-1110;
www.omnihotels.com
The focus at this Chinese restaurant located in the Hotel Omni Mont-Royal is on the food. The decor is modern minimalist. The evening prix-fixe menu allows patrons to sample every item on the menu.
Chinese menu. Reservations recommended. **$$$**

QUÉBEC CITY

The provincial capital of Québec, one of the most beautiful in the Western Hemisphere, is 150 miles 240 kilometers. northeast of Montreal. Nestled on a historic rampart, Québec is antique, medieval and lofty, a place of mellowed stone buildings and weathered cannon, horse-drawn calches, ancient trees and narrow, steeply angled streets. Once the "Gibraltar of the North," Québec's Upper Town is built high on the cliff and surrounded by fortress-like walls. One of the split-level city's best-known landmarks, Le Chateau Frontenac, is a hotel towering so high that it's visible 10 miles 16 kilometers. away. The Lower Town surrounds Cape Diamond and spreads up the valley of the St. Charles River, a tributary of the St. Lawrence. The two sections are divided by the Funicular, which affords magnificent views of the harbor, river and hills beyond.

In this heart of Canada's francophone soul, English is understood in many places. However Québec's soul and spirit is vibrantly French.
Information: www.quebecregion.com

WHAT TO SEE AND DO

Artillery Park National Historic Site

2 d'Auteuil St., Québec City,
St. Jean and D'Auteuil Sts.,
418-648-4205;

www.pc.qc.ca/ihn-nhs/qc/artiller
A 4-acre 2-hectare. site built by the French to defend the opening of the St. Charles River. By the end of the 17th century, it was known as a strategic site and military engi-

neers began to build fortifications here. Until 1871, the park housed French and British soldiers, eventually becoming a large industrial complex. Dauphine Redoubt 1712-1748., gun carriage shed 1813-1815., officers' quarters 1818. and arsenal foundry 1903. have been restored. Interpretation center.

Baillairge Cultural Tours
Québec City, 418-692-5737
Group tours lasting between three days and one week focus on art, cuisine and education. Late June-mid-October.

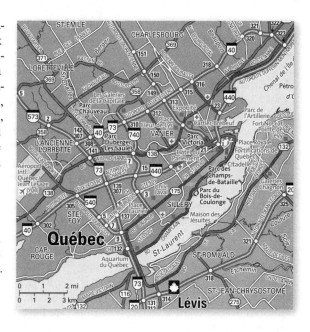

Basilica of Ste. Anne-de-Beaupre
10018 Royale Ave., Québec City, 418-827-3781; www.ssadb.qc.ca
This basilica is noted as the oldest pilgrimage in North America. The first chapel was built on this site in 1658; the present basilica, built in 1923, is made of white Canadian granite and is regarded as a Romanesque masterpiece. Capitals tell the story of Jesus' life in 88 scenes; vaults are decorated with mosaics; unusual techniques were used for 240 stained-glass windows outlined in concrete. Fourteen life-size Stations of the Cross and Scala Santa Holy Stairs. are located on the hillside.

Calèches
Take a tour of the historic district in a horse-drawn carriage. Most leave from the Esplanade parking lot on d'Auteuil Street, next to the Tourist Bureau.

Explore
63 rue Dalhousie, Québec City, 418-692-1759.
This 30-minute high-tech sound and visual arts show illustrates the founding of Québec and the beginnings of New France during the Golden Age of Exploration, when Columbus, Cartier, Champlain and others began to venture into the Americas.

Gaspé Peninsula
Québec City, 418-775-2223, 800-463-0323; www.tourisme-gaspesie.com
Jutting out into the Gulf of St. Laurent, the Gaspe Peninsula is a region of varying landforms including mountains, plateaus, beaches and cliffs. It is blessed with abundant and rare wildlife and some unique flora, including 12-foot-high 4-meter-high., centuries-old fir trees. The rivers, teeming with trout, flow to meet the salmon coming from the sea. Called "Gespeg" meaning "land's end". by the Aborigines, the area was settled primarily by Basque, Breton and Norman fishermen, whose charming villages may be seen clinging to the shore beneath the gigantic cliffs. The French influence is strong, although English is spoken in a few villages.

Grand Theatre
269 boul. Rene-Levesque, Québec, 418-643-8131; www.grandtheatre.qc.ca
Ultramodern theater has giant mural by sculptor Jordi Bonet in lobby; home of the Québec Symphony Orchestra and Opera; theatrical performances, concerts.

187

QUÉBEC

Harbor Cruises

124 St. Pierre St., Québec City,
418-692-1159, 800-563-4643.

M/V Louis Jolliet offers daytime, evening dance and dinner cruises on the St. Lawrence River. Bar service, entertainment. May-October.

Ile d'Orléans

Québec City, across the bridge in the
St. Lawrence River,
418-828-9411

This 23-mile-long 37-kilometers. island was visited by Champlain in 1608 and colonized in 1648. Old stone farmhouses and churches of the 18th century remain. Farms grow an abundance of fruits and vegetables, especially strawberries, for which the island is famous.

Jacques-Cartier Park

700 Lebourgneuf, Québec City,
418-844-2358; www.jacques-cartier.com

This park features beautiful views in a boreal forest valley. Fishing, rafting, canoeing, mountain climbing, wilderness camping, cross-country skiing, hiking, mountain biking, snowshoeing, dogsledding and picnicking are among the many activities available here. Visitors may also enjoy the serenity of its wilderness by walking the magnificent nature trail, as well as through nature interpretation activities. Late May-mid-October, mid-December-mid-April.

Jeanne d'Arc Garden

835 Wilfrid Laurier, Québec City,
418-649-6159

This floral jewel was created in 1938 by landscape architect Louis Perron. It combines the French Classical style with British-style flower beds and features more than 150 species of annuals, bulbs and perennials.

La Citadelle

1 Cote de la Citadelle, Québec City
418-694-2815;
www.lacitadelle.qc.ca

Forming the eastern flank of the fortifications of Québec, La Citadelle was begun

in 1820. Work on it continued until 1850. Vestiges of the French regime, such as the Cap Diamant Redoubt 1693. and a powder magazine 1750., can still be seen. Panoramic views; 50-minute guided tours. Changing of the guard (late June-Labour Day: daily at 10 a.m.). Beating the Retreat, a re-creation of a 16th-century ceremony late June-Labour Day: Tuesday, Thursday, Saturday-Sunday..

Laurentides Wildlife Reserve

Québec City, 418-686-1717;
www.sepaq.com

A variety of animals including moose, wolves, bears and numerous birds can be found here. Outdoor-lovers will find many recreational opportunities like canoeing, fishing, hunting and camping, as well as boat, ski and snowshoe rental. Located here are 140 cabins and 134 campsites. Late May-Labour Day, mid-December-mid-April.

Mont-Ste. Anne Park

2000 boul. Beau Pre, C.P. 400, Beaurpre,
418-827-4561;
www.mont-sainte-anne.com

Gondola travels to summit of mountain 2,625 feet or 800 meters., affording beautiful view of St. Lawrence River late June-early September: daily.. Skiing November-May.: 12 lifts, 50 trails; 85 percent snowmaking; cross-country, full service. Two 18-hole golf courses; bicycle trail. 166 campsites. The migration of 250,000 snow geese occurs in spring and fall at nearby wildlife reserve Cap Tourmente. Park daily; closed May.. Some fees.

Musée de la Civilisation

85 rue Dalhousie, Québec, 418-643-2158;
www.mcq.org

At the entrance is La Debacle, a massive sculpture representing ice breaking up in spring. Separate exhibition halls present four permanent and several changing exhibitions dealing with history of Québec and the French Canadian culture, as well as cultures of other civilizations from around the world.

Musée du Fort

10 Sainte-Anne St., Québec City,

QUÉBEC

418-692-2175; www.museedufort.com
Narrated historical re-creation of the six
sieges of Québec between 1629 and 1775,
with a sound and light show.

Musée des Anciens Canadiens
332 avenue de Gaspe W.,
Saint-Jean-Port-Joli, 418-598-3392.
This museum features an impressive collection of wood carvings by St. Jean artisans,
as well as original carvings by the Bourgault brothers. Visitors may watch a wood-
carver at work and ask questions about his
craft and purchase wood carved pieces.
Mid-May-October: daily.

Musee national des beaux-arts du Québec
Parc des Champs-de-Bataille, Québec,
418-643-2150; www.mnba.qc.ca
Features collections of ancient, modern and
contemporary Québec paintings, sculpture,
photography, drawings and decorative arts.

Museum of the Royal 22e Regiment
Succursale Haute-Ville, Québec City,
418-694-2815.
Located in two buildings. Powder magazine circa 1750., flanked on both sides by
massive buttresses, contains replicas of old
uniforms of French regiments, war trophies,
17th- to 20th-century weapons; diorama
of historic battles under the French; old
military prison contains insignias, rifle
and bayonet collections, last cell left intact.
Mid-March-October: daily. Changing of
the guard mid-June-Labour Day: daily at
10 a.m..

National Assembly of Québec
Grande-Allee and Honore-Mercier Ave.,
Québec City, 418-643-7239;
www.assnat.qc.ca
Take a 30-minute guided tour of Québec's
Parliament Building, constructed between
1877 and 1886. Guides provide an inside
look into the proceedings of the Québec
National Assembly, while explaining the
building's architectural features.

National Battlefields Park
835 Wilfrid Laurier, Québec City,
entrances along Grand-Alle,
418-648-4071
Two hundred fifty acres 101 hectares. along
edge of bluff overlooking St. Lawrence
River from Citadel to Gilmour Hill. Also
called the Plains of Abraham, the park was
site of 1759 battle between the armies of
Wolfe and Montcalm and the 1760 battle
of Ste. Foy between the armies of Murray
and Levis. Visitor reception and interpretation center presents history of the Plains
of Abraham from the New France period to
the present. Bus tour of the park. In the park
are two Martello towers, part of the fortifications, a sunken garden, many statues and
the Jeanne d'Arc Garden.

Notre-Dame de Québec Basilica-Cathedral
20 De Buade St., Québec City,
418-694-0665;
www.patrimoine-religieux.com
View the richly decorated Cathedral, over
350 years old and the crypt, where most of
the governors and bishops of Québec are
buried. Guided tours offered daily from
early May to early November.

Old Port of Québec Interpretation Centre
100 St. Andre St., Québec City,
418-648-3300;
www.parcscanada.qc.ca/vieuxport
Located in an ancient cement works and
integrated into harbor installations of
Louise Basin. Permanent exhibit shows
importance of city as a gateway to America
in the mid-19th century; timber trade and
shipbuilding displays; films, exhibits;
guides.

Parc de la Chute-Montmorency
2490 ave Royale, Beauport, 418-663-3330;
www.sepaq.com
Visitors to this park can enjoy walking and
hiking in the summer and skiing, ice climbing and downhill sliding on Sugarloaf Ice
Hill and Slide in the winter. Sights to see
include Manoir Montgomery, a restored
villa built in 1780 that houses a restaurant,

QUÉBEC

café, bar and shops; the Panoramic Stairway, offering breathtaking views atop its 487 steps; Montmorency Falls, which are 100 feet 30 meters. higher than Niagara Falls and the subject of many 18th- and 19th-century paintings; and the Wolfe House and Redoubt, which served as the headquarters for English general James Wolfe before the battle of the Plains of Abraham.

Place-Royale
27 Notre Dame St., Québec City,
418-646-3167; www.mcq.org
This site encompasses the earliest vestiges of French civilization in North America. Once a marketplace and the city's social center, it has been restored to its historic appearance. Today, visitors come to enjoy the many restaurants and retail stores, as well as performances in shows that take place during summer.

Québec Aquarium
1675 avenue des Hotels, Sainte-Foy,
418-659-5264; www.spsnq.qc.ca
Extensive collection of tropical, fresh and saltwater fish, marine mammals and reptiles; overlooks St. Lawrence River.

Québec City Walls and Gates
Encompassing Old Québec. Eighteenth-century fortifications encircle the only fortified city in North America; includes Governor's Promenade and provides scenic view of The Citadel, St. Lawrence River and Levis. Daily except Governor's Promenade.

Québec Zoo
9300 Faune St., Charlesbourg,
418-622-0312; www.spsnq.qc.ca
More than 270 species of native and exotic animals and birds in a setting of forests, fields and streams; children's zoo, sea lion shows; restaurant, picnicking.

Sound and Light Show "Heavenly Lights"
20 De Buade St., Québec City,
418-694-0665
This 30-minute multimedia show in both French and English takes place on three giant screens within the cathedral. Early May-mid-

October: first show is at 3:30 p.m., then every 60 minutes. Last show is at 8:30 p.m..

St. Andrew's Presbyterian Church
5 Cook St., Québec City,
418-694-1347
Serving the oldest English-speaking congregation of Scottish origin in Canada, which traces back to 1759. The church itself was built in 1810. Its interior is distinguished by a long front wall with a high center pulpit, as well as stained-glass windows and historic plaques. The original petition to King George III asking for a "small plot of waste ground" on which to build a Scotch church is on display in the Church Vestry. A spiral stairway leads to the century-old organ. July-August.

St. Jean-Port-Joli
Approximately 60 miles/96.6 kilometers N.E. on Hwy. 132, halfway to the Gaspe Peninsula, 418-598-3084;
www.saintjeanportjoli.com
The tradition of wood sculpture began in this town about 1936, initiated by the famed Bourgault family. Other craftsmen came and made this a premier handicraft center for sculpture, enamels, mosaics in copper and wood, fabric and painting. Located here is a small church built in 1779 and renowned for the beauty of its lines and interior decor. It features a sculpted wood vault, tabernacle and reredos, all by different artisans and has not been altered since it was built. Outdoor enthusiasts can enjoy a golf club May-September., tennis courts, mountain bike trails and a marina.

Uplands Cultural and Heritage Centre
9 rue Speid, Lennoxville,
819-564-0409; www.uplands.ca
This neo-Georgian home built in 1862 is located on 4 acres 1.6 hectares. of beautifully wooded grounds. Changing exhibits interpret heritage of Lennoxville-Ascot and eastern townships. The Lennoxville-Ascot Historical and Museum Society on the second floor contains period furniture and a small room for temporary exhibits.

QUÉBEC

Afternoon tea served all year reservations required in winter..

SPECIAL EVENTS

Carnaval de Québec
290 rue Joly, Québec City,
418-626-3716; www.carnaval.qc.ca
This internationally acclaimed French Canadian festival, billed as the world's biggest winter carnival, is celebrated throughout Old Town. Activities include parades, a canoe race on the St. Lawrence River, a dogsled race, a snow and ice sculpture show, a soapbox derby and the "snow bath," where participants brave the snow in their bathing suits. Late January-mid-February.

du Maurier Québec Summer Festival
160 rue Saint-Paul, Québec City,
418-529-5200, 888-992-5200;
www.infofestival.com
This 11-day event is one of the largest music festivals in North America. Performances are held at various locations throughout Old Québec. Major local and international artists are showcased, but the festival also serves as a springboard for up-and-coming artists. Early-mid-July.

Expo Québec
250 Boul. Wilfrid-Hamel, Québec City,
418-691-7110; www.expocite.com
This commercial, agricultural and industrial fair attracts over 400,000 people each year. Taking place at Exhibition Park, the event features arts and science pavilions, rides, a sand sculpture competition and a food exhibit. Late August.

New France Celebration
Québec City, 418-694-3311, 866-391-3383;
www.nouvellefrance.qc.ca
This family-oriented historical event in Old Québec re-creates the life of the colonists in New France in the 16th and 17th centuries. During this festival, the streets are filled with theatrical events, storytellers, song and dance performances, and children's entertainment. Both children and adults

who attend often dress in period costumes. Early August.

HOTELS

★★★Auberge Saint-Antoine
8 rue Saint-Antoine, Québec City,
418-692-2211, 888-692-2211;
www.saint-antoine.com
Explore historic Québec City from this sleek hotel housed in a building that has been occupied since the beginning of the French colony. A cannon battery runs through the lobby. Stone walls and wooden beams enhance the decor in this small hotel, located in the middle of Old Quebec's Port District on the St. Lawrence River.
95 rooms. Restaurant, bar. Busn. Center. $$$

★★Best Western Hotel L'Aristocrate
3100 Chemin Ste. Louis, Ste. Foy,
418-653-2841; www.bestwestern.com
100 rooms. Restaurant, bar. Pool. $

★★★Chateau Bonne Entente
3400, Chemin Ste. Foy,
418-653-5221, 800-463-4390;
www.chateaubonneentente.com
This country inn offers a very relaxing stay. Situated on 11 acres (4 hectares) in the suburbs, the property is very quiet.
109 rooms. Restaurant, bar. Children's activity center. Pool. Tennis. Busn. Center. $$

★★Chateau Laurier Hotel
1220 Georges 5th Ouest, Québec City,
418-522-8108, 800-463-4453;
www.old-quebec.com/laurier
57 rooms. Restaurant, bar. $

★★Clarendon Hotel
57 rue Ste. Anne, Québec City,
418-692-2480, 888-222-4652;
www.hotelclarendon.com
Historic hotel 1870., the oldest in Québec.
151 rooms. Restaurant, bar. $

★★Courtyard By Marriott Québec City
850 Place d'Youville, Québec City,
418-694-4004.

191

QUÉBEC

★
★
★
★
★

102 rooms. Restaurant, bar. Busn. Center. $

★★★Fairmont Le Chateau Frontenac
1 Rue Des Carrieres, Québec City,
418-692-3861, 800-441-1414;
www.fairmont.com

Reigning over this historic walled city from its perch atop the roaring St. Lawrence River is the majestic Fairmont Le Chateau Frontenac. Classic European details define the interiors here, where the rooms and suites reflect a worldly sophistication. Skiing and other winter-weather activities are available nearby and the hotel offers a fitness center and spa.
613 rooms. Five restaurants, bar. Swim. Busn. Center. $$$

★★★Fairmont Le Manoir Richelieu
181 rue Richelieu, Charlevoix,
418-665-3703, 800-441-1414;
www.fairmont.com

This majestic hotel in the heart of Québec's scenic Charlevoix countryside welcomes visitors with historic charm and world-class sophistication. Rooms and suites have a classic country appeal and with the most modern amenities. Guests can opt for nearby skiing and golf, or enjoy the hotel's fitness and spa facilities.
405 rooms. Restaurant, bar. Swim. Busn. Center. $$$

★★★Hotel Dominion 1912
126 rue Saint-Pierre, Québec City,
418-692-2224, 888-833-5253;
www.hoteldominion.com

Old Québec is considered the cradle of French culture in North America, and Hotel Dominion 1912 is a wonderful place from which to explore it. This small, sleek hotel takes full advantage of the early-20th-century building's historic architectural features while providing the modern conveniences that travelers expect.
60 rooms. Restaurant, bar. $$

★★★Hotel Germain-des-Pres
1200 Ave. Germain-des-Pres, Ste. Foy,

418-658-1224, 800-463-5253;
www.germaindespres.com

The property is 15 minutes from Québec City, major shopping malls and several golf courses.
126 rooms. Restaurant, bar. $$$

★★★Loews Le Concorde
1225 Cours du General De Montcalm,
Québec City,
418-647-2222, 800-463-5256;
www.loewshotels.com

See a vision of Paris out your window from this hotel on Québec City's "Champs-Elysees." Just 15 minutes from the airport, the tower has views of the St. Lawrence River, the city lights, and the historic Plains of Abraham. A visit is not complete without a peek, and hopefully a meal, at L'Astral, the revolving rooftop restaurant.
404 rooms, 26 story. Restaurant, bar. Pets accepted, fees. Pool. Busn. Center. $

★★★Manoir du Lac Delage
40 Ave. du Lac, Ville du Lac Delage,
418-848-2551, 888-202-3242;
www.lacdelage.com

This hotel is located 20 minutes outside Québec City.
105 rooms. Restaurant, bar. Exercise room. Pool. Tennis. $$

★★★Québec Hilton
1100 Boul. Rene Levesque Est., Québec City, 418-647-2411.

Located next to the Congress Centre and a 10 minute walk to Old Town, and other local attractions, the hotel is convenient for the business traveler or families. After a busy day of sight seeing, enjoy the local flavors and modern art at the hotel's Allegro Restaurant.
571 rooms. Restaurant, bar. Pets accepted, fees. Pool. Busn. Center. $$

★★Selectotel Rond-Point
53 Kennedy Blvd., Levis,
418-833-4920.

Ferry five minutes to Old Québec. 124 rooms. Restaurant. Pool. $

SPECIALITY LODGINGS

Au Manoir Ste. Genevieve
13 Ave. Ste. Genevieve, Québec City,
418-694-1666, 877-694-1666;
www.quebecweb.com/msg
9 rooms. **$**

RESTAURANTS

★★Aux Anciens Canadiens
34 rue Ste. Louis, Québec City,
418-692-1627;
www.auxancienscanadiens.qc.ca
French menu. **$$$**

★★★Laurie Raphaël
117 Dalhousie St, Québec City,
418 692 4555;
www.laurieraphael.com
Named after their children, owners Daniel
Vezina and Suzanne Gagnon head this popu-
lar restaurant with well-known friendliness.
Focusing on simple, gourmet fusion cuisine
allows the flavor and taste of some of their
best dishes, like Jerusalem Artichoke Blinis
with Abitibi sturgeon egg cream to come
shining through. The impressive wine cel-
lar includes a broad range of countries.
French menu. Reservations recommended.
$$$

★★★L'Astral
1225 cours du General de Montcalm,
Québec City, 418-647-2222;
www.loewshotels.com
Each rotation of this rooftop restaurant atop
the Loews Le Concorde takes 90 minutes,
plenty of time to enjoy its fine cuisine as
well as the spectacular panoramic views of
Québec City.
French menu. Reservations recommended.
$$$

★L'Omelette
64 rue Ste. Louis, Québec City,
418-694-9626
Breakfast, lunch, dinner. Closed November-
March. **$**

★★Le Bonaparte
680 E Grande-Allee, Québec City,
514-844-4368;

www.bonaparte.ca
French menu. Dinner. **$$$**

★★★Le Champlain
1 rue des Carrieres, Québec City,
418-692-3861;
www.fairmont.com
Exquisite St. Lawrence River views frame
traditional service and excellent
French fare. Jacket required. **$$$**

★★★Le Continental
26 rue Ste. Louis, Québec City,
418-694-9995;
www.restaurantlecontinental.com
Deep colors and oak dominate the rich
decor and European atmosphere at this fine
dining restaurant in Upper Québec. Order
one of the flambé specialties for a unique
tableside show.
French menu. **$$$**

★Le Manoir du Spaghetti
3077 Chemin Ste. Louis, Ste. Foy,
418-659-5628
French and Italian menu. **$$**

★★★La Pinsonniere
124 Saint-Raphaël, La Malbaie,
418-665-4431, 800-387-4431;
www.lapinsonniere.com
High above the St. Lawrence, La Pinson-
nière provides personalized service and
attention to each of its guest. Once the home
of Senator Marc Drouin, it is now a luxury
and fine dining inn. Each room is unique in
size and shape, yet filled with modern ame-
nities. The restuarant menu changes daily,
based on season and local ingredients.
18 rooms. Restaurant, bar. Pool. **$$**

★★★Le Saint-Amour
48 rue Ste. Ursule, Québec City,
418-694-0667;
www.saint-amour.com
Family-owned and operated since opening
in the heart of Old Québec in 1978, this
charming restaurant is away from the bustle
of the tourist beat. Fresh, local products are
highlighted and the vast wine room houses
more than 12,000 bottles.

193

QUÉBEC

French menu. Outdoor seating. **$$$**

★★Le Vendome
36 Cote de la Montagne, Québec City,
418-692-0557
French menu. Outdoor seating. **$$**

★★★Monte Cristo
3400 Chemin Ste. Foy, Québec City,
418-653-5221;
www.chateaubonneentente.com
Monte Cristo is a relaxed yet contemporary restaurant where guests are treated to traditional and original Québec cooking that emphasizes the use of local products. **$$$**

★★Restaurant au Parmesan
38 rue Ste. Louis, Québec City,
418-692-0341.
Italian, French menu. **$$$**

★★★★Restaurant Initiale
54 rue Saint-Pierre, Québec City,
418-694-1818;
www.restaurantinitiale.com
This modern French-cuisine restaurant is located in a former bank about one block from the St. Lawrence River in the Old Port district. Country products from local producers result in fresh, pure flavors.
French menu. Closed Sunday-Monday; also first two weeks in January. Reservations recommended. **$$$**

SAINT-JOVITE

Nestled in the valley of the du Diable River close to Mont Tremblant, this all-season destination is one of the oldest in the Laurentians. Visitors settle in to mountain cabins, lakeside cottages and heritage villages and venture from there to hunt, fish, snowmobile and ski in true alpine style. Three gorgeous beaches on the shores of Lac des Sables in Ste. Agathe make this a water sports paradise, and in the winter, international dogsled races at nearby Ste. Agathe-des-Monts are an exciting diversion. From open-air theater in the summer to mountain climbing on Monts Condor and Csaire, from antique shops to a Santa Claus Village, this region is an evocative mix of delight all year.
Information: www.laurentides.com

WHAT TO SEE AND DO
Antiques, arts and crafts
Interesting artisan's shops and galleries: Le Coq Rouge, an antique shop 819-425-3205.; Alain Plourde, Artisan 819-425-7873..

RESTAURANTS
★Antipasto
855 Rue Ouimet, Saint-Jovite,
819-425-7580;
www.tremblant.com
Italian menu. **$$**

SHERBROOKE

Nestled in a land of natural beauty at the juncture of the Magog and Saint-Francois rivers, Sherbrooke is a bilingual and bicultural community. The principal city of Québec's Eastern Townships, Sherbrooke is the center of one of Canada's fastest developing winter sports areas. In summer, its historic river system forms a vast linear park right through the centre of the city, allowing visitors and residents to benefit from nearly 20 kilometers of walking and cycling paths along the banks of the lovely Magog River. The region also bustles with entertainment: outdoor concerts, shows and performances, bistros, cafés and plentiful pubs. Sherbrooke's downtown offers nature, culture and architecture, with lively people, wide green spaces and an undeniable charm.
Information: www.tourismesherbrooke.com

194

QUÉBEC

WHAT TO SEE AND DO

Basilique-Cathedrale de Saint-Michel

130 rue de la Cathedral,
Sherbrooke,
819-563-9934

This Gothic-style cathedral is decorated with sculptures, mosaics and other works of art.

Beauvoir Sanctuary

169 Chemin Beauvoir,
Bromptomville, 819-569-2535;
www.sanctuairedebeauvoir.qc.ca

Built in 1920, this church is located in a setting of natural splendor on a hill. A statue of the Sacred Heart has been here since 1916, making it a regional pilgrimage site. May-October: daily; November-April, Sunday. Summer: picnic tables, restaurant, gift shop.

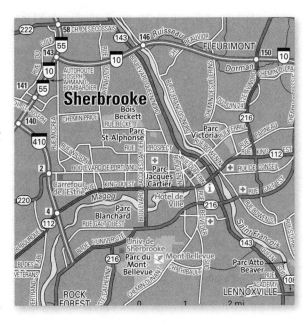

Louis S. St. Laurent National Historic Site

6790 Rte Louis-St-Laurent, Compton,
819-835-5448, 800-463-6769;
www.parcscanada.qc.ca/stlaurent

Birthplace of Louis S. St. Laurent 1882-1973., Prime Minister of Canada from 1948-1957; landscaped grounds; general store and adjacent warehouse with sound and light show. May-September: daily.

Mena'Sen Place

Site of large illuminated cross. Many legends surround the island and its original lone pine, destroyed in a storm in 1913 and replaced by the cross in 1934.

Musée du Séminaire de Sherbrooke

225 rue Frontenac, Sherbrooke,
819-564-3200; www.expoconcept.com

More than 90,000 objects of natural history. Tuesday-Sunday afternoons.

Parc du Mont-Orford

3321 Chemin du Parc Canton, Orford,
819-843-9855, 800-665-6527;
www.sepaq.com/montorford

Parc du Mont-Orford offers a wide array of both summer and winter activities, like golfing, cycling, swimming, backpacking, hiking, snowboarding, downhill and cross-country skiing and snowshoeing. For visitors wanting a more relaxed experience, there are walking trails, camp sites and opportunities for viewing wildlife. Some may also choose to sit back and relax and take in the spectacular views of the park's many mountains and peaks.

Orford Arts Centre

3165 Chemin Du Parc, Orford,
819-843-9871, 800-567-6155.

Located here are a pavilion with teaching and practice studios and 500-seat concert hall, where performances are given by noted artists during Orford Summer Festival. The center also features a visual arts program. May-September.

Ski Mont Orford

4380 Chemin du Parc, Orford,
22 miles/35 kilometers S.W.,
819-843-6548, 866-673-6731.

Mount Orford features some of the best facilities in Québec. It includes 54 runs the longest being 2 1/2 miles, or 4 kilometers.

QUÉBEC

and eight lifts, as well as 20 acres 8.09 hectares. of glade and 25 miles 40.2 hectares. of cross-country skiing. November-April: daily.

HOTEL

★★Hotel Gouverneur Sherbrooke
3131 King St. Ouest, Sherbrooke,
819-565-0464, 888-910-1111;
www.gouverneur.com
124 rooms. Restaurant, bar. Pool. **$**

ST. JÉRÔME

Founded in 1834 on the Riviere du Nord, St. Jerome is nestled in a magnificent setting of mountains, forests, lakes and rivers that offer all-season recreational delights. In summer, water sports head the field with more than 9,000 lakes and rivers to choose from. In fall, a cycling tour or a long or short-distance hike transports into fall's glory. In winter, snowshoing or skiing through snowy forests hark back to the days of the early pioneers. And in spring, rivers run high and fast, making for both exciting whitewater rafting and prolific fishing.
Information: www.laurentides.com

WHAT TO SEE AND DO

Centre d'exposition du Vieux Palais
185 rue du Palais, St. Jerome,
514-432-7171
An exhibition center of the visual arts.

TROIS-Rivières

Considered the second-oldest French city in North America, Trois-Rivieres was founded in 1634 and many 17th- and 18th-century buildings remain today. The St. Maurice River splits into three channels here as it joins the St. Lawrence, giving the name to this major commercial and industrial center and important inland seaport.

WHAT TO SEE AND DO

Cathedrale de l'Assumption
363 rue Bonaventure, Trois-Rivieres,
819-374-2409.
Built in 1858 in the Gothic Westminster style, this cathedral contains huge stained-glass windows, brilliantly designed by Nincheri. The cathedral was renovated in 1967.

Le Manoir de Tonnancour
864 rue des Ursulines, Trois-Rivieres,
819-374-2355;
www.galeriedartduparc.qc.ca
This historic structure is the oldest house in the city. It was built between 1723 and 1725 and rebuilt in 1795. When the government acquired the house in 1812, it was used as a barracks for soldiers. In 1852, it became the bishop's home. Today, the house is occupied by the Art Gallery in the Park and features displays of paintings, pottery, sculpture, engravings, serigraphy and jewelry.

Les Forges du St. Maurice National Historic Site
10000 boul. des Forges, Trois-Rivieres,
819-378-5116, 800-463-6769;
www.pc.qc.ca/ihn-nhs/
qc/saintmaurice
This site commemorates the founding of Canada's first industrial community. Visitors may see the remains of the first ironworks industry in Canada, the blast furnace and Ironmaster's House interpretation centers and a sound-and-light show at the Grande Maison. Mid-May-mid-October: daily 9:30 a.m.-5 p.m.; after Labor Day: daily 9:30 a.m.-4:30 p.m..

Notre Dame-du-Cap Shrine
626 rue Notre Dame Est.,
Cap-de-la-Madeleine,
819-374-2441; www.sanctuaire-ndc.ca
The site includes a small church that was built in 1714, making it the oldest preserved

stone church in Canada. It was turned into a shrine in 1888. Also here is a large octagonal basilica featuring stained-glass windows made by Dutch glassmaker Jan Tillemans, as well as neoclassic Casavant organ with 5,425 pipes. Summer organ recitals are held here from June to September. May-October: daily.

Old Port
800 Parc Portuaire, Trois-Rivieres, 819-372-4633

Magnificent view of the St. Lawrence River. Built over part of the old fortifications. Pulp and paper interpretation center; riverside park; monument to La Vrendrye, discoverer of the Rockies 1743..

Sightseeing tour: M/S Jacques-Cartier
1515 rue de Fleuve, Trois-Rivieres, 819-375-3000;
www.jacquescartier.croisieres.qc.ca

A 400-passenger ship offering cruises around Trois-Rivieres Harbor and on the St. Lawrence River. Options include dinner cruises, country cruises, fireworks cruises and a Captain's Christmas cruise. Late May-mid-September.

St. James Anglican Church
811 rue des Ursulines, Trois-Rivieres, 819-374-6010.

Constructed in 1699 and rebuilt in 1754, at various times the building was used as a storehouse and court; the rectory was used as a prison, hospital and sheriff's office. In 1823, it became an Anglican church and is now shared with the United Church. Carved woodwork was added in 1917; the cemetery dates from 1808. The church is still used for services today.

Ursuline Museum
734 rue des Ursulines, Trois-Rivieres, 819-375-7922;
www.ursulines-uc.com

Constructed in 1700, this Norman-style building has been enlarged and restored many times. A historic chapel, museum and art collection are located here. May-August, Tuesday-Sunday; October-April, Wednesday-Sunday.

SPECIAL EVENT
Trois-Rivieres International Vocal Arts Festival
Bonavanture and Royale, Trois-Rivieres, 819-372-4635;
www.artvocal.com

A celebration of song. Religious, lyrical, popular, ethnic, traditional singing. Late June-early July.

HOTELS
★★Delta Trois-Rivieres
1620 rue Notre-Dame, Trois-Rivieres, 819-376-1991, 888-890-3222;
www.deltahotels.com

159 rooms. Restaurant, bar. Pets accepted, fees. Exercise room. Pool. $

★★Hotel Gouverneur Trois-Rivieres
975 rue Hart, Trois-Rivieres, 888-910-1111; www.gouverneur.com

127 rooms. Complimentary continental breakfast. Restaurant. Pool. $

197

QUÉBEC

SASKATCHEWAN

SASKATCHEWAN, THE MIDDLE OF CANADA'S THREE PRAIRIE PROVINCES, IS GEOGRAPHICALLY located in the heart of North America. Within its borders is more road surface than in any other province, totaling 150,000 miles (241,400 kilometers). Half of the province is covered by forest, one-third is farmland and one-eighth is fresh water, with nearly 100,000 lakes. The province is a paradise of unspoiled hunting and fishing, with extraordinary sunshine to boot—the city of Estevan in the southeastern region is Canada's sunshine capital, averaging 106 sun-filled days each year. These sunny days make it easy to enjoy close to five million acres (more than two million hectares) of parkland, including two national and 26 provincial parks.

The province is popularly explored from behind the wheel of a car or recreational vehicle—roads are easy going, amenities along the way are plentiful, and the experiences are authentic prairie. Follow the route taken in 1874 by the North West Mounted Police, forerunners of today's Mounties, when they came west to quell the whiskey trade. Take in historic sites, panoramic views, cultural icons and friendly people, along with a slew of museums celebrating everything from the province's love of the sport of curling, its wild west beginnings and its discovery of vast deposits of dinosaur fossils. Wander through what locals call "parkland," a rolling and evocative combination of "not quite prairie and not quite forest." This was fur trade country, where rivers run clear, lakes are inviting and well-tended campgrounds are plentiful.

Provincial Capital: Regina
Information: www.sasktourism.com

 **SPOTLIGHT**

★ Near Regina is North America's oldest bird sanctuary, established in 1887 at Last Mountain Lake.

★ Curling was named Saskatchewan's official sport in 2001, although many have considered it so for years. Once called the "roaring game" because of the thunderous noise made by corn brooms used to sweep rocks down the ice, curling has a rich history and enthusiastic following in the province.

MOOSE JAW

Despite its humble beginnings as a village of sod huts and shanties, the city of Moose Jaw offers everything from high-energy adrenaline to laid-back relaxation. The city's "Tunnels of Little Chicago," an underground network of passages built to smuggle liquor during the Prohibition era, are a wink to the city's raucous history, which is well represented across several museums and sites. Take in sporting events, cultural extravaganzas, mineral spas and walking trails along with a small-town friendliness that makes Moose Jaw a must-see prairie destination.

Information: www.citymoosejaw.com

WHAT TO SEE AND DO

Buffalo Pound Provincial Park/White Track Ski Area
Moose Jaw, 306-694-3659

This 4,770-acre (1,930-hectare) park was established in 1963 and is known for its free-ranging buffalo in the Qu'Appelle River Valley. The name of the park refers to the aboriginal people's method of corralling bison by using the topography as a means to hold the animals in place. The park has a large outdoor pool, beaches, fishing, boating, mini-golf and hiking trails. It is also home to the White Track Ski Resort, with downhill skiing opportunities, as well as a number of snowshoeing and cross-country skiing trails.

Casino Moose Jaw
21 Fairford St. E., Moose Jaw,
306-694-3888, 800-555-3189

This casino has a 1920s theme and embraces Moose Jaw's unique history. It also has 20 indoor and outdoor wall murals that portray specific periods of the city's history. There are more than 150 slot machines to test your luck, as well as all the table game favorites, including blackjack, roulette and "Let It Ride" Bonus.

Cranberry Rose Gallery and Gifts
436 Langdon Crescent, Moose Jaw,
306-693-7779, 800-970-7328

The Cranberry Rose Gallery and Gifts shop is located in one of Moose Jaw's most elegant and historic houses. While here, you may shop, enjoy a cup of tea, or indulge your sweet tooth with one of their scrumptious homemade desserts.

Crescent Park
One block E. of Main St., 100 and 200 blocks of Fairford St. E.

Crescent Park is a beautiful place to enjoy spring flowers and grand trees. Take advantage of an outdoor pool, tennis courts, lawn bowling, an outdoor amphitheater, library, art gallery, museum and auditorium. For something more relaxing, simply walk along its bridges and watch the stunning waterfall.

Deer Ridge Golf Course
1375 Manitoba Expy. E., Moose Jaw,
306-693-4653

Most of the short course features Par 3 holes, good for the golfer who wants to play a round but doesn't want to spend the entire day on the links. Call in advance to make sure that tee times are available. Pull carts, power carts and club rentals are available.

Moose Jaw Museum and Art Gallery
461 Langdon Crescent, Moose Jaw,
306-692-4471; www.mjmag.ca

The permanent collections of the Moose Jaw Museum & Art Gallery feature a wide variety of works from a vast collection of local, provincial, national and international artists. The pieces from this collection are on exhibit at various times throughout the year. Don't miss the Norma Lang Gallery and the discovery center.

Moose Jaw River Park
276 Home St. E., Moose Jaw,
306-694-4447

There are eight miles (13 kilometers) of groomed cross-country trails located in the Makamow Valley. The park is a convenient outdoor option because it is located within the city.

St. Victor Petroglyph Park
206-110 Ominica St. W., Moose Jaw,
306-662-5411; www.saskparks.net

At this mysterious place, there are more than 300 carvings in the sandstone of a huge exposed rock that depict stories of ancient times. At different times of the day you can see different aspects of the petroglyphs.

Sukanen Ship and Pioneer Village & Museum
Hwy. 2, Moose Jaw Hwy. 2 S.,
306-693-7315; www.sukanenmuseum.ca

This 40-acre (16-hectare) museum includes an old village, an old farm, Tom Sukanen's ship and a collection of many vintage cars and tractors, as well as additional buildings containing various antiquities. The Sukanen ship stands as one of the strangest sights in western Canada and a marvel of ingenuity.

199

SASKATCHEWAN

★
★
★
★
★

Tunnels of Moose Jaw
18 Main St. N., Moose Jaw,
306-693-5261;
www.tunnelsofmoosejaw.com
These tunnels between many of the buildings in Moose Jaw's downtown are said to have been dug by Chinese immigrants in the late 1800s. Rumors surround all aspects of the tunnels; they are said to have been used during the Prohibition years by bootleggers and smugglers trying to avoid the law. Two 50-minute tours can help visitors draw your own conclusions.

Western Development Museum
50 Diefenbaker Dr., Moose Jaw,
306-693-5989;
www.wdm.ca
There are four Western Development Museums across Saskatchewan, each focusing on a different form of history of the province. The Moose Jaw location traces the development of transportation in the west through displays and artifacts.

Wood Mountain Post Provincial Historical Park
206-110 Ominica St. W., Moose Jaw,
306-694-3659, 800-205-7070;
www.saskparks.net
At this historic site, learn about how the Northwest Mounted Police arrived in the area and designated it as a post. The stories told during a visit through the historic buildings and sites paint a vivid picture of the important history that unfolded while

people here policed the Northwest. June-mid-August, daily 10 a.m.-5 p.m.

Yvette Moore Gallery
76 Fairford St. W., Moose Jaw,
866-693-7600;
www.yvettemoore.com
Here you will find reproductions, framed art cards and art plaques, as well as Moore's original artwork. She has won many awards for her art and is a source of pride for the city of Moose Jaw.

HOTELS
★★Heritage Inn
1590 Main St. N., Moose Jaw,
306-693-7550, 888-888-4374;
www.heritageinn.net
104 rooms. Restaurant, bar. Pool. $

★★Temple Gardens Mineral Spa
24 Fairford St. E., Moose Jaw,
306-694-5055;
www.templegardens.sk.ca
181 rooms. Restaurant, bar, spa. Pool. $

RESTAURANTS
★Houston Pizza & Steak House
117 Main St. N., Moose Jaw,
306-693-3934
Pizza, steak menu. $$

★Wayne and Laverne's Pizza and Steak House
622 Main St. N., Moose Jaw,
306-694-1777
Pizza, steak menu. $$

NORTH BATTLEFORD
The city of North Battleford and its neighbor, the town of Battleford, are located in the historic heart of Saskatchewan. Despite a relatively small population (less than 14,000), attractions abound—the city's northern lakes offer fishing, boating, swimming and camping, and nearby Table Mountain is one of the best ski hills in Saskatchewan. Fort Battleford National Historic Site, an old North West Mounted Police post, dates to the late 1800s and offers fresh air, big skies and living heritage.
Information: www.city.north-battleford.sk.ca

WHAT TO SEE AND DO
Allen Sapp Gallery
1 Railway Ave. E., North Battleford,

306-445-1760; www.allensapp.com
In May 1989, this gallery opened to display the works of Cree artist Allen Sapp.

The gallery sustains a theme of artwork of the Northern Plains Cree. Recently, the collection of Sapp's work has increased dramatically and the permanent collection has widened its scope by including First Nation and Inuit artists.

Battlefords Provincial Park
Cochin, 30 minutes from North Battleford, 306-386-2212
The park offers something for everyone, from family picnics to parasailing and golf. It is also great for cross-country skiing—nestled within its large rolling hills and forests are 25 miles (40 kilometers) of trails for all skill levels.

Blue Mountain Outdoor Adventure Centre
RR1, North Battleford, 306-445-4941;
www.bluemountaincanada.com
These 2,400 wooded acres (971 hectares) have some of the best trails and facilities in the world for cross-country skiing. The 25 miles (40 kilometers) of trails can be used by skiers of all levels and are rated according to ability. If you're feeling adventurous, you can take a shot at skate skiing, a form of skiing resembling skating on ice.

Finlayson Island
North Battleford on the North Saskatchewan River less than 10 minutes from downtown, 306-445-1740, 800-243-0394;
www.tourismbattlefords.com
This island was named in honor of Donald (Dan) Matheson Finlayson, who served as Member of Parliament from 1908 until 1934. It is a popular hiking and cross-country skiing destination with many miles of groomed ski trails that can be enjoyed in a beautiful setting.

Fort Battleford National Historical Park
Box 70, Battleford, 306-937-2621
Located at the confluence of the North Saskatchewan and Battle Rivers, Fort Battleford is an excellent site to achieve a better understanding of the historic role of the area's North West Mounted Police. The fort came

into being in 1876 and was maintained until 1924. Learn its story through its five original buildings, reconstructed stockades and bastions, and other period pieces. Victoria Day weekend to Labor Day weekend.

Gold Eagle Casino
11902 Railway Ave., North Battleford, 306-446-3833, 877-446-3833;
www.siga.sk.ca
The 15,000-square-foot (1,394-square-meter) casino features traditional casino games as well as "Let It Ride," Caribbean Stud Poker, progressive jackpots and Sega horse racing. Enjoy its lounge, restaurant and a nightclub that features weekend entertainment.

Makwa Lake Provincial Park
Loon Lake, 306-837-2410
Makwa Lake Provincial Park is a beautiful site that offers boating and fishing on five connected lakes. Try the beautiful 9-hole golf course in the summer and the 12 miles (19 kilometers) of intermediate cross-country ski trails in the winter. Those trails double as hiking paths in the summertime; there are many camping opportunities as well.

Meadow Lake Provincial Park
Dorintosh, 306-236-7680
Meadow Lake Provincial Park covers over 600 square miles (1,554 square kilometers) and is one of the most popular vacation spots in Saskatchewan. The area is a combination of several lakes and beautiful forests. This region provides a great area for many outdoor recreation opportunities like camping, swimming, boating, fishing, hiking, bird watching and canoeing. Winter activities include snowmobiling, ice fishing and cross-country skiing.

North Battleford Golf and Country Club
North Battleford, 306-937-5659
This 18-hole country club course is open for the public to enjoy. Its well-manicured greens are challenging and require excellent course management.

Steele Narrows
Loon Lake, 306-837-2410

201

SASKATCHEWAN

This site owes its existence to a battle between the North West Mounted Police and the Cree tribe. Named after Inspector Sam Steele, it is the site where he and his troops fought a three-hour battle with the Cree. This battle left several dead and was the last of the Northwest Rebellion.

Western Development Museum Heritage Farm and Village
North Battleford at Hwys. 16 and 40,
306-445-8033; www.wdm.ca
Visitors will find a large barn filled with livestock and see how a typical farmer of the 1920s spent his workday in the fields. Walk along the boardwalk and enter the town, where you can experience more aspects of this lifestyle, such as a co-op store, a church, or a typical home or business of the period.

PRINCE ALBERT

Prince Albert is located in the broad valley of the North Saskatchewan River near the geographical center of the province, where the agricultural prairie of the south and the rich forest belt of the north meet. The province's third-largest city, Prince Albert is a gateway to the recreational opportunities in the far northern region. Its center bustles with attractions, festivals, golf courses, casinos and museums. At theFort Carlton Provincial Historic Site in the city's southwest, see how life was lived in the days of the fur trade from the vantage point of a booming trading post circa mid-1800s, when swarthy trappers ruled along the North Saskatchewan River.
Information: www.citypa.ca

WHAT TO SEE AND DO

Athabasca Sand Dunes
La Ronge, 150 miles/241 kilometers N. of Prince Albert, accessible only by air or by boat from the Lake Athabasca communities,
306-425-4234
The Athabasca Sand Dunes, northernmost dunes in the world, are located along the south shore of Lake Athabasca in northwest Saskatchewan. This untarnished area has several dune fields that extend for approximately 60 miles (96.5 kilometers). Two major rivers in the park, the William and the MacFarlane, help create the unforgettable scenery here. Visitors must be self-sufficient for wilderness travel, taking along all food and supplies. All garbage must be packed out and visitors must be aware of special park regulations designed to protect the fragile environment.

Candle Lake Provincial Park
Candle Lake, 306-929-8400
Candle Lake has more than 19,457 acres (7,874 hectares) of recreational park and is known for its stunning waters, great beaches and sand dunes. Visitors can enjoy a number of activities in this nature park, including swimming, fishing, waterskiing, golfing, camping, hiking, biking and horseback riding. Many facilities and services are located in the nearby community of the Resort Village of Candle Lake.

Clarence-Steepbank Lakes Provincial Park
Smeaton, 90 miles/145 kilometers N.E. of Prince Albert. Access road runs W. of Hwy. 297 and approximately 7 miles/11 kilometers N. from Hwy. 913,
306-426-2622
This park encompasses 43,365 acres (17,549 hectares) and is the most accessible of the province's wilderness parks.

Elk Ridge Resort and Golf Course
Waskesiu Lake, 45 minutes N. of Prince Albert, about 4 miles/6.4 kilometers off Hwy. 2, on the outskirts of Prince Albert National Park,
306-663-4653, 800-510-1824;
www.elkridgeresort.com
The par-72, 6,796-yard (6,214-meters), 18-hole course is cut narrowly through the

SASKATCHEWAN

thick forest. It is a nature lover's dream, with scenery and wildlife that complement the course well. Call ahead to reserve a tee time. Proper golf attire is requested. For wintertime fun, the resort also has more than five miles (eight kilometers) of cross-country ski trails, both classic and skate-style.

Lac La Ronge Provincial Park
La Ronge, 145 miles/233 kilometers N. of Prince Albert, 306-425-4234
Lac La Ronge Provincial Park is Saskatchewan's largest provincial park, covering 851,204 acres (344,470 hectares) and containing more than 100 lakes. There are beautiful waterfalls on the Churchill River and the park is famous for its whitewater rapids. It also has excellent canoeing, fishing and hiking. If you enjoy skiing, you can bask in the beautifully diverse scenery along the 35 miles (56 kilometers) of cross-country trails, including three miles (five kilometers) of lighted trails for night skiing.

Northern Lights Casino
44 Marquis Rd. W., Prince Albert, 306-764-4777, 888-604-7711; www.siga.sk.ca
Northern Lights appends its casino games with monthly blackjack and slot tournaments. The casino also promotes and showcases Aboriginal artists on its stage. The Northstar

Restaurant and Prince Albert Inn are part of the complex.

Prince Albert Historical Museum
10 River St. E., Prince Albert, 306-764-2992
The Historical Museum began using the building in 1975 after the fire department vacated it. The museum contains exhibits that showcase Prince Albert's rich past. Visitors also enjoy a beautiful view of the river.

SPECIAL EVENTS
Prince Albert Canada Day Celebration
17 11th St. W., Prince Albert, 306-922-0405
Canada Day celebrations take place at Kinsmen Park during the day and at D.G. Steuart Park at night. Festivities include sports, picnics, flag raising, a color ceremony, contests and children's games. Early July.

Prince Albert Metis Fall Festival
14th St. W., Prince Albert, 306-763-7936
This annual cultural event features dancing and musical competitions. Late September.

Prince Albert Winter Festival
1211 First Ave. W., Prince Albert, 306-764-7595
Among the activities offered are dog pull and sled races, a snow sculpture competition and a trapping competition. For the less adventurous, there are arts and crafts, a wine and cheese show, talent shows, a chili cook-off, kid's carnival and a fiddlers' championship. February.

REGINA
The capital acts as the commercial, industrial and financial center of the province while still maintaining a small-town feel. Since the first pioneers homesteaded in the early 1880s, local residents have worked by hand to transform the flat, treeless prairie into a city of shaded parks and streets. Regina sparkles with rich artistic and multicultural traditions, with Canada's longest continuously operating symphony orchestra as well as the Globe Theatre, a company that stages innovative productions in the round. The Wascana Centre, in the heart of Regina, is one of North America's largest urban parks, measuring 2,300 acres (931 hectares). Regina is also the home of the Royal Canadian Mounted Police.
Information: www.tourismregina.com

WHAT TO SEE AND DO

Casino Regina
1880 Saskatchewan Dr.,
Regina,
306-565-3000, 800-555-3189;
www.casinoregina.com
Casino Regina boasts over
600 slot machines, more than
35 table games and features a
spectacular showroom.

Deer Valley Golf and Estates
Regina, 20 minutes N.W. of
Regina off Hwy. 11 to Hwy.
734,
306-731-1445;
www.deervalleygolfestates.
com
Many people consider Deer
Valley, an 18-hole championship golf course located along Wascana Creek in the beautiful Qu'Appelle
Valley, the best new course in Saskatchewan.

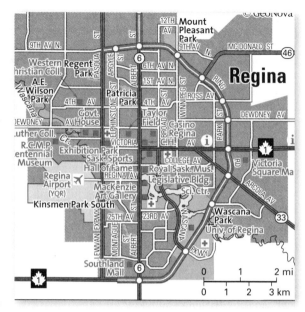

Echo Valley Provincial Park
Fort Qu'Appelle, 45 miles/72 kilometers E.
of Regina,
306-332-3215
In this 1,606-acre (650-hectare) park, enjoy
the picturesque Qu'Appelle Valley in addition to Echo and Pasqua lakes, where the
fishing is excellent. Other activities like
swimming, waterskiing, sailing and bird
watching await visitors to the park. In addition, six miles (9.6 kilometers) of groomed
cross-country trails are popular in winter
and may be used in the summer for walking
or biking.

Globe Theatre
1801 Scarth St., Regina,
306-525-6400;
www.globetheatrelive.com
View plays performed by the province's
oldest professional theater company. Season
runs September to May.

Government House Museum and Heritage Property
4607 Dewdney Ave., Regina,
306-787-5773;
www.graa.gov.sk.ca/govhouse
Opened in 1891 as the residence of the
Queen's representative, then became the
official residence of Saskatchewan's Lieutenant Governor from 1905 until 1945.
Fourteen rooms decorated with period furnishings and almost 100,000 artifacts.

Last Mountain House
146-3211 Albert St., Regina, 5 miles/8
kilometers N.W. of Craven on Hwy. 20,
approximately 45 minutes from Regina,
306-787-2790;
www.se.gov.sk.ca/saskparks
Last Mountain House is a reconstructed
Hudson's Bay Company post from 1869.
While touring the area, visitors will see the
Master's House and Last Mountain House,
as well as artifacts that give the history of the
area and show how the fur trade in this part
of Saskatchewan ended. July 1-Labor Day.

Mackenzie Art Gallery
3745 Albert St., Regina, Wascana Centre,
T.C. Douglas Building, 306-584-4250;
www.mackenzieartgallery.sk.ca

SASKATCHEWAN

The focus of this 100,000-square-foot (8,290-square-meter), tri-level gallery is Canadian and Saskatchewan artists. The collection of 1,600 works also features contemporary American artists and 15th- to 19th-century European prints, drawings and paintings.

Regina Symphony Orchestra
Saskatchewan Centre of the Arts,
200 Lakeshore Dr., Regina,
306-586-9555;
www.reginasymphony.com
Canada's longest continuously operating symphony.

Royal Canadian Mounted Police Training Academy and Museum
5607 Dewdney Ave., Regina,
306-522-7333;
www.rcmpmuseum.com
The Royal Canadian Mounted Police have been located in Regina since 1885. The museum explains the RCMP's role in Canadian. The tour shows visitors the oldest building in Regina, the chapel and provides a chance to view cadets in training.

Royal Saskatchewan Museum
2445 Albert St., Regina, Wascana Centre at Albert St. and College Ave,
306-787-2815;
www.royalsaskmuseum.ca
Visitors to this museum learn about the anthropological and natural history of the province. The museum houses earth and life science galleries, a fossil station, and exhibits that appeal to children.

Sask Power Building
2025 Victoria Ave., Regina,
306-566-2553
This building's covered outdoor observation deck offers a great view of Regina in an unexpected place. Also in the building is The Gallery on the Roof, which features works by a variety of Saskatchewan artists.

Saskatchewan Legislative Building
123 Legislative Bldg., 2405 Legislative Dr., Regina, Wascana Centre,

306-787-2376;
www.legassembly.sk.ca
The building was completed in 1912 and houses many provincial governmental activities. The building itself is worth a look, but if you take the tour, you will get a better feel for how Canadian government functions.

Saskatchewan Roughriders (CFL)
Taylor Field, Regina,
306-525-2181, 888-474-3377;
www.saskriders.com
Professional football team.

Saskatchewan Science Centre
2903 Powerhouse Dr., Regina, Wascana Centre at Winnipeg St. and Wascana Dr,
306-522-4629, 800-667-6300;
www.sasksciencecentre.com
Visitors will enjoy the vast array of exhibits and opportunities for discovery here. Hands-on exhibits explore physics, genetics, biology, ecology, geology and space and a Discovery Lab houses an array of reptiles and amphibians. Live demonstrations of static electricity, cryogenics, lasers, sound, ecology and anatomy are given daily. The SaskTel 3D Laser Theatre (one of only ten in the world) provides a unique experience. Visitors can also climb the 60-foot (18-meters) climbing wall or take in one of the many entertaining and informative stage shows. The Kramer IMAX Theatre has a five-story screen and powerful surround sound to immerse you in the films shown. It is one of the most dynamic ways to experience the places, people and principles of science and nature.

Wascana Centre
2900 Wascana Dr., Regina,
306-522-3661;
www.wascana.sk.ca
Visitors can partake of several activities within its perimeter, including parks, picnic areas and sports fields. At Wascana Lake (manmade), take a ferry to Willow Island for a picnic or just to enjoy the area. Swimming in the lake is prohibited, but once it freezes, ice skating is encouraged. Ski trails

205

SASKATCHEWAN

★
★
★
★
★

are groomed on the north shore from the Royal Saskatchewan Museum to Douglas Park. Phone ahead for trail conditions. The headquarters of the park, Wascana Place, is on Wascana Dr, north of the marina, west of Broad St. and east of Wascana Lake.

SPECIAL EVENTS

Buffalo Days
Ipsco Place, Lewvan Dr., Regina,
306-781-9200;
www.ipscoplace.com
At this city festival, enjoy activities ranging from midway rides to livestock shows to a parade. Late July.

Mosaic
2144 Cornwall St., Regina,
306-757-5990;
www.reginamosaic.com
Mosaic is an annual three-day festival of cultures that celebrates the rich ethnic history of the prairie settlers of this area. Experience 17 different countries and their cultures through food and dance. Early June.

Queen City Marathon
306-584-9270;
www.runqcm.ifchosting.com
Established in 2001, the Queen City Marathon has quickly become one of the most popular running events in Canada. Runners from all across North America participate and proceeds benefit a different charity each year. Mid-September.

RCMP Sunset Retreat Ceremonies
RCMP Training Academy,
Dewdney Ave. W., Regina,
306-780-5777
Traditional lowering of the flag, drill display by cadet band and march performed by the troops. Held on Parade Square, weather permitting. July-mid-August; Tuesday 6:45-7:30 p.m.

Regina Spring Sale of Antiques
306-522-7580
Since the late 1970s, vendors from all the nearby provinces have come to sell their collectibles and antiques at this annual event. Late April.

HOTELS

★Country Inn & Suites By Carlson
3321 Eastgate Dr., Regina,
306-789-9117;
www.countryinns.com
76 rooms. Complimentary continental breakfast. Pets accepted, fee. **$**

★Travelodge
4177 Albert St. S., Regina,
306-586-3443;
www.travelodgeregina.com
200 rooms. Restaurant, bar. Pool. **$**

★★West Harvest Inn
4025 Albert St., Regina,
306-586-6755, 800-858-8471;
www.westharvest.com
105 rooms. Restaurant, bar. **$**

★★★Delta Regina
1919 Saskatchewan Dr., Regina,
306-525-5255, 888-890-3222;
www.deltahotels.com
Contemporary and comfortable, the Delta Regina offers a range of accommodations to fit each guest's needs. Have some aquatic fun at the on-site Waterworks Recreation Complex, complete with a waterslide, pool, children's pool and whirlpool. Families are particularly welcomed here with children's menus, individual check-in cards for kids, and age-specific Kids' Essentials kits.
274 rooms. Restaurant, bar, children's activity center. Pets accepted, fee. Exercise room.Pool. **$$**

★★★Radisson Plaza Hotel Saskatchewan
2125 Victoria Ave., Regina,
306-522-7691, 800-667-5828;
www.hotelsask.com
Overlooking Regina Park, this historic landmark is elegant and welcoming to both business and leisure guests. The Cortlandt Dining Room offers fine dining and Sunday bruch and Sunday buffet. Enjoy high tea in

the Victoria Tea Room or something a bit stronger in Monnarch's Lounge
224 rooms. Restaurant, bar. Pets accepted, fee. **$$**

Regina Inn Hotel And Conference Centre
1975 Broad St., Regina,
306-525-6767, 800-667-8162;
www.reginainn.com
Located in the heart of Regina's downtown, the hotel is close to all local attractions and shopping. Guest will enjoy balconies with a city view, complimentary Internet and Starbucks coffee in their rooms. Enjoy dinner and entertainment at Applause Feast and Folly Dinner Theatre or a quiet drink at the VIC's lounge.
235 rooms. Restaurant, bar. Pets accepted, fee. **$**

RESTAURANTS
★★★Cortlandt Hall Dining Room
2125 Victoria Ave., Regina,
306-522-8972, 800-667-5828;
www.hotelsask.com
Situated in the Radisson Plaza Hotel Saskatchewan, the Cortlandt Hall Dining Room offers fine dining in an elegant and relaxing atmosphere. Memorable entrée options include grilled swordfish, proscuitto-wrapped pork tenderloin, and smoked duck breast. Traditional favorites are offered at the Sunday brunch and Sunday evening buffet.
International menu. **$**

★★★Danbry's Contemporary Cuisine
1925 Victoria Ave., Regina,
306-525-8777
Creative menu selections with locally produced products are offered at this casual, elegant restaurant housed in the historic Assiniboia Club building. An extensive cocktail menu is offered, as well as a cigar menu.
International menu. Closed Sunday. Outdoor seating. **$$$**

★Mediterranean Bistro
2589 Quance St. E., Regina,
306-757-1666
Mediterranean menu. Outdoor seating. **$$**

SASKATOON
Saskatoon is Saskatchewan's largest city, named from "mis-sask-quah-toomina," the Cree name for an indigenous berry. The jams and pies made from those berries are still local specialties. The South Saskatchewan River is the main waterway; bike, jog, or take a stroll along its banks. Along the river and in the downtown are many craft shops and galleries, a fine symphony orchestra, a plethora of summer festivals, four professional theater companies and an active amateur theater community.
Information: www.tourismsaskatoon.com

WHAT TO SEE AND DO
Blackstrap Provincial Park
102-112 Research Dr., Saskatoon,
306-492-5675.
This park is located on Blackstrap Lake near Mount Blackstrap. Many activities can be enjoyed on the lake, such as windsurfing, waterskiing and swimming; fishing is popular as well. If you're truly adventurous, climb Mount Blackstrap and take in the scenery of the lake and more than 1,310 acres (530 hectares) of park below. The hill at Blackstrap was built to accommodate events of the 1971 Canada Winter Games. There are a couple of sections for skiing along the three miles (five kilometers) available, though the trails are not terribly long.

Auto Clearing Motor Speedway
Range Rd., Saskatoon,
306-651-3278;
www.autoclearingmotorspeedway.ca
CASCAR, Thunderstock, Street Stock and Super Late Model series racing takes place on this one-third mile (one-half kilometer)

★
★
★
★
★

banked asphalt oval in Saskatoon. The city's motor speedway attracts around 2,000 racing enthusiasts on Friday, Saturday and Sunday from May to September.

Danceland
RR #1, Watrous,
306-946-2743, 800-267-5037;
www.danceland.ca
This 5,000 square-foot (465-square-meter) dance floor has been attracting fans of rock, bluegrass, swing, gospel, country and other musical genres since 1928. Whether hosting a big band orchestra or a square dancing event, the hall fills with crowds who dance the night away. Still here is the original maple floor, built on top of horsehair.

Emerald Casino
2606 Lorne Ave., Ruth and Herman Sts.,
306-683-8840
The 16,000-square-foot (1,486-square-meter) Emerald Casino features a variety of slot machines, as well as 38 game tables that invite gamblers to play favorites as baccarat, blackjack and seven-card stud poker.

Fort Carlton Provincial Historical Park
102-112 Research Dr., Saskatoon,
306-467-5205
This is the original site of a Hudson's Bay Company fur trading post that operated between 1810 and 1885 on the North Saskatchewan River. Today, visitors can check out a reconstructed stockade, fur and provisions store, trade store and clerks quarters. Each of the buildings appears much like it would have in the 1860s. See, touch and smell items such as buffalo hides, beaver pelts, war clubs, blankets, guns, twist tobacco and birch bark baskets. Mid-May-early September.

Greenbryre Country Club
Boychuk Dr., Saskatoon,
306-373-7600; www.greenbryre.com

Opened in 1979, this public course is located on 160 acres (65 hectares) and is perfect for all skill levels. The course's beautiful scenery features rolling fairways and many birch, ash and maple trees. Club and golf cart rental is available onsite.

Meewasin Valley
402 3rd Ave. S., Saskatoon,
306-665-6887; www.meewasin.com
The Meewasin Valley Trail is located in the center of Saskatoon and offers over 13 miles (21 kilometers) of cross-country trails along the South Saskatchewan River. In the summer, travel the river in an eight-person Voyager Clipper canoe, with a Meewasin guide. Canoeing and kayaking; hiking; fishing except in conservation areas.

Mendel Art Gallery & Civic Conservatory
950 Spadina Crescent E., Saskatoon,
306-975-7610; www.mendel.ca
Both permanent and temporary exhibits showcase historical and contemporary art by international, national and regional artists. The gallery holds a number of special programs, including "ART for LIFE," "Something on Sundays," and the annual "School Art" exhibit, which presents the works of Saskatoon's students.

208

SASKATCHEWAN

Pike Lake Provincial Park
102-112 Research Dr., Saskatoon,
306-933-6966; www.se.gov.sk.ca
Just 20 minutes south of Saskatoon, Pike Lake is an escape that has something for everyone: swimming, fishing, boating, nature trails, tennis courts, golfing, picnicking and year-round camping. The Leisure Pool and Waterslide Complex is designed for all, from first-time water sliders to the more experienced.

Saskatoon Blades
201-3515 Thatcher Ave., Saskatoon,
306-975-8847, 800-970-7328;
www.saskatoonblades.com
A member of the Western Hockey League. Games are played at the 11,310-seat Credit Union Center.

Saskatoon Golf and Country Club
865 Cartwright St. W., Saskatoon,
306-931-0022;
www.saskatoongcc.com/west.html
Although the main course is for members only, the beautiful (and challenging) West Course is open to the public. Huge bunkers and several water hazards make this a difficult course to negotiate. Rental of clubs and pull or power carts is available.

Wanuskewin Heritage Park
RR #4 Penner Rd., Saskatoon,
306-931-6767;
www.wanuskewin.com
Wanuskewin Heritage Park is set on 760 Acres (308 Hectares) along the South Saskatchewan River, 10 miles (16 kilometers) from Saskatoon in the Opamihaw Valley. The park focuses on the rich native heritage of the aboriginal people who lived here 6,000 years ago through cultural, archaeological, historical and geographical interpretation. There are self-guided trails, an interpretation center and a 500-seat amphitheater where native dances and songs are performed and stories are told.

Western Development Museum
2610 Lorne Ave. S., Saskatoon,
306-931-1910; www.wdm.ca
This tour shows many of the aspects of life in a typical prairie town. Through the many displays you will be transported to this time in history and learn what life was like.

Wilkie's Antique Clocks
1202 22nd St. W., Saskatoon,
306-665-2888.
Wilkie's is an antique clock-lover's dream. This shop specializes in hard-to-find clocks dating to the 1700s, as well as vintage and high-grade men's wristwatches. Repairs and new parts are available for all types of timepieces.

SPECIAL EVENTS
Cameco Victoria Park Summer Festival
233 Ave. C South, Saskatoon,
306-242-2711;
www.saskatoonsummerfestival.com
This unique festival offers fun for all ages with cultural and ethnic entertainment and excellent food. Throw in some Dragon Boat competitions and the whole family can enjoy this unique event. Mid-June.

Canada Remembers International Air Show
101-3515 Thatcher Ave., Saskatoon,
306-975-3155;
www.canadaremembersairshow.com
This popular air show is held as a tribute to Canadian veterans. Opening ceremonies feature a parade of veterans and are followed by performances from the Canadian Armed Forces, the U.S. Air Force, the U.S. Air National Guard and the Royal Canadian Air Force. Mid-August.

Clarica Mid-Summer Masters
Ebon Stables, Hwy. 16 E., Saskatoon,
306-477-0199;
www.ebonstables.com
This five-day event attracts the best equestrian athletes in Western Canada, who compete for $20,000 in prizes. Mid-August.

SaskTel Saskatchewan Jazz Festival
701-601 Spadina Crescent E., Saskatoon,

SASKATCHEWAN

★
★
★
★
★

306-652-1421;
www.saskjazz.com
At the end of June, thousands of visitors and local residents come together to enjoy the sounds of more than 800 of the best provincial, national and international jazz, blues, gospel and world-beat musicians. Events are held in venues like the Broadway Theatre and the Adam Ballroom and require tickets, but there are also many free staged events throughout downtown and in parks. Late June.

Shakespeare on the Saskatchewan
602-245 Third Ave. S., Saskatoon,
306-653-2300;
www.shakespeareonthesaskatchewan.com
This annual festival features outdoor performances of different plays written by the Bard. July-mid-August.

HOTELS
★Country Inn & Suites By Carlson
617 Cynthia St., Saskatoon,
306-934-3900, 888-201-1746;
www.countryinns.com
77 rooms. Pets accepted, fee. $

★★Radisson Hotel Saskatoon
405 20th St. E., Saskatoon,
306-665-3322.
291 rooms. Restaurant, bar. Pets accepted, fee. Pool. $

★★★Delta Bessborough
601 Spadina Crescent E., Saskatoon,

306-244-5521, 888-890-3222;
www.deltahotels.com
This full-service chateau-style hotel overlooks the Saskatchewan River. Guests can relax by the indoor pool or whirlpool. Children have fun here as well with activities and a playground. Enjoy a dinner at the Japanese steakhouse.
225 rooms. Restaurant, bar, spa. Exercise room.Pool. $$

★★★Sheraton Cavalier Hotel
612 Spadina Crescent, E. Saskatoon,
306-652-6770;
www.sheratonsaskatoon.com
Located in a business and shopping district, six miles from downtown and five miles from Calgary International Airport, this recently renovated hotel offers a variety of amenities. The Carvers Steakhouse provide a wonderful steak and seafood menu. Complimentary shuttle service is offered
249 rooms. Restaurant, bar. Exercise room. Pool. $

RESTAURANTS
★★2nd Ave Grill
123 Second Ave. S., Saskatoon,
306-244-9899;
www.2ndavegrill.com
International menu. Outdoor seating. $$

★Chianti
102 Idlwyld Dr. N., Saskatoon,
306-665-8466.
Italian menu. Outdoor seating. $$

SWIFT CURRENT
Swift Current's plentiful sunshine and passing chinooks (warm winds that blow in periodically from the Rocky Mountains) make it warmer than other parts of the province in winter. With a population of more than 15,000 and plentiful amenities, events and sights, Swift Current is an excellent jumping-off point for exploring Grasslands National Park, one of Canada's best.
Information: www.tourismswiftcurrent.ca

WHAT TO SEE AND DO
Chinook Golf Course
663-6th Ave. S.E., Swift Current,
306-778-2776;
www.westerngolf.ca/chinook

Playing conditions here are excellent year-round and the course is perfect for beginners as well as seasoned golfers. April-October.

Grasslands National Park
Val Marie,
306-298-2257;
www.parcscanada.gc.ca
Grasslands National Park preserves a wide expanse of the broad Frenchman River Valley with its weathered badlands, untouched native prairie and grassland flora and fauna. It is home to a unique blend of common and endangered species. Waterways such as the Frenchman River add to the diversity and are important habitats. The expansive valley, with its coulees and buttes, provides an impressive view. Exposed sedimentary rock enables visitors to see the first recorded find of dinosaur remains in western Canada.

SPECIAL EVENT
Frontier Days Regional Fair and Rodeo
Kinetic Exhibition Park, Swift Current,
306-773-2944;
www.swiftcurrentex.com
This annual professional rodeo features both American and Canadian cowboys who compete for a purse that totals close to $50,000. Late June.

HOTELS
★Best Western Inn
105 George St. W., Swift Current,
306-773-4660, 888-773-8818;
www.bestwestern.sk.ca
59 rooms. Complimentary continental breakfast. Exercise room.Pool. **$**

★Super 8
405 N. Service Rd. E., Swift Current,
306-778-6088.
63 rooms. Pets accepted, fee. Exercise room.Pool. **$**

RESTAURANTS
★Springs Garden Restaurant
3231 Springs Dr., Swift Current,
306-773-2021
Greek menu. **$$**

★Wong's Kitchen
320 S. Service Rd. E., Swift Current,
306-773-6244
Chinese menu. **$**

YORKTON
In Yorkton, immigrants primarily from the Ukraine, well experienced in plains farming, settled the fertile region. These pioneers brought with them a philosophy of community cooperation and cultural pride—and their legacy is that the city of Yorkton still boasts a rich ethnic diversity evident in the architecture of its churches, museums and handcrafts.
Information: www.tourismyorkton.com

WHAT TO SEE AND DO
Cannington Manor Provincial Historical Park
Kenosee Lake, 306-787-2700
Cannington Manor, built in the early 1880s by a British captain who lost his fortune in England, is located in southeast Saskatchewan. The captain wanted to create an aristocratic society of British people living in western Canada. Inside the house, learn the history of Captain Edward Pierce, the founder, as well of the house itself. Mid-May-Labour Day, Wednesday-Monday; closed Tuesday.

Deer Park Golf Course
Yorkton, 306-786-1711
This course has recently undertaken the reconstruction of seven holes to improve its appearance and to become more challenging.

Duck Mountain Provincial Park
Kamsack, 306-542-5500.
Enjoy the highlands of east-central Saskatchewan in beautiful contrast to its prairies. The park also offers a vista of aspen forests and gorgeous valleys that cradle the sparkling Madge Lake. There are beautiful beaches, convenient campgrounds and

lake fishing, along with golf, boating and hiking to enjoy. At the southern end of the park, find downhill skiing and 45 miles (72 kilometers) of cross-country ski trails.

Moose Mountain Provincial Park
306-577-2600; www.se.gov.sk.ca
This park features many lakes and forests and offers such recreational opportunities as horseback riding, bird watching, hiking, camping and cross-country skiing. Also here are two 18-hole golf courses, a 36-hole miniature golf course and a casino.

Painted Hand Casino
30 Third Ave. N., Yorkton,
306-786-6777, 888-604-7711;
www.siga.sk.ca
This 25,000-square-foot (2,323-square-meter), Native American owned-and-operated casino features 134 slot machines and 12 table games, including blackjack, progressive jackpots, slot machines, Red Dog, poker and roulette. The casino also hosts major events, such as curling tournaments.

St. Mary's Ukrainian Catholic Church
155 Catherine St., Yorkton, 306-783-4594
St. Mary's was built in 1914 and is Yorkton's most unique feature. On the inside of the dome of the church is the "Coronation of the Virgin," painted by Steven Meush from 1939 to 1941. This beautiful painting is as similar to the Baroque painted domes in German and Italian churches as you will find in this part of Canada.

Western Development Museum
Hwy. 16 W., Yorkton, 306-783-8361;
www.wdm.ca
The Yorkton Western Development Museum has re-created the times and styles of some of the many immigrants who settled in western Canada. Scenes illustrate the cultural roots of many of these new peoples: Ukrainians, English, Swedes, Germans, Doukhobors and Icelanders. Outdoors, the challenge of turning sod is demonstrated in the lineup of agricultural equipment, which includes the gigantic 1916 Twin City gas tractor, one of only two in North America.

SPECIAL EVENTS
Ukrainian Dance Festival
306-783-9538
This annual festival celebrates the Ukrainian heritage and ancestry of the area. Dance companies and bands from Manitoba, Saskatchewan, Alberta and North Dakota participate in the event. Early May.

York Colony Quilters Guild Quilt Fair and Tea
Yorkton, 306-783-8361
This two-day fair has been going strong for more than a decade. Its quilt show celebrating the York Colony Quilters Guild is a major attraction of the event. Early May.

HOTELS
★Comfort Inn
22 Dracup Ave., N. Yorkton,
306-783-0333, 800-228-5150
80 rooms. Complimentary continental breakfast. Pets accepted, fee. Exercise room.Pool. $

★Days Inn
2 Kelsey Bay, Yorkton, 306-783-3297, 800-544-8313; www.daysinn.com
74 rooms. Complimentary continental breakfast. Pool. $

INDEX

Blomidon Inn (Wolfville, NS), 89

Bloor Yorkville Wine Festival (Toronto, ON), 148

Bloor/Yorkville area (Toronto, ON), 140

Blue Crab Bar and Grill (Victoria, BC), 56

Blue Mountain (Collingwood, ON), 104

Blue Mountain Outdoor Adventure Centre (North Battleford, SK), 200

Bluenose II (Lunenburg, NS), 96

Boat Cruises (Sault Ste. Marie, ON), 132

Boscawen Inn (Lunenburg, NS), 96

Botanical Gardens (St. John's, NL), 81

Bow Valley Grill (Banff, AB), 4

Bowen Park (Nanaimo, BC), 29

Boxing Day Polar Bear Swim (Nanaimo, BC), 29

Brant County Museum (Brantford, ON), 102

Brewster Canada Motorcoach Tours (Banff, AB), 2

Brewster's Mountain Lodge (Banff, AB), 4

British Columbia Forest Discovery Centre (Duncan, BC), 26

Brock's Monument (Niagara-on-the-Lake, ON), 123

Brockville Museum (Brockville, ON), 103

Bruce Trail/Toronto Bruce Trail Club (Toronto, ON), 140

Buchanan's Chophouse (Niagara Falls, ON), 123

Buffalo Days (Regina, SK), 205

Buffalo Mountain Lodge (Banff, AB), 4

Buffalo Mountain Lodge Dining Room (Banff, AB), 4

Buffalo Pound Provincial Park/ White Track Ski Area (Moose Jaw, SK), 198

Bumpkins (Toronto, ON), 153

Burnaby Village Museum (Vancouver, BC), 34

Butchart Gardens (Victoria, BC), 51

Buttery Theatre (Niagara-on-the-Lake, ON), 125

Bytown Museum (Ottawa, ON), 126

ByWard Market (Ottawa, ON), 126

C

C Restaurant (Vancouver, BC), 45

Cafe Brio (Victoria, BC), 56

Cafe De Paris (Vancouver, BC), 45

Cafe De Paris (Montreal, QC), 180

Cafe Ferreira (Montreal, QC), 180

Cafe Ste. Alexandre (Montreal, QC), 181

Calaway Park (Calgary, AB), 6

Caleche Tours (Montreal, QC), 171

Calèches (Québec City, QC), 186

Calgary Flames (NHL) (Calgary, AB), 6

Calgary Science Centre (Calgary, AB), 6

Calgary Stampede (Calgary, AB), 7

Calgary Tower (Calgary, AB), 6

Calgary Winter Festival (Calgary, AB), 7

Cambridge Suites Hotel (Halifax, NS), 94

Cameco Victoria Park Summer Festival (Saskatoon, SK), 208

Camille's (Victoria, BC), 56

Canada Day (Ottawa, ON), 129

Canada Day Celebration (Fredericton, NB), 72

Canada Olympic Park (Calgary, AB), 6

Canada One Factory Outlets (Niagara Falls, ON), 120

Canada Remembers International Air Show (Saskatoon, SK), 209

Canada's Aviation Hall of Fame (Wetaskiwin, AB), 13

Canada's Sports Hall of Fame (Toronto, ON), 140

Canadian Empress (Kingston, ON), 111

Canadian Finals Rodeo (Edmonton, AB), 14

Canadian Football Hall of Fame and Museum (Hamilton, ON), 108

Canadian Grand Prix (Montreal, QC), 176

Canadian International (Toronto, ON), 148

Canadian Museum of Contemporary Photography (Ottawa, ON), 127

Canadian Museum of Nature (Ottawa, ON), 127

Canadian National Exhibition (Toronto, ON), 148

Canadian Parliament Buildings (Ottawa, ON), 127

Canadian Ski Museum (Ottawa, ON), 127

Canadian Trophy Fishing (Toronto, ON), 140

Canadian Tulip Festival (Ottawa, ON), 129

Can-Am Soapbox Derby (St. Catharines, ON), 134

Canatara Park (Sarnia, ON), 131

Candle Lake Provincial Park (Candle Lake, SK), 202

Canmore Children's Festival (Canmore, AB), 10

Cannington Manor Provincial Historical Park (Kenosee Lake, SK), 211

Canoe (Toronto, ON), 154

Canyon Ski Area (Red Deer, AB), 23

Cape Breton Centre for Craft & Design (Sydney, NS), 86

Cape Breton Highlands National Park (Cheticamp, NS), 86

Cape Breton's Celtic Music Interpretive Centre (Judique, NS), 86

Cape Forchu Lighthouse (Cape Forchu Island, NS), 98

Cape Spear National Historic Site (St. John's, NL), 81

Capilano Suspension Bridge (Vancouver, BC), 34

Capital City Recreation Park (Edmonton, AB), 12

Capital City Tally-Ho and Sightseeing Company (Victoria, BC), 51

Capri (Niagara Falls, ON), 123

Capri Conference Centre (Red Deer, AB), 24

Caribana (Toronto, ON), 149

Caribbean Days Festival (North Vancouver, BC), 41

Carillon (Victoria, BC), 53

Carlton Martello Tower National Historic Park (Saint John, NB), 75

Carman's Club (Toronto, ON), 154

Carnaval de Québec (Québec City, QC), 190

Carr House (Victoria, BC), 51

Carriages (Niagara-on-the-Lake, ON), 125

Carrousel of the Nations (Windsor, ON), 159

215

★ **INDEX**

★

★

★

☆

☆

217

INDEX

★
★
★
★

Fredericton Exhibition (Fredericton, NB), 72

Fredericton Golf and Curling Club (Fredericton, NB), 71

Fredericton Playhouse (Fredericton, NB), 71

Fringe Theatre Festival (Edmonton, AB), 14

Frontier (Revelstoke, BC), 32

Frontier Days Regional Fair and Rodeo (Swift Current, SK), 210

Fun in the Sun Festival (Fort Frances, ON), 106

Fundy National Park (Alma, NB), 73

Fundy Restaurant (Digby, NS), 88

G

Gaelic College (St. Ann's, NS), 86

Gallery at Ceperley House (Vancouver, BC), 35

Gallery of Stratford (Stratford, ON), 135

Gananoque Boat Line (Gananoque, ON), 107

Gananoque Historical Museum (Gananoque, ON), 107

Gananoque Inn (Gananoque, ON), 107

Gardens (Sarnia, ON), 131

Gaspé Peninsula (Québec City, QC), 186

Gasthaus Switzerland Inn (Ottawa, ON), 130

Gastown (Vancouver, BC), 35

Gate House Hotel (Niagara-on-the-Lake, ON), 125

Gatsby Mansion B&B (Victoria, BC), 55, 56

Geology Museum (Kingston, ON), 113

George R. Gardiner Museum of Ceramic Art (Toronto, ON), 143

Giant Waterslide (Gananoque, ON), 107

Gibson House (North York, ON), 143

Giorgio's Trattoria (Banff, AB), 5

Giovanni's (Sault Ste. Marie, ON), 133

Glenbow Museum (Calgary, AB), 7

Glenhyrst Art Gallery of Brant (Brantford, ON), 102

Glenora Distillery (Glenville, NS), 87

Globe (Montreal, QC), 181

Globe Theatre (Regina, SK), 203

Glockenspiel (Hamilton, ON), 114

Gold Eagle Casino (North Battleford, SK), 200

Golden Apple (Gananoque, ON), 107

Golden Tulip Georgian Court Hotel (Vancouver, BC), 43

Golden Tulip Valhalla Inn Thunder Bay (Thunder Bay, ON), 138

Gotham Steakhouse and Cocktail Bar (Vancouver, BC), 46

Government House (Charlottetown, PE), 165

Government House Museum and Heritage Property (Regina, SK), 204

Granby International (Granby, QC), 169

Granby Zoo (Granby, QC), 168

Grand Concourse Walkways (St. John's, NL), 82

Grand Falls (Edmundston, NB), 69

Grand Pré National Historic Site (Grand Pré, NS), 89

Grand Theatre (Kingston, ON), 112

Grand Theatre (London, ON), 117

Grand Theatre (Québec City, QC), 186

Grange Park (Toronto, ON), 141

Grano (Toronto, ON), 154

Granville Island (Vancouver, BC), 35

Granville Island Kids' Market (Vancouver, BC), 35

Grasslands National Park (Val Marie, SK), 210

Gray Line Bus Tours (Toronto, ON), 143

Gray Line Bus Tours (Montreal, QC), 171

Gray Line Bus Tours (Québec City, QC), 186

Gray Rocks Resort and Convention Centre (Mont Tremblant, QC), 170

Grazie (Toronto, ON), 154

Great Gorge Adventure (Niagara Falls, ON), 120

Great Hall of the Clans (St. Ann's, NS), 87

Greater Vancouver Zoo (Aldergrove, BC), 36

Green Acres Inn (Kingston, ON), 113

Green Gables (Cavendish, PE), 163

Green Park Shipbuilding Museum (Port Hill, PE), 165

Greenbryre Country Club (Saskatoon, SK), 207

Greenhouse (Niagara Falls, ON), 121

Greenwood Inn Calgary (Calgary, AB), 8

Grouse Mountain (North Vancouver, BC), 36

Grubstake (Louisbourg, NS), 87

Guinness World of Records Museum (Niagara Falls, ON), 120

Guy Lombardo Music Centre (London, ON), 117

H

Halifax Citadel National Historic Park (Halifax, NS), 90

Halifax Highland Games & Scottish Festival (Halifax, NS), 93

Halifax Marriott Harborfront (Halifax, NS), 94

Hamachi Grill & Sushi House (Dartmouth, NS), 95

Hamilton International Air Show (Hamilton, ON), 110

Hamilton Military Museum (Hamilton, ON), 109

Hamilton Mum Show (Hamilton, ON), 110

Hamilton Place (Hamilton, ON), 109

Hamilton's Farmers' Market (Hamilton, ON), 109

Hampton Inn & Suites (Vancouver, BC), 43

Hampton Inn Vancouver Airport (Richmond, BC), 44

Happy Rolph Bird Sanctuary & Children's Farm (St. Catharines, ON), 133

Harbor Cruises (Québec City, QC), 187

Harbor Cruises Ltd. (Vancouver, BC), 36

Harbor Towers Hotel & Suites (Victoria, BC), 55

Harbour Hopper Tours (Halifax, NS), 91

Harbourfront Centre (Toronto, ON), 143

220

INDEX

★
★
★
☆
☆

Imperial Chinese Seafood Restaurant (Vancouver, BC), 46

Indian Village (London, ON), 118

Inn on the Lake (Waverley, NS), 94

Insectarium de Montreal (Montreal, QC), 172

Institute for Ocean Technology (St. John's, NL), 82

InterContinental Hotel Toronto Centre (Toronto, ON), 151

InterContinental Toronto (Toronto, ON), 151

International Air Show (Lethbridge, AB), 21

International Air Show (Kamloops, BC), 27

International Buskerfest (Halifax, NS), 93

International Fireworks Competition (Montreal, QC), 176

International Freedom Festival (Windsor, ON), 159

International Friendship Gardens (Thunder Bay, ON), 137

International Hotel Suites Calgary (Calgary, AB), 8

International Ice Hockey Federation Museum (Kingston, ON), 112

International Snowmobilers Festival (Edmundston, NB), 69

International Tulip Festival (Truro, NS), 97

International Villages Festival (Brantford, ON), 102

Inuit Gallery of Vancouver (Vancouver, BC), 36

Inverarden Regency Cottage Museum (Cornwall, ON), 105

Inverary Resort (Baddeck, NS), 87

Ironman Canada Championship Triathlon (Penticton, BC), 30

Irving House Historic Centre (Vancouver, BC), 36

Irving Nature Park (Saint John, NB), 75

Isaiah Tubbs Resort & Conference Centre (Picton, ON), 113

Island Queen (Kingston, ON), 111

It's a Grand Summer (Kingston, ON), 113

J

Jack Miner Bird Sanctuary (Kingsville, ON), 158

Jacques-Cartier Park (Québec City, QC), 187

Jamieson's Irish-House & Grill (Dartmouth, NS), 95

Japanese Village Steak and Seafood House (Victoria, BC), 57

Jardin Nelson (Montreal, QC), 181

Jasper Tramway (Jasper, AB), 17

Jazz City International Music Festival (Edmonton, AB), 14

Jazz Festival (Edmundston, NB), 70

Jeanne d'Arc Garden (Québec City, QC), 188

John Freeman Walls Historic Site and Underground Railroad Museum (Windsor, ON), 158

John Janzen Nature Centre (Edmonton, AB), 12

Johnson Geo Centre (St. John's, NL), 82

Johnston Canyon (Banff, AB), 3

Joseph Schneider Haus (Kitchener-Waterloo, ON), 114

Joso's (Toronto, ON), 154

Journey Behind the Falls (Niagara Falls, ON), 121

Just for Laughs Festival (Montreal, QC), 176

K

Kakabeka Falls Provincial Park (Thunder Bay, ON), 137

Kamloops Museum and Archives (Kamloops, BC), 27

Kamloops Wildlife Park (Kamloops, BC), 27

Kaulbach House (Lunenburg, NS), 96

Kelowna Regatta (Kelowna, BC), 28

Keltic Lodge Resort and Spa (Ingonish Beach, NS), 87

Kenora Agricultural Fair (Kenora, ON), 111

Kenora International Bass Fishing Tournament (Kenora, ON), 111

Kensington Market (Toronto, ON), 144

Keystone Alley Cafe (Stratford, ON), 136

Kingfisher Oceanside Resort and Spa (Courtenay, BC), 30

Kingfisher Restaurant (Courtenay, BC), 57

Kings Landing Historical Settlement (Kings Landing, NB), 71

Kingsbrae Arms (St. Andrews, NB), 78

Kingsbrae Garden (St. Andrews, NB), 77

Kinsmen Antique Show (Stratford, ON), 135

Kinsmen Sports Centre (Edmonton, AB), 12

Kitchener-Waterloo Art Gallery (Kitchener-Waterloo, ON), 114

Kitchener-Waterloo Multicultural Festival (Kitchener-Waterloo, ON), 115

Kluane National Park (Haines Junction, YT), 215

Knights Inn (Kingston, ON), 113

Kortright Centre for Conservation (Woodbridge, ON), 144

L

L & W (Jasper, AB), 18

La Belle Auberge (Ladner, BC), 46

La Boheme (Edmonton, AB), 15

La Citadelle (Québec City, QC), 187

La Fenice (Toronto, ON), 154

La Foire Brayonne (Edmundston, NB), 70

La Fontaine Park (Montreal, QC), 171

La Gaudriole (Montreal, QC), 181

La Gondola (Ottawa, ON), 130

La Louisiane (Montreal, QC), 181

La Maree (Montreal, QC), 181

La Perla Dining Room (Dartmouth, NS), 95

La Pinsonniere (Montreal, QC), 179

La Place Rendez-vous (Fort Frances, ON), 106

La Rapiere (Montreal, QC), 182

La Ronde (Edmonton, AB), 15

La Ronde (Montreal, QC), 174

La Rua (Whistler, BC), 60

La Sauvagine (Ste. Agathe, QC), 182

La Spiga (Edmonton, AB), 15

La Terrazza (Vancouver, BC), 46

221

INDEX

★
★
★
★
★
★

223

INDEX

225

INDEX

★

★

★

☆

☆

227

INDEX

★

★

★

★

228

INDEX

★ ★ ★ ★ ★

INDEX

230

INDEX

231

INDEX

NOTES

★
★
★
★
★